# BRAIN & BELIEF

## An Exploration of the Human Soul

with

## John J. McGraw

AEGIS PRESS

Aegis Press

P.O. Box 3023
Del Mar, CA 92014

www.theaegispress.com

Copyright © 2004 by John J. McGraw

LCCN: 2003098895

ISBN 0-9747645-0-7

Design and layout
BBD / Jonathan Gullery
9 Washington Avenue
Pleasantville, NY 10570

Manufactured in the United States of America
by BooksJustBooks

First Aegis Press paperback edition published 2004

*To my father,*
*who instilled in me the sense of wonder.*

# CONTENTS

*Man is neither angel nor beast,*

*and the unfortunate thing is that*

*he who would act the angel acts the beast.*

—Blaise Pascal, *Pensées*

# PREFACE

One Sunday morning in 1980, my mother took my three older siblings and me to visit our great-grandfather who lived in a nearby hospital. I know we had visited him before, I believe we visited him again, but this is the only visit I can still remember. Why he lived in the hospital, I wasn't sure. I was told that he was very, very old and senile—a word which meant nothing to me.

As we departed the warmth and light of that August morning to enter the hospital, I noticed the smell foremost. To this day, I could be taken blindfolded into any hospital and know instantly that's where I stood, for all hospitals have *that* smell. At the time, though, the surroundings were truly novel for me, as far as I know I had not been in a hospital for about six years—since I was born. So, with the typical mystery and fear that all first hospital visits impart—sickness, bandages, crying people, doctors, nurses—the whole carnival of death and decay—we proceeded through the vast, fluorescent lit halls and up the elevator until we reached my great-grandfather's private room. I believe I was holding the hand of my mother or an older brother— my father had opted out of the visit—as we walked into the room, but still the fear overwhelmed me. There perched in the bed was a thin, bright blue-eyed old man who stared straight ahead at an empty wall.

The room was cozy but filled with a stench even more memorable than the hospital's more general aroma. The smell was somehow familiar but rotten—one I couldn't quite place. My mother went to her grandfather, kissed him on the cheek, and greeted him with an unnatural, carefully spoken set of words, as if she were speaking to a child smaller than myself. My three siblings and I stood near the foot of the bed and waited awkwardly, unsure what to make of the scene. Here before us, frail and bed-ridden, lay the oldest living member of our family—the great father, the living seed. My dad's mental puzzles, the ones he had begun to quiz me with, filled my head and I thought how if this old man had not been born then neither would we have been born. My mother and all her brood—*poof!*—never to exist. Without this relic lying before us, without this strangely staring old creature, all of us would disintegrate into so much nothingness. I marveled at the thought and felt the visit proper and right, though I was scared.

My mother shuttled each of us to his side for an introduction. I watched my brothers and sister go one by one right up to him while my mother said something to the old man. Finally, my turn came. A light feeling overtook my stomach and my legs seemed unsure of themselves. My mother crouched over the bed and softly announced my presence to him. I looked at my great-grandfather's long, thin head—so like the one I now possess—as it turned towards me and stared. The pale blue eyes frightened me but far more horrifying were their emptiness and vague confusion. Something human looked at me but something human was missing. I shuddered. I had never seen anything like it before. This man was the origin and this man was the end, and I knew it. The experience reminds me of the Sphinx's classic riddle, the one that only Oedipus solved: "What has four legs in the morning, two legs in the afternoon, and three legs at night?" Oedipus rightly answered "MAN!"—who begins as a crawling child, grows into a sure-footed adult, and ages into a cane-supported geriatric.

I left the hospital changed. Some original innocence had been lost to an uncanny experience. I contracted an illness that day from the unsettling old man. It was the sickness unto death that Kierkegaard wrote about—despair. Often I didn't know I was ill, often I neared death from a despair I couldn't understand, but I think I have finally healed myself of it. This book, a book about brains and souls, about death and life, is my headlong attempt to understand the sickness that infected me that summer day in 1980.

# INTRODUCTION

Of this experience called life we are told two basic stories; one story for one ear, a second story for the other. We are told that we are born and die, that we possess no essential difference from other animals. We grow and as we grow our minds mature until—from nothing—we possess a self. As we age that self, like an electric bulb, grows brighter and brighter and then its filament decays and begins to dim. Towards the end of the bulb's life, one solid shake will break the filament and forever darken the lamp. If one lives long enough, then like my ninety-something great-grandfather, one's body lives on after one's mind has dimmed with the nightfall. This story tells us that the self is the brain. When we visited my great-grandfather I found out about this story's end. For the first time I truly understood the scope of this story and I felt it's truth rattle my bones.

The second story I had also heard by the time I was six. In fact, that very day, earlier that morning, I had probably heard a rendition of it in my Sunday school class. This story tells us that human existence is a farce. Life on Earth is a brief test. The results of this test are momentous: they determine one's real 'placement,' one's eternal existence. We are not animals born to die but souls born to live forever, souls born to outlive stars and night. No mystic can tell you the scope of this tale for no one really knows it. Vague secrets are whispered about the true life that begins after one's death.

The story begins: for an unknown reason, the very Creator of all that is fashioned us of the Earth, a relatively base substance, and from Himself, the omniscient, eternal essence from which everything derives. We are not simply animals but animals with souls, animals with God-stuff infused in our hearts and minds. The story ends: when the animal in us decays and dies the pure God-stuff begins some more important and everlasting journey whose depth we cannot fathom.

So where was my great-grandfather's God-stuff? Where was the old man's soul—his will, his conscience, his understanding, compassion, love? This question was the sickness that infected me that morning. For in the back of my mind, I knew, forever after, that this second story was fable. A dissonance, a clanging bell, would resound in my head for many years—for as much as I'd seek God and deepen my faith, I'd also know that there was none to be had. In silence, and with merely a glance, my great-grandfather had informed me that Santa Claus was not real that day, that Jesus cared not for me, that despair is genuine, that all comes to naught, that in the end I—like all other things—would cease to be. The gifts of life were not something of myth and magic or a carefully staged scene, but a tale told by an idiot, full of sound and fury, that signified nothing. All the fables were something kind-hearted parents gave as gifts to their children, but which their children must someday find out about on their own. I didn't understand the full importance of this at the time. I sensed something in me change but it would take many years, a great deal of study, and ceaseless reflection to uncover the truth. My great-grandfather had scribbled down the meaning of life and passed it to me in a thoughtless stare. Where was my great-grandfather's God-stuff? When his ninety year old brain shriveled and tangled so did his human essence disappear with it. The look he gave told the whole story for that look conveyed matter without spirit, form without substance.

But let us not settle on any firm conclusion. Let us carefully read the history of the soul and understand this Shakespearean drama in all its epic proportions. Afterwards, we will learn of the brain and the many things in our lives which alter and effect the brain. Perhaps then you'll come to understand human existence as I have come to understand it. Or perhaps you'll come to think differently than I do. I have sampled many solutions and have alternately been a born-again Christian and an atheist, I have been a studied Catholic and an evangelical Fundamentalist. Lately I am a humanist informed by our most modern of myths—science. I understand these different perspectives and, more importantly, I have felt each of their soul-shaking truths. We are emotional beings after all and our thoughts are more often the reasoned expression of our feelings than some distilled logic. With a full respect for the different 'takes' on the human drama let us begin with a careful study of brain and belief.

# Matter and Spirit

Man is dual. He knows his consciousness—his sense of self, his perception of thoughts, his emotions—and objects in the world, all the material things—dogs, trees, toads, and the like. We can see, hear, touch, taste, and smell physical things but cannot perceive thoughts in these ways. Both are real, aren't they? In philosophical jargon this phenomenon is called *mind/body dualism*. Duality can be understood in two different fashions—as substance dualism or as property dualism. Substance dualism proclaims there to be just two fundamental substances in the universe: the mental and the physical. The mental realm exists as spirit and the physical realm as matter. In more scientific terms, matter is built of atoms and their interactions while spirit does not depend on atoms. While the spiritual cannot die, matter, as we all perceive, readily decays—its molecules break apart to create endless other things out of the same atoms. While the most famous champion of this argument was the 17th century French philosopher René Descartes, dualism was, in fact, a thoroughly entrenched position long before Descartes.

But why duality? Why have people everywhere come up with this notion? Why not unity or some greater plurality? Isn't splitting up our experience simply an illusion, aren't we part and parcel of everything around us? Well, yes… kind of. But our very bodies create a thin wall between what we perceive as our core selves and the world outside. Such is property dualism, a distinction between the properties of subjective mental life and the properties of inanimate, thoughtless objects. According to property dualism there are not two different substances but only one substance, a substance composed entirely of atoms. According to this doctrine, the atoms that make up the molecules that make up the brain give rise to the very thoughts you possess at this moment. Isn't that stunning! These seemingly immaterial thoughts and feelings are, in fact, just as material as your hands and your furniture. Atoms are so bizarre that they create all these different properties—solidity, fluidity, sharpness, brightness, cheerfulness, sadness. Everything we see and think is part of one substance expressed in different ways. There is nothing *more* than atoms, nothing beyond atoms. Your bed and your mind are both just atoms behaving in different ways—pure energy frozen into varied forms.

While the debate over a theory of substance—the unity of materialism (everything comes from matter alone) or the duality of spirit/matter—appears the height of a useless academic exercise, in reality, it shapes our most crucial ideas about human existence. This question is not limited to college philosophy classes. This same question has started wars, sent countless people to burn at the stake, imprisoned hordes of people, and liberated many more. Depending on how one answers this question he will be a Jew or a Christian, a Muslim or a Buddhist, an atheist or a fundamentalist. With this question lies most political power and the entire command of priests and churches. From this question the Pharaoh derived sovereignty over Egypt and from it a Jewish carpenter transformed himself into God Himself. The two basic notions—man as animal or man as spirit—are the direct conclusions of this philosophic debate. If truth resides in dualism then man is likely divine. But if materialism proves correct then the whole Darwinian damnation—death and all—has become our lot... and we had best get on with it.

## *The Perennial Soul*

Science teaches us that nature embedded in all creatures some rudimentary sense of self. Without the self, survival would be a lost cause. To survive and adapt, one must perceive the unity of one's actions. What fitness has a toad, a dog, or a human being if, devoid of self-concern, it walks into a predator's toothy mouth? "But this foremost—To thyself be true," is not only a father's sage advice to his son but nature's to each of its children. Watch a child jerk back from the pain of her first contact with fire and you'll witness the same instinctive retreat that keeps the fish wary of the hook. Skin, which provides a thin barrier between the inner and the outer, gives rise to the experience of duality. The duty to keep this membrane free of tears remains among our top priorities. And the duty to stuff this skin with all the foods and liquids necessary for its many functions keeps us ever busy. All our attempts at safety and comfort—the amassing of wealth, the achievement of status, the power of command—are different ways to ensure our body's integrity and, finally, to avoid dismemberment and death.

This first duality, the basic perception of self and other, the interior and the exterior, streams through our categories of thought and forms a pillar in our construction of culture. How do we take this natural heritage and humanize it? Among the most noteworthy of ideas, we 'split' ourselves; we insist that one part of us is a soul—immaterial, immortal, and eminently important—while the other part is merely a vessel or a shell. This idea has taken such root that many have sacrificed themselves for it: believers everywhere have endangered their bodies for what they considered the protection of their souls.

Without this understanding, without an unflinching faith in its truth, how could the educated, postmodern martyrs of Islam—the terrorists of 9/11—rush into certain death? These men lived in the twenty first century with the rest of us. They were not cave-dwelling brutes but scientists and engineers; capable individuals who managed to obtain pilot licenses in American training programs. These men had undoubtedly used drugs in their lifetimes and had perceived head trauma in their lifetimes, but still they failed to see the all-important connection of mind and body. These men believed in ghosts. They did not fear the destruction of their bodies because they *knew* that their souls would flutter off to paradise moments after their religiously-inspired act had come to fruition. Instead, they destroyed thousands of lives, including their own. The martyrs of 9/11 did not release their souls but they did diminish the human spirit.

Somewhere along the journey from apes to poets, we humans developed the ability to see 'objectively.' That is, we gained an imagination that allowed us to perceive ourselves as actors in a larger drama. This aptitude became so sophisticated that we could make objects of everything, including our very bodies. The chimpanzee, after all, doesn't prattle on and on about being fat the way we commonly do. The chimp doesn't loathe himself when his form slackens with age. Of all reactive creatures, only man's sense of self, due to his enormously complex brain, developed to the point where it could objectify even itself. Only the human animal can experience the strange torment of alienation. Now a person can disparage himself as so many drives and desires, so much foible and folly. The individual can be, and usually is, his own worst enemy. While a simpler creature might identify its whole body as 'itself,' man has the ability to perceive body as 'not-self.' The happy-go-lucky dog sniffs his fellows' netherparts and licks his own—fully identified with all aspects of himself, high and low—while even the relatively unfettered man of modernity treats such issues with Victorian shame. And the anorexic who overcomes all instinct and avoids sustenance: how else could an anorexic starve the very flesh that keeps her alive, rejecting it like a transplanted organ? The anorexic has dissociated body and mind, denying their absolute union. No other animal is capable of such perverted self-harm. The self, to man, can be reduced down to its most basic element—the mental realm—and even then to a sparse series of programs and routines such as the need to be thin or the ambition to be powerful. The sum of one's efforts may revolve around just a bare few routines.

The perception of duality—of the interior self and the exterior world, including the body—is a double-edged sword. On one side it cleaves a massive wound in our psyche, the most horrid realization: that we, housed as we are in bodies, are mortal and shall pass. Not only have we experienced the deadening loss of those dear to us, people who lived, loved, breathed, and laughed with us, but we infer this fate to be our own. It is nothing less than psychological trauma to realize that one's individual self is housed in a flawed shell— flawed because it ages, decays, and dies. The truth is too terrible, our will to deny may save us from it.

While one side of the sword cleaves, its other side heals. For the same mental agility that led to the troubling 'problem' of death also created its hopeful solution: a different kind of life, in a whis- per—*life after death*. "Life after death," it's a phrase so hopelessly inept in logic that it defines the word oxymoron. But the concept, as imaginative—indeed infantile—as it is has its root in experience. The sense of self appears so rugged in comparison to our fragile bodies that we imagine it to be an entirely separate substance—a soul.

Consider a marathon runner. After battering her body with twenty six miles of pounding exertion, pushed to the very limits of human physiology, she can go ever farther. With incredible willpower the tiny form of a woman can do this and more, beyond all limits of reason, because she finds meaning in the meaningless act. This isn't a hunt for food after all, nor is the endurance run an adrenaline- fueled flight from death—no pouncing tiger or charging rhinoceros lies in wait. No, one signs up for the marathon, one *pays* to do such a thing. And just when the body seems on the verge of collapse a loud cheer from a friend or a thoughtful mantra one whispers to oneself rejuvenates the will and enlivens the body for more punishment.

So, that such a thing as the soul might exist, that one's mind may be *stronger* than one's body, is not out of the question for our experience teaches us to expect the improbable. And with the soul, with the concept of this persevering center, we may perceive the decay of the world around and within us and yet feel protected—*we shall endure*. Though friends and family have passed on, they are simply in another plane, ready to meet us when we ourselves depart from this one. Claims to personal immortality almost always come from a belief in this immaterial soul. The dogma is a near universal one in the religions of the world—concerned, as they must be, with the meaning of life.

Ultimately, the soul and immortality arise from two sources: the ontological and the historical. Ontology refers here to the very structure of one's organism—the core of sensations inside the body and the fear of death. As a concept, the soul will appear time and again without any outside instruction. It issues from needs that our bodies will always possess and is part of our very nature. So long as we live in aging and frail bodies we will fear death and seek comfort in the face of it. Historically, this self-evident fear has been shored up by all sorts of soul philosophies and immortality doctrines. When one first hears such a doctrine, a bell of recognition rings—this is the answer I've always sought. My 'I' will not disappear. In the end, both our natural structure and our cultural heritage confirms the reality of dualism for us. Few needs are so dire and universal among human animals. Roy Batty, the sympathetic madman of *Bladerunner*, when facing his creator, Dr. Tyrell, demands just one thing: "I want more life!" This is the theological universal, it's what all men want from their gods. Like an entirely different kind of appetite, we mentally and verbally hunger for more and ever more: *I want more life!* Because of this urgency in the face of death, the doctrine of the soul is practically unassailable.

Why bring up the debate about the human soul once again? If thousands of years of careful thinkers could not resolve the arguments, why should we expect anything more? We can now expect better answers—or at least better arguments—because science has provided us with new tools and new information about this all-important matter. In particular, the findings of neuroscience demand a reassessment of the substance dualism argument for they assert the truth of the materialist position. We near the end of an epic quest. We can finally know the truth about the soul.

# PART I

# A HISTORY OF THE SOUL

When the body (*soma*) becomes the tomb (*sema*) of the soul, the true home of the soul is sought beyond this world. Thus the soul is the source of the supernatural. As long as man does not feel divided against himself, he lacks the notion of the supernatural. The supernatural is a projection of man's sense of alienation from nature.

—Walter Kaufmann, *Tragedy and Philosophy*

# *Ghosts*

Long a favorite of our kind, ghost stories fill us with wonder and instill in us a sense of the eerie and unknown. Plucking many chords, these tales resonate powerfully within us. No wonder, these tales reflect our condition—we are haunted.

For thousands of years the dead have pestered the living. They share our space and occasionally drive us crazy. The dead live inside each of us. The history of our words and the meanings through which we come to understand the world commingle the living and the dead. Side by side within us, the latest scientific findings provide one way of understanding while ancient traditions linger on to create contradictory understandings. We are thoroughly clogged with the thick residue of dead and dying conceptions of the world. As individuals and societies, we are passionately confused.

Freshly minted world-views and Stone Age ones struggle for dominance within the same human mind. The Stone Age descriptions, born of battle and accustomed to the gore of hacking, often win out over the modern ones that seek too casually to win peace through concession. In their victory, roughshod viewpoints mirror the violence and conquest that barbarian hordes have shown time and again when they topple refined civilizations long unpracticed in the arts of war. While science will require you to hold many difficult ideas at once, and leave them unsettled or dependent on further data and argument, many religions will assure you of a particular truth and demand that you think no more of it. Let your questions disappear and be replaced with a certain faith—the simplest solution to impossible mysteries.

The methods by which we acquire knowledge are also haunted. Many prefer the methods of science while others cling to mythologies of another time and place, long out of date. Until we banish our ghosts we will remain haunted, stretched between an ancient world—unfamiliar to us—and the one which is our true and present home.

*Chapter 1*

# WHERE WE ARE—
# THE CARTESIAN SPLIT

While Descartes achieved a reputation for diverse philosophic achievements, his description of mind/body dualism won him lasting fame. He details the two basic components of life as that which can be handled, measured, and extended in space—body (or matter); and that which is equally real but finds no proper measurement or extension in space—consciousness (or mind). For instance, while we can experience this manuscript as a physical thing—measure its height, determine its weight, count its words, burn its paper—we cannot measure or touch the very consciousness, our own, which makes sense of its symbolic contents. Which is more real? While the book can be carried and shown to all who possess sense, its more important fact, its usage as a communication device, cannot be had without that invisible, untouchable substance we call human consciousness.

Descartes's first thoughts on dualism appear in his essay, *Discourse on the Method*. He continues this theme in *Meditations on First Philosophy*. Descartes uses doubt as his most important philosophic tool. Beginning with the most extreme worries, Descartes attempts to get to the absolute truth:

> I will suppose...that there is an evil demon, supremely powerful and cunning, who works as hard as he can to deceive me. I will say that sky, air, earth, color, shape, sound, and other external things are just dreamed illusions which the demon uses to ensnare my judgment. I will regard myself as not having hands, eyes, flesh, blood, and senses—but as having the false belief that I have all these things.[1]

Through a steadfast exercise of such doubt, he destroys one after another of his most basic assumptions. Finally, he comes to a concept that he cannot doubt—his own existence as a thinking being. Descartes wrote one of philosophy's most famous statements: "*Cogito ergo sum* (I think therefore I am)."[2] Through doubt he reached philosophic bedrock: if he didn't exist as a thinking being, then who did all the doubting?

Philosophers often spend a great deal of time and ink reiterating an argument that, in its essence, is quite simple. Descartes's dualism provides us the crucial case in point. Instead of lumbering over each and every syllable of this earnest thinker's careful words, let's get to the meat of the matter: the human person possesses an immaterial mind and a physical body. In his sixth meditation, Descartes writes:

> ...from the fact that I have gained knowledge of my existence without noticing anything about my nature or essence except that I am a thinking thing, I can rightly conclude that my essence consists solely in the fact that I am a thinking thing. It's possible (or, as I will say later, it's certain) that I have a body which is very tightly bound to me. But, on the other hand, I have a clear and distinct idea of myself insofar as I am just a thinking and unextended thing, and, on the other hand, I have a distinct idea of my body insofar as it is just an extended and unthinking thing. It's certain, then, that I am really distinct from my body and can exist without it.[3]

The person, therefore, is a dual being composed of a spirit and a body. That, in reality, is all Descartes sought to flesh out and, in doing so, he illuminated no one for all had long accepted this truth—it is the very backbone of all Christian theology and Western culture.

The teaching of dualism is repeated hundreds of times per day whenever and wherever people celebrate the Catholic Mass. According to the doctrine of transubstantiation, the physical host—the wafer of unleavened bread—mystically transforms into the very body of Christ. Obviously, though, the piece of bread doesn't turn into a bloody piece of flesh. Christ's body, then, must be a nonphysical thing—in short, a bodiless body, better known as a spirit. During the Mass, then, the bread turns into the very spirit of God—God stuff. By eating it you gain more soul. You become less animal and more spirit, you get a boost of grace, a protein shake for the soul.

Why, then, did Descartes obtain such fame for putting into

words what everyone had already understood to happen during the Mass? Descartes represented the up and coming heresy—science. The rise of science posed a great threat to theology in Descartes's time. Galileo had just been arrested, Bacon had recently published his important *Novum Organum,* and creative theorists were rapidly transforming the rediscovered Greek ideas into an assortment of anti-Church theologies. On many intellectual fronts, the Church had begun to fight an all out war. To have Descartes repeat its highest truths in the new language seemed a tremendous victory. For this, his name would long be revered, a scientific saint of the Church.

Descartes's doctrines produced immediate, far-reaching effects, including a new degree of freedom for science, which had been tightly holstered by the Church. Cartesian dualism supported the Church's critical role in the sphere of man's soul and its salvation. No amount of science would take away the Church's supremacy. This assurance from Descartes made the Church more secure. Consequently, the Church allowed the scientists a freer hand in the material matters of the here and now; science's tinkering no longer presented a threat to spiritual authority. At the time, this parceling out of mental real estate seemed a striking bargain to the Church. A celebrated philosopher-scientist had proved their total sovereignty in the most important of realms—the spiritual one. Looking back, this 'deal' turned out to be an enormous rip-off. Science, as we well know, quickly peopled and expanded its parcel until it became the New York of our worldview. The Church, in contrast, seems to reside in some rustic, non-arable acreage, as archaic and useless as a crumbling castle in the moors, the shadow of a once great fiefdom.

We must not forget that during this time all things occurred under the Church's supervision. The New World, at that moment already plundered and ransacked, had not been conquered and annexed for the glory (or wealth) of any European power, but under the pretext of saving heathen souls. Around the same time, the Inquisition mercifully marched onward.

Imprisoning Jews and non-believers (people, that is, who believed in things other than the Christian Truth), the Inquisition presented them with the option of admitting their unbelief and accepting Christ as Lord and Savior, or being tortured to death. And such torture the Christians developed! Torture had never achieved such heights of creativity and art. No Chinese water torture or bamboo under the fingernails could compare with the high art of Catholic torture. The mechanical geniuses of this time created devices of pain whose divine inspiration is clear. With these brutal machines the Inquisitors could attack the devilish flesh from above, below, from the side, backwards. These virtuosos played bones, ligaments, and nerves like musical instruments in a symphony of agony. And why not? Surely any means is permissible if it helped to accomplish the ultimate end—the salvation of the soul. The Inquisition's methods reflected a faultless logic. In the redemption of a non-believer's soul, any amount of pain was both merciful and just. What are some few moments of agony and indignity, what is enfeeblement or death itself, when compared to one's eternal salvation? If human consciousness resides in the transcendent soul then whatever material need be cut from that jewel, in the quest for salvation, becomes superfluous. The Church was anything if not rational. It accepted a set of assumptions and acted accordingly. Were it still so logical (or shall we say powerful) it would continue the Inquisition. However bizarre and inhuman this may seem to us, the Inquisition was a campaign of the purest mercy. Believers genuinely hoped to divert non-believers away from their hellward path. And by saving their fellows, inquisitors assured their loyalty and faith to the great Lord, in whose service they were performing these tortures.

In an era when Church/State boundaries were unknown, all political and legal matters had some recourse to faith and Christian authority. The Church possessed the keys to man's most important endeavors. If a king thought of moving an inch, he had to seek approval from the Church. He may have resented its power but he could not deny it. While a king might control his peoples' lives, the Church possessed far more powerful control over the masses. Descartes's swindle helped to dethrone the Church from its imperial seat.

Dualism appeared long before Descartes in places far afield, a spontaneous discovery that came from man looking death in the face and seeking some escape. Dualism had always been observed and used, but never so carefully articulated. It took Descartes's philosophic genius to clarify dualism and make it a subject of debate. Before it had been a religious assumption, after Descartes it became philosophy's keystone.

*Chapter 2*

# THE PREHISTORIC BEGINNINGS
# OF THE SOUL

The first prehistoric man who recounted a vivid, action-packed dream to his clan members, only to be told that he hadn't left his spot in the cave all evening, knew something of his dual self. The reality of his dream and his voyages in the dreamworld must have convinced him of a two-fold existence, a first separation of body and soul.

In addition to one's experience of a dream alter ego, the common experience of encountering a dead loved one in dreams lends support to the soul and the afterlife. The incredibly detailed reality of the person we know to be dead is often difficult to 'explain' in our own time. To a pre-scientific, pre-Freudian people this experience confirmed the reality of the afterlife and the continuing existence of the dead in a supernatural place separate from the physical world.

Some anthropologists estimate the concept of the soul to be 30,000 years old. The excavations of caves used as prehistoric dwellings reveal that the Cro-Magnon, some of the earliest of our species, buried the dead with ritual objects and coated the corpses in red ocher paint. As Mircea Eliade notes in *A History of Religious Ideas*: "Belief in a survival after death seems to be demonstrated, from the earliest times, by the use of red ocher as a ritual substitute for blood, hence as a symbol of life."[1] Like the ancient Egyptians, the Cro-Magnon buried personal objects with the dead for usage in the afterlife. In these burials corpses were set in a fetal position that also suggests rebirth.[2] If this interpretation is correct, it marks the notion of the soul as tremendously ancient. If the idea of a soul existed in early human communities as long as 30,000 thousand years ago then as these communities explored and peopled diverse sections of the globe, the seed idea of a soul would be found in mythologies the world over—as it is.

In addition to care-intensive burials, cave art portrays a visionary interpretation of the world. The art, with its depictions of strange symbols, animals, hand prints, and half-man, half-animal creatures could have only come from powerful imaginations. Carved and painted by humans in Paleolithic (Old Stone Age) times, the detailed images that adorn subterranean chambers and vaults reveal magico-shamanic motifs.[3] The Koonalda cave in Australia possesses art dated more than 20,000 years old.[4] Cave art found throughout Europe similarly dates back tens of millennia. The fabulous Dordogne region of France is rich in these sacred caves, including the celebrated Lascaux. More recent finds, like the Chauvet Cave, push back the dates of this evocative art even further. The art of the Chauvet Cave may be 35,000 years old.[5]

Most of the caves where art is found remain thoroughly out of the way and difficult to access. The artistically rendered images often lie hundreds of meters deep in places where natural light does not penetrate. This art was not prehistoric doodling; rather, these places were religious sites, their art an overlay of magical imagery upon sacred stone. Some of the images were elaborately painted while others were deeply carved into the stone and colored with pigment. Such care requires the concentrated talents of a capable human artist. When one ventures into the dark stillness of these caves, the flickering fire of torchlight transforms these glyphs into moving images full of supernatural meaning and vitality—this is indeed a sacred experience.

One of the most striking depictions in European cave art is the "Shaman of Les Trois Freres," discovered by a French Count and his three sons in 1914. The artistically rendered shaman possesses human and animal features akin to the pictures of Egyptian gods with their jackal heads and eagle wings. The scene details a human-like figure, thickly dressed in animal skins and donned with a large set of antlers. The shaman seems to be performing a dance. The magical overtones in this art suggest a religious inspiration that stretches back into our kind's very beginnings.

## Animism

> ...animism, surely the most absurd and most punished error in
> the history of sapiens, the triple paradox: that all things can
> think; that thinking can be disembodied from any thinking
> thing; and that thinking (soul, spirit) is a thing more immor-
> tal than matter—whereas actually mind is always and only a
> contingent and temporary function of a thing, the brain.
> —Weston LaBarre, *Culture in Context*[6]

Before strict dualism came into vogue and divorced man's soul
from his body, the system of belief called animism taught man that
all things possessed souls—the stone no less than the man. For ani-
mists, our modern notion of 'dead matter' would make no sense. To
early man everything seemed alive. The ancient sense of self differed
greatly from our own because of this belief system. Living deeply
embedded in his environment and lacking control over natural
processes, prehistoric man lived interdependently with all other
things. Though he perceived its many mysteries, man still understood the world around him in an intimate fashion—he perceived it
as a part of his community and understood its processes in his own
terms. There was no idea of 'man versus nature' in ancient times,
men and nature were one and the same.

For ancient man, all natural processes were understood as
'willed' in the same fashion that we perceive our own actions to be
self-directed. The term for this belief is imposing—anthropomorphism. Anthropomorphism defines a simple idea, that we project
human-like features onto a non-human process. Animism is one version of anthropomorphism—the projection of the human psyche
upon the world at large, the understanding that objects have minds.
Things behave the way they do because of a set of feelings and
thoughts like our own. All things exist like humans do, they just possess differently shaped bodies and speak a different language.

Animism informed the world-view of people at least as far back
as the Cro-Magnon. The Paleolithic art of ancient peoples is best
viewed through the lens of animism. By recognizing the spiritual
powers in things and seeking their help, man obtained harmony
with his environment—his predators and prey. Cave art seems to

depend on 'sympathetic magic.' The performance of rituals in sacred art affects the 'real' things depicted, the idea being that a sympathy exists between the mental/spiritual world and the real one. The voodoo doll, for instance, is a tool for sympathetic magic. By hurting the doll, you hurt the real person that the doll represents. In ancient times, a ritual hunt was portrayed by the shaman in magical art before undertaking the actual hunt. The modern practice of visualizing an athletic success and 'psyching oneself up' to improve performance attests to the adaptive success of such 'magic.'

Animism fostered an intimate relationship between ancient men and their environment. If nature did something 'unkind,' it was as punishment for some fault of man's—he either forgot some ritual or broke some rule. A peace must be made: the ancients needed to persuade the various agents of the natural world be made to forgive their our transgression. Some healing ritual would rekindle our friendship with nature. All this is quite similar to the gift exchange system of primitive societies. Insults and misunderstandings are a common feature of living in a community and must be righted with gifts and exchanges of respect to restore social order. Animals, plants, insects, weather—the whole spectrum of nature—were 'persons' in community with oneself. Though one could not talk to these different beings in the way one talked to his friend, they were still as person-like as the clan two valleys over who spoke a different dialect. Religion and sacred rites emerged as a non-verbal language to communicate with nature for the exchange of respect. The Winnebago Trickster Cycle provides an example of the personification of nature assumed in animism. This Native American tale, just a few centuries old, indicates how 'natural man' understands his surroundings through animistic mythology:

> He [Trickster] went all over the Earth, and one day he came to a place where he found a large waterfall. It was very high. Then he said to the waterfall, 'Remove yourself to some other location for the people are going to inhabit this place and you will annoy them.' Then the waterfall said, 'I will not go away. I chose this place and I am going to stay here.' 'I tell you, you are going to some other place,' said the Trickster. The waterfall, however, refused to go. 'I am telling you that the Earth was made for man to live on and you will annoy him if you stay here. I came to this Earth to rearrange it. If you don't do what I tell you, I will not use you very gently.' Then the water-

fall said, 'I told you when I first spoke to you that I would not move and I am not going to.' Then the Trickster cut a stick for himself and shot it into the falls and pushed the falls on to the land.[7]

The natural world of ancient times made sense as much, if not more, than the scientific world that we now inhabit. We may marvel at the beauty and power of a waterfall but now try to imagine the waterfall as a person. Imagine that you really believe that the waterfall possesses a mind. You might then have something like a human relationship with the waterfall, you could talk to it and listen to it. The world, then, was not something external and different from you but a part of your society. When all things can be viewed in the same language as human intention, a profound sense of community prevails. If a stone rolled down a cliff it was not because of gravity or some 'objective' chain of causes; obviously the cliff had spit out or rejected the stone in the same way we spit out a splinter of bone when chewing a sinewy piece of meat. If you needed to climb that cliff you could utter a chant or entreaty and be assured that your respect for the cliff, as another living being, would forge an understanding and provide you safety. Rain fell for a 'reason'—the clouds either wept or urinated or fulfilled a wish, as evinced in Native American rain dances. Myths, like the Greek one about Helios the Sun god, proposed a 'plot' behind the sun's daily journey that gave a human explanation to its regular behavior.

Ancient man personalized everything. By attributing the complex causes of the world to human willing, man could gain an understanding otherwise prohibited to him. Just as a child talks to his doll or his dog as if they understand him, primitive man believes that the storm-cloud is aware of him and pursues him particularly. As the philosopher Unamuno wrote:

> The divine, therefore, was not originally something objective, but was rather the subjectivity of consciousness projected outwardly, the personalization of the world. The concept of divinity arose out of the sense of divinity, and the sense of divinity is naught but the dim and nascent sense of personality turned upon the outer world.[8]

As a way to understand mysteries, anthropomorphism makes a lot of sense—it is quite 'rational.' When looking through our modern eyes, anthropomorphic explanations—the typical explanations in most myths—seem silly and immature. They are not. Though we rarely notice, every one of us still portrays things anthropomorphically to a surprising degree: we get 'mad' at our cars (as if this could coerce the machine to perform) and infer every accident and chance event in our lives as divinely sanctioned events. We punch the soda machine if it does not give us what we paid for, like we might punch a person who cheated us. The soda machine neither intends an insult nor feels our injury. But it is not easy to understand this inhumanity, to casually forget the mishap as an accident of the machinery in front of us. Before the careful methods of science were devised, anthropomorphic notions were the best explanations of life's mysteries. Without explanations, the world would appear less comprehensible and people would feel less 'at home'—a state of anxiety would prevail were we to constantly perceive everything around us as casually inhuman.

## I Think/I Believe

Anthropomorphism always leads to interpretations of existence based on dogma, interpretations that must be accepted as articles of faith. Science explains mystery by different—and faithless—means. Science, like religion, informs us through belief. Propositions and explanations must be believed, at least for a time, in order to construct further beliefs. Religion and science differ in their conservatism about these beliefs. Religion, by posing strict dogma, changes far more slowly than science. The frontiers of science reshape themselves every few decades, discoveries in techniques and theories constantly revamp entire systems of scientific thought from the ground up.

Science and religion affect men in fundamentally different ways. Within the believing group, religion often ties people closer together. However, as groups with differing beliefs begin to communicate more often, as in the modern/post-modern world, religion poses a great problem: the beliefs of different groups are different! Since the character of dogma does not allow for any quick revisions, religion leads to serious crises between groups of differing faiths. The conflict of Christians and Muslims in the Crusades continues to this very day. Science, on the other hand, brings together people of many different regions, languages, and cultures. Its relatively universal methods and humility before phenomena allow people of diverse backgrounds a common language and platform for interaction. In its worst instances, of course, science gets conscripted to serve the more powerful faith systems of ideology and religion. In such cases, the fruits of science are mere weapons for those with the most fanatical beliefs.

The great complexity man perceives in his environment leads to a state of fear and wonder. Such a state of mind can alternate quite unpredictably between one pole and the other—profound wonder and overwhelming fear. Without reasons and stories to structure this raw state of mind, man would be drowned in the terror of isolation. It seems that he alone—in all the cold universe—exists as a sensitive being invested with emotion and reason.

The split between the scientific (which depends upon perception and testing) and the mythico-religious (a matter of faith) exists in the minds of most people today. Either interpretation gives the world an explanation, something man always and everywhere needs. Of the two types of knowledge, religious/mythological interpretations usually offer more in the way of answering the great mystery of existence since the imagination of the priest or shaman will always outpace the slow-going rigor of the scientist with his tangle of instruments and equations. The religious world-view will also remain more popular since it promises the fulfillment of man's desires. In contrast, science emphasizes the limitations of an impersonal natural world. To assure ourselves, we always frame things to make us feel cared for like children by an all-powerful, all knowing parent. Science will never be able to tell such bedtime stories to its 'believers.'

## A Reasonable God

The tendency to anthropomorphize the natural world, projecting our human intentions upon it, appears time and again in our creative attempts to explain life's mysteries. Shortly after thousands of the most pious European Christians descended upon the Middle East in the 11th century after the birth of their savior, slaughtering swaths of Muslims all along the way, a new principle appeared in discussions about the Christian God—the principle of reason. The booty that Christians brought back from the Holy Land included ancient Greek writings. The Muslims, confident in their political strength, happily studied and discussed the wisdom of the ancients. Europeans, long since cut off from Greek thought, began to ponder this curious, pagan philosophy. The ancients seemed especially enamored of reason—applying rigorous analysis and scrutinizing logic to the great questions. When Medieval theologians tried to align the mythology of Christianity with this newly found 'reason,' the assumption of anthropomorphism crept in still.

The medieval theologian, Saint Thomas Aquinas, devised various 'proofs' for the existence of God, the belief in the Resurrection, the divinity of Jesus, etc., like so many puzzles out of Euclid's geometry (a bit of plunder that instigated the Cathedral Age of Europe).

One of Aquinas's proofs of God, entitled "the Unmoved Mover," reflects the tendency to imagine the actions of the universe in terms of human will and mentality. According to the proof, since all motion must have a cause, including the beginning of the universe, then something 'unmoved' must have started the ball rolling. This first step of creation must simply be God's doing. Unfortunately, Aquinas fails to clarify the assumption that the Unmoved Mover is specifically 'humanlike.' What he forgets to explain is why the Unmoved Mover would be conscious and intentional, 'will-like', rather than blind and unconscious. When we consider a smaller problem, such as a rock falling from a cliff, we impose no human 'reasons' whatsoever. In its essence, the 'Unmoved Mover' might be as blind and thoughtless as the rock's descent. The scientific theory of the 'Big Bang' provides us just such an explanation. But an even larger hole in Aquinas's proof of God is that a God who is merely the initiator of this first movement implies absolutely nothing about the very personal God that religious people hold dear. The God who is the Unmoved Mover might just as easily be cruel and insane as thoughtful and benevolent.

Steeped in anthropomorphism throughout our history, we encounter in ourselves a tremendous resistance when we try to explain something in impersonal (that is, scientific) terms. It took centuries, and not a few scientific martyrs, before people came to believe Copernicus's blasphemous doctrine that the Earth revolved around the Sun. That our world is not the very center of the universe—anything but that!

The lineage of our thinking patterns from prehistory, to ancient history, to modern times, preserves its anthropomorphic tendencies. The universe fundamentally does not make sense to us unless some form of human-like will directs it. Xenophanes, one of the original critics of our self-centered ideas about the universe, joked about man's propensity to think of everything in terms of his own experience: "…if oxen and horses and lions…could create works of art like those made by men, horses would draw pictures of gods like horses, and oxen of gods like oxen…"[9] Using a more human example Xenophanes wrote, "Ethiopians have gods with snub noses and black hair, Thracians have gods with grey eyes and red hair."[10]

Animism and its magico-religious beliefs set the stage for dualism by supposing that a spiritual substance persists behind all material things. The animistic world that had once imbued soul upon all things eventually receded leaving its tidal pools of soul-substance in humans alone. By holding on too tightly for too long, the animistic notions that bound ancient man to his environment later drove them apart; now everything seemed patently 'inhuman.' During the maturing process mankind came to recognize subtle patterns in nature. Things were not as clearly 'alive' as before. The patterns of nature, like the paths of the stars, could be recognized, charted, and accurately predicted. No longer were the processes of nature person-like, they were entirely thing-like. Nature was no longer 'ensouled' but mechanistic. The psychological poetry of human intention gave way to the cold language of mathematics. The objective study of nature, stripping it of its imagined subjectivity, provided an accuracy of comprehension that religious mythology had never offered. Adolescent mankind no longer needed gods or souls to explain the processes of the world outside of him. Having disposed of nature's 'soul,' man recognized soul to be his own unique possession.

## *Chapter 3*

# SHAMANISM

Shamanism is the ancient and universal institution of spiritual 'specialists'; call them priests, witch-doctors, medicine men, or wizards, these specially trained and unusual people held a power in their community of the first order. These spiritual specialists possessed the techniques and magical abilities that gave man knowledge of the 'causes' behind things and the ability to influence the unseen world. Shamans played crucial roles in their clans, acting as spiritual warriors to defend: "...life, health, fertility, the world of 'light,' against death, diseases, sterility, disaster, and the world of 'darkness.'"[1] Our knowledge of shamanism makes it certain that the idea of the soul existed for thousands of years before the high-culture of the ancient Egyptians. The shamanically-oriented Central Asian tribes that stretched across that continent and eventually peopled the Americas articulated a clear notion of the soul. As a cultural artifact, shamanism existed in a circumpolar ring that united ancient peoples all the way from Ireland to the Americas. Currently, shamanism retains a strong presence in the traditional cultures of rural South America. Many cultures, ancient and modern, rely on shamans for their spiritual wellbeing.

The need for explanation and a modicum of power in the face of nature's mysterious ways are fulfilled in the character of the shaman. Mircea Eliade explains in his book *Shamanism: Archaic Techniques of Ecstasy*:

> It is hard for us to imagine what...shamanism can represent for an archaic society... The shaman's essential role in the defense of the psychic integrity of the community depends above all on this: men are sure that one of them is able to help them in the critical circumstances produced by the inhabitants of the invisible world. It

is consoling and comforting to know that a member of the community is able to see what is hidden and invisible to the rest and to bring back direct and reliable information from the supernatural worlds.[2]

Shamanism has played a vital role in human culture for thousands of years. Besides the Shaman of Les Trois Freres, another strange figure, painted on the walls of the nearby Lascaux cavern, also appears to be a shaman. The scene shows a bison nudging a man on the ground. Most unusual about this figure is his bird-head, complete with beak. Next to him stands a perched bird. These motifs are suggestive of shamanism which commonly uses the bird as symbol of the shaman's transcendental abilities.[3] The bird defies the law of gravity that keeps men and most other animals glued to the Earth. The bird seemed the fitting animal of the shaman who himself, of all his tribe, had the secret knowledge to alter the laws of nature. Given the age of shamanically-influenced cave art, shamanism proves to be the oldest surviving religion on Earth. Shamanism's institutions, practices, and world-views informed much later religion with its typical reliance on 'specialists' (prophets, mystics, seers, priests) in dealing with the spirit-world.

## *Ecstasy*

Shamanism is less a religion than a complex of religious methods and ideas. Shamans knew various ways to access the spirit-world. They were masters of the techniques of ecstasy.[4] Ecstasy, an alternate state of consciousness, provided an entrance to the world of spirits and magic. Through ecstasy the shaman voyaged to the world behind our own, the source of the great mysteries. The mystical strand woven into virtually every religious tradition utilizes and explores ecstasy. Aldous Huxley entitled mysticism the "perennial philosophy"[5] because of its seeming universality and importance. To this day ecstasy is the core method of mysticism.

The central feature of ecstasy, as its Greek etymology suggests, is the ability to stand outside of oneself. It is, in short, a temporary release from the body. The concept of ecstasy employs some of the features we've seen in animism; in particular, ecstasy assumes the separation of reality's two principles—matter and spirit. The dualism spawned by animism provides the background for the talents of the shaman who specializes in the spiritual realm.

The great shamans could enter states of ecstasy at will. Conditions such as mild schizophrenia, autism, or bipolar depression, seen as congenital defects in our own time and culture, would have endowed their ancient sufferers with a kind of shamanic vocation—a divine madness. Instead of condemning these people to social disfavor and poverty, such proclivities may have thrust them into positions of authority. Indeed, the cultural notion that madness and genius are paired reveals a bit of our shamanic heritage. And the very word, genius, refers to a spirit guide—imbued with special knowledge—reminiscent of this ancient belief system. In the original usage of the word, a person was not a genius but *had* a genius.

The more even-keeled shamans relied on means such as drumming, singing, dancing, fasting, and the use of hallucinogenic plants to achieve ecstatic states. In Siberia, the hallucinogenic mushroom *Amanita muscaria* provided a foolproof method for this. Both North and South American shamanism makes extensive use of psychoactive plants to enter shamanic states of consciousness. If the American strain of shamanism accurately reflects an age-old tradition of plant-induced ecstasy then the history of drug use and humanity go hand in hand. Our own dismal take on drugs results from the modern, recreational abuse of them—a fundamental disrespect of their great power. Drug-assisted shamanic ecstasy is as sanctioned and controlled in its cultures as the distribution of Eucharist is in the Catholic Communion. Both the ingestion of the Eucharist and the consumption of sacred plants are sacraments in these respective traditions. The thought of using sacred plants recreationally would have been as abominable to the members of a shamanic culture as the defilement of the Eucharist is to Catholics.

## The Shaman's Call

The predisposition of those who would become shamans included mental instability. Often sickly, sometimes bizarre, the future shamans possessed many of the traits that we now associate with mental illness. Many scholars of shamanism decry the insinuation that the great shamans of the past were the prehistorical analogues of our contemporary insane. The mythologist Joseph Campbell feels that the abnormal temperaments of shamans were reflective of the initiatory crisis of their provocative roles. In his mind, these were not disturbed individuals. Rather, they were the ancient equivalents of the creative, sensitive artists of our own time:

> ...though the temporary unbalance precipitated by such a crisis may resemble a nervous breakdown, it cannot be dismissed as such. For it is a phenomenon *sui generis*; not a pathological but a normal event for the gifted mind in these societies, when struck by and absorbing the force of what for lack of a better term we may call a hierophantic realization: the realization of 'something far more deeply interfused,' inhabiting both the round Earth and one's own interior, which gives to the world a sacred character; an intuition of depth, absolutely inaccessible to the 'tough minded'...[6]

Because the main role of shamans involved healing, the shamans could not be sick people themselves. Despite the fact that the initiatory shamans showed all the signs of a psychological 'crack-up,' they came to heal themselves. Having been exposed early, by fate, to the venom of contingency—innately at the mercy of a kinked brain or a tempestuous and delicate constitution—the proto-shaman had to master life's most poignant truth and integrate it in order to take on the more robust personality of the healer. Even so, history could probably tell a much longer tale about the failed shaman initiates than those who succeeded. Eliade explains the shamanic vocation:

> Like the sick man, the religious man is projected onto a vital plane that shows him the fundamental data of human existence, that is, solitude, danger, hostility of the surrounding world. But the primitive magician, the medicine man, or the shaman is not only a sick man; he is, above all, a sick man who has been cured, who has succeeded in curing himself.[7]

In addition to having a unique constitution, the shaman needed to undergo thorough training. The shaman could not take his role in the community until two highly elaborate forms of knowledge were mastered. He needed the spirit-guided instruction of ecstasy through dreams, trances, and visions; and he needed the traditional education by a former shaman, training in the techniques, tricks, mythology, secret language, and the like. For instance, in the traditional Yakut culture of Siberia most individuals learn about 4000 words. The

Yakut shaman, though, uses a poetic vocabulary of some 12,000 words.[8] Like the Catholic priests of old, who performed all rituals in Latin, the shamans possessed special languages for their religious rites.

After a complete education, the shaman underwent the initiation of ritual death. During this horrific process, a spirit-guide dismembers the shaman's flesh and gives the pieces to evil spirits. Through his self-sacrifice, the shaman gains the power of healing the diseases inflicted by these very spirits. The shaman awakes, reborn into a new body replete with magical powers. While most cultures practice rites of passage, the shaman undergoes the ultimate rite of passage—the most rigorous and difficult dissolution and reconstruction of character.

The shaman's unusual character, thorough education, and ritual death bestowed not only perception of the spirit-world but free access to it. The shaman derives much of his abilities from contact with spirits and supernatural helpers. Eliade explains the importance of spirit contact as a source of knowledge:

> 'Seeing spirits,' in dream or awake, is the determining sign of the shamanic vocation… For, in a manner, having contact with the souls of the dead signifies being dead oneself. …the shaman must so die that he may meet the souls of the dead and receive their teaching; for the dead know everything.[9]

Shamanic healing required secret knowledge and spiritual ability. The etiology of disease in shamanic cultures is quite different from our own. It is recognizable, though, in many ancient cultures and represented in the New Testament. Disease comes from evil spirits. One cures such disease by removing ('casting out') these spirits. Disease can also be the result of the soul having strayed away from its body or being stolen. To cure, the shaman must search high and far to find the soul and then return it to the ill person. One can imagine how adept a shaman must be to perform these harrowing tasks and usher in a convincing 'cure.'

One must carefully plumb ancient man's ideas about disease, for only then can the shaman's importance be appreciated. Ancient peoples believed disease—including the final disease of death—to be against the natural course of things. The only explanation for a disruption in the flow of life was another's evildoing. To the ancients, only murder could cause death. If one died from 'natural causes,' then obviously black magic lay somewhere behind it. Even to those of our contemporaries who still live in traditional cultures (e.g. those cloistered in the jungles of Papua-New Guinea or the Amazon), disease originates from another's curse or an evil shaman's doings. Death, as an event, made no sense to a people who perceived only life all around them. Death was a sudden and complete cessation, a bizarre implosion of life and the erasure of a personality. If a perception lay behind the dualizing tendencies of animism, it was likely the astonishing contrast of death and life—common to all but absolutely irreconcilable to each other. The ancient Greek philosopher Epicurus expresses this perception cogently: "Death...is nothing to us, since while we exist, death is not present, and whenever death is present, we do not exist."[10] But while the sage Epicurus accepted the finality of death, most would not so easily accept his conclusion. A fundamental disbelief clings to death. This disbelief accounts for the heartfelt denial we experience when faced with the death of one close to us. No matter how seasoned we are, no matter how closely we wed ourselves to nature's principles, it just does not seem possible that one we knew in life—someone who ate with us, shared her dreams and desires with us, and laughed with us—just disappeared into oblivion. Dread follows upon the heels of this disbelief.

Death belies all experience and perception for it opposes the rhythm of so many natural processes. The rhythm of the natural world always illustrates a circular pattern, not a linear one. The year has neither beginning nor end, only the individual animal exhibits such a book-ended passage through time. When the sun fell, all knew it would rise again the following morning. When the leaves withered away in autumn, everyone casually expected their bountiful return in the buds of spring. When men fell, though, they did not come back. Only human death seemed final to ancient peoples and, therefore, aroused a sense of poignant strangeness and illogic. Even the renewal of generations could not replace the dead. Children unfold into a distinction whose uniqueness is often jarring to those who parented them. Once an individual passes away, none can renew her form or personality.

Thoroughly versed in life alone, we—like our Stone Age fore-bears—find it impossible to describe such a thing as non-life and have no bearings for doing so. The vast body of people then and now avoid any consideration of death. If the moment turns him to death, the typical person will quickly mutter the most hackneyed phrases to himself and others—eyes downturned—and hope to bring a speedy close to the discussion. The wise majority profess no real knowledge of death. If we are forced to discuss the issue we'll describe death as a transition from this life to another whose terrain can be fathomed only by a marvelous inflation of the experiences and con-ditions of this world. The afterlife of such creative persons usually takes on the sheen of a transcendental Disneyland. Stripped of any fanat-ically-won credos, people of all places and times consider death the most unusual of life's phenomena and stand in utter humiliation before its power.

The task of the shaman, seen specifically in the context of man's humility before life's mysteries, resembles the modern role of the psychotherapist. Both of these specialists help us to regain stability after a disorienting confrontation with dread. The dread of death and sickness shock man to the core because they strip away the garb of life, health, and the illusion of control. The experiences of sickness and death reveal that none hold reins, but that all are yoked in the train of more powerful forces. The retreat of health and the advance towards death alert any thoughtful person to life's most dangerous truths. Comfortable in these truths, for his training and initiation have instructed him in their ways, the shaman walks the uninitiated down the darker halls of the human condition.

## *Shadow of the Shaman*

By knowing techniques of ecstasy, the shaman can explore the spirit-world. In shamanic cultures, it is thought that everyone goes to these other worlds after death. One doesn't have to be a shaman to learn the secrets of existence, one has only to wait. The shaman, in contrast, can go to this other world as often as he likes—during life. Enjoying his ability to travel as a soul, away from the body, the shaman can tell us about the other side of reality.

The shaman's adventures led to some of the earliest conceptions of life after death. Common features about the afterlife appeared in these shaman-informed communities. Upon death, the individual generally faced a trial to weigh his good and evil deeds. In many of these traditions, the recently deceased would have to cross a bridge that, for the good, widened and led to paradise. For the wicked, this bridge narrowed to a razor's edge.

After millennia of shamanic soul-traveling, a standard set of myths began to proliferate. At last, a spiritual geography had come into being. A heaven, an underworld, and a host of spiritual beings became recognized features of the spirit world. With an elaborate spiritual geography and a complex of myths about these planes of existence, the stage was set for profound religious creativity. The abstract worlds and the divine beings who peopled them forged the mythology of the world's great religions. Only through the original animistic dualism and then the shaman's spiritual geography could later mythologies come into being and lead to religion as we know it.

The influence of shamanism on human culture cannot be overstated. Through archeology we have learned that this eclectic set of religious beliefs possesses roots in the most ancient stratum of human prehistory. Anthropology has shown the presence of shamanism in cultures all over the world. Due to its age and importance in early human communities, shamanism spread with the roving tribes to cover Asia, the Americas, and even the remote outposts of Oceania. Historians of religion have shown us that the fundamental concerns of many world religions—concerns about an immaterial soul, about supernatural powers and gods, healing, and the afterlife—were clearly articulated in shamanic traditions that stretch back into remote prehistory.

Whatever its true influence on later faiths, shamanism possessed a well-developed notion of the immaterial soul. Perhaps other religions, in other times and places, developed the idea of the soul independent of any shamanic inspiration. Such convergence is fairly common in the realm of nature. However, evolution, whether of organisms or culture, usually works geologically, one layer gradually forming from the layer beneath and before it. The retention, and subsequent proliferation, of adaptive and useful forms seems as common a process in culture as in biology. However old the idea of the soul is, it was a prominent and useful feature of shamanism.

*Chapter 4*

# THE ANCIENT EGYPTIANS

The ancient Egyptians, living as they did along the Mediterranean Sea, certainly informed Hebrew and Greek notions about the soul. These latter two cultures served as parents to all Western ideas about the soul.

If we take the Bible literally, then the Egyptian influence on Jewish culture must have been tremendous. Indeed, even Rabbi Jesus spent some time living in Egypt. The *Gospel of Matthew* records that: "...an angel of the Lord appeared to Joseph in a dream and said, 'Get up, take the child and his mother, and flee to Egypt...' Then Joseph got up, took the child and his mother by night, and went to Egypt..."[1]

According to the Hebrew Bible, the Jews were enslaved by the Egyptians for centuries.[2] The whole drama of the *Exodus* and story of Moses centers around the escape of the Jews from their Egyptian masters. The larger part of the Jewish religion attributes its identity to this momentous intervention of God against the Egyptians. In spite of the Bible, there is no archeological evidence of this bondage. This controversy aside, the Egyptian culture certainly influenced all Mediterranean cultures due to its tremendously long history.

Like all things Egyptian, their idea of the soul was complex and thoroughly developed. For all this development, though, Egyptian conceptions of the soul are difficult to characterize and entail a host of themes about the afterlife. When summarizing the religion of Egypt, one must keep in mind that this culture persisted for thousands of years. Due to this endurance, ideas about the soul and the religious order changed somewhat over time. Central to the theme of dualism, they believed the soul to be a separate part of the human being that survived death.

## *Re and The Osiris Cycle*

For the Egyptians, the sun, known as the god Re, controlled order in the universe. Re emerged as the original divinity, his daily ordering of the heavens showcased the working harmony of the universe. Part of that harmony, the annual flood of the Nile, enriched the valley and made Egyptian life possible in an otherwise rock-strewn, barren landscape.

The most persisting Egyptian myth, that of the Osiris cycle, reflects this culture's obsession with rejuvenation and order amid the threat of chaos and destruction. The Osiris cycle, along with underlying reverence for Re, formed the central cosmology of the Egyptians. Stephen Quirke describes the Egyptian cosmology in *Ancient Egyptian Religion*: "The cosmic environment installed by Re and the mythic cycle of Osiris and Horus created the framework of space and time for human existence."[3] The cycle myth distilled the principles of order and disorder, death and fertility.

The death of Osiris, murdered and dismembered by his brother, Seth, threatened chaos—the dread fear of all Egyptian mythology. Osiris's wife, Isis, collected his pieces and, achieving some success in his revitalization, was able to conceive a son, Horus, by him. Osiris then retreated to the underworld and became the god of the blessed dead. He provided everlasting life to those who lived well on Earth. Isis, still protecting order, hid Horus in the marshes to protect him from the destructive Seth and guarded him from other natural enemies. Seth, hoping to seize power after Osiris's death, now had to face the grown Horus, the seed of order come to fruition.

Quirke expresses the many meanings of this cycle:

> In all three stages the Osiris cycle yielded guarantees for the Egyptians: the first stage, the murder and revivification of Osiris, promised fresh life in the ground, fresh plant life after the flood and fresh human existence after death; the second stage, the protection of the infant Horus, offered survival in the face of natural attack from venomous neighbors in the Nile Valley; the third stage, the struggle for victory over Seth, offered the model for kingship, for all good in the fight against evil, and for eternal life, available only to those who could prove that they had lived good lives on Earth.[4]

In some mythologies, Seth and Horus, as symbols of destruction and order, constantly struggle, splitting control of Egypt. In other ones, Horus triumphs completely though Seth remains a menacing influence.

This myth not only provided a framework for understanding the delicate balance of life in Egypt, but permeated the political order itself. The Pharaoh came to be the literal embodiment of the god Horus. As one Pharaoh died, going to and becoming Osiris, the next Pharaoh was installed as his son Horus.

## *Taking Care of the Dead*

The stunning grandeur of the pyramids and the better-hidden kings' tombs attest to the importance of Egyptian religious beliefs. These impressive monuments were not simply mortuaries for com-memoration of the dead but played important roles as the Pharaohs' 'death vehicles.' The Pharaoh, leader on Earth and in the afterlife, assured prosperity for his people both here and there. The great pyr-amids and tombs played an essential role in this preservation of order. From the collective social body at the base, the chain of com-mand strives heavenward to the pinnacle, Pharaoh himself.

Along with the tombs, the temples formed a seamless chain for the greater aims of Egyptian life here and hereafter. The temples func-tioned as religious machines, delicate clockwork representations of the larger order. With a highly specialized staff, engineers of religious harmony, the temples could be carefully maintained assuring the preservation of life and order in the cosmos.

The Egyptians, given the importance of the mythology of life and death, developed the intricate arts of mummification and tomb con-struction. Andreu summarizes in *Egypt in the Age of the Pyramids*:

> ...the question of human destiny after death was the great affair of the living, who spent their whole lifetimes preparing for it... To accept this inevitable end and assist the human mind in envis-aging the passage to the realm of the great unknown, the Egyptians invented a whole arsenal of material procedures and magico-reli-gious ceremonies...[5]

If the Egyptians believed in life after death, which their entire culture confirms, then why this insistence on mummification? Why the elaborate and quite expensive practices? The Egyptians, in con-trast to the ancient Israelites, never believed in a bodily resurrection;

they didn't think the body would be resuscitated to walk again in the flesh. Though they didn't believe in resurrection, the care with which they preserved the body indicates the close association they understood to exist between physical life and spiritual life. No simple mind/body dualism is this, but one which, at some level, emphasizes the person's wholly physical existence. So many spiritual traditions perceive the body to be an impediment, or at least an inessential part of the person. The Egyptians understood the body to be a great necessity, a counterpart for the immaterial soul which it needed in some way. Though the body remains lifeless, the Egyptians understood the vitality of the soul to depend on it. The stuffing of tombs with food and other material possessions portrays this crucial, if confused, dependence. A kind of receptive/transmissive exchange of power shuffled between the two.

The Egyptian afterlife, a slightly improved version of earthly life, also shows their love of the physical. In that place, the crops grew to ever richer harvests, the game made easy hunting, the tables were covered with foods of all types and the serving girls were especially attractive: a visit to Hooters after a good hunt. The Egyptian preoccupation with death and the afterlife reflects a deep love for all things worldly and a desire for their extension.

## Egyptian Souls

Most religions settle into a simple schema of body and soul. For the ancient Egyptians, a number of souls were at work serving different functions. The *ka*, which existed in this life and the next, is something like the person's essential nature, his true identity, mind, and vital force.[6]

In contrast, the *ba* exists only after death, and represents the person's mobility. Usually symbolized as a bird, the *ba* traveled between the tomb and the spirit-world. The careful preservation of the features of the mummy and its masks or headgear have been thought necessary so that the *ba* could recognize the appropriate mummy.

The *ab* represented the person's conscience. It was thought that the conscience and seat of intelligence rested in the heart so the *ab* appears as that organ. The majestic *Book of the Dead*, many copies of which have been found in tomb treasures, describes various beliefs about the *ab*. The Egyptian afterlife expressed here may seem familiar, for its basic plot revolves around the moral judgment of the recently deceased. In his article on ancient conceptions of the soul, Davies writes of the judgment:

> Each person was taken after death before Osiris... and his or her heart weighed on scales against the figure of the goddess Right [represented as a feather]; the good passed through to the new life as transfigured spirits, but the hearts of the wicked were tossed to Amemet, 'the swallower', portrayed with the rear of a hippopotamus, the fore of a lion and the head of a crocodile.[7]

These three components of soul loom large in the various mythologies of ancient Egypt and their notions of afterlife. Another component, the *akh*, is the "transfigured spirit" mentioned in the passage above that comes after death. People are often referred to after death as *akhs*—beings of light. Along with the mummy, all these parts of the soul had to be nurtured after death.

The strict notions of caste and wealth that existed in Egyptian society persisted in the afterlife; though this didn't prevent the wicked of any class, dying with heavy hearts, from falling to destruction in the jaws of Amemet. To those with means, careful preservation of the body through mummification and the fabrication of exquisite tombs became important priorities during life. Further, no 'one-time' storing of provisions sufficed. The energy which the food provided to the mummy and souls became depleted over time. A constant replenishment of the tomb became necessary. On special days and festivals the tombs of the dead needed to be restocked by the living.

Given the continued role of the Pharaoh in the afterlife, it was necessary to keep him stocked with lavish supplies through a funerary cult. The services of this cult carried on for hundreds of years and required a large staff to meet all its daily rituals.[8] The discovery of the sealed tomb of Tutankhamun with its riches intact gave testimony to the importance religious beliefs played in the Egyptian social order. By the time of Tutankhamun, the construction of tombs was performed in great secrecy to forestall the threat of desecration created by the roving class of tomb robbers.

The reality of the dead to the living is also exhibited in the letters written to the dead. Tombs often possessed chapel areas where the living could come to visit the dead. As if the dead were completely accessible, the living left letters asking their dearly departed for some helpful intercession. Andreu cites a heartfelt letter from a wife to her husband:

> As for this servant Imiu who is ill, can you not fight night and day for her against any man or any woman who wishes her harm? Why do you want to spoil everything? Fight for her again! Now! Then her household will be restored and libations will be made for you. If you do not help us, your house will be destroyed! Don't you know that it is this servant who does everything amongst the people? Fight for her! Watch over her! Then your house and your children will be well. Hear me well![9]

The ancient Egyptian culture, spanning thousands of years and representative of the highest order imaginable in its time and place, deeply influenced its neighbors and supported the notion of an immaterial self. Much of this refined culture depended on a powerful religious mythology. Due to the fundamental importance of religion in their culture, the ancient Egyptians may be the truest example of a working theocracy. Pharaoh lived as both god and king to his people in this life and the next. He represented the victory over death and chaos to his people. The fantastically elaborate beliefs, rituals, and structures that helped Pharaoh in his transition to the heavens constantly reminded the common folk that this life was but one part of a much larger whole. The Egyptians, for all their insistence on the importance of spiritual existence, always perceived the mysterious alliance of the soul and the body. Their careful practices of mummification and the provision of material necessities reflects the idea that all magic, all power, comes from the properties of material things.

# Chapter 5

## ZOROASTRIANISM

As an adolescent I used to tremble when thinking about good and evil. I'd hearten myself with the credo that I was put on this Earth to do good and to fight evil, to take up arms against forces seen and invisible, to oppose the Saddams of the world and the archangel Lucifer in the hidden realms of existence. I once collected comic books and became enthralled by the cosmic battles of superheroes and villains. These wonderfully simple, clear-cut plots made sense and kept you cheering. Among my friends are people who passionately believe these things still. They risk their lives and fortunes committed to the simple principle that there is an evident good and evil at work in the world. Some are police officers, some Mormons, some soldiers, but all believe the same thing. All of these good people practice the same religion, though they'd never admit it. Indicative of the belief's power, they do not know the source of their thoughts, nor the name of its founder; indeed, they assume that these principles of theirs are not beliefs—they are *the way things are*.

I myself have outgrown such a perspective. I see sides and nuances and rhetoric. I live with doubt and skepticism and when someone uses the word evil I begin to wonder about their honesty or sanity or both. But I do not wrest my friends from their beliefs—there are worse things to believe after all. If one matures philosophically, though, the very words good and evil come to seem a bit innocent, *unworldly* that is. The real illusion of good and evil is that no one believes himself to be evil. In the end, everyone, *everyone* seeks the good. Hitler, for instance, did not crush human beings out of a tongue-wagging bloodlust. Hitler crushed subhuman vermin, *evil* things, to protect his good, unblemished—*chosen*—people. And the tens of thousands of people in his armies who killed for him, who killed the enemy, did not drink blood or worship the devil at Black Masses—most were good Christian *volk*. A person like Hitler believed in good and evil, just as the Ayatollahs of the world breathe the concept. The difference between them and their actions and us and ours is one of definition—what is good to us is evil to them and vice-versa. Our freedoms and lifestyles are to them the very pattern of devilry. The more passionately they believe in this simplistic schema and the more they are willing to fight evil, the more damage they do to themselves, others, and our very complex—and *shared*—world.

Zoroastrianism is the source of all this confusion. Your very thoughts about morality and meaning can be traced back to a Persian shepherd-prophet who lived three thousand years ago. His name was Zarathushtra. We come to the title Zoroastrianism through the ancient Greeks who translated Zarathushtra into Zoroaster. Zarathushtra developed one of the fundamental cosmologies of all later Western religion and philosophy. He portrayed reality as a battleground between good and evil. Scholars call this idea cosmic dualism. Cosmic dualism usually imports substance dualism—the differentiation between soul and body—into its ideologies.

## Dualism

According to Zarathushtra's teachings, one god stands above others. This god, Ahura Mazda (wise lord), had twin children—Spenta Mainyu (beneficent spirit) and Angra Mainyu (hostile spirit)—whose influences spread throughout the entire universe. Such a conception is not strictly a cosmic dualism since one god subsequently created two contrary forces. A truly dualistic system would have only two forces from the beginning.[1] One could argue that Christianity similarly constructs a 'removed' dualism (see Milton's *Paradise Lost*). For here, the single God creates both Satan, who does evil in the universe, and Jesus, who opposes evil and promises total salvation from it. In both cases, Zoroastrianism and Christianity, the 'evil' characters should not be understood as original creations of God, but as free beings who chose the evil path.

The existence of evil in the universe, what philosophers term "the problem of evil," implicates God in the following manner: if we affirm the existence of evil then either God is not all powerful or God is not all good. Whether a religious system is strictly dualistic or dualism 'removed,' either explanation comes as a logical consequence from the "problem of evil."

For a long time, man has recognized the harmful and destructive elements in his environment and in himself: things like plague, war, disease, and death. If one believes in a good God and has any sensitivity at all, these malignant elements cannot be seen as products of his workings. The need for a cosmic 'split' occurs; something besides God must account for the evil. With tremendous creativity, religious innovators create frightful mythic antagonists—devils. These evil characters stir up trouble and are responsible for the ugly parts of existence. Sometimes God Himself wars with the evil Lord throughout history (a true dualism), while in other instances, various prophets and saviors battle evil. Such an alien or removed God must wield slightly less than omnipotent powers or possess some mysterious reason for allowing the evil spirit to flourish. As a piece of logic, though, the creation of the evil character staves off the first barrage of man's questions about the presence of evil in the world.

The great spiritual insight of Zoroastrianism is that man fulfills a crucial role and will decide the battle between good and evil. Each person, through her life and actions, helps good or evil towards final victory.[2] The individual dignity derived from this critical role became a keystone of many religious faiths and secular philosophies alike. In Zoroastrianism, one is not merely doing good for practical reasons or to ease conscience but for the very salvation of the universe. One could argue that this dogma unifies many faiths of the world. Zoroastrianism conveys an ultimately ethical message. Allied with one spirit or another, the source of the good or the source of evil, the individual furthers either good or evil in the universal drama.

Religions based on cosmic dualism necessitate substance dualism. In faiths that demand a rigorously moral life, one makes many sacrifices and often places himself in a position of danger. Standing up against evildoers is never a task for the weak-hearted, as Batman, the Lone Ranger, Captain America, and the Green Lantern prove time and again. Suppose one endures in supporting good and fighting evil, both in himself and the world, but is killed by an evil person. Such a case does not seem just, yet a system that promises the eventual victory of good over evil must ultimately be just. Did the good person gain anything by going out of his way to do good? It seems not. In the grand scheme of existence, these actions made his short life even more difficult. Not many would opt for such a life. Indeed, Zarathushtra obsessed over this problem and often dwelled on the punishment of the wicked and the reward of the virtuous. By assuming an afterlife this problem encounters an elegant solution for in the afterlife the good find their rewards and the evil their punishment.

To further the notion of an afterlife, Zarathushtra imagined two basic substances in the universe, one of these substances was the vehicle of spirit and good, the other of decay and evil. The celestial essence—*menok*—made up the originally resplendent cosmos. Aggressing against Ahura Mazda's creation, Angra Mainyu contaminated *menok* with *getik*—pure material existence. Perhaps a way to understand *getik* is as a veil which hangs on the spiritual *menok* and causes its decay. The ultimate redemption of the world will be a separation of these mingled elements and the final dissolution of *getik*. At the end of time, a general resurrection will occur and the righteous will inhabit the 'improved' world with their pure *menok* bodies, eternal and everlasting. Man's efforts to support Spenta Mainyu against the malevolence of Angra Mainyu obviously succeed, for at the end of time it is told that a transfiguration of the entire world will occur for the better.

The doctrine of the transfiguration strikes one as eminently Jewish, yet these ideas were present in the oldest literature of Zoroastrianism.[3] The intriguing character referred to as the Saoshyant (savior) delivers the resurrection at the end of time.[4] At this time death will cease in the world.

Despite the end-time resurrection, one still possesses a soul which, upon death, retreats to its purely spiritual state. Shortly after dying, the soul meets its essential self (in the good, a beautiful young woman; in the wicked, a gnarled hag) who then escorts it to the bridge of Paradise. For the wicked, this bridge narrows to a razor's edge causing them to fall to hell. How do the good find refuge immediately after death and also 'resurrect' to live in something like a material world at the end of time? This incomprehensible doctrine will pervade Christianity as well.

With the advent of Zoroastrianism and its impressive depiction of reality as a war of good and evil, the importance of the individual and his morality take primacy in religious philosophy. Forever after, the human person becomes a crucial soldier in the fight for cosmic order and ultimate justice. And from this deep structure, people will forever search out 'evil' and accuse their enemies of being evil's representatives. Lacking subtlety of thought, the Christian or Muslim 'Zoroastrian' will only see good or evil. This individual importance, quite a revolution for a tribal society, leads to the notion of a soul and an afterlife. The mind/body dichotomy becomes an essential tenet in this type of world-view and lies at the core of Western culture, responsible for both its glories and its holocausts.

*Chapter 6*

# THE SOUL OF PLATO

It was Socrates who, so far as can be seen, created the conception of the soul which has ever since dominated European thinking.
—A.E. Taylor, *Socrates*[1]

As one chronologically traces the history of the soul, it begins to resemble modern conceptions more and more. In point of fact, though, virtually the same 'soul' has bee n in currency since man first began to shamanize. From the Greeks' rich culture comes much of what we consider to be modern and Western. The thinkers of this time and place articulated the foundational ideas of Western arts and sciences. From tragedy and democracy to atomic theory, the Greeks hold supremacy in our intellectual tradition. It is no surprise that the core doctrine of Western spirituality derives from the ancient Greeks in general, and the philosopher Socrates, in particular.

> Once we see clearly how after Socrates…one philosophical school succeeds another, wave upon wave; how the hunger for knowledge reached a never suspected universality in the widest domain of the educated world…became the real task for every person of higher gifts…how this universality first spread a common net of thought over the whole globe, actually holding out the prospect of the lawfulness of an entire solar system; once we see all this clearly, along with the amazingly high pyramid of knowledge in our own time—we cannot fail to see in Socrates the one turning point and vortex of so-called world history.[2]

Nietzsche's hyperbole does not stretch the truth much—the importance of Socrates and his chronicler, Plato, cannot be overestimated. The completeness and inestimable quality of Plato's writings about Socrates is a testimony of the disciple's deep admiration for his teacher and the result of a lifelong exploration of his charismatic ideas. To separate what in the dialogues derives truly from Socrates and what from Plato is a near impossible task. We will, according to a common practice, use the terms 'Platonic' and 'Socratic' interchangeably. The fusion of ideas accomplished by these men provided the framework for all Western thought and religion.

Of interest here, the lingering theme of the imprisonment of the soul in the body, of the insignificance of the material in contrast to the spiritual, in short—the whole complex of dualistic thinking—appears time and again as the focal point of Socratic-Platonic thought.

Those who lived in the harsh day-to-day world of the ancient Greeks knew that things came and went: plants, animals, friends. In that foregone world—where the infant mortality was atrocious, where diseases progressed without treatment, where hygiene and public sanitation were virtually unknown—death dwelled everywhere, fearsome and unabashed. There were no hospitals to siphon off the dying from the eyes of the common lot; no funeral parlors to make a corpse look ruddy-cheeked and unperturbed in its final hour of agony. Death, once upon a time, was common and accepted, as well as it could be, that is. So things pass, it keeps man humble. But Plato thought differently. Humans, as we all know, seem different from the other animals—we stand out. Since we see ourselves as quite exceptional in the realm of nature, why not extend that sense of 'specialness' just a bit? Rather than imagining anything less of the afterlife, as Homer taught, why not expect much more, why not expect our true, supernatural, and transcendent birthright? Man—an animal? Why not imagine him a god, or something like a god-in-training? Walter Burkert, in his classic *Greek Religion*, sums up Plato's world-changing doctrines:

> Since Plato and through him, religion has been essentially different from what it had been before. For the Greeks as we know them since Homer, religion had always meant acceptance of reality, in a naïve and yet adult way, acceptance of a reality that included corporeality, transitoriness, and destruction, in heroic defiance or in tragic insight. Through Plato reality is made unreal in favor of

an incorporeal, unchangeable other world which is to be regarded as primary. The ego is concentrated in an immortal soul which is alien to the body and captive in it.[3]

This new Socratic-Platonic philosophy was so utterly bizarre, so truly unique, that it forced its listeners to gasp in astonishment; it seemed alien wisdom from another world. The gnomish Socrates, in an imaginary conversation with his peers, befuddled all who would oppose him and each of their arguments, be they silly or sophisticated. Philosophy's first martyr quietly reasoned through the greatest questions of life like a geometer at play, tracing figures in the dust with his bare feet and countering the ingenious retorts of his high-stationed interlocutors with simple examples from everyday life. The eccentric dialogues continue to impress the best-trained intellects of our own time though they were inspired and completed dozens of generations before any Shakespeare or Newton, long before a Kant or Einstein. In fact, all these late-born luminaries inherited a considerable largesse from the poor Athenian workingman and his noble apprentice.

The foundation of philosophy came from ideas fully reasoned through without the application of any advanced mathematics. They were forcefully demonstrated with just a meager few references and fruited in a mind uncultivated by any real education—Socrates possessed no Ph.D. All these stunning ideas—the fascinating, diamondlike arguments that would tease the best thinkers of each generation—originated from the intense curiosity of an able-brained fellow stimulated by a few writings and conversations. These revolutionary ideas were created by men who rarely possessed materials to write with and who lacked assistance from computers or other 'information technologies.'

The whole scenario—the origin of the Western mind in the whimsical conversations of an ill-born savant and his usually inept challengers rustling through a marketplace in ancient Athens—all seems as exceedingly improbable as the emergence of life itself. As the early Christian theologian Tertullian wrote about the physical resurrection of Christ: *credo absurdum est* (I believe because it's absurd).[4] Tertullian thought the Christian mystery too vastly unbelievable to have found its inspiration in any human mind. The concept that God would become a man in order to sacrifice Himself—to

Himself—and thus save a 'fallen' mankind; and then rise—after a prolonged and painful death—from the inescapable state of death; and then promise all who would swear an unflagging allegiance to— the man-God/Father-son—an indescribably perfect and eternal life after their own deaths… no, even the most creative thinkers could not fabricate such a notion. Only God Himself could spin such a fantastically original tale and only such a tale could reliably dislodge the hearts of men from their adherence to illuminating reason and cast it far beyond into the murky realm of faith. When a belief is sufficiently bizarre and cordially promises us the moon and all the stars besides, it cannot fail to persuade—such a creature is man; the less he uses his reason, the higher the hope. As faith systems from Platonism to Islam prove—if a notion of something 'more' (more happiness, more wealth, life eternal…) is too common and close-to-home then it is unconvincing and easily disproved; too humble and it fails to wrangle one away from his better judgment. The master poets/prophets know that for a faith to arouse zeal it must be incredibly bizarre and play to mankind's insatiable vanity.

The history of strange cults always follows the same progression: first, a passing moment of sheer disbelief often accompanied with a raucous scorn of the cult's believers as gullible simpletons; second, a stage of temporary uncertainty, a restraint of judgment and entertainment of the cult's tenets—the 'what if' stage; and finally, the far more enduring history that stretches across whole lives and epochs. Alas, what was initially strange can later proclaim itself a success of the most lasting type. All and sundry profess the cult's quite perfect inspiration and wonder who might have ever imagined it strange— it is the quintessence of the normal, the gold standard of whole peoples and the touchstone of all thought and action, no matter the context. Plato had all the eccentric ideas that answered man's perennial questions and a mind capable of conveying them in the most rational, believable terms. One comes to moments, reading Plato, or the much later Aquinas, when reason seems a hopeless tool; for no matter what the thesis, if one wishes enough that it be true and has a brain for argument then it is true. The influence of his thought is in a word—vast. Of Plato, Burkert says: "…there has been no theology which has not stood in his shadow."[5] If ever there was a 'voice in the wilderness, preparing the path for the Lord,' it was certainly not

John the Baptist, but Plato. It was his ideas that made Christianity a viable institution in the Greco-Roman world.

Socrates is the founding father of Western philosophy but who was he? No other thinker possessed such seeming contradictions of character. Through his student Plato, Socrates's teachings led to the formation of the first institute of higher learning—the Academy in Athens. In spite of this, Socrates was anything but 'academic.' Most of his thinking is related through Plato's writing, a very lucid and complex style that records and develops the brilliant subtleties of the master's ideas. Even so, there are other, more rustic accounts of the philosopher.

Xenophon, a contemporary of Plato unconcerned with the higher mysteries, recorded the gentle, homespun wisdom that Socrates shared with the commoners who came to him complaining of domestic disputes and the like.[6] Hardly 'lost in the clouds,' (as another contemporary, Aristophanes, portrayed him[7]) Socrates furnished sage, easy-to-understand council to all who approached him in need.

While all around him spurious teachers charged their wealthy apprentices exorbitant fees for bits of advice on oratory and social advancement, Socrates shared his teachings and advice with everyone free of charge. The public philosopher spent the majority of his time in the *agora*—the marketplace where news and wares from all lands converged to meet the practical necessities of life.[8]

The world over knows Socrates as an ingenious philosopher but in his life the man served all the typical duties of an Athenian male: he fought with the utmost bravery in its wars and served with ability and justice during his terms in democratic office. Perhaps his least successful role was as husband and father. His love of wisdom so exceeded his practical duties that he provided less for his wife than was needed and spent less time as *paterfamilias* than as marketplace prophet.

Alone of the Athenians in his time, Socrates passed between the highest and lowest classes, able to address each in his own terms and respected by most for his character and dignity (though despised for his 'uppity' wisdom by some members of the higher classes). Among his unique traits, Socrates's appearance marked him well. In addition to his rather poor dress and bare feet, the man's ugliness was common knowledge and public joke. Socrates accepted his unattractive looks with equanimity and even joined in the jokes in the same fashion as his latter-day analogue, Cyrano de Bergerac. In spite of his looks—and also like Cyrano—the inner beauty of Socrates and the elegance of his words endeared him to all who would listen and led to a few notable infatuations. But there was no Roxanne for Socrates, all the raciest liaisons were male-male.

Socrates lived a blameless life but humiliated enough important people to bring ruin upon himself. His tireless challenges to everything established and respected tickled those with flexible minds but aroused hatred from many who found Socrates's stances too critical. Though he considered himself the most civic person, Socrates would be the very type to burn his country's flag in order to make a point. Just as those who knew him might appreciate the message, though become embarrassed by the act, those who would misinterpret him eventually lost their tolerance. The rigorously ethical lifestyle that Socrates taught presented a challenge to traditional Athenian mores and its culture of public honor. Insensitive or aloof to the warnings sent his way, the troublesome Socrates eventually received, and accepted, a death sentence. Having become a martyr for his beliefs, the ideas that Plato recorded would never die. The essential message of the Socratic-Platonic philosophy can be distilled into the statements, "know thy self (soul)" and "take care of yourself (soul)." Considering it his spiritual duty to inform people of these all-important tasks, Socrates's death became the great vehicle of his ideas.

## Orphism and Pythagoreanism

> ...Plato regarded the speculations of the Orphic theologians not only with interest but with a respect that was near akin to reverence. They did much more than simply serve to illustrate his points, and must indeed have powerfully affected the form which his own religion took.
> —W.K.C. Guthrie, *Orpheus and Greek Religion*[9]

The most striking features of Platonic philosophy resemble doctrines of Orphism popular during Plato's time. In Plato the influence of Socrates's rigorous logic mixed with an innately poetic constitution and love for divine mysteries. The Orphic ideas that Plato institutionalized appeared in the writings of numerous classical poets and were obviously well-discussed, public notions.[10] Yet, until Plato, these ideas could be appealing only as something foreign and exotic, tantalizing but difficult to swallow. The Orphic tenets suffered great criticism at the hands of Athens's more traditional minds.[11] Orphism required Plato's genius to make its notions acceptable to a mindset that had all but relinquished mythology.

Orphism came from Thrace, a land to the north of Greece whose people still retained the primitive culture of prehistoric Europe. The Greeks thought the Thracians a wild bunch. Like most of ancient Europe, shamanic religious influences interfused the local Thracian beliefs. The parallels of Orphism with shamanism are many though in Orphism one begins to see a patterning of shamanic motifs into an increasingly complex and dogmatic religious system more appropriate to this time and place.

That shamanism influenced Platonism through the intermediary of Orphism can scarcely be doubted. In his classic study, *The Greeks and the Irrational*, E.R. Dodds charts this lineage carefully. As he writes near the end of that work, "...Plato in effect cross-fertilized the tradition of Greek rationalism with magico-religious ideas whose remoter origins belong to the northern Shamanistic culture."[12] Macchioro, another scholar of Orphism, also proposes the shamanic origin of the Orphic soul. He notes that, "...the starting point of the Orphic ideas of the after-life was in visions."[13] Of course, the visionary tradition is a distinct trait of shamanism with its ecstatic retreats from the body. The pervasive influences of the incorporeal soul and of a merit-justified afterlife linked non-Greek, shamanic traditions to Platonism.

Orphism originated in the teachings of the legendary Orpheus. One scholar writes:

> He was a singer and player of the lyre who could charm and soften the violence of nature. Trees and animals came to his song. Birds flew above his head and fishes swam behind his boat. He was a prophet and religious teacher who knew the secrets of the world of the dead; a shaman and magician who had crossed over into that

world and used his spells to bring the dead back to the world of the living.[14]

The traits of Orpheus—his skill in music, his connection with nature and the animals, and secret knowledge, especially of the dead— identify him as a shaman of old.

In contrast to the more traditional shamans, Orpheus taught a set of refined religious dogmas. Also different from other shamans, whose culture was an oral one, the Orphic movement disseminated its message through writing. Plato noted the, "…mass of books of Orpheus and Musaios [student of Orpheus]."[15] A revolution occurred in man's religious life when ideas could be separated from their prophet. The charismatic presence of the shaman had been central to the whole tradition. In contrast, Orphic writings moved its readers merely through the consideration of its tenets. This marks a crucial psychic transition: man had separated the influence of ideas from the influence of their messenger. At this time, and for the first time, one could be one's own priest. No longer was the religious specialist—the shaman—necessary. Religion had become word, specifically, it had become sacred text.

Through a similar turn, the Platonic dialogues assisted in converting the rudiments of culture from an oral to a written foundation. The genius and skill of Plato as a writer can be seen in the subtlety of the revolution he effected among his compatriots. The Platonic dialogues retain the atmosphere of a verbal discussion, the preferred method of communication in ancient Greece. But the dialogues were obviously not real conversations—they were words set upon paper. The Platonic dialogues are the birthing ground of a totally different genre altogether—the modern treatise with its reliance upon argumentation and reasoning. From the most ancient system of knowledge coming down through the oral transmission of the king, prophet, or shaman, to the rhetorical swaying of the masses by a philosopher or elected leader, evolved the treatise in which the illusion of a fictional conversation revealed, in fact, the reader's own conversation within himself.

Orphism taught that man possesses a spiritual core at odds with his physical body. Mortal life—life in the body—resulted from a divine punishment, a fall from the original state of divinity. Because of the fall, man had to incarnate many times on Earth in various physical bodies to expiate his spiritual impurity. In the *Phaedrus* dialogue Socrates relates ideas seemingly plucked right from the Orphic texts:

> Whatsoever soul has followed in the train of a god, and discerned something of truth, shall be kept from sorrow until a new revolution shall begin, and if she can do this always, she shall remain always free from hurt. But when she is not able so to follow...but meeting with some mischance comes to be burdened with a load of forgetfulness and wrongdoing, and because of that burden sheds her wings and falls to the Earth, then thus runs the law. In her first birth she shall not be planted in any brute beast, but the soul that hath seen the most of being shall enter into the human babe that shall grow into a seeker after wisdom or beauty, a follower of the Muses and a lover; the next, having seen less, shall dwell in a king that abides by law, or a warrior and ruler...

Orphism developed a set of initiations and purifications intended to speed the expiation of sin so that, upon death at the end of this very life, the Orphic could escape the mortal round to a paradisal afterlife and reconnect to the true state of human (in fact, 'superhuman') existence.

Pythagoreanism, also a very popular school around the time of Plato, came along after the Orphic doctrines had already achieved popularity. In some ways, Plato more closely resembles a Pythagorean than a pure Orphic. Pythagoras, the mathematical theorist to whom we owe the Pythagorean theorem at the base of all geometry, seems to have adopted the Orphic beliefs. With his own slight revisions and a different set of methods, including the religious study of science and mathematics, Pythagoras helped to further popularize Orphic notions. Pythagoreanism emphasized exercise of the intellect as a more appropriate, and perhaps more Greek, path to liberation. Socrates and Plato seem to have followed this approach though neither admitted themselves to be Pythagoreans.

The beliefs of Orphism (and now Pythagoreanism) entailed a radical change in one's way of living. Certain principles were to be followed: strict vegetarianism, a celibate lifestyle, and the devotion of this life's energies towards the liberation of the soul upon death. Even pleasure, since it opposed the concept of life as punishment, must be avoided. The Orphic lifestyle considered the body to be a tomb or prison of the soul. A popular Orphic trope was the similarity, in words, between *soma* (body) and *sema* (tomb). This questionable etymology seemed to encapsulate their take on the human condition. By promoting 'good behavior' the Orphic could more quickly escape from the shackles of mortal existence and live as an immortal in the blessed afterlife. The puritanical lifestyle of the Orphics, the rule they followed that good must always oppose evil and that the soul must reign superior over the body, assumes cosmic dualism. The classicist F.M. Cornford addresses this issue: "...throughout the mystical systems inspired by Orphism, we shall find the fundamental contrast between the two principles of Light and Darkness, identified with Good and Evil. This cosmic dualism is the counterpart of the dualism in the nature of the soul..."[16] The affiliation of cosmic dualism and mind/body dualism reflects the intuition that nature and the individual possess similar constitutions. This is an example of the anthropomorphism dear to all mythological systems of thought. The ardency of religious belief precludes any recognition of mythology as symbol, so the Orphics considered their alliance with one side of the world and of their own constitution to be of the gravest importance. The Orphic's actions determined his state in the hereafter and the merit-based afterlife took primacy as religious dogma.

The great aim of Orphism, which Plato took upon as his own, taught that earthly life is inconsequential—if not inherently a form of punishment—and that escape from the mortal plane to the afterlife is the true purpose of human existence. No idea could have posed a greater contrast to traditional Greek religion. The religion of the Greeks did not prescribe an impossible, transcendental goal for the individual. The greatest achievement in Greek life involved the full exercise of one's individual talents and abilities on Earth and in the present. Grave epitaphs from this period portray the traditional view: "Once I was not, then I was, and now I am no more: what further is there to be said?" and "Live! For there is nothing sweeter granted to us mortals than this life in the sunlight."[17]

H.D.F. Kitto describes the ancient Greeks as an 'embodied' culture, scarcely able to imagine the dualism which most of us blandly accept:

The sharp distinction which the Christian and the Oriental world has normally drawn between the body and the soul, the physical and the spiritual, was foreign to the Greek—at least until the time of Socrates and Plato. To him there was simply the whole man... The Greek made physical training an important part of education, not because he said to himself, 'Look here, we mustn't forget the body,' but because it could never occur to him to train anything but the whole man.[18]

To Greeks bathed in the lines of Homer, the body, especially the robust and beautiful body of the hero, was life's only vehicle. They celebrated the body and its activities at every turn. In the ancient Olympics, the athletes performed in the nude—none could imagine that a future people of their stock would turn ashen at the sight of uncovered flesh. Puritanism, with its hatred of the body and repugnance of sexuality, would have moved these hardy Greeks to laughter.

Being grounded in the body, the ancient Greeks knew that its loss spelled one's certain end. Immortality belonged to the gods alone and neither was, nor should be, man's destiny. The fact of immortality served as the chief difference between men and gods. Of course, the gods wielded greater power—they controlled the sky, the sea, and the battlefield, venues in which human control could be mighty but always begged the mercy of higher forces. The true character of the gods, though—their essential nature—did not convey an existence superior to the lives and victories of traditional Greek heroes. The gods looked and acted like normal people—they fought in wars, they made love, they fed upon nectar and ambrosia. Nothing in their nature was foreign or unknown to the well-rounded man. Nothing about these gods was 'transcendental' or unknown in the human sphere. The Greek pantheon lived through as many family squabbles, tragic misfortunes, and lapses into temptation as any group of humans ever did; they were, in effect, human people living human lives. Like human beings, they too had a greater power above them. The gods always lived under the demands and constrictions of *moira/Ananke*—the unbending laws of necessity. Certain things, for gods as for men, were simply the way they must be and could not be changed—none could alter the essential fabric of reality. Fate, once woven, could not be undone. What really distinguished ancient Greek gods from men? They lived, they loved, they feasted—but *they did not die.* Immortality was the gods' chief blessing, the essential distinction between them and 'mortals.'

Strongly based in their senses, the ancient Greeks had never before entertained anything like the Orphic doctrine of the soul. Somewhere in their prehistory they had lost connection to shamanic ideas about the soul. When reading Homer, the canonical source of ancient Greek culture, one encounters extravagantly detailed, and thoroughly physical, descriptions of men and their circumstances. When, for instance, he suffers the insult of Agamemnon in the *Iliad*: "...anguish gripped Achilles. The heart in his rugged chest was pounding, torn...Should he draw the long sharp sword slung at his hip, thrust through the ranks and kill Agamemnon now?—or check his rage and beat his fury down?" Achilles, the great hero of ancient Greek culture, could not be described in our modern, highly mental terms. The modern hero, so often a paragon of repression and checked emotions—like a well-practiced poker player—is anything but Greek. Consider Hamlet's painful indecision: "To be, or not to be, that is the question..." To be or not to be was never a question for the Greeks. When anguish filled Achilles, his heart beat with fury and he quickly settled on his terrible, unbending choice to fight no more for his king. When anguish filled Hamlet, his wits strained to their breaking point and so was his action stifled by every consideration. What can one imagine of Hamlet except his mentality? We remember less his actions than his honeyed words. Like Descartes's distinction between matter and spirit, Achilles was extended in space and time but Hamlet was a mental substance, timeless and immaterial. As he himself confessed: "I could be bounded in a nutshell and count myself a king of infinite space, were it not that I have bad dreams." Everything to this modern Achilles resides in the mind: "...there is nothing either good or bad but thinking makes it so." The physical had long since marked the individual by Shakespeare's time. In contemporary literature the physical feeling and location of emotions is all but forgotten. To the Greeks, the body is the very person. Life finds its home therein and without it death follows.

The only time Homer discusses anything like an afterlife, in Book XI of the *Odyssey*, he portrays a shadowy existence at best. In Hades, to which Odysseus descends to gather information, the once-living are mere shadows of their former persons and can only speak when revitalized by fresh blood—otherwise they squeak like bats. So grounded in the body were these Greeks that they could not imagine any state of existence, even after death, without the body. When Odysseus meets the crowds of dead who flock to him: "…many were there, too, torn by brazen lanceheads, battle-slain, bearing still their bloody gear." These were no purified spirits free from the mortal coil, these freshly fallen still bore the very marks and gore that they suffered in their last living moments. In Homer's afterlife, the hero Achilles laments his state in Hades. Odysseus praises Achilles as greatest among men in life and now, the very lord of the dead: "Let me hear no smooth talk of death from you, Odysseus, light of councils. Better, I say, to break sod as a farm hand for some poor country man, on iron rations, than lord it over all the exhausted dead." The wisdom of Achilles, who had once lusted after fame more than any man, now understood life—without qualification—to be the only good. For heroes and martyrs alike, death holds no glories.

To the ancient Greeks, the rewards of life—other than happiness and honor—were the esteem with which the community kept their memory. It was this very fame that had once dictated Achilles's actions. Honor and reputation were the currency of life and the proper aim of one's efforts. The idea of a spiritual purpose to life would have appeared quite fantastic. Macchioro describes the clash of traditional Greek religion and Orphism:

> Greek religion and Orphic religion represent historically two different worlds, which never understood and never fully accepted each other, and the history of Greek thought consisted…in a gradual victory of the Orphic religion over the Greek religion. Christianity marks the climax of this process.[19]

Orphism promised much more to the individual, thus helping the individual think of himself as an entity separate from his community. This radical individuality had never before been a convention of the community-minded Greeks. Jaeger writes:

> The Orphic conception of the soul marks an important advance in the development of man's consciousness of selfhood. Without it Plato and Aristotle could never have developed the theory that the human spirit is divine, and that man's sensual nature can be dissociated from his real self, which it is his true function to bring to perfection.[20]

The strange influence that Orphism gained over the Greek mind forever changed the spirit of that place. Only with the charismatic Socrates and his eminent powers of persuasion could such a transformation occur. It paved the way for the spiritualization of all European culture.

## *Socrates, Seal of the Shamans*

Many elements in Socrates's character parallel the typical shaman's way of life. Socrates was definitely not a shaman in the traditional sense but a key figure in the evolution from shamanism to later religious traditions.

According to Eliade's formulation, the shaman can be characterized as a master of the techniques of ecstasy. In other words, the shaman must possess the peculiar ability to leave his body and travel to the spirit world. The actions he performs there affect the fate of his clients and community. The shaman frequently falls into trances or otherwise takes soul journeys. What, in Socrates's character, fulfills this criterion? Socrates's reliance upon the doctrine of the immaterial soul points in this direction. As will be discussed below in the exploration of the *Phaedo* dialogue, Socrates, at the end of his life, affirmed the notion of an immortal soul as the keystone of his thought. Socrates's insistence about the soul reveals the importance of the doctrine to all of his philosophy.

Whenever Socrates puts forth anything resembling a doctrine the reader must take careful note. The majority of the time Socrates claimed neither to know nor teach anything at all. His genius lay primarily in his ability to spur others towards a constant meditation upon knowledge and its shaky foundations on opinion. His 'teachings,' if ever there were any, sought to dislodge people from their preconceived notions. In countless dialogues and individual arguments, Socrates proves that most peoples' conceptions of knowledge rely upon the unfounded and arbitrary assumptions of time and place—culture. By illustrating and demolishing these convictions Socrates sets the seeker on an endless, and more humble, quest for truth. The concept of the soul—which he glorifies as the key to his ideas about knowledge in the *Phaedo*—establishes Socrates as an idealist (spiritualist) as opposed to a materialist. Shamanic notions, of any type, rely upon spiritual realities as the backbone of their doctrines.

Beyond his assumptions of spirituality, Socrates often falls into trances—the classic shamanic technique. Without warning, Socrates would become transfixed by a peculiar idea or thought. Insensate to his surroundings, Socrates might remain entranced for hours. In a revealing dialogue, the *Symposium*, Socrates falls into one of his fits at the outset. His friend, Aristodemus, and he were walking towards a party when Socrates lagged behind and retreated into a nearby porch. Aristodemus, knowing full well of Socrates's predilection, went unaccompanied to the party. When the host, Agathon, sent a servant to fetch Socrates, Aristodemus urged him against it: "You'd much better leave him to himself. It's quite a habit of his, you know; off he goes and there he stands, no matter where it is. I've no doubt he'll be with us before long, so I really don't think you'd better worry him." The most famous occurrence of this happened while Socrates fought at Potidaea. Alcibiades, Socrates's most notorious student, recalls:

> He [Socrates] started wrestling with some problem or other about sunrise one morning, and stood there lost in thought, and when the answer wouldn't come he still stood there thinking and refused to give it up. Time went on, and by about midday the troops noticed what was happening, and naturally they were rather surprised and began telling each other how Socrates had been standing there thinking ever since daybreak. ... Well, there he stood till morning and then at sunrise he said his prayers to the sun and went away.[21]

While Alcibiades assigns Socrates's state of mind to mental wrestling, in fact, we don't know what was going on in Socrates's head. That he would stand in one place for a full day is quite out of line with the way people generally think over problems. Also, since Socrates later defines higher thought as a meditation on the transcendent ideas, we might understand these states of his as closer to ecstatic meditation than to thinking.

Cornford, an esteemed classicist who thought shamanic elements in early Greek philosophy an important influence, did not consider Socrates's lapses to be classic instances of ecstasy.[22] But, we must infer that these episodes, which we can analyze, are merely a sample of his normal 'meditations.' That these curious trances of Socrates were common enough to have been noticed and recorded suggests them to be part of the Socratic technique hitherto underestimated and unexplored. Just as the fossils we find of ancient creatures represent only a tiny fraction of the ranges and forms of creatures that once existed, so do these few recorded instances of Socrates's trances suggest the varied alterations in his consciousness to be an essential part of his character. There is more concrete evidence, though, about Socrates's ability to experience sudden 'illuminations' than this inference alone.

In discussing the concept of beauty in the *Symposium* Socrates claims to follow the path taught him by a priestess named Diotima. Diotima discusses beauty—the aim of all philosophy—in mystical terms hardly appropriate to the kind of logical reasoning we understand to be philosophy's method:

> Whoever has been initiated so far in the mysteries of Love...is at last drawing near the final revelation. And now, Socrates, there bursts upon him that wondrous vision which is the very soul of the beauty he has toiled so long for. It is an everlasting loveliness which neither comes nor goes, which neither flowers nor fades, for such beauty is the same on every hand, the same then as now, here as there, this way as that way, the same to every worshiper as it is to every other.

Using Socratic methods, it seems, one comes to know the good and the beautiful in terms far more in line with spiritual traditions than logical analysis. These insights show us that Socrates, for all his argumentation, holds in heart ideas and conceptions closer to shamanism than rationalism. Diotima taught Socrates that the true path to human excellence is spiritual:

> And remember, she said, that it is only when he discerns beauty itself through what makes it visible that a man will be quickened with the true, and not the seeming, virtue—for it is virtue's self that quickens him, not virtue's semblance. And when he has brought forth and reared this perfect virtue, he shall be called the friend of god, and if ever it is given to man to put on immortality, it shall be given to him.

In the *Phaedo*, Socrates discusses knowledge in terms quite familiar to the shaman: "We are in fact convinced that if we are ever to have pure knowledge of anything, we must get rid of the body and contemplate things by themselves with the soul by itself." In light of these revelations, it seems that Socrates's trances may have resembled shamanic states of consciousness.

The shaman, in his strange dreams and trances, appears quite insane to common folk. Similarly, Socrates claimed that the highest knowledge arrived through a type of madness. In the *Phaedrus*, during one of his rare jaunts outside the city walls, Socrates discusses madness as the fount of prophecy, poetry, religious practices, and love: "...the greatest blessings come by way of madness..." Socrates seems almost to recount his shamanic predecessors directly: "...it is in place to appeal to the fact that madness was accounted no shame nor disgrace by the men of old who gave things their names..." Shortly thereafter, Socrates shows roundabout how both madness and the highest gifts depend upon the immortal soul, his catch-all doctrine. The hallmark practices and ideas of the shamans find a comfortable home in Socrates's 'new' system.

Other passages portray Socrates as possessing a strange mastery over his mental states akin to the shaman. While drinking, for instance, Socrates shows no signs of drunkenness. Alcibiades doles out a generous volume of wine for Socrates but despairs of getting him drunk: "...I shan't get any change out of him. It doesn't matter how much you make him drink, it never makes him drunk."[23] At the end of the dialogue, when morning has broken, all lay about in a drunken stupor, or asleep. In the midst of this, and after having drunk more than any other, Socrates finishes debating with the last of the muddle-headed revelers, themselves beyond hope, and leaves for a morning bath so that he can begin his day as usual.

Like the classic shaman, Socrates possessed a robust constitution, unflagging endurance, and even the unusual stare common to the powerful sorcerers. Again, Alcibiades recounts many of these important features of the philosopher when he remembers their time together in battle:

> ...he stood the hardships of the campaign far better than I did, or anyone else, for that matter. And if—and it's always liable to happen when there's fighting going on—we were cut off from our supplies, there was no one who put such a good face on it as he. ...the way he got through that winter was most impressive, and the winters over there are pretty shocking. There was one time when the frost was harder than ever, and all the rest of us stayed inside, or if we did go out we wrapped ourselves up to the eyes and tied bits of felt and sheepskins over our shoes, but Socrates went out in the

same old coat he'd always worn, and made less fuss about walking on the ice in his bare feet than we did in our shoes. ...And then, gentlemen, you should have seen him when we were in retreat from Delium. ...I noticed for one thing how much cooler he was...and for another how—to borrow from a line of yours, Aristophanes—he was walking with the same 'lofty strut and sideways glance' that he goes about with here in Athens. His 'sideways glance' was just as unconcerned whether he was looking at his own friends or at the enemy, and you could see from half a mile away that if you tackled him you'd get as good as you gave...[24]

In short, the Socrates that we see in this frank narrative possesses all the eccentricities of the reconstituted shaman. Sieroszewski paints a portrait of 'the perfect shaman' as one who: "...must be serious, possess tact, be able to convince his neighbors; above all, he must not be presumptuous, proud, ill-tempered. One must feel an inner force in him that does not offend yet is conscious of its power."[25] Such a description matches Socrates precisely. Karjalainen writes that the shaman must possess: "...keen intelligence, a perfectly supple body, and an energy that appears unbounded. His very preparation for his future work leads the neophyte to strengthen his body and perfect his intellectual qualities."[26] These characteristics, too, resemble Socrates at his best.

To become a shaman, one must possess a distinct calling. Some kind of revelatory dream or other sign alights upon the initiate who then cannot divorce himself from the call to destiny. Socrates received such a calling to his role as public philosopher. He describes his vocation in the *Apology*. Upon learning that the oracle at Delphi had deemed him wisest among men, Socrates set out on a mission to see what the oracle could possibly have meant. He did not understand the divine pronouncement for he himself knew that he possessed no knowledge to speak of. He began his tireless search for truth by visiting all of Athens's greatest minds. Hoping to find someone with superior wisdom, he would come to understand the significance of the oracle. In fact, he could find no one who possessed superior wisdom. As aforementioned, all possessed an esteemed knowledge that showed limitation upon closer scrutiny. Of course, in such a quest Socrates offended and disgruntled many. He accepted this consequence as part of his religious duty to teach people that only those who profess no real knowledge are truly wise. Such people must be tireless students with fresh and flexible minds:

> That is why I still go about seeking and searching in obedience to
> the divine command, if I think that anyone is wise, whether citi-
> zen or stranger, and when I think that any person is not wise, I try
> to help the cause of God by proving that he is not. This occupa-
> tion has kept me too busy to do much either in politics or in my
> own affairs. In fact, my service to God has reduced me to extreme
> poverty.[27]

Socrates claims neither pleasure nor reward from this duty of his,
a duty which: "I have accepted...in obedience to God's commands
given in oracles and dreams and in every other way that any other
divine dispensation has ever impressed a duty upon man."[28] His
understanding of it as a divine calling, without real compensation,
closely parallels the difficult tasks that the shaman takes upon himself for the same reasons.

One of the shaman's crucial techniques is his reliance upon
spirit helpers. Perhaps Socrates's most unusual trait was his own
dependence upon a personal *daemonion*—a voice which speaks to
him and directs him to the good: "In the past the prophetic voice to
which I have become accustomed has always been my constant com-
panion, opposing me even in quite trivial things if I was going to
take the wrong course."[29] Socrates's voice is not the call of conscience
that we each possess but something altogether more radical. He
believed in it so strongly that, in the *Apology*, he credits its silence, as
he faces the death sentence, as indicative that in death lies a great
good rather than the evil traditionally supposed. Sensitive to
Aristophanes's insults and the public's conception of the philosopher as a fool, Socrates explains his true state of mind as one of possession: "Standing aside from the busy doings of mankind, and
drawing nigh to the divine, he [the philosopher] is rebuked by the
multitude as being out of his wits, for they know not that he is possessed by a deity."[30]

All the shaman's bizarre traits mean nothing if he doesn't actually perform his duties. And what are these? The shaman acts as healer
and protector to his community. Socrates described himself in these
terms foremost:

> It is literally true, even if it sounds rather comical, that God has spe-

cially appointed me to this city, as though it were a large thoroughbred horse which because of its great size is inclined to be lazy and needs the stimulation of some stinging fly. It seems to me that God has attached me to this city to perform the office of such a fly, and all day long I never cease to settle here, there, and everywhere, rousing, persuading, reproving every one of you.[31]

Predicting his case lost, Socrates says that the court will slap him like the stinging fly he is: "…and then you will go on sleeping till the end of your days, unless God in his care for you sends someone to take my place."[32] Socrates perceives himself in the most sacred terms as a divinely sent guardian to fight the spiritual complacency of his beloved Athens.

For all his similarities, Socrates lacks some of the shaman's notable qualities. So far as we know, Socrates did not undergo any of the ritual training and initiation universal to shamanic traditions. He received a calling and did seem to possess a disposition perfectly fitted to his occupation. His training, though, if there were any, appears to have been self-directed. The shaman usually possesses an uncanny connection to nature. In spite of his supernatural capabilities, the shaman always retained a fondness for nature that allowed him special insights. He usually possessed animal helpers of some type or another and identified himself with various power animals. In contrast to this rich heritage, Socrates seemed anti-natural at every turn. He is the original city-dweller who ventured outside his urban home on only the rarest occasions. Neither did he show a fondness for or special connection to animals of any type.

Given that Socrates possesses many of the rare and unique traits of the shaman, we must ask, "To what purpose?" For all his similarities, Socrates did not fit the bill as a classic shaman. But, indeed, what ideal exists in reality? With his peculiar mix and match of shamanic traits, one sees in Socrates the transition at the heart of European religious thought as it left its ancient matrix of shamanism and evolved into its individualistic stage. The age-old notions of spiritual and animistic tendencies present in shamanism met the highly rationalistic hero ethic of the Greeks. While the animist ideas had once forged a deep-connection between man and his environment, in the peculiar Orphic-Platonic blend these ideas served as the crucial determinant to alienate man from his environment. The ancient ideas that had served a primordial hunting people came to serve urban man in his enthronement of the artificial world and its unholy progeny, the stark individual.

In his essence, Socrates was the last shaman of European culture. With him the ancient lineage that had enchained hundreds of generations of archaic peoples to their environments was broken. To borrow the language of Islam, Socrates was the seal of the shamans.

## Phaedo

Plato's dialogue, *Phaedo*, recounts the last day of Socrates and how the legendary philosopher faced death with a tranquil heart. It is no coincidence that we learn most about the life-extending doctrine of dualism in this dialogue, as Socrates himself faces death. As described in the introduction, death, with its full accompaniment of annihilation fear, creates the need for dualism. This subtext, the feared enemy that opposes the entire activity and passion of life, forms a key focal point that any understanding of the world must address.

To set the stage for the dialogue: Socrates, loved by some, despised by many more, was taken to court for charges of impiety and corruption of the youth. Though Socrates represented himself in the trial with aplomb, he nevertheless lost his case. He is sentenced to death, freely accepting his fate (rather than escaping Athens, as his friends planned), though he knows his condemnation is a sham. Despite the corruption and injustice inflicted on him, Socrates remains in good spirits.

Socrates's friends congregate to spend the fleeting hours with him. His wife and children have already visited and Socrates had them escorted away as they were too emotional for the crowd of sober thinkers. Nevertheless, as his final hour approaches his emotionally reserved friends break down as well. Socrates is so endearing to those who know him well that even his prison guard becomes teary-eyed in the last moments. This turbulent climate of emotions does not impress Socrates who has long taught the restriction of passions and the insignificance of the body.

Now, in the presence of his friends, shortly before he himself will carry out the death sentence by drinking a poisonous concoction,

Socrates spends his time discussing the essence of the soul and its immortality.

The setting of the dialogue rings allegorical: the entire discussion of the *Phaedo* occurs in Socrates's prison cell after his unhappy condemnation. The poetic context efficiently parallels the content of the dialogue and drives the subliminal message of Orphism, namely, that the body is a tomb and life in the body merely a period of imprisonment. Socrates's death at the end of the dialogue suggests that, while all he left behind remain in the prison house, he himself has achieved a liberation from the torment of bodily existence. It is within this context that his final words, a request for his friend Crito to pay a debt to Asclepius—the god of healing—make sense. Socrates, whom his friends declare, "...the bravest and also the wisest and most upright man," had been healed of the disease of life.

In the *Phaedo*, Socrates seeks to alleviate his friends' sadness and clarify their ideas about death: "I suppose that for one who is soon to leave this world there is no more suitable occupation than inquiring into our views about the future life, and trying to imagine what it is like. What else can one do in the time before sunset?"

Beginning with suicide (he's against it) and a positive attitude towards death (he's for it) Socrates's beliefs about the afterlife change from place to place throughout the dialogue. As is common in the dialogues, where the hand of reason cannot stretch—the realm of death in this case—various mythologies are compared in an attempt to make sense of life's puzzles. At one point Socrates discusses the belief in reincarnation; at another, a standard 'judgment' belief—one often discussed by the Orphics. Later he becomes less formulaic, and merely 'hopes': "...I have a firm hope that there is something in store for those who have died, and...something much better for the good than for the wicked." His best-reasoned argument stipulates that philosophers go to a heavenly place of truth and presence with God while those direly attached to the body haunt the Earth until some future incarnation. In short, lacking any real footing, Socrates's ideas about the afterlife appear unsettled and vague. Toward the end of the dialogue, after an almost unrelated, yet elaborate, description of another type of afterlife, the philosopher admits his uncertainty:

Of course, no reasonable man ought to insist that the facts are exactly as I have described them. But that either this or something very like it is a true account of our souls and their future habitations—since we have clear evidence that the soul is immortal—this, I think, is both a reasonable contention and a belief worth risking, for the risk is a noble one. We should use such accounts to inspire ourselves with confidence, and that is why I have already drawn out my tale so long.

Socrates thinks the belief in an enduring soul and its afterlife imbues man with confidence. This much needed assurance in the face of death fits with another statement he made earlier: "Anyone who does not know and cannot prove that the soul is immortal must be afraid, unless he is a fool." Socrates shows no fear towards death which he defines in the rhetorical question: "Is death nothing more or less than this, the separate condition of the body by itself when it is released from the soul, and the separate condition by itself of the soul when released from the body? Is death anything else than this?"

## The Doctrine of Recollection and the Theory of Forms

But how does Socrates get to the idea of an afterlife? How does he prove that the soul is immortal? He begins with his doctrine of recollection, touched upon in a number of dialogues. It is one of the key Platonic doctrines. Socrates wondered how people came to know anything, how we determined the true from the false, the real from the illusory. In hypothesizing an answer, he both created a theory of knowledge and a proof of the soul. Since he hadn't recourse to educational psychology or even the simplest notions of how the brain works, he proposed knowledge through recollection. He thought that the soul, having lived before birth with tremendous knowledge, came to recollect this knowledge during its life on Earth. Education is merely a 'drawing-out' of this previously held knowledge.

At a famous instance in the *Meno*, Socrates takes a young slave and teaches the child some elementary geometry. The totally uneducated child reasons through Socrates's questions after brief instruction. This instance proved that all were secretly in possession of great knowledge and that the teacher needed only to draw out the knowledge from his student. One can only imagine how Socrates would explain a learning disability. Perhaps the shamans would attribute such phenomena to 'soul-theft.'

If knowledge arrives through the process of recollection, what do we recall? What is the world from which we came? Plato faced some major obstacles with this theory. For instance, if we come to understand through a process of recall then what do we make of something that is truly novel, or is nothing truly novel?

Suppose one encounters a new chair in his neighbor's home. Surely that particular chair wasn't part of the soul's experience before birth so how could one even identify the thing as a chair? Of course, this is a trivial example; more importantly, how does one ever decide upon a particular course of action—if all is recollection then how do we act morally in any situation; have we previously lived through all situations and thus learned every appropriate course of action? These enigmas all came to be revealed in Plato's theory of forms. The doctrine of recollection relies entirely on this theory for its intelligibility.

In the ideal world from which the soul 'fell,' forms of each thing exist in their perfection. These are the archetypes or quintessential examples of all things. In the world of forms exists a form of justice, a form of chair, a form of good, a form of man, woman, *ad infinitum*. Whenever one recognizes a dirty sofa at a garage sale, whenever one feels that a certain decision is the most just, the same thing occurs— a recollection of the ideal forms and a juxtaposition of a worldly counterpart with these forms. If the thing we perceive roughly parallels the form, or has the 'essential' attributes, then it can be recognized and understood. According to Plato, this is how we 'know' things, how we ever feel right about making decisions. In this theory, there is a spirit-world full of all the perfect things and the base material world in which everything is but a poor and varied replica. Socrates describes the theory in brief:

> Suppose that when you see something you say to yourself, this thing which I can see has a tendency to be like something else, but it falls short and cannot be really like it, only a poor imitation. Don't you agree with me that anyone who receives that impression must in fact have previous knowledge of that thing which he says that the other resembles, but inadequately?"[33]

This theory of forms also led to a theory of beauty. Beauty, in large part, derives from an object closely resembling its ideal. If we find ourselves attracted to a particular man or woman it is because these individuals are closer to the 'ideal' than others. Forget Freud, forget individual desires, according to Plato, we all seek the same thing. Given that we live in a much broader world than ancient Greece, full of varied peoples and varied 'ideals,' the Socratic theory of beauty begins to falter. Consider the Venus de Milo: surely, it must come close to the ideal of woman for its radiant beauty still dazzles all who see the statue. Or does it? The average Eskimo might think the Venus a bit waifish and prefer instead a broad-hipped Earth mother *a là* the Venus of Willendorf. In contrast, the adolescent clubgoer would think the Greek goddess positively mannish and select a Twiggy-type anorectic as the contemporary ideal.

Considering the soul to be the true reservoir of knowledge, Socrates distrusted the testimony of the senses. Truth cannot be found 'out there' but must be sought in the soul, through the process of recollection. In the Platonic view, the whole body—the whole world—presents an impediment to real knowledge. The philosopher's life: "…consists in separating the soul as much as possible from the body, and accustoming it to withdraw from all contact with the body and concentrate itself by itself, and to have its dwelling, so far as it can, both now and in the future, alone by itself, freed from the shackles of the body."[34]

Socrates disparaged the body. Was this because he himself possessed a unattractive one? After Socrates the soul, bank of knowledge and trustee of goodness, became the philosopher's wealth. Death seemed the grand consummation of the philosopher's life, the release to a pure existence of soul and soul's truth:

> So long as we keep to the body and our soul is contaminated with this imperfection, there is no chance of our ever attaining satisfactorily to our object, which we assert to be truth. …the body provides us with innumerable distractions in the pursuit of our necessary sustenance, and any diseases which attack us hinder our quest for reality. Besides, the body fills us with loves and desires and fears and all sorts of fancies and a great deal of nonsense, with the result that we literally never get an opportunity to think at all about anything… If no pure knowledge is possible in the com-

pany of the body, then either it is totally impossible to acquire knowledge, or it is only possible after death, because it is only then that the soul will be separate and independent of the body...[35]

The Platonic notion of a better state after death became a permanent fixture of Western mentality. Most subscribers to the Platonically-inspired afterlife don't envision, as Plato himself did, an eternity of philosophic adventure spurred on by the sublime contemplation of truth. Nevertheless, Plato's idea attracted a large audience with its promises that upon death, all the tough questions of life will find their solution. The idea that forever onward, one resides in a 'better place' cools the burning fear of annihilation and rescinds one's obligation and responsibility to the sacred moment. Unfortunately, many silly notions about the afterlife proliferated in this newly opened land; the only ingredient lacking in this untilled soil was rich fertilizer. Soon people described the afterlife, quite rationally, with such attributes as: the fulfillment of all desires (food, sex, continuous NFL, and the like), the investiture of material riches and power, and an assortment of sundry pleasures whose extent would be exhausted after the first few centuries of one's eternity. The *shameless vanity of the soul* reflected by this Platonic notion of the afterlife attracted a following whose lusty imaginations quickly outran their stumbling logic. Additionally, the Platonic dislike of the body anchored itself deep into the Western-Puritanical tradition. Only recently, in the wide expanse of European history, has this traditional culture of physical prudishness swayed to one whose *shameless vanity of the body* crafts idols from the spindly flesh of young women, promotes a morality of muscle-tone, and whose consummate end lies in the flesh-cut abdominal 'six-pack.' From one extreme end of the spectrum, the pendulum has swung to its opposite absurdity.

Plato believed in the soul's existence before birth, during life (trapped, as it were, in the prison of the body), and after death. For Plato, the soul is eternal; yet, for some strange reason one's individual soul gets trapped for a brief moment in this body, in this place. During this infinitesimal moment of eternity, recollection of one's pre-birth eternity appears lost. Many mysteries arise from this idea. Why do people receive varying 'sentences' of life? One soul escapes in infancy before the growth of any apparent identity or reason, another crosses-over during childhood, or after parenting a family, yet another lives to a ripe old age, as Socrates did, before sloughing off the mortal coil.

Where does memory come from—that other place? How is it facilitated or hampered? Is intelligence merely the practice of recollection? Some early Greek thinkers challenged all such notions of immortality with the following argument from memory and recollection: since we don't remember the soul's existence before the birth of the body, then neither should we expect an existence after its death. For these philosophers (and many modern ones, as well), the soul emerges in life and disappears at the end of life. Coming from nothingness, to nothingness it returns. Two thousand years later, the sometimes pessimistic Mark Twain, with his trademark (and Greek-like) irony, quipped:

> Annihilation has no terrors for me, because I have already tried it before I was born—a hundred million years—and I have suffered more in an hour, in this life, than I remember to have suffered in the whole hundred million years put together. There was a peace, a serenity, an absence of all sense of responsibility, an absence of worry, an absence of care, grief, perplexity; and the presence of a deep content and unbroken satisfaction in that hundred million years of holiday which I look back upon with a tender longing and with a grateful desire to resume, when the opportunity comes.[36]

## The Platonic Attempt

While the Platonic idea of the soul created a typhoon of problems, one must appreciate the elegance of this primitive 'solution' to the mysteries of the mind. The doctrine of recollection and the theory of forms roughly parallel a natural process of brain-mediated memory. To the ancients, it was probably just as unbelievable that memory could arise out of a piece of meat than from some other world. We moderns should know better since we've long accepted the function of our organs as the source of the body's many 'miracles.' We are not surprised to learn that our energy comes from our hearts, our lungs, our adrenals. We do not suppose that energy angels deposit the necessary fuel when required. The concepts of metabolism, while not on everyone's mind, still do not incite disbelief when they are posed as an explanation for our living body. The step from this to the notion of the mind/brain presents no great leap. The Greek notion, the shamanic prejudice, leaves a deep mark in our presumptions—we cannot easily accept the mind's source in matter because of our dualistic inheritance. It is still preferable to believe in another, higher world—the source of the human being's origin and the place of destiny.

Even without a good understanding of the brain, the fact that ancient philosophers could accept Plato's doctrines surprises anyone who has ever attempted to learn a new skill. The vividness of an idea or skill never renders itself after some practice of transcendental ecstasy. Only through long, varied practice can something be mastered. Any sport, for instance, necessitates careful habituation and rigorous training. The ice skater does not contemplate the eternal forms to improve her abilities but spends thousands of hours on the ice allowing her brain and body to enrich themselves with massive connections and sensitize themselves to increasingly subtle and complicated maneuvers. No spiritual plane dumps perfection from heaven to Earth. As the master of any discipline will testify, long is the road to success. The reality of learning teaches study and discipline, not recollection of a supernatural world. This process, despite being wholly material and taking place within one's head, is as miraculous as any ghostly Platonic doctrine. The sheer computing power and ingenuity of the brain's structure permits a process nearly impossible to explain or replicate. For all his error, Plato was not so far off in his wonder over these seemingly supernatural capacities. In the modern world, blessed with great knowledge and tools for knowledge, we can understand processes in great detail that Plato could only guess at through his reasoning and mythologizing. We know that 'recollection' and a comparison of 'forms' takes place in the brain according to the experiences amassed during a lifetime, not through the soul from pre-birth experience.

Plato's audience, as well-educated and sophisticated as they were, knew nothing of the brain's mechanisms of memory and were not privy to scientific knowledge. Most didn't even consider the brain to be the source of one's mental aptitudes. The heart was, to many, a more likely center for the mind. Explanations through mythology and metaphor provided understandings of the world which, if not true and predictable, were at least tenable. When we have nothing else, even the small footholds of speculation confer a sense of stability which the human mind relishes.

Plato reinvigorated the chasm between the physical and the immaterial that the shaman had assumed and perpetuated it into modern, Western consciousness. Since Platonism directly shaped Christianity and likewise Christianity influenced all modern conceptions of the person, one discerns that shamanism—through the intermediary of Orphism—is the grandparent of all Western spirituality. Something like an underlying template lies beneath all religions, particularly Western religions; this template possesses a multitude of shamanic elements. Modern man can achieve greater unity by seeing the family resemblance in all of his spiritual doctrines. He will find this unity undeniable when he realizes that all such doctrines are wrong for the same reason, namely—that there is no such thing as a spirit.

# Chapter 7

# JUDAISM

In early Judaism, the concept of soul did not support the mind/body split present in so many other religions and philosophies. In her article on the afterlife in the *Encyclopedia of Religion*, Jane Smith explains:

> In the Hebrew view, a person was not understood so much as having a body, something essentially different and apart from the nonphysical side of one's being, as being a body, which implies the totality of the individual and the inseparability of the life principle from the fleshly form.[1]

## *The Breath of God*

Soul in the Hebrew Bible means 'breath' or 'vital principle,' that which gives life to all God's creatures.[2] One need only think of the word, 'inspiration,' to understand what the Jews meant when they talked about the soul. To come to life was to be literally 'breathed into' by God. The majestic beginning of humanity in *Genesis* illustrates this belief, "...then the Lord God formed man from the dust of the ground, and breathed into his nostrils the breath of life; and the man became a living being." This emphasis on breath and respiration is not a surprising one: breathing is the ever-present, yet mysterious, action of the living. At the moment of death, breathing and life cease together.

The magical quality of receiving the invisible life-force into one's body seemed a great mystery to the ancients. Only with our modern understandings of chemistry do we understand that the invisible is still material, the gaseous. This gaseous substance, only twenty-one percent of which is the relevant oxygen, goes through a chemical process to provide the body energy. Around the world words for soul often relate it to breath or breathing. Common notions of the soul perceive it to be a kind of gaseous substance. This is no surprise given the long history of confusing oxygen with the invisible life force. This wondrous but wholly natural process seemed much more 'spiritual' before science.

The Jews considered the soul the action-giving principle of the body. The Hebrew word, *nefesh*, is commonly translated 'soul' but never referred to a soul distinct from the body. Because of this close tie to the body, the Jews did not originally conceive of an immaterial existence after death. In the earliest biblical times, if the afterlife was mentioned at all, it came in the idea of Sheol. Sheol, never discussed at length in Scripture, referred to a dark, lifeless place where the dead go. In the despairing *Book of Job*, during a point when Job laments being born, he suggests death as one's consummate end with only the tombs and burial goods to represent the person's previous position in life:

> Now I would be lying down in quiet; I would be asleep; then I would be at rest with kings and counselors of the Earth who rebuild ruins for themselves, or with princes who have gold, who fill their houses with silver... There the wicked cease from troubling, and there the weary are at rest. There the prisoners are at peace together; they do not hear the voice of the taskmaster. The small and the great are there, and the slaves are free from their masters.

During the early part of Judaism—a relative golden age of the Hebrew nation when they genuinely seemed to be the chosen nation of God—the afterlife didn't enter into religious thought. Their god was of the living and his favor could be seen in the strength of the community of Jews.

## *Jewish Apocalypticism*

In a dark period, when one persists in righteousness, following the holy laws and carrying out the rites, the misery of existence seems inexplicable. It is not right for God's people to suffer through life. To suffer or die for one's faith, when there is no possibility of reward, goes against all good sense. If God is just then there must be a reversal; if not now then at the end of time. Stern relates the historical timing of the doctrine of resurrection:

> ...it is likely the prominence the idea of resurrection began to assume in this period was a result of the political and religious crises in which significant numbers of Jews suffered martyrdom. In order to maintain a belief in God's justice and in his promises to the righteous that they would enjoy the restoration of Israel, it became necessary to extend the doctrine of reward and punishment beyond this life to the hereafter.[3]

The first clear instance of the doctrine of resurrection occurs in the *Book of Daniel*, written during the time of the Hasmonean Revolt (c. 165 B.C.E.). The earlier prophets Isaiah and Ezekiel, themselves living in times of Jewish bondage, also composed apocalyptic, or 'end-time' literature. All of these writers foresaw God's revenge on Israel's enemies and a glorious renewal of Israel's power. It was Daniel, though, who first envisioned the resurrection of the dead in Jewish Scripture.

With his fourth century B.C.E. victories throughout the ancient world, Alexander the Great started a Hellenizing influence that threatened the traditional cultures of the time. The strong political control that Greece possessed during this period resulted in a dissemination of their culture and philosophy. As a consequence of this, just two centuries later, the cosmopolitan ruler Antiochus IV defiled the temple in Jerusalem, making it a sanctuary of Zeus. In our modern world an analogy of such a disturbing act is lacking. It could be equivalent to having our next president destroy the Statue of Liberty and erect a mosque in its place. Only with a horrific war, the Hasmonean revolt, did the Jews reclaim and purify their temple, an event now commemorated annually in the Jewish festival of Hanukkah.

The times were so anti-traditional and anti-religious that the prophet Daniel considered it proof of the impending end of the world. His writings predicted the fall of this wicked world and a restoration of God's chosen people:

> There shall be a time of anguish such as has never occurred since nations first came into existence. But at that time your people shall be delivered, everyone who is found written in the book. Many of

those who sleep in the dust of the Earth shall awake, some to ever-lasting life, and some to shame and everlasting contempt.

This version of the resurrection implies a novel conception of life and afterlife. In the prophet Daniel's take, one retreats to the grave right after death. Sometime later, when the end of the world comes, the dead 'awake': "But you, go your way, and rest; you shall rise for your reward at the end of days." From these descriptions, it's clear that nothing like a disembodied spirit leaves the flesh to find a transcendental abode. God has the power to restore the flesh. This, and this alone, creates the person. Life without the body did not enter into Jewish ideas about existence.

The apocalyptic atmosphere of the time also gave rise to sectarian groups like the Essenes of the Qumran community. Apocalyptic groups, convinced that the end of the world approached, lived in the desert and prepared for the end by living a strict life of purity. The Qumran Essenes are responsible for the famous Dead Sea Scrolls found in 1947. Of interest in this context is the marked language used in some of the Dead Sea Scrolls. Using terms such as "sons of light" and "Prince of Darkness," many scholars now think this Jewish community to have been thoroughly influenced by Zoroastrianism.[4]

During their times of troubles, the Jews assumed that the end of the world was at hand. A monotheistic religion that doesn't split either themselves or the world into the seen and the unseen, the spiritual and the material, cannot easily make sense of troubled times. If one believes one's god the most powerful, indeed the only god, then no other people should pose a threat. The comically universal idea that 'God is on our side' shone strong in Hebrew culture. During crisis periods, two interpretations occur in such faiths: the times of trouble are proof that God is angry with and punishing his people or that he has started the chain of events to end the world. This theme plays itself out again and again in the Hebrew Bible. The conceptual model presents a god so authoritarian and judgmental that his anger at disobedience causes either an abandonment or some punishment against his chosen people and the world at large.

Shortly before Christianity, when the Romans had total dominion of the region, the righteous Jews knew that they hadn't broken God's covenant. They could account no reasons for God's punishment. Their suffering under the Romans made the outlook bleak… yet they kindled a spark of hope. For those affected by the apocalyptic literature, all seemed clear: the last days were at hand. The resurrection of the dead would soon come to pass and the long-awaited Messiah would free God's chosen.

# Chapter 8

# THE BODY OF CHRIST

The dualism that defined Platonic thought might have been an interesting footnote in history, the kind of theory that a small group appreciates, occasionally philosophizing upon the subject. However, with the entrenchment of Christianity into the Western tradition, the notion of an immortal soul became more than theory, more than philosophy, it became dogma... *terra firma*.

## The Christian Mind

The history of Christianity, with all its delicate transitions and transformations in doctrine and theology, remains the key to any understanding of the modern mind. The idea that two thousand years ago a rag-tag group, a baker's dozen of uneducated artisans and fishermen, changed history more radically than any empire or group of geniuses truly astounds. No imaginative novel, no play of Shakespeare, could capture the unbelievable plot that the world over now knows so well. The very nature of our beliefs and perceptions, the way that we understand the world and, most importantly, envision ourselves, came from the mind of a single man—a carpenter with a penchant for religion.

Of course, during the stream of history each culture produced its brilliant prophets. The life of the Buddha influences more people today than Christianity. The religion of Muhammad, a prophet called to record the Koran and teach 'submission to the will of God' (Islam), now rules the entire Middle East and a good deal of Southeast Asia. Nor can one easily overlook the other faith traditions and their respective seers. However, because Christianity created the Western tradition and because of its zeal for missionary work, it has come to influence the world more profoundly than less 'invasive' faiths.

European culture dominates the world more than any other. After all, the great mass of China, once organized and mobilized by a tradition of Emperors and home-grown bureaucracy, now regulates itself by a communist model developed by a couple of nineteenth century European intellectuals. But how do the philosophies and ideals of Europe relate to Christianity? To ask that question is like asking how the branches are related to the trunk and root system of the tree. All things, at one time or another, had to seek accord with Christian dogma or the emotions and psychology that it engendered. Dualism, that once and future theme, lies at the heart of all this hubbub. Without death and the fear of death and the soul and hope of salvation, little of what we call the world would now exist. Who knows how things would be different?

Perhaps the most remarkable fact about Christianity and dualism is that Christianity isn't really dualistic! As an outgrowth of Judaism, early Christianity espoused the resurrection of the body as its doctrine of immortality. Strict dualism, with its insistence on a transcendent soul, does not have a solid basis in the Scripture. In *A History of Heaven*, Jeffery Burton Russell had the following to say: "Given the overwhelming testimony to the salvation of the body in both Jewish and Christian Scripture, the separate immortality of the soul is incompatible with Biblical teaching."[1] And Russell is not alone. Many contemporary theologians and historians think that the early Church had no belief in the detachable soul. The soul, to them, must always be part of the whole person, body and all.

Then how did Christianity become the great vehicle for the dualistic message? Though deriving from the tradition and philosophy of Judaism, the New Testament makes noteworthy revisions to the Jewish faith. While there is nothing of dualism in the New Testament so blatant as in Plato's *Phaedo*, there are ambiguous passages which could be interpreted with the disembodied soul in mind. That tear combined with the gradual pull of Platonism and the many Gnostic influences eventually wrought the chasm between the body and soul in Western mentality.

Much of this controversy derives from the different words for soul in Hebrew, Aramaic, and Greek. When speaking of psychological matters—how we think, the difference between mental substance and physical substance, how emotions enter into behavior—the ancients were worse off than we confused moderns. Ancient conceptions about the soul employed a vague set of psychological terminology. Moreover, since Jesus himself never wrote anything, we can't be sure that his usage of words (in Aramaic) regarding the soul were properly translated in the early Scripture which was written primarily in Greek.

While the psychological vocabulary of Judaism proved to be vague at times, the Greeks' vocabulary abounded in equivocation. Greece, the original land of philosophizing, had been dealing with various definitions of soul for centuries by the time Christianity began employing its words. In utilizing Greek terms for soul, the Jewish writers unwittingly complicated matters. The variant meanings of this terminology furthered the confusion. The Greek words employed in describing the human person included *psyche, pneuma, soma,* and *sarx.* As was common with that highly philosophical language, these words changed meaning as different nuances were considered. *Psyche,* from the Greek verb *to breathe,* indicated 'life' and sometimes meant spirit as separable from the body. *Pneuma,* so similar to our word for air driven—pneumatic—possessed a similar meaning to *psyche,* though later Christian thinkers would distinguish the two words more drastically. In some circles, the pneumatic self indicated a higher, more purely spiritual part of the person while his psyche might correspond more generally to something like his ego or personality. Part of our continuing usage, in English, of the two words 'soul' and 'spirit' reflect this Greek inheritance. *Soma* often referred to the body animated by soul. *Sarx* is usually a disparaging word for the body—the sinful flesh. Theologians have had no easy task in pulling these terms apart from their written context in the hopes of better understanding their subtleties, accidental or otherwise.[2]

The competing understandings of soul terminology make it very difficult to understand scriptural ideas about the soul. While the vocabulary poses its own problems, Scripture itself seems to revel in ambiguity. A careful inspection of the passages reveals how confusion about the soul emerged in Christian thought.

## The Dual Substance of Christ

A caution needs to be raised before we turn to the passages in question. First, most biblical scholars are in agreement that the early Christian writings do not represent a single view. Rather, the various Gospels and the many letters attributed to Paul represent a number of different 'communities' in the early church. Furthermore, not a single gospel was written any earlier than 70 c.e. That's nearly forty years after Jesus's death! Imagine taking any set of events in your life, even the most luminous, from forty years prior and trying to reconstruct the exact sequence of events, the exact play of words and nuances. One must expect, with that background, a certain amount of imprecision.

In many ways, early Christianity was marked by conflict. Each community sought to establish Christianity after its own fashion. One might look upon Kurosawa's masterful tale, *Rashomon*, as an instructive analogy. In that film one occurrence came to be seen in many, sometimes radically different, ways. Similarly, we must assume that the various apostles and disciples experienced Christ in different ways. It is more than likely that some apostles were present for such and such an experience with Jesus while others were present at other times. That means that, from the very beginning, Christ was known through multiple stories and perspectives.

Numerous Hellenistic doctrines also influenced each community. In the first two centuries, at least, Christianity was a swirling mass of writings, ideas, and contradictions. The 'one true faith' of orthodoxy had yet to develop. As time passed ideological controversies caused these different perspectives to widen and deepen. At some point in history, one may wonder if the various ideologies caused the stories to be shaped more radically. Unfortunately, this is impossible to know. What we must accept, as a principle, is that any one passage may or may not have been the virtual words of Jesus, Paul, or any other figure. Many early writings are known to be forgeries. Finally, whether a particular set of words truly was from Jesus or not ceased to be important. As the Church gained power and sought to unify its doctrines a set canon was determined. From that day until our own, believers accepted the fact that the Bible was divinely inspired and faultless. In other words, for most of history the confusions and controversies that are an inherent part of this conglomerate of literary and philosophical influences were accepted without reservation—contradictions and all.

The passages we'll consider pose two major theological problems: what is the afterlife condition of the human being and when does the afterlife begin? Upon death, does the person live as a spirit—that is, without a body—or does she 'sleep' until obtaining a body at the Resurrection? The New Testament offers both alternatives in different passages. Even Jesus (or the words attributed to him) seems unclear in respect to these questions.

In the *Gospel of Luke's* "The Rich Man and Lazarus" passage, Christ purportedly describes immediate spiritual (incorporeal) entry into the afterlife upon death:

> The poor man died and was carried away by the angels to Abraham's bosom. The rich man also died and was buried; and in Hades, being in torment, he lifted up his eyes, and saw Abraham far off and Lazarus in his bosom. And he called out, 'Father Abraham, have mercy upon me, and send Lazarus to dip the end of his finger in water and cool my tongue; for I am in anguish in this flame.' But Abraham said, 'Son, remember that you in your lifetime received your good things, and Lazarus in like manner evil things; but now he is comforted here, and you are in anguish. And besides all this, between us and you a great chasm has been fixed, in order that those who would pass from here to you may not be able, and none may cross from there to us.' And he said, 'Then I beg you, father, to send him to my father's house, for I have five brothers, so that he may warn them, lest they also come into this place of torment.' But Abraham said, 'They have Moses and the prophets, let them hear them.' And he said, 'No, father Abraham; but if someone goes to them from the dead, they will repent.' He said to him, 'If they do not hear Moses and the prophets, neither will they be convinced if someone should rise from the dead.'

This short passage implies a great deal about early Christian notions of the soul and the afterlife. The souls of the rich man and Lazarus, here implied as separate from the body, go to either heaven or hell. And though no worldwide resurrection has occurred, they have been sent, immediately upon death, to their respective fates. Such events suggest their afterlife to be a spiritual one. Yet, we see the rich man asks Abraham to send Lazarus with some water to cool his burning tongue. Such details hardly imply a spiritual existence.

Interestingly, these men are not referred to as Christians; their respective afterlife fates result from their obedience to Jewish law and custom. At no point does Jesus relate, as elsewhere, that: "I am the way and the truth and the life. No one comes to the Father except through me." The rich man and Lazarus achieve their deserved afterlives without the intercession of Jesus, quite a blasphemous doctrine if stated by anyone but Christ.

Christ's words to one of the criminals who died beside him also implies immediate, incorporeal existence upon death. The *Gospel of Luke* records: "Then he [the criminal] said, 'Jesus, remember me when you come into your kingdom.' He [Jesus] replied, 'Truly I tell you, today you will be with me in Paradise.'" Jesus essentially tells the criminal that, though their corpses will still be hanging from crosses, they will enter paradise upon death.

In contrast to this immediate entry into heaven or hell, elsewhere Jesus teaches the Resurrection. The Resurrection, when all are judged at the end of time, involves literally raising the dead from their graves and doling out new bodies to them. Christ definitely believed, and taught, the Resurrection. The *Gospel of Luke* records these words of Jesus: "…when you give a banquet invite the poor, the crippled, the lame, the blind. And you will be blessed, because they cannot repay you, you will be repaid at the resurrection of the righteous."

In a clever passage in the *Gospel of Mark*, the Sadducees, who denied bodily resurrection, tried to trick Christ by a *reductio ad absurdum* argument. Using the laws of Moses as a starting point, the Sadducees devised a scenario that, if it were true, would make a mockery of Jesus's idea about life after death:

> 'Teacher, Moses wrote for us that if a man's brother dies, leaving a wife but no child, the man shall marry the widow and raise up children for his brother. There were seven brothers; the first married and, when he died, left no children; and the second married the widow and he died, leaving no children; and the third likewise; none of the seven left children… In the resurrection whose wife will she be? For the seven had married to her?'

Jesus said to them, 'Is not this the reason you are wrong, that you know neither the Scriptures nor the power of God? For when they rise from the dead, they neither marry nor are given in marriage, but are like angels in heaven. And as for the dead being raised, have you not read in the book of Moses, in the story about the bush, how God said to him, 'I am the God of Abraham, the God of Isaac, and the God of Jacob?' He is God not of the dead, but of the living; you are quite wrong!'

As complex a passage as any, what Jesus means by they "...are like angels in heaven" is not clear. Perhaps he is reiterating that all social and familial ties cease to be important in the Christian realm, a point Jesus emphasized many times. But Christ could mean something more esoteric with this answer. Whatever Jesus intended the Sadducees to understand by this has been lost to us. One should not conclude, though, that living as angels conveys living without a body for angels always existed in bodily form whenever the Jews encountered them.

In some radical way, Jesus hints that people will not be the same as they are in the here and now. The afterlife will be different enough from this one that those who are married here will not be married there. In spite of this difference, Jesus insists that any life worthy of the word requires a body. He tells the Sadducees that they are wrong in doubting resurrection, that God holds power over living things, not inanimate, dead things. Life requires a body and until the body returns the person to life, there is none at all. This directly opposes the ideas in "The Rich Man and Lazarus" discussed earlier.

In addition to these confusions, an inherent tension between body and soul appears throughout the New Testament. As Jesus directs in the *Gospel of Matthew*: "Do not fear those who kill the body but cannot kill the soul; rather fear him who can destroy both soul and body in hell." Jesus suggests a physical redemption of martyrs' bodies in the *Gospel of Luke*: "...and they will put some of you to death. You will be hated by all because of my name. But not a hair on your head will perish. By your endurance you will gain your souls." It probably goes too far to imagine a spiritual being with imperishable hair.

Sin, which jeopardizes a person's chance of salvation, makes the body suspicious since it is the vehicle of sinning. Jesus uses graphic words in the *Gospel of Matthew* to indicate the body's relative worthlessness:

> If your hand or your foot causes you to stumble, cut it off and throw it away; it is better for you to enter life maimed or lame than to have two hands or two feet and to be thrown into eternal fire. And if your eye causes you to stumble, tear it out and throw it away; it is better for you to enter life with one eye than to have two eyes and to be thrown into the hell of fire.

In the *Gospel of Matthew*, Jesus sets up a very dangerous division: "Stay awake and pray that you may not come into the time of trial; the spirit indeed is willing, but the flesh is weak." Here, explicitly, the immaterial soul wars against the physical body. A distrust of the body, that constant theme of Platonism, becomes a mainstay of Christianity as well.

Jesus confuses the spirit/body split in other passages. When discussing the importance of baptism in the *Gospel of John*, he suggests an immaterial 'something' which sanctifies the person receiving baptism: "…no one can enter the kingdom of God without being born of water and Spirit. What is born of the flesh is flesh, and what is born of the Spirit is spirit." In the same text, Christ identifies spirit as physical breath, in line with Jewish tradition: "…Jesus said to them again, 'Peace be with you. As the Father has sent me, so I send you.' When he had said this, he breathed on them and said to them, 'Receive the Holy Spirit…'" Which is it then? Should we conceive of the spirit as merely a vital principle in the body, like breath, or should we think it a transcendent and mysterious 'something'? Unfortunately, Christ cannot help us on this matter since he uses different understandings throughout the Scriptures never settling on a single concept.

In determining whether Christianity implies bodily resurrection or immediate spiritual reception into the afterlife, the most important evidence for the debate comes from the very actions of Christ. Jesus returned to his disciples in the resurrected flesh. There is no uncertainty on this point, it is dogma.

Christ had predicted his resurrection so often that the Pharisees worried that his disciples might steal his body and claim the prophesied Resurrection. Along with the chief priests, the Pharisees went to Pilate to obtain guards to watch over the tomb and prevent just such a hoax. In spite of their careful tactics, an angel came and rolled away the boulder at the entrance of the tomb so that Jesus could physically depart it. As noted in the *Gospel of Luke*, Christ came to the whole group of disciples:

> ...Jesus himself stood among them and said to them, 'Peace be with you.' They were startled and terrified, and thought that they were seeing a ghost. He said to them, 'Why are you frightened, and why do doubts arise in your hearts? Look at my hands and my feet; see that it is I myself! Touch me and see; for a ghost does not have flesh and bones, as you see that I have.' ...he asked them, 'Have you here anything to eat?' They gave him a piece of broiled fish, and he took it and ate in their presence.

As the prototype for every 'saved' person's resurrection, Jesus exists in bodily form. There is no spirit here, no immaterial 'ghost-like' nature. He came back "flesh and bones" and even felt hunger and wanted to eat. Such a powerful statement all but negates ideas of a spiritual afterlife. The dead will come back, as Jesus did, in bodily form; they must wait, though, until the Second Coming. As an aside, one wonders whether those who lived their entire lives overweight will likewise spend eternity in their overweight bodies. Such are the vagaries of the literal Resurrection that Jesus taught and lived.

According to the Scripture, though, not quite everyone has to wait until the Resurrection. A sort of preemptive Resurrection occurs in the *Gospel of Matthew* right after Christ dies on the cross: "The tombs also were opened, and many bodies of the saints who had fallen asleep were raised. After this resurrection they came out of the tombs and entered the holy city and appeared to many." What should we make of this passage? What happened to these 'early risers?' Did they ascend to heaven, with Jesus, after a stroll about town? Perhaps they returned to their graves after this three day sojourn into the daylight? Whatever we decide about this peculiar incident, it reiterates the prominence of bodily resurrection as the Christian way to understand life after death.

Looking over these Scriptures, it is apparent what difficulties the early Church faced in discussing the afterlife: in one place we talk about spirit and immediate access to the afterlife while elsewhere we note 'sleeping' until the Resurrection. Indeed, the many gravestone epitaphs 'Rest in Peace' rely on the latter notion. Many great minds would ponder these issues. The Church fathers, both leaders and theologians, struggled with many doctrines of the soul and the afterlife.

# Paul

By the time Paul came to Christianity and served as its most prolific and ingenious lobbyist, infighting about the soul and the afterlife was well underway. As the first theologian of the Church, Paul's thoughts, which according to him proceeded directly from the Holy Spirit ("And I think that I have the Spirit of God[3]"), served as a continued testament of Christian belief.

Paul was not one of the original apostles but, at first, persecuted the Christians. As a headstrong Jew he felt the Christians (an entirely Jewish sect at that time) were betraying their true faith and disobeying the laws of Moses. Only after a miraculous vision of the risen Christ did he switch sides. For those who didn't know, Paul never met the living person, Jesus. And, having never known the person, one wonders how much easier it was for Paul to make of him a god. After his miraculous vision, Paul became Christianity's most important apostle and, in opening the faith to the Gentiles, made of this strange sect a world religion. A number of biblical scholars consider Paul the true founder of Christianity.[4]

To discuss the afterlife and the significance of Jesus, Paul needed to clarify just what death is and how it came about. By no means the natural state of man, death derived from sin; in fact, through the sin of one man, Adam. The following ideas from *Letters to the Romans* (Paul's most complete work of theology) uncover the origins of death:

> ...just as sin came into the world through one man, and death came through sin, and so death spread to all because all have sinned— sin was indeed in the world before the law, but sin is not reckoned when there is no law. Yet death exercised dominion from Adam to Moses, even over those whose sins were not like the transgression of Adam...

Such a doctrine claims an utter divorce between man and the rest of nature. For while all natural things decay and die, man originally did not know death. Only because of that little incident in the garden, when Eve ate the forbidden fruit and cajoled Adam into doing the same, did the curse of death begin. The entire history of human existence—banishment from the Garden of Eden, natural death, every catastrophe of the human race throughout history, and even the requisite emergence of Jesus Christ to atone for the sin of Adam—all these cosmic events occurred because of one, half-witted transgression by a couple of childlike people. It is as if the history of the world hinged upon the act of a mentally handicapped person. A sin as horrible as this could only be reconciled through the sacrifice of God's only Son… to Himself.

Christ came as the divine sacrifice to regain eternal life for man. Sin results in death and only in the forgiveness of sins, through Christ, does one gain eternal life. Again, the *Letter to the Romans*: "For the wages of sin is death, but the free gift of God is eternal life in Christ Jesus our Lord."

As elsewhere in the Scripture, Paul emphasizes a warring between spirit and body. The body should be viewed with extreme suspicion for it can jeopardize the great reward of the righteous, eternal presence with the Lord. Paul explains the importance of repudiating the body in *Letter to the Romans*: "…if you live according to the flesh, you will die; but if by the Spirit you put to death the deeds of the body, you will live." Paul discussed this eternal conflict between spirit and body in many of his letters. He regularly sent letters to churches throughout the Near East. In his *Letter to the Galatians*, Paul emphasizes the spirit/body distinction: "Live by the Spirit, I say, and do not gratify the desires of the flesh. For what the flesh desires is opposed to the Spirit, and what the Spirit desires is opposed to the flesh; for these are opposed to each other, to prevent you from doing what you want." Only with such continued emphasis to the Christian communities could this unhappy teaching lodge itself in the very center of Christian psychology. Such a dislike for the body made it less and less acceptable as the source of the soul. Though Paul would explicitly fight against Plato's notion of a dualistic soul, his more intense crusade against the body had the ironic result of 'tilling the theological field' so that Platonic doctrines could flourish.

Paul's distaste for all things physical augmented his desire to leave the world. He would much prefer a cessation of this conflict, this living in the world, and opt for the blessed afterlife. He states as much in his *Second Letter to the Corinthians*: "So we are always confident; even though we know that while we are at home in the body we are away from the Lord—for we walk by faith, not by sight. Yes, we do have confidence, and we would rather be away from the body and at home with the Lord." He considers life a vehicle to demonstrate devotion to Jesus. One can tell when reading his letters that, in the face of all his difficulties, Paul derives tremendous meaning from his work. He considered it something of a duty to remain in his body, though he loves the idea of "departing." In the *Letter to the Philippians* Paul discusses his ambivalence in whether to seek death or life in the world: "For to me, living is Christ and dying is gain. If I am to live in the flesh, that means fruitful labor for me; and I do not know which I prefer. I am hard pressed between the two: my desire is to depart and be with Christ, for that is far better; but to remain in the flesh is more necessary for you."

Paul also furthered the spiritual/material split by creating a division between the visible and the invisible, much like Plato. This distinction shows the disparaging way Paul views reality. For him, all is not what it seems. The world remains an impediment to the higher spiritual life divorced from the world. In his *Second Letter to the Corinthians*, Paul writes:

> Even though our outer nature is wasting away, our inner nature is being renewed day by day. For this slight momentary affliction is preparing for us an eternal weight of glory beyond all measure, because we look not at what can be seen but at what cannot be seen; for what can be seen is temporary, but what cannot be seen is eternal.

Paul's words emphasized the latent dualism in Christianity. However, when push came to shove, he—like Christ—staunchly supported the physical doctrine of the Resurrection. How both these beliefs can exist, side by side, in the mind of anyone remains the great mystery of Christianity. To set the corrupted body against the purity of one's spirit while also believing in the glory of the Resurrection as the acme of God's plan, requires the Christian to live amid contradiction. A similar contradiction would develop around sexuality. It was, on the one hand, the source of sacred life but also considered to be filthy and devilish, depending on one's disposition. In the *Letter to the Colossians*, Paul went so far as to say that: "...in him [Jesus] the whole fullness of deity dwells bodily." One detects in Paul's writings, as he changes from a loathing of the body to a reverence for it, a profound confusion about the subject. The same confusion that existed in the Holy Spirit, then in Paul (for he claimed to be informed by the Holy Spirit), now exists in the minds of most Scripturally-trained Christians. This grand mystery passes from generation to generation leading to mind-twisting interpretations within the official doctrine. Though others, led by the Gnostics, had begun to deny the literal implications of the Resurrection, Paul remained a Resurrectionist rather than a dualist.

The Corinthians of Greece, living as Christian believers but fifty miles from the home of Socrates and the Platonic Academy, faced a host of philosophic challenges. The intellectuals of Greece considered the Christian belief in physical resurrection silly. A superb proselytizer, Paul molded his language and ideas to the respective cultures wherever he taught the new faith of Christianity. To the Corinthians he was a logician, to the Hebrews a Rabbinical scholar. Paul tried his best to make the Christian beliefs 'fit-in.' As Paul wrote in *First Letter to the Corinthians*: "For Jews demand signs and Greeks seek wisdom, but we preach Christ crucified, a stumbling block to Jews and folly to Gentiles." To the Greeks, as to most of us who have inherited Greek notions, the non-physical soul provided a much more reasonable understanding of the afterlife.

Paul seems to have devoted great thought to the issues surrounding the Resurrection. He did not budge, though, on this point. In the *Letter to the Corinthians*, Paul responds to the arguments as the logician the Greeks preferred:

> Now if Christ is proclaimed as raised from the dead, how can some of you say there is no resurrection of the dead? If there is no resurrection of the dead, then Christ has not been raised; and if Christ has not been raised, then our proclamation has been in vain and your faith has been in vain. We are even found to be misrepresenting God, because we testified of God that he raised Christ—whom he did not raise if it is true that the dead are not raised. If Christ has not been raised, your faith is futile and you are still in your sins. Then those also who have fallen asleep in Christ have perished.

Here Paul vehemently affirms both Christ's Resurrection and the doctrine in general. He even links the two, holding Christ's Resurrection as proof of each believer's individual resurrection. To Paul, there could be no doubting either Christ's physical return as fact or the implications that this had for the doctrine of the Resurrection. To be resurrected was to be embodied. Paul would not accept a doctrine of spirit without the body, for the body itself was part of God's plan. In his interpretation of the *First Letter to the Corinthians*, theologian Karl Barth concludes: "To wish to be God's *without* the body is rebellion against God's will, is secret denial of God; ...The truth of God requires and establishes the Resurrection of the Dead, the Resurrection of the Body."[5]

Further on in the *First Letter to the Corinthians*, Paul makes life after death, in the form of the Resurrection, the Christian pillar of faith. Without this essential piece of the Christian message, Paul pronounces the entire venture absurd. He even claims he would live a different kind of life:

> If for this life only we have hoped in Christ, we are of all people most to be pitied. But in fact Christ has been raised from the dead, the first fruits of those who have fallen asleep. For as by a man came death, by a man has come also the resurrection of the dead. For as in Adam all die, so also in Christ shall all be made alive. ... Why am I in peril every hour? I protest, my brethren ... I die every day! What do I gain if, humanly speaking, I fought with beasts at Ephesus? If the dead are not raised, 'Let us eat and drink, for tomorrow we die.'

Paul, the great teacher of Christian abstinence, claims we should live as hedonists ('eat, drink, and be merry') if we lose the prospect of an afterlife! For Paul, Christianity's true promise comes in the reward of life after death. As he wrote above: "If only for this life we have hope in Christ, we are to be pitied more than all men." The difficulties of the early Christians made living as one a true challenge. The world seemed pitted against the early Christians and they against the world. These adversities, combined with the essentially abstinent behavior they taught, made of life an uneasy passage. Without the promise of reward in the hereafter, Paul would find his philosophy of life elsewhere.

Other Christians of the time fought against the emerging orthodoxy; indeed, they helped to define it. After all, a church doesn't achieve orthodoxy until it can kick out a few members and scorn them as heretics. These early heretics found Paul's theology of physical resurrection both simple-minded and a bit revolting. Furthermore, part of the promise of the physical resurrection was its linkage to the end of the world. The Christians of the time, Paul in particular, had reckoned the end of the world to be coming any day. But the days passed, and still Rome ruled Israel, and still Christ was gone. Faithfully, though, they awaited for the glorious transformation. Worries arose that those who had already died would somehow miss out on the spectacle of the Second Coming, while those who still lived would witness it more completely. In his *First Letter to the Thessalonians*, Paul writes to these doubters:

> ...we would not have you ignorant, brethren, concerning those who are asleep, that you may not grieve as others do who have no hope. For since we believe that Jesus died and rose again, even so, through Jesus, God will bring with him those who have fallen asleep. For this we declare to you by the word of the Lord, that we who are alive, who are left until the coming of the Lord, shall not preceded those who have fallen asleep. For the Lord himself will descend from heaven with a cry of command, with the archangel's call, and with the sound of the trumpet of God. And the dead in Christ will rise first; then we who are alive, who are left, shall be caught up together with them in the clouds to meet the Lord in the air...

Paul evidently thought that he and many of his contemporaries would be alive to witness the Second Coming. Of course, Paul died before this momentous event and the doubts about the Second Coming only worsened. It became an urgent task to rectify this theological cataclysm. In his *Death and Eternal Life*, John Hick describes the atmosphere: "As time went on without the *parousia* (Second Coming) occurring, and as more and more believers 'fell asleep,' the sense of living in the last hours of a dying Age gradually faded and the church had to adjust itself to the prospect of an indefinitely long future in this world."[6] Part of this "adjustment" was to interpret the Second Coming less literally. Since Christ had insisted that the time was at hand, yet nothing seemed to change, people began to think this revolution might be invisible and already present in the here and now. The metaphorical take on the

Second Coming made more sense than a physical transfiguration of the world. Taking a more Platonic spin on things, some early Christians, who called themselves Gnostics, nearly swung Christianity in an entirely different direction. Had they succeeded an entirely different history of the Western world would have followed.

## *The Gnostics*

The Gnostic idea of the soul utilized a Platonic understanding of man's duality. By no means though was Gnosticism merely a 'Platonic Christianity.' Gnosticism drew from Zoroastrian traditions, mystery cults, and Greek philosophy. Only recently, with the discovery of a buried cache of Gnostic writings in Egypt, have we begun to understand the details of these teachings.

Though it had a relatively short history, flourishing between 100-350 C.E., the effects of Gnosticism should not be minimized. Many of the early Church fathers defined the orthodox faith against Gnosticism. The irony about defining oneself against another is that elements of the 'other' always tend to suffuse one's identity. Like the elegant dialectic of Hegel, a thesis generally gives rise to its opposite—its antithesis. Thereafter the two merge to form a synthesis. Gnosticism has remained the unseen shadow of Christianity for fifteen hundred years trailing behind—and within—the Church's official canon.

Gnosticism thrived on creativity in Christian thought. We have lived with a 'strict' Christianity for so long that it is difficult to imagine it as a liberal, creative tradition. The Gnostics fostered individual insight. In fact, one didn't show her true spiritual connection with God until she revealed some new understanding or teaching.

Along with this creativity came the difficulties of keeping any central tenets. A variety of factions and traditions quickly emerged like sprouts in fertile soil. Orthodoxy, in attempting to sustain a faith system, rightfully combated this liberalizing influence.

In one sense, Gnostics were more 'spiritual,' that is, always seeking, and attempting to connect with, the Godhead. This created something of a Gnostic elitism. As in all human endeavors, some will stand out in skill or talent while others will congeal into the common horde. Orthodox Christianity, by creating a faith system, enabled all and sundry to achieve the highest goal—the promise of Heaven and presence with Christ. Living a set of explicit rules and believing an 'accepted' faith—which came to be formulized in the official creeds of the Church—conferred everyone an equal share in Christ's promise.

Gnosticism, as a whole, set itself up as an exclusive tradition. Its teachings and way of life implied an extraordinary commitment of physical and mental energy. One had to be sophisticated enough to understand its various doctrines and mentally disciplined enough to explore them.

The extreme divergence between the Gnostics and the orthodoxy posed a real threat to early Christianity. Barely surviving under the persecution of its challengers—mainly Romans—the Christians now faced a threat from within, the threat of doctrinal splintering. Today, the world is witness to hundreds of 'brands' of Christianity, each with its fine distinctions in practice and doctrine. In the early days of its persecution, such splintering would have spelled a quick end to the faith.

What is Gnosticism? The name itself relays its means and message: *gnosis* means knowledge. Like Plato, who thought the unexamined life not worth living, the Gnostics felt the purpose of life could be found in knowledge—in their traditions, secret knowledge. In her excellent survey, *The Gnostic Gospels*, Elaine Pagels describes the essence of this message: "…to know oneself, at the deepest level, is simultaneously to know God; this is the secret of *gnosis*."[7] In the *Book of Thomas the Contender*, one of our recently unearthed Gnostic gospels, the ancient author states the case well: "For he who has not known himself has known nothing, but he who has known himself has at the same time already achieved knowledge about the depth of the all."[8] Knowledge, not faith—experience, not hearsay—forged the core of Gnosticism and set it against the traditions of orthodoxy.

The Gnostics pursued the esoteric path in Christianity. They believed there were, as yet, secrets to be uncovered in the religion. Rumors of 'secret teachings' of Christ, the disciples, and even Paul quickly gained currency. The strange nature of Christ's Resurrection, the many parables he taught, and the overall mystique of his character suggested much more than the simple-minded faith that the traditional Church espoused. But don't be fooled into thinking this another heresy—Gnostic Christianity had a solid basis in Scripture.

Christ first propagated a distinction in his public teachings and his private, secret teachings. In the *Gospel of Mark*, Jesus purportedly says:

> ...to you has been given the secret of the kingdom of God, but for those outside, everything comes in parables; in order that 'they may indeed look, but not perceive, and may indeed listen, but not understand; so that they may not turn and be forgiven.'

Moderns, well-versed in analogy and metaphor (at least some of us), understand how parables work. To an ancient people, though, who had little education and thought in terms of the concrete, such parables needed careful explanation to unlock their true meaning. Christ would traditionally relate a parable and then teach its meaning, or save these teachings for later discussion with his disciples alone. Like speaking in code, the message expressed in parables needed a careful decipherment to be understood and appreciated. To outsiders—Romans and traditional Jews—the teachings would seem harmless babble about farming, fishing and such, but to the insiders was disclosed a revolution in thought.

The Gnostics believed that Christ had taught many arcane and difficult truths to the hidden community of the Church and to those he thought capable of understanding. These often eccentric doctrines served as the basis for the many Gnostic writings that blossomed during this period.

Among the most interesting of the Gnostic texts, the *Gospel of Thomas* begins with this tantalizing challenge: "These are the secret sayings which the living Jesus spoke and which Didymos Judas Thomas wrote down. And he said, 'Whoever finds the interpretation of these sayings will not experience death.'"[9] The discovery of secrets seems the aim of many Gnostic writings. This tradition had a thorough basis in the orthodox Church Scripture as well.

The *Book of Revelation*, an 'official' book of the New Testament, stands out as the best example of the esoteric tradition retained by the orthodoxy. It is, at once, a text in the apocalyptic tradition—

always popular in times of trouble (and all times are times of trouble)—and a secret message to its author's Christian compatriots. This book, laden with metaphors and bizarre imagery, has been rich fodder for every Christian with a bent for mysteries and has destroyed whole cities of paranoid minds. Originally sent out to the early Christian communities, the book utilized its lurid language because of official persecution. As tradition would have it, the book was written by a prisoner of the Romans, John, banished to the tiny island of Patmos in the Aegean. The Empire had exiled John to this island because they knew he would have no audience and could do no harm. John taught in a way that aroused the suspicion of the Romans. He was probably clever enough to avoid outright sedition, which would mean death, but suggestive enough that the Romans felt banishment necessary. To get a potentially treasonous letter out to the churches, he had to clothe his meaning in extremely obscure language. What all his symbolism conveyed to these churches, we cannot fully unravel. Like an encrypted message whose code has been lost, Christians have come to decode this text in manifold ways through the centuries. Each generation gives it a try, finds a meaning, and passes it on to the next. The *Book of Revelation* is the original crossword puzzle of the Bible, except we don't know what the words mean.

Paul, too, partook in secret teachings and mysteries. In some of his letters, he refers to the special knowledge given by God to the Christian Church. In the same way that Christ created an 'in-group' which shared his saving teachings and an 'out-group' destined for damnation, so Paul consolidates esoteric knowledge against the ignorance outside the Church. In the *First Letter to the Corinthians*, Paul writes:

> ...we speak of God's wisdom, secret and hidden, which God decreed before the ages and for our glory. None of the rulers of this age understood this; for if they had, they would not have crucified the Lord of glory. But, as it is written: 'What no eye has seen, nor ear heard, nor the human heart conceived, what God has prepared for those who love him' –these things God has revealed to us through the Spirit...

The teaching of special wisdom characterizes all religions. If there were no distinction between those in a religious group and those outside of it, we would all be of one faith.

The more dangerous tendency in early Christianity came through divisions within the body of the Church itself. Some, the Gnostics thought, were ready for the secret, and by implication, higher wisdom. The Gnostic *Gospel of Philip* suggests that there are different teachings for different levels. In a highly allegorical passage, the writer states:

> There are many animals in the world which are in human form. When he identifies them, to the swine he will throw acorns, to the cattle he will throw barley and chaff and grass, to the dogs he will throw bones. To the slaves he will give only the elementary lessons, to the children he will give the complete instruction.[10]

Unfortunately, even this most dangerous doctrine found its parallel in Paul's letters. In his *Letter to the Hebrews*, Paul makes a distinction between simple and advanced doctrine likening it to "milk" and "solid food":

> ...we have much to say that is hard to explain, since you have become dull in understanding. For though by this time you ought to be teachers, you need someone to teach you again the basic elements of the oracles of God. You need milk, not solid food; for everyone who lives on milk, being still an infant, is unskilled in the word of righteousness. But solid food is for the mature, for those whose faculties have been trained by practice to distinguish good from evil.

Gnostics followed these tendencies claiming secret teaching, hidden traditions, and saving knowledge to be the real treasure of Christianity. Their prolific writings created many complicated doctrines. Despite all this, a few major themes run throughout the many schools and writings of Gnosticism.

The Gnostics greatly amplified the Christian tradition of bodily distrust. The soul became all-important and the body an impoverished housing. In the *Gospel of Thomas*, Jesus expresses an ironic sentiment about the body: "...If the flesh came into being because of the spirit, it is a wonder. But if spirit came into being because of the body, it is a wonder of wonders. Indeed, I am amazed at how this great wealth has made its home in this poverty."[11] Like so many of us today who remain befuddled when told that the three pound mass of jelly between one's ears is the source of one's thoughts, neither could the Christ of Thomas believe such a thing. Surely, the nobility of reason and the innate spirituality of people could not reside, in any substantial way, in the contemptible body with all of its stinks, farts, and spit. The *Gospel of Philip* expresses a similar disfavor: "No one will hide a large valuable object in something large, but many a time one has tossed countless thousands into a thing worth a penny. Compare the soul. It is a precious thing and it came to be in a contemptible body."[12] The parallel between this Gnostic understanding of the body and the Orphic-Platonic one appears too remarkable to have occurred independently. In fact, Gnosticism, with its liberal and intellectual tradition, likely absorbed elements from the rich mythologies and teachings present in the Mediterranean at the time. Among these, Platonism and Orphism remained a powerful force during the early Christian centuries. Gnosticism took the core idea of bodily distrust and fashioned it after its own unique style, motifs abundant.

The *Corpus Hermeticum* makes the body the vehicle through which demonic forces tarnish the human spirit:

> Those who are enlightened in their spiritual part by a ray from the divine light—and they are but few—from these the demons desist. ...all the others are driven and carried along in their souls and their bodies by the demons, loving and cherishing their works. ...All this terrestrial rule the demons exercise through the organs of our bodies...[13]

As creatures of the Earth we must, like other creatures, physically ingest life to feed our own. This sad notion of life feeding on life, the tragic game which nature plays with all her creatures, implicates humans. Our refined sensitivities against destruction cry out against the fertilizer that makes the crops grow. The dead feed the living. *Soylent Green*, that campy sci-fi movie of the sixties in which people live on the reduced sludge of the recently deceased, is a poetic truth. Something of an 'existential embarrassment' occurs when recognizing, high though we feel, that our life depends on the same basic processes as all primitive life. We eat, we excrete, we get fat, and we find our consummate pleasure in the bliss of reproducing—doing the duty that our genes demand of us. Often thought a purely mod-

ern insight—limited to the works of Jean-Paul Sartre, Tennessee
Williams, and the like—we find this same existential embarrassment
in *The Book of Thomas the Contender*:

> …these visible bodies survive by devouring creatures similar to
> them with the result that the bodies change. Now that which
> changes will decay and perish, and has no hope of life from then
> on, since that body is bestial. So just as the body of the beast per-
> ishes, so also will these formations perish. Do they not derive from
> intercourse like that of the beasts? If it, (the body) too derives from
> intercourse, how will it beget anything different from beasts? So,
> therefore, you are babes until you become perfect.[14]

For Gnostics, the body and soul exist in a strictly dualistic fashion. War between them occurs for the fate of the soul and cosmos.
While traditional Christianity had made this an unhappy enough
philosophy, Gnostic Christianity built its entire world-myth around
it. Not only was the Earth an obstacle in the pursuit of heaven, it was
not even created by the God! In fact, God's enemies, the demigods
called the Archons, created the universe as a means to entrap our
souls and prevent us from reuniting with the God who made us!
This fantastic myth makes of human life a hideous bondage.
Everything we've come to think holy—birth, marriage, food, reproduction—the very things that orthodox Christianity hallow as sacraments are, in fact, links in the chain by which the Archons bound our
souls to this wicked world, away from our true Creator. We are cast-
aways and prisoners on this planet. The Gnostics among us yearn
for another world and another life.

The Gnostics fashioned complex cosmologies. The God whom
Jesus represents, the truly good God, exists far away from this world.
He is alien to the Earth and to the known universe. The gods who rule
this plane, like the Old Testament Yahweh, are wicked offspring of the
alien God who, like Pontius Pilate, seems to have washed his hands
clean of all this dirty business. Hans Jonas, in his classic text, *The
Gnostic Religion*, describes the alien God:

> The Gnostic God is not merely extra-mundane and supra-mun-
> dane, but in his ultimate meaning contra-mundane. The sublime
> unity of cosmos and God is broken up, the two are torn apart, and
> a gulf never completely to be closed again is opened: God and
> world, God and nature, spirit and nature, become divorced, alien

to each other, even contraries. But if these two are alien to each other, then also man and world are alien to each other...[15]

The suspicious dualism that early Christianity developed transformed itself into a dark abyss. The body isn't merely a shoddy vehicle for the soul, it is the means by which the soul forgets its true nature and its true God. In his attempt to outwit the Archons, Jesus Christ, an agent of the alien God, appeared in fleshly form to teach mankind its secret history and the techniques to escape this evil world. The salvation Jesus taught begins with *gnosis*, knowledge of one's true nature, an apprehension of the battling we feel against the world, and secret methods to escape the physical world upon death. The nature of dualism implies one's true sentiment—the agony of physical existence, the ever-present longing for release from it, and a return of one's inner spirit to the divine world of love and light. This cosmic dualism, which enters us in the form of substance dualism, pits the truly spiritual against the physical in a frightening way.

In light of these teachings, some of the more enigmatic passages from the *Gospel of John* begin to take on a new character. The fourth gospel was deeply influenced by Gnostic ideas. In one section Jesus explains why the world "hates" him: "The world cannot hate you, but it hates me because I testify against it that its works are evil." He goes on to describe the heavy burden the Christian takes on and why it occurs: "If the world hates you, be aware that it hated me before it hated you. If you belonged to the world, it would love you as its own. Because you do not belong to the world, but I have chosen you out of the world—therefore the world hates you." In a striking passage, Christ seems to identify his God as someone besides the Lord of the Jews, Yahweh: "Then Jesus cried out as he was teaching in the temple, 'You know me, and you know where I am from. I have not come on my own. But the one who sent me is true, and you do not know him. I know him, because I am from him, and he sent me." And finally, Christ describes his promise of salvation, a promise that encourages hatred of the world: "Those who love their life lose it, and those who hate their life in this world will keep it for eternal life."

Re-reading official Scripture in light of Gnostic writings sounds a certain resonance. Gnosticism didn't threaten to overturn Christianity because it was foreign but because it was a different reflection of the same.

The strangeness of man's fall, his exile from the garden on the basis of gaining the *knowledge* of good and evil, finds its answer not in the sacrifice of Christ's body on the cross but only through the secret knowledge that he taught to a chosen few—*gnosis*. Now the "lamps in the darkness" take on a new meaning. This knowledge, coming through divine revelation, begins with the feeling of difference, the true awareness of exile. Gaining this knowledge, man cannot easily be returned to his chains. Having come to the realization, the Gnostic cannot 'unlearn' the revealed truth of her situation. The conventions of the world, all the careful rituals that the Jews followed with such fastidiousness, including the countless injunctions of *Leviticus*, were useful precepts to keep the life of the physical person in order but were also designed to keep him deaf to his higher calling. Like the dutiful husband who, burdened with countless responsibilities, forgets what freedom and happiness are and thus creates a family devoid of love, the dutiful Jew of Christ's time—the judicial Pharisees—trudged through the legalistic swamp of Old Testament teachings and forgot their own divinity. Not from sinister intentions did they fall. By their own righteousness these old model Jews forgot their divinity. Perhaps this notion is best expressed in a light passage from the *Gospel of Thomas*: "Jesus said, 'Do not be concerned from morning until evening and from evening until morning about what you will wear.'"[16] Through forgetfulness and getting caught up in the business of daily life, the spirit forgets its true identity. Even then, though, the knowledge whispers—behind and below—encouraging one to fight the gods of the world and seek the alien God.

Another common feature of Gnosticism, it emphasized individual growth. Though the Gnostics possessed community and even looked to the advanced among them as leaders, the Gnostic path ultimately lay between the person and his God. No one could die for another, no one be another's revelation. This tendency, of course, is the most threatening revolt against a shared religion. The Church does not want the individual to be her own priest. The *Gospel of Thomas* reveals the special calling of the solitary seeker: "Jesus said, 'Blessed are the solitary and elect, for you will find the kingdom. For you are from it, and to it you will return.'"[17]

Divorcing God from the world, the individual from the community, and the individual's soul from his body, Gnosticism pursued an increasingly dangerous and anti-religious aim. Jonas summarizes the unique message of Gnosticism: "Never before or after had such a gulf opened between man and the world, between life and its begetter, and such a feeling of cosmic solitude, abandonment, and transcendental superiority of self taken hold of man's consciousness."[18]

## *Later Christianity*

The Gnostic heresy gave the early Church leaders a real war to fight. The often brilliant Gnostics managed to formulate systematic theologies more appealing to the thinkers of the early Christian communities. Orthodox Christianity felt threatened by these Gnostics' arguments and learned authority. In their letters to each other and the churches, the patriarchs of the orthodoxy spent much time arguing against the Gnostics. Not only did their appeal seem a threat to the 'true faith,' but their criticisms of the world in general appeared the height of blasphemy. In *Genesis*, after God had created man and given him dominion over the Earth, He: "...saw everything that he had made, and indeed, it was very good." Of course, the Gnostics thought the god of *Genesis* an evil one, not the true God. The orthodox Christians raged against such complex nonsense. They often overlooked the fact that all this heresy found its basis in Scripture.

In response to the Gnostics, patriarchs such as Irenaeus, Tertullian, and Augustine (the most influential of early Christian theologians) formed very physical interpretations of the Resurrection. Augustine, once a Gnostic in the highly dualistic tradition of Manichaeism, eventually converted to Christianity proper and opposed the Gnostic tendencies that had tempted him as a young man.

Other important theologians, like Origen and Clement, were less sure about the arguments. While opposing Gnostic interpretations, the inherent appeal of Platonic thought could not be left behind. Origen often went back and forth in his theology about the soul and the Resurrection. Again, ambiguity endured in the Christian teachings.

Over time, Catholics (as the orthodox came to be called) began to rely on the importance of saints in their faith. Saintly intercession, the practice of praying to a saint for help in various affairs (St. Christopher for traveling, etc.), depended heavily on the immaterial basis of the soul. If the saints were asleep in their graves, silently awaiting the Second Coming and the Resurrection, then what good were the prayers of the living to them?

Theological issues and folk traditions never held a true consistency. Around 1300 C.E., the debate came to a head: theologians arrived at the idea that upon death the soul met with its particular judgment—heaven, hell, or purgatory (a place for the cleansing of sins). After this particular judgment the soul departed to its assigned destination. Later, at the final judgment, the souls in hell would stay in hell, the ones in purgatory get 'bumped up' to heaven, and, at the same time, all those in heaven come back to Earth for re-embodiment and deployment to the New Jerusalem of the *Book of Revelation*. The final judgment seemed less the epiphany it promised to be since the souls really faced judgement upon death. In this theology, the final judgment would only apply to those living on Earth at the time. John Hick describes the doctrine's sobering influence:

> In this conflation of the individual judgment at death with the universal judgment at the end of the world faith was following (perhaps unconsciously) not only the logic of the imagination but also the logic of the intellect; for once the individual's eternal fate has been settled, and he has begun to enjoy or endure his appropriate destiny, the second judgment becomes an anti-climax, if not an empty form.[19]

In 1336, Pope Benedict XII sanctified the outlines of this theology in his *Benedictus Deus*. In the pronouncement, the notion of the immaterial soul became Catholic dogma. To settle on this dogma, Benedict XII had to overlook a load of Scriptural evidence to the contrary; he needed to overturn the thoughts of such brilliant Church fathers as Irenaeus, Tertullian, and Augustine. Finally, Benedict had to avoid many logical difficulties. For instance, hell—that place of endless burning and physical torture—could no longer make sense: people had no bodies! Incapable of corporal punishments, the immaterial soul demonstrated a marked deficiency. Even such conventions of heaven and hell as real 'places' no longer sufficed. Defining the soul as a 'spook' would necessarily entail one's eternal residence in an immaterial place. In short, the *Benedictus Deus* overturned all of the root Jewish conceptions of the Resurrection and much of the New Testament Scriptures. This statement transformed Christianity into a wholly spiritual, non-physical religion. The invisible now reigned supreme over the visible. Plato had won. A mere three centuries later, Descartes formulized his philosophy of mind/body dualism.

*Chapter 9*

# RECAPITULATION OF THE SOUL

The soul—the conception of it that we hold as that immaterial, immortal part of us that endures after death—has accompanied mankind since our very beginnings. Through a long process of diffusion and occasional cross-fertilization between cultures, the soul fulfilled an adaptive role in the philosophy of the human condition.

In animism, the first spiritual tendencies of man shone forth in the idea that all things were 'ensouled.' Projecting his subjectivity outwards, everything, like man, possessed some form of consciousness. Religious practices sought harmony with these entities.

As shamanism developed and extended across the great landmasses, the notion of man's soul became increasingly complex and refined. Through their practices of ecstasy, the shamans found that the soul could be separated from the body and travel to various planes of existence. A geography and characterization of the afterlife began. The authority and influence of shamans lasted for millennia and influenced every notion of spirituality.

In ancient Egyptian religion we see the importance of the immaterial soul in the massive construction of pyramids and temples. To the Egyptians, the soul, though it retained a material connection with the world (thus the importance of mummification), crossed the threshold from life into the great realm of the afterlife. In the *Egyptian Book of the Dead* (a.k.a. *Book of Going Forth by Day*) incantations are taught which ensure success in the afterlife. Perhaps originally from shamanism, this same doctrine appears in *The Tibetan Book of the Dead*, in secret teachings of the Gnostics, and in various mystery religions (esp. The Eleusinian Mysteries).

The Zoroastrian tradition began to definitively 'split' the world.

Now a radical division existed between good and evil; these were the activities of two warring gods who sought fresh conscripts from each generation. Naturally, this split came into the very essence of the human being; the body and the soul became polarized. One served the good Lord while the other reflected the Evil One.

The ancient Jews avoided incorporeal conceptions of the soul altogether. A culture with firm roots in the world, the Jews hadn't felt the need for a soul until they were enslaved by the Babylonians in the sixth century B.C.E. During the Babylonian Exile, the Jews had access to the rich Zoroastrian traditions popular in that region. Suddenly, we see in Judaism a proliferation of end-time prophecies remarkably similar to the Zoroastrian ones. A logical solution to the persecution of the righteous presents itself in the promise of an afterlife. The Zoroastrian Saoshyant, the representative of the good powers and the deliverer of the great transfiguration of the world, intrigues the Jews. The hope of a Messiah emerges in Judaism. During the apocalyptic era of the Hasmoneans a renaissance of these themes occur. The end of the world is at hand. When shall the Messiah come to deliver his chosen?

Meanwhile, hundreds of miles away, the scurrying influences of Northern tribes along the edges of Greece imports shamanic trends into Greek mystery religions. Though small, these religions promise something new and different. Eventually, through the creativity and genius of Plato, the soul becomes a popular idea. With the Platonic soul comes a new understanding of life, the individual, and morality. The Greek model of life, once based in the pride and vigor of life in this world, is turned upside down—the deep distrust of all things material supplants the older, humanistic model.

In Nazareth—as the Gospel of John notes: "Nazareth! Can anything good come from there?,"—the Messiah begins to preach. In an apocalyptic age, a new rabbi full of revolutionary ideas sways a small group to follow Him unto death. Speaking of "light" and "darkness" like an Essene or Zoroastrian, the Christ teaches a bipolar doctrine between physical resurrection and spiritual life. No small symbol, the arrival of the Magi (from whom we derive the word 'magic')—traditional priests of the Zoroastrians—at the birth of Jesus means a transfiguration of the world, the presence of the Saoshyant, and the triumph of good over evil.

The soul, the discovery of the shamans, fulfills a critical role in the intense dualism of Zoroastrianism. A splitting of the world down the middle occurs—the good soul and the corrupt, evil body. This play of opposites rests at the core of Western mentality.

# PART II

# THE SOUL MATTER

Men ought to know that from the brain, and from the brain only, arise our pleasures, joys, laughter and jests, as well as our sorrows, pains, griefs and tears. Through it, in particular, we think, see, hear, and distinguish the ugly from the beautiful, the bad from the good, the pleasant from the unpleasant... It is the same thing which makes us mad or delirious, inspires us with dread and fear, whether by night or by day, brings sleeplessness, inopportune mistakes, aimless anxieties, absent-mindedness, and acts that are contrary to habit. These things that we suffer all come from the brain, when it is not healthy...
—Hippocrates, c. 400 B.C.E.

# A Conflict of Soul

Hippocrates's statement reveals that people have been correctly identifying the brain as the source of human consciousness for many thousands of years. Besides Hippocrates, those who have opposed the concept of spirit and endowed the brain with the prominence it deserves includes luminaries of many times and places. Despite these thinkers, it has only been recently, in the last 150 years, that people have begun to seriously attribute mental abilities to the brain. By and far, most people have always considered such abilities to issue from the immaterial soul. People thought of themselves as ghosts moving around bodies—almost like a state of possession.

In his detailed history, *The Origins of Neuroscience*, Stanley Finger proposes that prehistoric man performed basic head surgery. Called trephination, skulls from all over the world—many quite ancient— show evidence of having been intentionally bored into and subsequently healed over prior to death. The exact meaning behind such operations remains unclear. Some suggest that such holes provided the exit point for evil spirits. Others think the breached skulls were the best means of releasing the pressure of excess fluid caused by a blow to the head—to treat concussions, that is. Either way, one must infer ancient man's identification of the head as the location of mental attributes. The convergence of the major organs of perception— the eyes, the ears, the nose, and the mouth—in the head also led to the conclusion that this area had more to do with one's mental life than other zones of the body. And if the head was the central point of all these senses, then the brain must have something to do with them.

If one assigns consciousness to the brain, one is a materialist. However, our look at shamanism, the evidence of dreams, and early philosophy also attests to humanity's notion of the world as an essentially spiritual place. The body belonged to one level of reality, the mind to another one. The coexistence of materialist theories and dualist theories, since the beginning, suggests a muddled approach towards the brain and consciousness. This same confusion remains commonplace since, as a culture, we've never fully resolved these issues. The staggering amount of denial involved in holding both the materialist and dualist theories suggests a deep-seated inability to accept materialism outright. From one line of evidence, we conclude that man has always known the mind's material basis. The other line of thought proves that humanity has always been unable to accept this knowledge. Why have we never found peace with this issue?

A peculiar thing occurs when one learns that the brain is the source of all mental activity. A fundamental revulsion issues from this recognition. Why? The dread rises up as a sickening, gut-wrenching fear that everything we cherish can be reduced to the chemical and electrical pulses racing through three pounds of flesh. This vulnerability seems far more hostile than our arch-enemy—death itself—because it threatens the very essence of the person, the sacred center of the self.

What is a person? Is it the miracle of life and the creation of the world; the experience, on the personal level, of the powers and forces of eternal nature and the genius of individuality? Is it the ability to feel deeply and to see far, to ponder the nature of the universe and to be moved by the living words of dead poets? Mustn't this beautiful, unique existence be eternal? If the self can be distilled down into three pounds of gelatinous meat housed in a thin, bony shell then the self can die. Worse yet, the self can whither away, piece by piece, resection by resection, until one meekly asks the question, "What am I?"

An especially disturbing description in Thomas Harris's *Hannibal* features just such an example. Harris's arch-villain, Hannibal Lecter, does the unthinkable to a backbiting FBI agent by the name of Paul Krendler. Lecter binds and drugs Krendler before violating his mind. As Lecter shaves off one slice after another from the frontal cortex of Krendler, the fellow loses more and more of his human attributes then becomes a babbling infant.

The gruesomeness of Harris's example is not far from the truth for we are filled with sheer dread whenever we contemplate the nature of physical decay at work within our brains. To consider the material basis of our minds and to understand that a stroke can zap away our ability to speak or to understand speech, to recognize that a motorcycle accident can erase one's childhood memories, for instance, or sense of morality is, in a word, gruesome. That this recognition occurs somewhere inside of us is witnessed by the difficulty of accepting the brain as the sole source of consciousness. These are fearful things. The most threatening challenges are those whose existence we deny most—the truths of life, death, and contingency—the truths that Alzheimer's and drug addiction whisper into our ringing ears.

The collision of our cherished belief in an imperturbable sense of self with the harsh reality of materialism needs no Descartes or similarly gifted discoverer. Any individual who can interpret his experience with faultless honesty will quickly recognize humanity's essence in the brain. Each time we hear of an old person who slowly loses himself along with his memory, each time we note a friend's mood disorder improve after taking psychotropic medication, and after each acknowledgment of changes in an acquaintance who has suffered some head trauma, we understand the difficult truth that our deep selves are not permanent things which find their final repose in some transcendent heaven or hell but are as delicate as a spider's web. Call them selves or personality traits, these subtle properties originate in the structure and chemistry of our brains; change that structure or chemistry and the properties change, *we change*. This remarkably simple observation remains elusive since we will go to almost any length to avoid or deny it. While dramatic events— Alzheimer's, drug therapy, and head trauma—stun us with their teachings, it's easy to find more common analogues in our day-to-day reality. Most of us know the charm of coffee, the intoxication of alcohol, and the pang of drowsiness. All these things express a material basis and daily remind us that the properties of mind are results of body. It is part of our animal heritage to avoid this realization and part of our human destiny to make a conscious peace with it. The solution to this tangle is the solution to so many of life's difficulties—a hearty acceptance of the values we talk about but do not practice, the exercise of honesty, integrity, and courage.

What lesson do we learn from all this? What do we think about life when we accept that our very essence is a three pound jumble of protein, water, and fat housed between our ears? Should we conclude, as many do, that life is meaningless and fleeting? That short of a spiritual existence which pierces the veil of mortality and extends limitlessly into the future, we have no real meaning or purpose? Shall we agree with the Greek poet Pindar, who two-thousand years ago wrote a bitter victory ode to a haughty Olympic athlete, "...brief is the season of man's delight. Soon it falls to the ground... Thing of a day! Such is man; a shadow in a dream."[1]

The fact of our mortality, of our delicate equilibrium within the web of body and environment, does not necessitate a bleak despair. All things, in a cosmological understanding of time, pass away. Whether a mind is constructed from water-engorged flesh or silicon and steel, its elements will always find their final destination, as they found their origination, in the fusion reactions of stars. So even if our structure was built on a more rugged frame, we'd still die eventually. While we can imagine a vast stretch of time and space through our fabulous mathematics and our limitless creative capacities, the cosmological scale should not take away from our daily experience within the closer neighborhood of history and place. Our seventy or so years still seem a healthy chunk of existence when experienced through the senses and mentality so carefully adapted to the world in which we live.

The appreciation of our mortality leads just as easily to a philosophy of fulfillment and appreciation as to one of despair and delusion. With it comes the choice the living must never postpone: will I live poorly or well? And while lives two thousand or ten thousand years past seem a curious thing to consider; archaic in their languages and behaviors, and somehow beaten—because dead—they existed, as fully human and alive as we, caught up in the gossip and intrigue of friends and neighbors, critical of politicians, and occasionally musing on the significance of things. Life, always and everywhere, commands us to give it its full due, to be caught up in the seeming trivialities, to be absorbed in our talents and others', and captivated by a sense of wonder when reflecting on it all. Any philosophy that decries this, or persuades us to mock it, is a philosophy for another world. The higher road intersects our lives with humane values and religiously binds us to the living, the dead, and the yet-to-come. It inspires a more respectful attitude towards every natural thing that supports and affects our mental lives. We come to realize the importance of nutrition and sleep, the necessity of social relationships, and of love.

To know oneself fully, accounting all limitations, effects an attitude of sanctity and grace, an attitude that repudiates despair. Despair results from a frightening half-formed thought; something that's been partially-digested and spit out, left to infect the world. We despair not from seeing something terrible but from not looking at it directly. It is the sideways glance, the eyes peeking between the fingers of a hand, that leads to fear and hopelessness. Fear without response creates despair. The human spirit possesses something akin to a liver—for even the most toxic of thoughts swallowed down whole can be filtered and transformed into nutrient. The conscious understanding and acceptance of a fearful consequence, while it may naturally generate sadness and grief, does not create the cancer of despair. When all things are reckoned there will be tragedy and comedy, epic and fable, never some wholesale judgment of good or bad. Death, like the frame of a picture, though important, remains merely a frame while art lies always at the center of things.

Our ancient defenses, to defeat death and vulnerability by a combination of delusion, ignorance, and faith continues to influence our world-view in fundamental ways. This is an unfortunate and vestigial series of conceptions since contemporary insights deliver us an innovative understanding of self and world. The new philosophy does not disintegrate our traditional time-honored values, washing all into a sea of nihilism, but underscores the importance of human values.

Some fear that with the rejection of traditional religion comes a rejection of values. Such fear is groundless; values have never found their sources in the injunctions of gods and prophets, gods and prophets always found their beginnings in values. Is Christ worshiped because he claimed to be the son of God or because he taught and lived the ideal of love? Which is a truly believable notion anyway? Shall we believe that the creator of the entire cosmos had a brief, and single, union with an ancient Israeli who spawned His 'only begotten son,' or that a brilliant man developed a philosophy of love and forgiveness? In every generation lunatics have claimed to be the son of God but are quickly forgotten because their actions are needy, not generous. The medium is not the message.

While religion portrays values as the ornaments of faith—the shimmering stained-glass windows seen from within—in reality, values are the bulky flying buttresses which, outside, secretly hold everything together. Morality circumscribes divine actions as much as mortal ones. Consider the great gods of Greece who, despite their powers, still had their foibles and suffered the social consequences of them. Zeus, the prototype of all executive philanderers, got into more than a little trouble in his day. He met the stern gaze of an upset wife and felt the judgment of his peers. When we excuse the immorality of a god we accept evil into our midst. If we declare all actions of a god as correct then we confirm the ancient fallacy of identifying 'might with right.' If we blindly accept evil in the world as just part of a 'divine plan' and somehow learn to ignore the suffering all around us, we murder the very best parts of ourselves and dirty our most sacred conceptions. So long as there is great suffering we should experience some distress. Such pain proves that we would have it otherwise, that we would prefer a world free of malicious suffering and senseless destruction. Such unease is the whisper of our finest feelings.

Values serve structure and growth and oppose the destructive characteristic of reality. In the human sphere, values create the framework from which institutions are built. Organization is the key that opens the door to human intelligence and social sophistication alike. Just as our personalities represent a miraculous apex of organizing principles in evolution, so the discovery and utilization of genuine human values illustrate that man has the ability to overcome and surpass the parts of his nature that would break organization apart. This insight should align us in battle against those parts of nature which have always threatened to blindly destroy both the common and precious alike. The doctor declares this oath, the protector takes this stand, and the healthy person always chooses creation and life over destruction and death. Our effort to preserve both our selves and our highest principles is the very culmination of that organizing, intelligent principle; the same which protects complex structures as different as stars and beating hearts against the haphazard destruction of black holes and genocide. While all things pass, it is the human's, and distinctly human burden, to construct, preserve, and remember. Call it soul, call it spirit, it begins with the neuron.

*Chapter 10*

# THE BASICS

The mind is the processes of the brain. The mental world, the interior world of the self, arises from the pieces of the brain at work. Difficult to accept at first, because so much is apparently at stake, we'll come to see that this process of 'emergence' occurs in nearly everything around and within us. The brain, while certainly the most interesting organ, is no different in kind from the other organs of the body. How do the cells of the liver filter and purify the blood so well? How does it transform 'mere chemicals' into the essential 'life-force' of the body? And what about the pancreas, the kidneys, the lungs, or the heart? All these cells, tissues, organs, and systems work together to produce the improbable human creature.

We experience hunger for food as a state of mind; we don't think of it as the motion of our guts or as the messages of our hormones. Nevertheless, when we're told this truth in biology class we don't storm out of the room and ban the teaching of metabolism. When our hearts beat quickly and deliver a load of oxygen to our various organs we experience energy. When told that this energetic feeling could not happen without the heart functioning correctly, we don't marvel over it and debate the point. While we tacitly accept the findings of science about our hearts and stomachs we explode in protest when science outlines similar understandings of the brain and its cellular product—consciousness. Certainly, consciousness must derive from some beauteous and eternal plane far from our ephemeral, accident-prone world. *How could these puny cells create my spirit?* We persist in this vein despite the fact that we know Alzheimer's—that eradicator of human personhood—arises from a diseased brain or that Prozac, by affecting the levels of brain chemicals, can restore the feeling of hope to a person imprisoned by despair. Hope? Despair? How could these spiritual states have anything to do with the levels of particular chemicals in our brains?

## *Emergence*

The most complex phenomena of nature come from the 'emergent properties' of very simple functional units through their interactions and arrangement. From atomic elements to molecules to compounds to people—the way of nature is the construction of the complex, with all its behaviors and properties, from the simple. This remains a staggering proposal because we generally think about the world in a primitive manner. Even if we vault that gaping hole of ignorance called the middle ages and explore the early scientific world-view of the Greek philosophers, we are still only two millennia removed from the archaic mind set of demons and spirits, the world of the shaman. Though modern science can provide an updated, increasingly accurate understanding of nature, it cannot provide a simple one. Science does not write off mysteries to God or prohibit difficult questions. We still prefer the simple, animistic world of spirits and the projection of human motives upon the natural world. Natural processes simply have nothing to do with human psychology and emotions—which are but a few of its infinite creations.

From one small particle to the next we perceive that everything physical results from the emergent properties of elemental particles. In *From Soul to Self*, Crabbe writes:

> Atoms, the chemical building blocks of nature, are ordered into complex biological molecules such as proteins and nucleic acids. As we step up the hierarchy of order, novel properties emerge that were not present at simpler levels of organization. These emergent properties result from interactions between components that make the whole greater than the sum of the parts. Unique properties arise from how parts are arranged and interact, not from supernatural powers.[1]

Water is the preeminent example of emergence. By combining two atoms of hydrogen gas and one of oxygen gas, one receives liquid water—an entirely different 'thing' altogether! The water apparently 'emerged' when these distinct elements bonded. When we describe physical processes in this fashion all goes well enough. Using the same logic on the organ of perception itself, we find there is no reason to think of it as different in kind from any other material structure. When we declare that the brain and the mind can only be described in terms of will or thought we assert the properties of the brain as the sole reality. But these processes result from the underlying structure of the brain. The words used in psychotherapy can be just as useful as the drugs administered in psychiatry, but neither denies the other's reality. We are merely speaking a different language and seeing a different perspective of the same object—the brain. The whole 'experience' of the person, her appearance, her personality, her voice, could not exist without the patterns of molecules that make her up. One can either study her pieces, as a physician must do when treating an illness, for example, or one can love her entire form and essence, overlooking the amalgam of chemicals, as her husband does. In the end, both these 'takes' of the person refer to the same entity.

Acceleration, deceleration, braking, maneuvering—these are all words we use in describing car function. These descriptive properties do not come from, nor belong to, another world—they are the result of the peculiar organization of the engine, the brakes, and the steering system. The car needs an exceedingly precise arrangement of metals, chemicals, and electricity to function in such a way that it can exert these properties. Just as the car's many abilities derive from its physical structure, so our perceptions, judgments, and emotions originate in our physical brains. Were we logically consistent dualists, we would discuss the car in the same dual terms that we use to describe ourselves. We would declare the steering and acceleration properties of the car to be immortal. In some other plane, we would expect our car to continue in existence long after it has crumbled into a heap of rust. When the matter of the car erodes, its spiritual essence will thus be released to rev away perfectly, along a heavenly highway in the sky, forever.

Many car buffs personalize their vehicles and treat them with tender loving care. But none of these people feel 'cheated' or stand in disbelief when they contemplate the sheer materiality of their cars. In contrast, those who really value their cars learn as much as possible about mechanics so they can properly care for their vehicles. At some level the car buff may conceive his vehicle as human-like but on another level he easily accepts the reality of the vehicle and attributes its functioning not to personality but to physics. Anyone who looks into the mechanisms of the automobile accepts science's explanations readily enough and for good reason—science created this device, not religion. No matter how many times you pummel the steering wheel with a clenched fist or pray to the divine Creator, the car will not bend to your desires nor will it suffer the fate of the damned or the destiny of the chosen. Fresh oil and new spark plugs go a lot further in keeping a vehicle going than prayers or wishes. You must bend to the car's necessities and follow its rules if you expect it to work properly. When it comes to our consciousness and its underlying matter, we scarcely know—or care to know—how it all works.

It is a great tragedy that we don't treat our own brains, or our bodies in general, with the same rational approach that we reserve for our cars. We are practically anti-brain when it comes to our physical maintenance: we commonly provide the body with the least expensive, toxin-laden fuel. We rarely rest enough and commonly work ourselves into frenzies of activity and worry. Instead of regular oil changes and tune-ups—frequent vacations and retreats, that is—we run our brains without reprieve until they all but break down or come near to it. Those who treat their automobiles in a similar fashion rapidly destroy their engines. The things that function best, like the human brain, are the same we take for granted most. We generally concern ourselves with proper maintenance only during, or as a result of, a major crisis. Defiance seems to be at work in this relationship: it's as if the individual proclaims, "I am more than this physical condition and I will prove it by abusing my brain as much as possible." Such people, though, learn many terrible truths—the least of which are depression and addiction. Were our brains as poorly engineered as our cars, they would have ceased working long ago from our relentless abuse.

The miracle that is consciousness and selfhood depends on the emergent properties of things like neurons and neurotransmitters. Just as government comes from the total activity of many individuals, computer functions from chips and bits, and speed and maneuvering from gas and oil, so do all things proceed from the combinations of the few and the simple. Many parts of ourselves (subunits and patterns in our brain) will reject this notion because of its consequences. Consequences of this understanding (such as death) fearful though they are, are as natural a part of our shared world as governments, computers, and cars.

## Chapter 11

# OF NEURONS AND NEUROTRANSMITTERS

The human brain, the most complex physical phenomenon ever studied, possesses nearly one hundred billion neurons. These cells are the functional units of the nervous system. The structure and function of these cells determine our mental and behavioral existence. For each neuron there are roughly ten additional cells (called *glia*, Greek for "glue") that insulate the neuron and assist with its cellular needs. Besides these sentry-like cells, the blood vessels of the brain have unique properties that give rise to the 'blood-brain barrier.' Only a very small range of materials in the blood can reach the precious neurons through this barrier. The blood channels of the brain supply the glia with the brain's required nutrients. These cells then shuttle 'brain food' to the neurons. Why does the brain have so many safeguards against toxins from the blood? Neurons do not regenerate with the same ease as most other cells. For a very long time, it was thought that neurons didn't grow back at all. Scientists long considered that people were born with a finite number of neurons and spent their lives shedding these miraculous little cells. Fred Gage and colleagues at The Salk Institute recently overturned this dogma by showing that new neurons can be created and integrated into adult brains.[1] Even so, the lion's share of neural growth occurs during the earliest stages of life. The elaborate protection provided throughout the brain slows the decay of neurons as best as it can, protecting them from the dangers of the environment like a princess guarded in a castle tower.

While there are many types of neurons, most possess the same basic characteristics. They have a spindly architecture with a small number of filaments called axons that lead into the cell body.

Opposite the axon (or axons, depending on the type of neuron), the cell body thins out into a nest of filaments called dendrites. Axons and dendrites connect neurons to each other. They are the 'electrical wires' that allow neurons to construct circuits. The many dendrites provide reception of signals from other neurons while the axon(s) allow the cell body to signal other neurons. The overall look of a neuron, with all these arms branching from its cell body, is akin to a foliage-stripped tree in the winter.

The neuronal axon usually connects neurons in very small reaches of matter. A few specialized neurons possess axons that stretch the whole distance from the spinal column e to the toes. Even in those neurons that possess just one axon, the axon can branch to form hundreds of connections. Axons transmit electrical action potentials while dendrites receive them. Action potentials are the subtle charges of electricity that serve as the nervous system's means of communication. Just like the battery in your car, charged chemicals generate this electricity. In the nervous system, most electricity comes from the interaction of sodium (positively charged), potassium (positively charged), chlorine (negatively charged), and calcium (positively charged).

When the axon is long, as in the case of motor neurons that connect to glands or muscle tissue, myelination of the axon makes electrical conductance much more efficient. Myelination is a process in which pale sheaths of fat coat small, interspersed sections along the axon. With these fatty sheaths, the myelinated axon resembles a thick-linked chain. Without myelination, the long axons of our nervous system would be turtle-like in their ability to relay information. No doubt, animals would be very different creatures (if not dead altogether!) had this ingenious little process never developed. Indeed, some tragic diseases, like multiple sclerosis, result from a loss of myelination and lead to a disruption between mind and muscle.

Most of the neurons in the brain are interneurons. When connecting to each other interneurons often lack myelinated axons; their tight proximity makes the accelerated speed and efficiency of myelination unnecessary. Because of this, a person with a demyelinating disease (like MS), usually has a completely normal mental life. The cell bodies of neurons and the unmyelinated axons of interneurons exhibit a grayish hue. When looking at the surface of the brain these bunches of unmyelinated neurons appear as a great gray mass—hence the name 'gray matter' for these parts of the brain. 'White matter' refers to the tracts of fatty myelinated axons that stretch down the spinal cord or connect distant parts of the brain. One of the more apparent stretches of white matter in the brain is the corpus callosum, a thick band of axons that forms the primary link between the left and right hemispheres of the brain. In a rare type of surgery, called a commissurotomy, doctors purposefully sever the corpus callosum. Without the corpus callosum, the two hemispheres cannot easily communicate. While this produces strange effects in consciousness, it is sometimes necessary in order to prevent the electrical storms of epilepsy from spreading.

The other branches of the neuron, called dendrites, receive the action potentials from neighboring axons and conduct them to the cell body. In contrast to the single axon, a neuron often has a vast number of dendrites capable of thousands of connections. This massive connectivity between the neurons allows a nearly infinite complexity of information exchange; it is to this that the nervous system owes its marvelous function.

In the cell body of the neuron something like a digital choice is made—yes or no/on or off—either propagate the electrical action potential or don't. At any moment, billions of neurons receive electrical stimulation. If these signals were always heeded the brain would seize up with overstimulation: you'd have the incessant urge to jump up, and sit down, run and stop, open your eyes and shut them close. In a healthy, undamaged brain, a single charge from an action potential is unlikely to cause the receiving neuron to relay its own action potential; a great flurry of electrical activity is necessary for this.

So far, the brain sounds little different than a computer: waves of electricity, digital-coding, and transmission/reception. In point of fact, many computer designers have done their best to replicate the findings of neuroscience. In other words, the forerunners in the field have always attempted to make an artificial brain. Where they don't understand how something works, the genius of engineering fills in. While we've made enormous leaps this way, we have a long way to go, both in our understanding of the brain and our understanding of computer modeling, before we create artificial intelligence.

Unlike any computer we've yet crafted, the brain uses an array of chemicals in addition to electricity. The combination of these two agents to create the electro-chemical processes of the nervous system gives far greater complexity to it than any computer. This should be no surprise: after all, we're the ones making the computers!

Wherever an axon of one neuron meets the dendrite of another neuron a gap exists; these are not 'hardwired' circuits, each neuron is always insulated by space. The gap between the axon of one neuron and the dendrite of another neuron is called a synapse. At the end of an axon, the axon terminal holds within it a bunch of chemical bags, or vesicles, like a vine of plump grapes. The action potential sent from the neuron's cell body, like an electrical jolt, cause these vesicles to flee to the end of the axon, fuse to its cell wall, and dump their contents of neurotransmitters (some of the most common are acetylcholine, serotonin, dopamine, epinephrine, and norepinephrine) into the divide between the axon and dendrite (the synaptic cleft). The neurotransmitters then float across this divide and bind to the receptors of the adjacent neuron's membrane. The neurotransmitters find matched receptors on the willowy dendrites of nearby neurons. Both neurotransmitter and receptor are intricately fashioned so that they fit perfectly like a lock and key. Many drugs work because they approximate the shape of neurotransmitters. By imperfectly binding to the dendrite they do not stimulate it in the way that the appropriate neurotransmitter does but they do block that neurotransmitter, preventing it from going about its normal business. It's as if one has gummed up the lock so that the key won't fit and the door won't open. At the receptor site, the bound neurotransmitter excites an electrical charge that, if great enough, will proceed to the neuron's cell body to be 'judged.' If the electrical action potential reaches a threshold level it will cause the cell body to fire its own action potential and repeat the routine; if it doesn't reach this threshold, it will all but end there, making some slight changes in neighboring neurons at most. This relatively simple sequence, performed throughout the nervous system all the time, creates the foundation for our mental and physical life. It seems improbable that this electro-chemical switching creates human personality but we must keep in mind that all the wonders of computers—their ability to calculate taxes, to schedule flights, and to simultaneously conduct and orchestrate thousands of different functions—arise from a bunch of on/off decisions as well. There is nothing more to computation than a binary code, a zero or a one. Most of the emergent properties of intelligence, be they artificial or human, come from the nearly infinite nesting of zeroes and ones interacting with each other in silicon or brain tissue.

The chemical environment around neurons creates subtle changes in their electrical sensitivity. Some synapses, called excitatory, increase their neuron's sensitivity to electrical change. Other synapses, called inhibitory, make their neurons less sensitive to change. Roughly equivalent to moods, our predominant neurochemistry at any moment thoroughly influences how the electrical activity of our brain functions. One has only to remember her last bout with drowsiness to realize how mood affects other brain processes, like thinking. Or recall the last time a dark cup of coffee was enjoyed and how quickly it changed one's mental activity/reactivity. Such examples are the large-scale experiences of what occurs throughout the brain at any moment.

Medications also reveal how changes in chemistry affect changes in mental functioning. Medications can lead to particular brain area of a. One medication may create a change in one brain area while a hormone, or another medication, will affect another area entirely. Suddenly, the well-coordinated workings of the brain are out of balance. The difficulties and dangers of medication interactions reveal the delicate equilibrium of our chemical brains on a large scale.

## *Neurotransmitters*

Neurotransmission, the process of using chemical neurotransmitters to convey a 'message,' involves four basic steps: (1) the synthesis of the neurotransmitter; (2) the storage of the chemical and the release from those storage sites; (3) the neurotransmitter's interaction with receptors across the synaptic cleft; and (4) the removal of the chemical from the synaptic cleft.[2] The chemical aspect of the nervous system lies in these basic processes and psychoactive drugs work by influencing them.

## Serotonin

Serotonin is a critical neurotransmitter involved in the regulation of emotions. Serotonin comes primarily from a cluster of cells in the base of the brain called the raphe nuclei. From these production sites, serotonin pathways project downward into the spinal cord and upward into various brain regions, especially the limbic system, an important region for emotion. Serotonin levels affect appetite, body temperature, levels of aggression, and mood. Low levels of serotonin are almost always associated with the state of mind we call depression. Violent suicides, the epitome of both depression and impulsive aggression, tend to be performed by people with abnormally low levels of serotonin, at least as measured by the products of serotonin breakdown.[3] Most of the hallucinogenic drugs, with their mind-altering affects on perception and thought, resemble the serotonin molecule and are thought to work by stimulating serotonin receptor sites.

## Norepinephrine (a.k.a. Noradrenaline)

Norepinephrine comes from an area in the base of the brain called the locus ceruleus. Like serotonin, its pathways innervate throughout much of the brain and are especially rich in the limbic region. Norepinephrine, related in its structure to the epinephrine (a.k.a. adrenaline) molecule (another neurotransmitter), adjusts one's level of arousal and attentiveness. Many of the stimulant medications work by influencing levels of norepinephrine.

## Dopamine

A versatile neurotransmitter, dopamine largely regulates processes such as movement and the sensation of pleasure and motivation. Much of the brain's dopamine comes from two cell clusters in the midbrain, the substantia nigra and the ventral tegmental area. The dopamine pathway from the substantia nigra, called the nigrostriatal dopamine pathway, is involved in motor control, our ability to coordinate movement. In Parkinson's disease, this dopamine pathway is damaged and leads to a lack of fluid movement and then to muscular rigidity. Two other pathways, the mesolimbic and the mesocortical, derive from the ventral tegmental area and distribute dopamine throughout the limbic system and the frontal cortex. Most of the pleasurable effects of drugs are thought to occur by stimulating these two pathways. Unfortunately, unusual levels of dopamine in these areas probably lead to the psychotic symptoms of schizophrenia.[4]

## Acetylcholine

Acetylcholine was the first discovered neurotransmitter (in 1921) and is one of the best understood, which isn't saying much! The production of acetylcholine occurs in a brain stem area called the nucleus basalis. Acetylcholine is the main neurotransmitter of muscle contraction. Acetylcholine provides the means of communication where the nervous system meets the skeletal muscles. It also appears necessary for the normal functioning of memory and learning. Distributed throughout the cerebral cortex, acetylcholine is acutely low in those who suffer from Alzheimer's Disease. In studying Alzheimer victims' brains, many neurotransmitters remained within normal ranges but acetylcholine was always deficient. Whether this can be considered a cause of the symptoms of that disease or just a symptom itself is uncertain. Some of the medications for this disease try to right this acetylcholine imbalance.

# Receptors

For all their importance, the neurotransmitters are hardly the end of the matter. Neurotransmitters only fit into specific receptors. Just as there are many types of neurotransmitters, a great many types of receptors are found throughout the nervous system. Serotonin, for instance, has at least 15 different types of receptors (called serotonergic receptors) that bind to it.[5] Depending on which receptors bind the serotonin, different effects follow. It's as if the serotonin key fits into one lock that opens Door A—certain moods, while it can also fit into the lock for Door B—hallucinations, Door C—appetite, and so on.

One of the processes that the nervous system does best is to keep a relative state of equilibrium. The world is a very dynamic place; if the nervous system lost its balance every time something drastic happened, few animals would pass from one era to the next. The key to survival is flexibility, having the ability to adapt to sudden changes.

Receptors allow such flexibility by providing a relatively balanced state of mind in a constantly changing environment.

An important part of this flexibility, receptors create a sense of stability in the nervous system even when a particular neurotransmitter gets very depleted or, conversely, floods the system. Like a home's thermostat, the receptors are constantly monitoring and adjusting so that everything stays within a narrow range of settings. If the nervous system has a sudden surplus of serotonin (as happens when people take certain anti-depressants) the serotonin receptors eventually 'downregulate.' This means that, sensing the presence of a high level of serotonin, the receptors prune themselves to a smaller number, minimizing the effect of the extra serotonin (at least as one theory goes).

One might think of the receptors as an assembly of microphones listening for a certain sound, in this case, the only tune they hear is created by serotonin. In a person with low levels of serotonin, such as a clinically depressed person, the 'listening system' has upped its number of receptors—it has hung as many microphones as it can to hear the faint sound of serotonin. This makes the serotonin system very, very sensitive. By taking anti-depressant medication and increasing the level of serotonin, the receptors alter themselves. It's as if the surplus of serotonin has caused too much feedback, too much noise. All the microphones get overloaded. Naturally, sensing all this tumult, the receptors downregulate, paring their numbers, until a nice middle ground is reached. Everything works just right now; they hear the tune they're trying to monitor and they've adjusted themselves so that it's neither too faint nor too loud. Such regulation of receptor numbers allows the nervous system greater versatility. By constantly monitoring its influences and adjusting receptor numbers through upregulation (hanging more microphones) or downregulation (reducing the number of microphones), the nervous system adapts to its environment. Of course, for all its relative success there are many casualties as well. Depression is, after all, the most common mental illness in the world. In some people, this delicate adjustment simply veers too far in one direction or another leading to (perhaps) depression or mania.

Given this constant regulation one wonders why the system ever loses balance, why the music gets 'out of tune.' We don't know the answers to such questions. Either because of unusual changes in the environment, genes, or in thinking patterns themselves, the brain has lost its appropriate settings—it has lost the sense of how loud the music should be.

*Chapter 12*

# HOW WE KNOW OUR BRAINS

Our understanding of the brain is far from complete and most theories about it are tentative, but given the immense complexity of the thing and the tiny scale on which all this takes place, it's striking that we know as much as we do. The greatest advances in this field come as a result of animal research performed during the last few decades. As glorious as the processes of the human nervous system are, they do not separate us from the rest of the animal kingdom. The same basic neurons and repertoire of neurotransmitters exist both in Mozart and in the common variety sea slug. While controversy continues about sacrificing animals for the sake of research, the therapeutic uses of this revolutionary knowledge helps countless people and enriches all our lives. Ultimately, these sacrifices lead to a greater recognition of our familial bonds with our fellow creatures. Science, that uniquely human endeavor, has come full circle to demonstrate how deep the bonds of kinship are between us and all other animals. Beginning with Darwin and continuing in our most innovative research, science closes the gap between human beings and the rest of nature.

Some still protest: humans are too unique for comparison to other animals. In some senses, we are. Though our neurons and our chemistry may be the same, it's in the organization of these materials that humans come to our wondrous gifts. Put a few thousand neurons together in the right way and you create the nervous system of the sea slug. Get a few billion and arrange them differently and human compassion emerges.

How we look at ourselves and the world will always be a matter of scale. On one level, we are identical with all other living things and share the same essential needs from our environment. For instance, we will always need to consume life to live. The needs of our cells are found in the products of other cells, be they plant or animal. On another scale, the scale of human experience, we cannot reasonably compare ourselves to animals. Our experience, in the form of our shared and individual meaning, is immutable. The goal of this book, indeed the goal and need of all modern rationality, is to make all levels of scale coherent and contiguous with one another. While there are gaps between these levels of scale, there are no leaps. Something at the scale of human experience, like compassion, should not contradict or be contradicted by something at the scale of our biology. When we attribute compassion to something external to nature, like soul, we separate one part of ourselves from the rest. In a more rational future, compassion will find description at the scale of neurotransmitters, through scientific knowledge, and at the scale human experience, through thought and action.

In addition to animal research, our most important methods of learning about the brain include imaging, like MRI (Magnetic Resonance Imaging) and PET (Positron Emission Tomography), and the study of people with brain damage.

Our powerful medical knowledge has given us the ability to keep injured people alive much longer than ever before. The proliferation of cardiovascular disease and the increase in life expectancy creates an abundance of stroke victims. Though there are many types of strokes, they always have the same effect—a deprivation of blood to brain tissue. When this occurs in large brain arteries, large sections of brain are lost. Such strokes, of course, tend to be fatal. Like other body parts, the brain is rife with very small blood vessels as well. Any dysfunction in these tiny vessels kills off a commensurably tiny amount of brain tissue. The results of such micro-strokes can be quite subtle. With the refinement in our medical methods and the use of tools like MRI and PET scanning devices, we are now able to locate these damaged areas and observe what their effects are upon the individual.

In addition to strokes, brain injury exists in many other forms. Psychosurgery (literally 'soul-surgery') provides us with sometimes frightening examples of brain function/dysfunction. The history of lobotomies, discussed later, led to important insights into the function of the frontal lobes of the cerebral cortex. In contrast to the horrible episode of misuse in Ken Kesey's novel *One Flew Over the Cuckoo's Nest,* the performance of psychosurgery is usually motivated by more humane concerns. The treatment of devastating epilepsy, for example, often involves life-saving psychosurgery. Without such surgical intervention, severe epileptics would face the prospect of an increasingly brutal, short existence.

Our knowledge of the brain derives from a variety of research methods. Animal studies, MRI and PET imaging studies, and injury studies are some of the most important types of research but are incomplete without the other fields and their respective knowledge and methods. Combined, these various perspectives have taught us much about the structure and function of the brain. For now, we'll take a quick look at the structure of the brain, its anatomy. Afterwards, we'll investigate functions more specifically and investigate how all our most unusual human qualities, that we once thought resided in the dualistic soul, are actually workings of the brain.

# Chapter 13

# ANATOMY OF THE BRAIN

Devoted to the structure and function of the brain, neuroanatomy attempts to define and explore specific regions of the brain. The work of the neuroanatomists gives us a rare look into the functional units of our brain tissue. Concerned with different scales of analysis, neuroanatomy looks both at the trees of individual neurons and explores the forests of cerebral structures. How clusters of neurons are arranged and interconnected with their neighbors provides the varied functions of brain regions.

Like cartography, the science of map-making, neuroanatomy should not be misinterpreted as 'the real thing.' Any time we compress the complexity of reality into a model, as in making a map of the world or of our brains, we overlook a great deal of information in order to simplify. Such convenient 'lies' should be taken for what they are: pointers to reality rather than reality itself.

## The Triune Model

Studying the mass of brain tissue and comparing it to other animals' brains, the neuroscientist Paul MacLean came up with the "triune model" of the human brain in 1970.[1] MacLean breaks up the human brain into three basic levels. The region of the brain stem, whose functions include the most essential parts of life—regulation of breathing/heart rate, the monitoring of blood sugar levels, and the control of wakefulness—MacLean refers to as the Reptilian brain because its structure and function is reminiscent of reptile brains. The structures above this regulate emotion and confer upon us the general set of behaviors common to all mammals. He calls this section the Paleomammalian ("old mammalian") brain. The final area, the cerebral cortex, or the human neo-cortex, provides human beings with our most distinguished abilities—planning, will, and abstract thought. MacLean calls this the Neomammalian ("new mammalian") brain.

Though an oversimplification, this model relates an important design strategy of evolution—building on top of what already exists. Throughout evolutionary history, we have been assembled from the ground up, from ancient to modern—the most essential structures being the oldest. The reptilian structures that serve us so well literally survive on their own in hundreds of species without all the "extras" (Paleomammalian and Neomammalian structures) that we count as blessings. The fundamental truth of evolution is that organisms must adapt to their environments if they are to survive. While the relative success of reptiles is demonstrated by their ancient lineage, the jury is still out on the upstart mammals and, of these, the trial has barely begun for the upstart of upstarts, the human being. Whether or not nature has come upon a good design scheme will be judged by our ability to survive over a long period of time. So far we have thrived but we are beginning to see the self-sabotage our species has inflicted upon its sustaining ecology. Hopefully, our brains will provide us both a recognition of this quandary and a hopeful solution.

A model like MacLean's is helpful in showing the fundamental architecture evolution has wrought in the human brain. Looking closer at the anatomy, contemporary scientists feel reticent breaking up the brain's interacting structures into such neat divisions. For ease of study, they do use three terms—the hindbrain, the midbrain, and the forebrain—though they do not assign these terms any overarching characteristics in the way MacLean's model does.

## *The Hindbrain*

The parts of the brain most essential for survival rest in the hindbrain, a tightly-packed collection of structures just atop the spinal cord. Damage to any part of brain tissue can be a life-threatening situation but damage to this region almost ensures death.

The medulla, seat of breathing, heart rate, salivation, vomiting, coughing, and sneezing, is just above the spinal cord. Another essential role this area plays is in the control of wakefulness through the reticular activating system, a collection of neurons that sends net-like projections throughout the brain. The wide-eyed, heart pounding, limb-tingling feeling that occurs when one hears a loud noise while asleep in bed is largely due to this system's alerting function. This high-powered concentration that focuses the whole brain may be related to small-scale processes of attention as well.

The cranial nerves connecting many of the organs of perception to the brain, do so through the medulla and pons (Latin for "bridge"), another hindbrain structure. The pons is also home to the raphe nuclei of cells, one of the major sources of the neurotransmitter serotonin. Working along with the reticular activating system, these structures modulate our basic level of conscious arousal. Since our most important mental functions require full consciousness, the role of these systems cannot be underestimated. Highly specific damage (lesions) done to these structures in rats leads to a coma-like state of unconsciousness.

The pons is also a bridge between the cerebellum and the rest of the brain. The cerebellum (Latin for "little brain"), nestled in the lower back part of the brain behind the medulla and pons, performs many functions relevant to movement. This distinctive mass, perhaps the most easily recognizable in the brain, possesses an enormous number of neurons. Though it composes only about 10% of the brain's volume, it contains perhaps half of the brain's total number of neurons![2]

The main function of the cerebellum involves precise coordination of movement and equilibrium. Anything athletic involves the cerebellum but some evidence even points to it's importance in mental processes.[3] In the same manner that it makes fluid the various movements of the body, it may also help to coordinate thoughts.

## The Midbrain

In the small zone between the hindbrain and forebrain lie tiny areas of brain involved in vision and hearing. The ability to orient towards a sound or sight, to sense in which direction it comes from and either turn the head or otherwise locate it, derives from these structures. In reptiles and birds these areas are quite developed while in mammals they are relatively underdeveloped.

Another structure in the midbrain, the substantia nigra, is the main site for the production of dopamine, an important neurotransmitter. The damaged substantia nigra leads to Parkinson's disease—that dreaded immobilization of movement and thought so well depicted in Oliver Sacks's *Awakenings* (an excellent novel and popular movie). As described by Sacks, a return of function can be achieved through medical intervention. The brain is able to synthesize more dopamine when it receives a boost of L-Dopa. This is no easy solution, though, for a range of side effects and other complications follows soon after. The brain's delicate processes make the most sophisticated medical therapies seem blunt.

## The Forebrain

The most 'human' characteristics we possess come from a few forebrain structures. The generation of emotions, thought, and the acquisition and storage of complex memories occur here. One must be especially wary about over-localizing such functions; in reality, they depend on many brain structures, of all three divisions, working in concert.

The forebrain includes a single structure, the cortex, and a collection of other structures below the cortex. Subcortical structures send pathways above and below, entwining the most essential functions of the hindbrain with the uniquely human ones of the cerebral cortex. Anyone who's stayed up all night studying for a test or otherwise tried to perform mental gymnastics on little sleep, knows how much these 'advanced' functions depend upon one's underlying mood and energy—in short, on the doings of the hindbrain. The interactions between forebrain structures can conflict among themselves as well: in the heat of some emotion, be it rage or grief, mental operations are a lost cause, or at least our courts tell us so. The mind is an uneasy alliance of brain structures and constantly reminds us how all things complex derive from the coordination of the simple.

### The Limbic System

Many of the structures that reside toward the center of the brain are grouped together and referred to as the limbic system. These structures which include the thalamus, the hypothalamus, the hippocampus, and the amygdala, interconnect the cortical and subcortical regions of the brain. And again, while such a neat division is certainly not accurate, it is useful. Many of the most important structures in the lower part of the forebrain—the thalamus, hypothalamus, and pituitary gland—are also the prime movers of the endocrine system, the system of hormone production and regulation. Because of this interconnection, hormones directly affect thinking and mood.[4] Any postpartum mother can tell you as much.

The hypothalamus is a structure of the nervous system and the endocrine system. Many of our daily motivations, the desire for eating, drinking, sex, and competition, find some regulation here. Consider how closely this localized function depends on many other brain parts for its actual performance. For instance, while one's libido may go up and down as the hypothalamus is activated, what one perceives as 'sexy' is not here. Gentlemen prefer blondes, or brunettes, or redheads, or other gentlemen, or whomever their culture tells them to prefer. The whole range of sexual experience is not localized to a tiny zone in the hypothalamus but results from this area's pathways as they connect with other brain parts.

When the hypothalamus is damaged bizarre and sometimes deadly results follow. Without delicate regulation of basic drives the individual faces a lot of trouble. A person without an appetite or a good sense of water regulation may haphazardly malnourish or dehydrate herself. Indeed, almost all of the deaths that have occurred from the use of the club drug 'Ecstasy' (MDMA) have been a result of overheating. This suggests that MDMA somehow blunts the body's normal sensitivity to heat and thirst, likely through an influence on the hypothalamus. As such, drug awareness programs have tried to emphasize the conscious necessity of drinking plenty of water and occasionally resting to prevent the unwanted side-effect of heat exhaustion among club-goers.[5]

The pituitary gland, the 'master gland' of the body that orchestrates many of the other endocrine organs, lies adjacent to the hypothalamus and is connected to it by a stalk. These two are intimately associated. The hypothalamus modulates hormone release from the pituitary by using an assortment of chemical messengers. As is always the case with the brain, hormones in the blood then provide feedback to the hypothalamus which will then alter its stimulation of the pituitary gland.

Given the preponderance of interaction between the endocrine system and the brain structures, some scientists advocate a breakdown of the distinction. The brain with all its related structures, they argue, is an outgrowth of the endocrine system.[6] Whether medical professionals eventually decide to make this dramatic move is of no importance. After all, these are just words. The vital message here, the meaning, involves a radical social understanding—the mind is the body. While we can continue to distinguish between perspectives; that is, talking about thoughts when appropriate and neuromodulation when appropriate, we must quibble no longer on the source of our mental life.

The thalamus, just above the hypothalamus, receives the varied information of the five senses and routes it to respective parts of the cerebral cortex. The thickest connections between the subcortical region and the cortex occurs in this structure.

The hippocampus (Latin for "sea horse," which the hippocampus resembles) is the brain structure most crucial for memory. Memory, due to its importance in our understanding of identity, is a burning question among brain researchers. Damage to the hippocampus prevents the further creation of long term memories. Short-term memory, the ability to hold something in the mind while one is actively engaged with the thing (like remembering a phone number between perceiving it and dialing it), continues unabated if this structure is damaged. The moment attention is lost, however, consciousness of what one was doing disappears without a trace. A person suffering damage to the hippocampus leads a bizarre life since what occurred a few moments before is continually lost.

The most famous case of this is a well-known figure in the neuroscience literature, H.M. H.M. suffered from terrible epilepsy and in an effort to control his seizures underwent brain surgery in 1953. A portion of his brain, (including the hippocampus and amygdala) were removed. For the last few decades H.M. has lived a bizarre existence for he is forever the young man he was shortly before 1953. He can be taught simple procedures, how to play a certain game or work a puzzle, but he cannot remember the daily narrative content of his life. In that regard, it is always the 1950s for H.M.

Emotions come from the interaction of many brain structures. One of the most important, the amygdala, gives us the ability to perceive emotional undertones in stimuli. It's greatly involved in the experience of fear and anger. Whether it's the rustling of leaves that we imagine to be a tiger awaiting to pounce or the subtle changes in tone during a conversation with our lover, the emotionality of the situation filters through this part of the brain. Given the dramatic emotionality of the human being, damage to this area leads to bizarre behavior and raises difficult questions about our humanity.

## The Cerebral Cortex

The surface of the human brain, that wrinkled mass of gray matter that has become an icon of science and pop culture alike, is called the cortex (Latin for "tree bark"). Looking at it, one is reminded of a wrinkled walnut. The mountain-like edges of these folds are called gyri while the valley-like rifts are called sulci. The reason for these deep wrinkles is to squeeze the maximal amount of surface area into a limited space. This need for surface area arises from the specialization of cortical neurons. Our most essentially human traits are a result of 'squeezing in' a collection of specialized cells that there simply wasn't any more room for in our head.

Anyone who's packed for an important journey has experienced stuffing in the last article; the article that, after all, isn't the most crucial but will assure us that extra comfort or insurance against some possible contingency—the rain poncho or the wool sweater. Nature performed the same feat when packing our head with the cortex. Barely able to 'zip our heads closed' (note the delicate fontanelle of the infant), our heads are truly 'bursting at the seams' as infants. The skull's sutures, where the pieces of bone come together, do not fully fuse for many years.

Why didn't nature just build a bigger head for this terribly cramped brain? As a species, we're intelligence-centric and tend to think every challenge merely an opportunity to exercise more cleverness. Looking at nature as a whole, one realizes this strategy to be rare. Evolution is a hack job—what works for the moment goes on, what doesn't dies out. The fact that human intelligence has done so well is a fluke, not Providence. Nature's just as concerned with things like movement and structural integrity (though you wouldn't think it, given the back problems so many of us suffer). We didn't get bigger heads because we didn't develop bigger hips to birth these heads. At a certain point, a woman's ability to move is hampered by elephantine hips. Between a maximum hip size and the brain's costly commandeering of fuel resources, evolution put a cap on our head (brain) size and our intelligence.

Size, though important, is not the end of the matter. The elephant or the killer whale have enormous brains, many times larger than the biggest human brains. Even when considering brain to body ratio (meaning the overall size of the animal in proportion to its brain), there are a few species out there that do slightly better than humans. The miraculous abilities of the human cortex derive not from the total number of the neurons but from the sophisticated organization and interconnection of these neurons.

In the cortex, sheets of neurons called laminae, are piled atop each other like leaves of paper. In some places, such as the area of the cortex involved in muscle control (the motor cortex), these laminae are six sheets deep. In addition to being organized into distinct sheets of laminae, the neurons are also organized into columns that go through the sheets from top to bottom. The neurons' organization into sheets and columns allows for area specialization. In fact, much like a map of the world, various zones, like countries, function in particular ways and for their own purposes. Those zones close together possess similar functions—speaking the same language—and are more interconnected than those elsewhere. After damage to a specific area, adjacent neurons often take over the routines previously run by the destroyed neurons. The rehabilitation that takes place after a stroke illustrates this ability of nearby cells to adapt.

In contrast to a map of the world, there are no vast oceans between cortical regions. Some deep crevices, called fissures, do separate a few adjacent zones, though all the different regions of the cortex are contiguous. If flattened out, the cortex would appear like a torn old parchment with uneven borders and peninsula-like edges.

Neuroanatomists have come up with various ways to distinguish zones of the cortex. The most basic representation breaks up the cortex into four major regions, called lobes. From front to back the frontal lobe, each hemisphere of the brain possesses: a temporal lobe, a parietal lobe, and an occipital lobe. A more detailed anatomical representation, called the Brodmann map, focuses on the structural differences in the neurons throughout the cortex. In this map, there are over fifty regions with distinguishable patterns of organization. Even such detail evades the more complex differences throughout the cortex.

The frontal lobe of the cortex is responsible for some of the most 'human' and mysterious functions of the brain. Executive functions, those things that involve 'will-like' properties of motivation and action, are found primarily in this lobe, especially the very front part. The great neuropsychologist, Alexandr Luria, referred to the frontal lobe as "the organ of culture."[7] Among other things, our ability to infer other people's assumptions, to predict their feelings and behaviors, in short, *to understand them* originates in this region. Damage to this area results in an ignorance of others' desires and expectations. Mentally sound in all other ways, the person with frontal lobe dysfunction may be crass and obtuse in social situations. Besides its social aspects, this inability to sense others' feelings may reflect a more profound loss, the failure to distinguish self and 'non-self.'[8] Damage to the frontal lobes, then, may render us less mature in our psychological development, reducing us to a state of childish vagueness about reality. Of all animals, we have the most robust and articulated frontal lobes accounting for some 30% of the brain's cortical surface. The development of these lobes seems to correspond to a creature's self-consciousness.

Some neuroscientists, like Antonio Damasio, would qualify the frontal lobe as the sole site of these executive functions.[9] In his book, *Descartes' Error*, he makes a convincing case for a different model of these 'higher' human capacities. He argues that such areas of the frontal lobe are thoroughly involved in the creation of things like will and motivation but that the complex of abilities we call reason depend upon our emotions as well. The basic repertoire of emotions provided by the limbic system give thought its most important support. According to Damasio, the creation of our intellect involves the whole body and many parts of the brain. He doesn't deny that these zones in the frontal lobe are of great importance in executive functions but thinks it a gross error to stop there. The age-old philosophic distinction -that the emotions and reason war against each other- is totally wrong. Damasio's observations are similar to many tempered neuroscientists' thoughts. Neat labels and precisely understood pathways are hard to find in the brain. Just when one begins to think a particular piece of brain responsible for some function, new evidence offers increased sophistication. It's clear, though, that when pieces of the frontal lobe are lost to injury or stroke profound changes occur in executive functions.

The frontal lobe is separated from the parietal lobe by the central sulcus. On the frontal part of this fissure, a band of tissue responsible for control of the body's movements stretches across the cortex. This is called the motor cortex. Parts of the body are literally 'mapped out' here in something like a sequential fashion: toes, feet, ankles, and so on. Neuroscientists often place the image of a ugly little man, called a homunculus, across this area to indicate which aspects of the body are controlled by which mass of neurons. As all over the cortex, the right side functions of the body are mapped onto the left side of the brain and vice-versa.

As one crosses the central fissure towards the back of the skull, the parietal lobe begins. Across the fissure from the motor cortex, on the parietal side, is a similar band of tissue responsible for our sense of touch in all these various parts of the body. This is called the somatosensory cortex. While the motor cortex gives command over movement, the somatosensory cortex provides a representation of the body and a constant processing of its touch receptors. The two work together in very important ways.

For instance, imagine a complex movement, like wielding a samurai sword. The first time one handles such a sword it is cumbersome and inaccurate. One's balance is thrown off, movements are slow and reactive—there is no art. But the great masters of the sword, through the continuous feedback of practice, gain a supernatural control over the blade. After a while it seems an extension of the samurai's body and he controls it as carefully as a pianist controls a finger. He is fully 'sensitized' to it. As the interrelationship develops in pathways between a few areas—the somatosensory cortex, the motor cortex, and the cerebellum to be sure—the individual achieves a staggering level of accuracy and control. Such a samurai can split a cantaloupe atop his son's head at full speed, stopping less than a millimeter from the scalp. DO NOT TRY THIS AT HOME! Such basic processes of practice and habituation result from years of careful training and the intricate linking of different parts of the brain.

The parietal lobe fills a number of roles. In addition to the somatosensory cortex, the parietal lobe serves as an 'association area,' mixing various sensory impressions to create a recognition. For example, if one's eyes are closed and an object is given to his, he may smell it, feel its edges and texture, and even come to visualize its shape. After feeling a firm texture, a round shape, and noticing a citrus-smell, the person will quickly determine that he's holding an orange. These are very different kinds of information but we have the ability to cross the boundaries from one sense to another and 'add them up' to an overall impression of the thing. The parietal lobe is one of the main places where divergent sources of information find unity.

The occipital lobe, which we'll cover in a moment, is the primary site for visual processing but a few other regions assist in creating vision. Some theorists make distinctions in our ability to see the 'what' of an object and the 'where' of an object. The parietal lobe defines the 'where' of an object in the visual field.

The temporal lobe, which drapes down the sides of the brain, takes a leading role in the ability to analyze sounds. A couple of structures, most commonly residing in the left side of the temporal lobe, give us the ability to understand and create language. Broca's area is involved in the creation of speech while Wernicke's area processes language and assists in linking meaning to the sounds of words. These two areas show a far greater proportion of tissue (and development of tissue) than other animals which makes a lot of sense given our sophisticated ability to communicate with language.

Aphasia, the inability to communicate, takes on two distinct forms because of these areas. If one has Broca's aphasia, he can understand language but is unable to respond verbally. Wernicke's aphasia is quite different: here one can speak words and sentences though they are totally devoid of meaning. Obviously, the interaction of these two areas is necessary for any full sense of verbal communication.

In addition to processing sounds, the temporal lobe also gives us the ability to recognize very specific patterns of visual information. In the breakdown of the 'what' and 'where' modalities of vision, the temporal lobe creates the 'what' allowing recognition of a particular face, for example. When an individual declares that he's bad with names but never forgets a face, there are good reasons for this: they are two very different processes in the brain. There isn't some single place where all our knowledge of a person (or anything else, for that matter) resides. Whenever we see or think about a person a great deal of 'parallel processing' occurs—face patterning, name recognition, 'feeling' about the person, and any number of other memories and information. These different functions occur all over the brain and create the overall sense of a person.

The occipital lobe, though farthest away from the eyes, is the hub of visual processing. A lot of pioneering research has been done to understand human vision, one of the best understood processes of the brain. Though counterintuitive, the processing of sights is not anything like a single process. Rather, many different zones of the occipital lobe process quite specific parts of visual information. One zone processes vertical types of visual data, another area processes horizontal data; one part color, another depth. Deeper parts of the brain, like those mentioned in the section on the midbrain, assist in perceiving movement. And, as we discovered, there are 'what' and 'where' modalities in vision processing.

*Chapter 14*

# THE BINDING PROBLEM— WHAT IS CONSCIOUSNESS?

The idea of 'breaking up' information, called parallel processing, seems to be the main strategy of the brain. Consider a commonplace example: a man speaking to his wife. The brain puts together so much information so well that we don't appreciate the complexity of the underlying processes. The various senses pick up hundreds of different 'streams' of data—color, sound, emotion— that get doled out to various neural circuits. The sound goes to one part of the brain which may then route through memory pathways and emotion 'detectors' to reroute, at some point, with visual information which has similarly been sent to memory and emotion circuits through different pathways altogether. Individual units become adept at performing a task and then link up with other units to create a total product: the basic sharing of vast amounts of meaning between husband and wife.

Think of the levels of subtlety at work! The husband may perceive the slightest droop around his wife's eyes, or the barely discernable lilt in her voice, which to him can be the most significant source of meaning in an otherwise humdrum conversation. How the various pieces of the brain yield the unified perception we take for granted is a great mystery. Called 'the binding problem' our ability to coordinate so many types of information, binding it into wholes, remains mysterious. How do the parallel processes come together? Parts of the brain called 'association areas' seem to play a key role but are not the only areas involved in the coordination of our seemingly unified consciousness. But to a larger question—is our consciousness truly unified?

The human brain is a bit like an eclectic Recreational Vehicle. Occasionally, driving down an interstate you'll encounter some improbable truck. It's not to be confused with the sleekly engineered, super-expensive, monster RV—satellite dish included. Instead, the truck I'm referring to possesses some simple form with lots of add-ons. Underneath the mass, driving the rig, is a solid, V-8 pick up that's buried beneath a camper fitted with after-market visors, antennae (CB and TV), power and water hook ups, all bedecked with bicycles and bumperstickers. A truck like that catches one's eye. Looking closely you can almost date each revision and predict what will next be added or taken away. The rig's jumble of parts were put together because each served some purpose, at least for a time. That does not mean that it is the best design nor does it mean that it's efficient in all ways. The addition of so many 'extras' may have turned the thing into a nightmare of aerodynamics and the balance of the vehicle may shift from one terrain to the next. All in all, though, what has come together holds together reasonably well.

Similarly, the human animal is no carefully planned affair but a medley of latter-day experiments and poorly tested gadgetry. In Paul Theroux's novel, *The Mosquito Coast*, a rebellious inventor sums up the mistakes in our body's design:

> Skin's not thick enough, bones aren't strong enough, too little hair, no claws, no fangs. Drop us and we break! Why, we're not even symmetrical. One foot bigger than the other, left-handed, right-handed, our noses run. Look where our heart is. We weren't meant to stand up straight—our posture exposes the most sensitive parts of the body, heart and genitals. We should be on all fours, hairier, more resistant to heat and cold, with tails. What happened to my tail, that's what I'd like to know.[1]

As the body has taken form over the last few million years numerous tools and tricks have been added, revised, bolstered, hindered, inflated, and deflated. At the end of all this a remarkably sturdy creature has evolved out of a lucky combination of gizmos.

While the unity of consciousness makes it seem that our senses and thoughts are nicely matched, pairing power to movement like a good transmission, in fact it's unclear whether this is the case. The supposed unity of consciousness may really just be an illusion. Anyone who does a good bit of introspection can see how, in fact, we're always checking our progress with doubts, engaging in spontaneous behaviors to destroy long-term efforts, and using terrible methods to render important decisions. Harking back to the example of Hamlet, the mind is more often in a state of indecision—bending to the chances of fate—than it is in seamless control of our emotions and ideas. Our senses work nicely, the association areas provide a high-fidelity representation of the world—otherwise we'd never be able to drive cars without crashing—but the 'higher-order' aspects of our minds are lucky to get into a comfortable and safe groove.

Buddhists compare the mind to a chattering monkey. Our heads are usually full of so many contrasting thoughts and musings that following a clear path becomes a near impossibility. The 'stream of consciousness,' to use William James's phrase, is too much like a flooding stream littered with flotsam and jetsam than it is a well-defined conduit of pure water. Heraclitus's classic statement about the world, that one cannot step into the same river twice, defines the always changing nature of our consciousness.

Considering that the brain is an amalgam of devices put together in drastically different historical periods, to adapt to widely variant ecosystems, it is a wonder we're not all mad. And when one witnesses the truly insane, absolutely fixated on some trivial act, or obsessed with sexuality, or adrift in a mental world of dreams, the truth comes out—the brain barely balances all its thrown-together gadgetry. The answer to the binding problem is this—the mechanisms of our mind are more often unbound than they are bound. The true binding problem is how the mind can convince us that, in fact, it is a unified affair. More likely, the poet Petrarch was right: "How many are the emotions and how adverse with which the human mind fights within itself; it is never whole, never one, it is at variance with itself, it is always at war."[2]

# *Chapter 15*

# PSYCHOACTIVITY

Psychoactive drugs have shaped history. From the prehistoric shamans and medicine men who possessed sacred knowledge of mind-altering plants to the latest magazine articles on alcoholism and drug addiction, we are alternately set free and put into abysmal bondage by the subtle changes these substances effect in our brain chemistry. Be it peyote or Prozac, caffeine or cocaine, we commonly use such a variety of mind-altering chemicals that we forget the implications of them. For nothing attests so well to the wholly material nature of our personhood than the ability of chemicals to affect our minds.

There is nothing 'as if' about drugs—they do not affect some physical component but leave another mental, or spiritual, counterpart untouched. Anyone who uses a powerful psychoactive drug realizes that what seemed predictable—the sense of self—transforms into the novel and uncertain. The testimony of millions of addicts, if errant, is not false—*drugs work*. Drugs can uplift the spirit, free the mind, convey bliss, and provide enlightenment. Humanity has always used/abused drugs and always will because of our physical, creaturely substratum. The ability of addictive chemicals to control a person's mind, to oppose all will power and better judgement, gives witness to the physical basis of the soul. The entwinement of drug abuse and despair results not simply from the horrors of addiction but also from the tacit proof relayed to the addict—that the mind is material and conscious life fleeting.

Virtually every person alive uses one or more of the chemicals outlined below. But besides these, there are hundreds of other substances that can make alterations in our mentality. Neither can we overlook the more common nutrients we use to change our moods. Who can keep a chipper attitude while desperately hungry and who deny the heavy-headed drunkenness experienced after a turkey-rich Thanksgiving dinner? In some very real way, everything one takes into the body—be it water, food, or medication—is psychoactive for all these things alter the chemical environment of the brain.

One can explore drugs from the vantage of history, pharmacology, anthropology, religion, and philosophy. Many books have viewed drugs through these various lenses. To accurately convey the significance that psychoactive substances play in human society some brief synopsis these varied traditions must be discussed.

Perhaps most significant of all, the influence of drugs on religious history is more profound than most would care to admit. The poignancy of the relationship between drugs and religion—and the intermingling of the two—lies at the foundation of our notions of a disembodied self. Perhaps more than any other single factor, drug experience 'invented' the soul. In truth, every drug has a sacred history and every sacred history, a drug.

## *Depressants*

Since society began, we've found many ways to medicate ourselves. One of the troublesome aspects of having such sensitive and complex brains is that they often become overactive. Consciousness, the final source of the self, is at times too much for we poor animals. By chemically 'depressing' the brain's activity, we 'take the edge off'— we become comfortably numb. For those suffering anxiety, depressants are sometimes the only means of drowning one's worries; and for those trying to forget, depressants are the surest way of misplacing the past.

Alcohol is the oldest and best-known depressant in humanity's medicine chest but in the last century we developed a whole new range of these substances. We're still experimenting with these new drugs and coming to know them better.

One should note that the substances we label 'depressants' are quite different from depression, the mood disorder. Clinical depression may or may not result from certain brain structures being electrically and chemically 'depressed.' In general, though, the effects of chemical depressants do not cause a state of psychological depression. It is misleading when we use similar terms for such dissimilar things.

Doctors prescribe depressant medications for many conditions. Depending on the dosage, they can be used as sedatives to allay anxiety or as hypnotics to induce sleep. These drugs are sometimes labeled sedative-hypnotics.

Millions of people use depressants as an aid to get through, in Hamlet's words, "...the slings and arrows of outrageous fortune." Hamlet himself, were he alive today, would probably be on a cocktail of these drugs. The travails of modern existence have made anxiety among the worst problems of our times. In measured doses, anxiety forms the backdrop of any meaningful activity. Out of balance, though, anxiety will prevent the individual from enjoying the company of others, lead to chronic depression, hinder sleep, and generally diminish any possibility for a pleasant life. The anxiety-reducing ability of depressants can help restore a balance to one's state of mind. Whether or not this is the appropriate manner to deal with anxiety poses a much grander question of philosophy and sociology. If we have to increasingly medicate ourselves to live within our current model of society then perhaps we should reevaluate this model.

In addition to helping with anxiety, depressants also provide a medical solution to insomnia. Like generalized anxiety (and probably because of it), insomnia seems to be a growing 'disease.' Chemical depressants can right this sleep disorder.

Because depressants lower nervous system activity, they can help to prevent the neural over-activity called epilepsy. The depressant effects of these substances keep the brain in a state less amenable to seizure activity. Unfortunately, the therapeutic doses used to prevent epilepsy may also keep the epileptic in a sluggish state. The dilemma in this area of research is to craft medications that can prevent seizures without leaving the epileptic in a state of chronic sedation.

## *Alcohol*

O God, that men should put an enemy in their mouths to steal away their brains! That we should with joy, pleasure, revel, and applause transform ourselves into beasts!
—William Shakespeare, Othello[1]

About ten thousand years ago mankind left the caves. Gone were the days of foraging and roving; never more would the seasons and whims of nature cause man to chase over the land, living a nomadic existence in search of food. Somehow and in some marvelous way the science of agriculture had found its way into the mind of man. With this bounty, the clans could establish permanent settlements and attend to the less mundane matters of existence. Though man was cursed with the "toil of the fields," he still led a much freer and richer life than ever before.

The fabulously crafted human brain, housed in a graceful but harmless physique, had elected early man a privileged position as king of the scavengers. The original jack-of-all trades, early man excelled in his environment by mastering nothing. Like no other animal, man's designer attempted a truly radical departure from the blueprints. Instead of focusing on an improved claw, a sharper fang, faster acceleration, or enormous size, nature began to innovate in the mental realm. A bigger brain with a host of excellent modalities and tools provided tremendous information processing and limitless recording capacity. Agriculture and primitive cities were the first fruits of this design innovation.

With an abundance of food, man's belly kept full while his mind soared. On an empty stomach, few are philosophers or scientists; on a full stomach, the hunger of the belly moves to the brain. An appetite for knowledge began to grow. Little tricks of the nomads, like charting stars to predict seasons, now blossomed into elaborate sciences and cosmologies. Math evolved from simple arithmetic into the complex geometry and trigonometry exhibited in the great pyramids of the Egyptians, hewn just a few thousand years after the first agricultural settlements. The nomad mentality of large patterns distilled into the scrutinizing love of detail born from a sense of place. Turned upon itself, the human nervous system expanded geometrically and continues apace.

This world, a world of wheat and time, observation and memory, is the world of alcohol. It took subtle minds to recognize the features of accident that had first caused alcoholic inebriation. Perhaps some great earthenware vessel, commonly used for grain storage, had been mistaken by a nearly blind old woman. Unable to see the golden contents at the bottom of the dark well, she filled it high with river water and sealed it for drier days. As the days became hot and dry and the creek first slowed to a trickle then became a clay-cracked arroyo, the family turned to their stores to slake their thirst. The old woman ladled out the woody concoction and was much teased by her doting brood. Soon the teasing became hilarious and the room spun, the lot of them were drunk. A rare spirit had descended to inspire and exhilarate. They stumbled out and shared the cereal water with their neighbors who also got caught up in the comedy. Alcohol had seeped into the human drama.

The secret ingredient that makes bread rise and turns a rotting liquid into an alcoholic beverage is yeast. In the presence of sugars and water, yeast thrives. Consuming the sugar and multiplying, yeast produces alcohol as a byproduct. Yeast will produce their waste until the alcohol approaches 15% of the solution; at that point, the alcohol kills its creator and stops its own production. Beer commonly possesses 4-5% alcohol while wine rarely surpasses 13%. For most of history humans only had access to beer or wine because of this natural production limit.

The ancient Egyptians' primary drink was a heavy type of beer. In ancient times, people drank alcoholic beverages out of necessity as much as for enjoyment. As Samuel Butler explains, "When the water of a place is bad it is safest to drink none that has not been filtered through either the berry of a grape, or else a tub of malt. These are the most reliable filters yet invented."[2] Wines and beers may have been among the purer, more reliable sources of water given the lack of sanitary measures before modernity. Throughout Europe wine, beer, and mead (a honey-based liquor) were popular drinks. In the Mediterranean regions, wine supplied enjoyment to the Greeks and Romans alike who sang its praises: *in vino veritas* (Latin for "truth in wine").

Sometime around the ninth century of the Common Era, scientifically minded Arabs distilled pure alcohol from wine. Because alcohol has a lower boiling point than water, it evaporates easily. With some tubing and glassware, the essential tools of the moonshiner and chemist alike, early experimenters collected alcoholic vapors. When the Muslim scientists distilled these subtle vapors, they encountered a colorless liquid that, left to itself, quickly disappeared.

They named it alcohol which means "finely divided spirit" in Arabic. When naming it, no doubt, they were talking about its physical properties rather than its affect on human behavior; they themselves were forbidden to delight in the revelrous stuff. The prophet Muhammad had condemned the consumption of alcoholic drinks in the seventh century. Though the Muslims were prohibited from enjoying alcohol, their poetic name for it, which describes the human being as well as his chief inebriant, gives lasting credit to the spirit of science that once flourished in the Middle East.

Distillation allowed a whole new range of alcoholic preparations and liquors. The process of alcohol distillation made its way quickly from the Muslim world into the Christian one with its sacred delight in the mind-altering affects of alcohol. After all, the Lord Savior's very first miracle involved turning water into wine at a festive wedding party in Cana. Jesus forever sanctified alcohol at the Last Supper. In remembrance of him, wine is exalted as the literal blood of Christ in the holy sacrament of Communion celebrated during the Catholic mass.

Just as wine represented the healing love of Christ, purer forms of alcohol became renowned for their own healing properties. A high dose of alcohol was touted as a cure for everything from arthritis to tuberculosis. The French physicians called it *aqua vitae* (Latin, "water of life"). This epithet showed up time and again in various countries as they specialized in their own preparations of alcoholic liquors. The Irish became famous for their Whiskey (*Uisgebeatha*, Irish for "water of life"). For about nine thousand years, people had access to only wine, beer, or mead but in less than three centuries dozens of throat-searing beverages came to the fore throughout the European continent and its outlying islands.

### Consumption

Drinking alcohol is part of the very fabric of Western culture. Without wine, the French would cease to be French; without beer, the Germans far less Germanic. All European cultures persist in their vast production and distinctive types of liquors. As for America, perhaps statistics best reflect its alcoholic tendencies.

According to the U.S. Census Bureau over half the U.S. population drinks alcohol on a regular basis. That means there are nearly 130 million drinkers in this country alone! The statistics for 1997 estimate that every adult in America drank about 39 gallons of beer in that year alone! In the same year, Americans imbibed three gallons of wine and nearly two gallons of assorted liquors.

Because of its widespread use and addictive properties, no other drug approaches the damage and destruction of alcohol. In 1997, 245,000 Americans were enrolled in drug treatment facilities for alcoholism. Every year in the U.S., a staggering number of deaths are alcohol-related. Throughout the 1990s, nearly 7% of all adult deaths were alcohol-related. Most acts of homicide are committed while intoxicated and similarly most sexual assaults occur under the influence. Aside from these, the number of injuries from drunk driving accidents alone is shocking. Roughly 50,000 Americans die every year in traffic accidents and about 30% of those involve drunk drivers.[3]

The amount of damage wreaked by alcohol has always been a problem in America. By the early 1900s, the temperance movement had won a great deal of support for the dissolution of drinking. In 1919, by tacking the Eighteenth Amendment to the Constitution, Americans hoped to finally rid themselves of alcohol. An enormous black market for the spirits ensued rife with gangsters and mob influence. The culture of moonshine and speakeasies flourished. Fourteen years later, the Constitution received another Amendment, the Twenty-first, which ushered alcohol right back. The government had received a stern lesson—human appetites cannot be so easily legislated.

The need to regulate alcohol did not end with the Prohibition. Left now to the individual states, an assortment of ordinances and state laws try to hedge the consumption of alcohol. In spite of these regulations, alcoholism and its sordid by-products remain all too common.

## Why Drink?

I have drunk since I was fifteen and few things have given me more pleasure. When you work hard all day with your head and know you must work again the next day what else can change your ideas and make them run on a different plane like whisky? When you are cold and wet what else can warm you? Before an

attack who can say anything that gives you the momentary well-being that rum does? I would as soon not eat at night as not to have red wine and water. The only time it isn't good for you is when you write or when you fight. You have to do that cold. But it always helps my shooting. Modern life, too, is often a mechanical oppression and liquor is the only mechanical relief.
  —Ernest Hemingway, *Selected Letters*[4]

When faced with the chaos provoked by alcohol, one wonders why it rests near and dear so many peoples' hearts. Certainly, to those who do not know its virtues, the vices seem overwhelming. Despite its dangers, few cultures have elected to deny themselves the pleasures of alcohol.

Alcohol produces changes in the brain felt on many levels of consciousness. A sense of relaxation accompanies an underlying vigor. Zest, zeal, and fun rise aloft on these spirits. Honesty with one-self and others may increase. Like most psychoactive drugs, atmosphere mediates the alcoholic experience. Put in an aggressive situation, the alcoholic will become more aggressive than normal; placed in a relaxed setting, the alcoholic achieves serenity. In short, alcohol diminishes the self's normal thresholds, its 'settings.' The boundary between individual and situation becomes hazier when inebriated. The voice of the self is quieted allowing all the other voices of the moment to speak louder.

The drunken experience is one of disinhibition. The structure of the self, with its complex of character traits, generally emerges by inhibiting all the forces that commonly filter through the brain. At any moment, a limitless amount of information streams through all the senses yet we are scarcely aware of more than a few paltry details. Our attention remains focused only on address to while all the rest seems to drain away unheeded by one's consciousness.

The four-year-old child expresses a humanity less constrained by inhibition. Caught up in glee one moment, the child may break down into a soul-stirring cry the next. An object of desire, be it some sugary treat or bright toy, achieves god-like status for a spell and is forgotten once out of sight. The skillful parent quickly learns how to negotiate the obsessions of the child by redirection, changing the object of fascination from one thing to the next. Even by that young age, inhibition has already set into many behaviors. Potty training lies as the first great hurtle that separates a feral child from an increasingly self-directed human being. Soon after, the child acquires the ability and habit of postponing gratification and strategizing for future indulgences. Only a matter of degree separates this child from her adult counterpart; they are of the same kind. As the child ages and becomes the adult, the great gray mass of the brain, especially the frontal lobes, have masterfully inhibited all manner of reactive behaviors. Every human personality is a fine orchestration of such inhibition and disinhibition. The individual becomes expert at alternately tapping on the gas and pressing on the brakes, following all the appropriate rules of the road that her society has lain down before her.

Alcohol disrupts all this. Alcohol disinhibits globally. As the level of alcohol increases in the blood and in the brain, the normal patterns of inhibition, the normal behaviors of the person, become jumbled. The drunk is closer to his environment and moves more freely with its rhythms, less caught up by his many inhibitions.

In small doses, such disinhibition provides a cozy respite for the self. The end of the day drink helps the busy person unwind, to step away from what she's been doing, and to rest, to simply 'be' in the moment. Moderate use of alcohol is not only pleasant, it is healthy. At these low doses, alcohol benefits mental life and helps various mechanisms of the body.

In higher doses, and with more chronic dependence, alcohol becomes a true monster that devours the self. The frightened self shies away from normal activities and becomes the weak-spirited servant of its alcoholic master. In the chronic alcoholic, the self is merely a means to procure more alcohol. The existence of the person diminishes to a drunken one disengaged from the world. An enormous feat of will or intervention or both becomes necessary to chain this beast and revitalize the individual's true humanity.

The experience of alcohol reveals an essential truth about many drugs. A life-saving drug in one dosage can become the deadliest of poisons in a slightly different dosage (or in a different person). Just as water radically transforms at zero degrees Celsius, becoming ice, so too may a drug change its overall effect from one dosage to the next, changing from a therapeutic medication into a whole new disease. Finding the golden mean relates just as aptly to these substances as to all manner of life's endeavors.

## How Does Alcohol Work?

Alcohol enters the bloodstream rapidly. It begins to do so in the stomach though the majority of its absorption occurs in the small intestine. When mixed with other liquids, alcohol dilutes and enters the blood in lower dosages. However, if swallowed with carbonated beverages alcohol gets into the bloodstream much quicker. The carbonation forces the liquids from the stomach into the small intestine where they are readily absorbed. When taken with food, some alcohol binds to the food's protein molecules and gets carried through the digestive system without being absorbed into the bloodstream.

Once present in the bloodstream, a small amount of alcohol escapes through the breath and skin. The liver clears the lion's share of alcohol from the blood. In the liver, an enzyme called alcohol dehydrogenase converts pure alcohol into acetaldehyde, a very poisonous substance. Acetaldehyde is then quickly transformed by the enzyme aldehyde dehydrogenase into acetic acid (vinegar) and water.

An unusual feature of the metabolism of alcohol is that its rate is constant—approximately one-quarter to one-third of an ounce per hour. For most chemicals in the body, a certain proportion gets metabolized in a certain amount of time. In other words, the rate of metabolism is proportional to the amount present in the bloodstream. Alcohol differs from these other substances. No matter how much alcohol is in the body, less than a third of an ounce per hour metabolizes into vinegar and water. This is why heavy drinkers often wake up the next morning still drunk—they truly are! The alcohol is still working its way through the liver at the same sluggish rate.

Once in the blood alcohol pervades all bodily tissue. Being both water soluble and fat soluble, alcohol breaches the blood-brain barrier.

The exact mechanism of alcohol is unknown. Most researchers feel that alcohol, like a general anesthetic, produces some of its effects by influencing all neural communication in the brain. Alcohol targets glutamate, serotonin, and GABA transmission. Much research has focused more specifically on alcohol's influence on the GABA receptor.

GABA (gamma-amino butyric acid) is one of the brain's more common neurotransmitters. Dr. James Ballenger describes GABA as, "...the major inhibitory neurotransmitter in the CNS, with receptors located on approximately 30% of cortical and thalamic neurons."[5] Like a great symphony, the music of the brain cannot occur if all the instruments are blaring at once. The orchestration of stops and goes, activity and reduction of activity, make the complex rhythms of the brain more like music. GABA is one of the primary means of stopping or slowing various parts of the brain.

Alcohol enhances GABA's inhibitory actions. By enhancing GABA's inhibitory action, the overall state of the brain becomes increasingly 'depressed.' It may seem contradictory that alcohol enhances neural *inhibition* while producing behavioral *disinhibition*. In fact, behavioral disinhibition is the logical consequence of neural inhibition—when parts of neural matter become inhibited people feel as if they are acting more 'on impulse.' In other words, the typical means of thinking through consequences, considering scenarios, checking one's values/principles—all those things that make us good thinkers—become silent allowing the moment to flow less 'thoughtfully.' Alcohol reduces the many voices of the brain to a relative few and not necessarily those who should be speaking in public.

### Detox

A true alcoholic, one who feels an intense compulsion to drink on a daily basis, alters his body chemistry. The constant introduction of alcohol into the system has changed many of the normal metabolic pathways. Most importantly, this habit has very seriously changed brain chemistry.

Most chemical systems seek equilibrium. Like any good piece of evolutionary hardware, chemical systems adapt dynamically to their environment. If alcohol is a relatively constant part of this environment, the nervous system adapts to alcohol.

Since alcohol enhances GABA's inhibition in neural tissue, not as much overall GABA is necessary for the system to attain something like a 'normal' state. In fact, either by reducing GABA levels overall or by making more receptors for GABA (which, in effect, 'dilutes' GABA's message to the cell body), the overall state of brain chemistry becomes more excitable. Now, the alcoholic must drink alcohol to achieve something closer to a normal state. This is part of the phenomenon of tolerance. Such tolerance can lead to dependence.

If the chronic alcoholic is now barred access to alcohol, his brain goes into a highly active/excited state. The normal levels of GABA are no longer present to do their job; the brain expects its daily introduction of alcohol. Until the brain recognizes this lack of alcohol and resumes normal production of GABA, it will be in a terrible state of excitation.

The overall physical effects of this neural excitation include dangerous changes in blood pressure, physical shaking, and even DTs (*delirium tremens*). *Delirium tremens*, the most serious withdrawal symptom, is essentially a state of psychosis. One may have intense visual, auditory, and even tactile hallucinations. The detoxification state of a chronic alcoholic poses severe dangers for everyone involved.

## What is a Hangover?

An occasion known by most drinkers is the dreaded hangover. What precisely is a hangover? A hangover results from a combination of alcohol's effects, as it lingers in the body.

The most important cause of the hangover experience is a mini-withdrawal from alcohol. Because alcohol so effectively alters a number of neurotransmitter systems, when they return to life without alcohol, even after a single drinking session, they have to undergo rapid change. The change of GABA function, in particular, may be an important source of this experience. Ingesting a smaller amount of alcohol during a hangover makes this withdrawal less drastic.

The metabolism of alcohol by alcohol dehydrogenase produces a toxic substance called acetaldehyde. Small amounts of this poison get into circulation and cause damage to body tissue. No doubt, this is one source of alcohol's dreaded shadow side. As the liver ages and gets less efficient at doing its constant busywork, the protection of the body from acetaldehyde lessens.

Hangovers can also be caused by congeners—byproducts of alcohol distillation. Many chemical processes occur in the journey from cereal grains, potatoes, or grapes to alcoholic beverage. The fermentation and processing of these organic compounds into alcohol containing liquors creates more than alcohol alone. Other types of alcohols and organic compounds end up as part of the solution guzzled down by drinkers. Though these poisons are in tiny proportions, some people ingest plenty of them during a festive drinking session. Combined with a poorly functioning liver these hazardous substances harm the body. Perhaps the worst result is an inflammation of the meninges. The meninges are the durable membranes that surround the brain and preserve its shape and form. When these become inflamed, they produce a crushing pain.

Another result of too much alcohol is an imbalance of the body's electrolytes. When electrolytes (sodium, chloride, and potassium) are depleted, which occurs whenever the body processes a lot of fluid, a state of fatigue follows. The normal operations of the nervous and endocrine systems are hampered by these deficits. Combine this state of electrolyte depletion with overall dehydration and a poor physical state results—one feels tired and sore. In a lot of ways, a binge-drinking episode runs the organs through something like a marathon. This taxing of the metabolic pathways, especially if repeated often and in quick succession, brings the body into a state of exhaustion. One needs only look at an 'old drunk' to see how haggard the body becomes after processing so much poison. Like a poorly maintained automobile, it's not surprising that all sorts of things fall apart after a lifetime of hard usage.

One final disruption of an alcohol binge involves the alteration of the digestive flora and the irritation of the stomach lining. Digestion relies on the presence of millions of helpful bacteria. These bacteria assist in the breakdown of foods. Strong alcohol consumption kills off many bacteria and inflames the membranes of the digestive tract. This state makes the digestion of food quite difficult. The nutrients provided by food often pass through the digestive system unabsorbed. Until the natural proliferation of this bacteria resumes, the body has trouble with digestion. Furthermore, other less friendly bacteria, yeast, and fungi can sometimes invade the digestive system while its defenses are down.

## *Barbiturates*

Barbiturates first came into use around the turn of the twentieth century. Some of the better known barbiturates include barbital (Veronal), phenobarbital (Luminal), amobarbital (Amytal), pentobarbital (Nembutal), and secobarbital (Seconal).[6] Barbiturates are organized according to their onset time and duration of activity. With chemically synthesized depressants, physicians have, in effect, a controllable alcohol. They know how quickly the depressant effects will occur and for how long they will last. If alcohol was the only color in the rainbow before, we now possess a full spectrum of depressants. With psychoactive drugs, the knowledgeable doctor has the ability to control a number of psychological symptoms. Scientists developed a wide range of promising barbiturates and some of them, like phenobarbital, were the first effective medications for the control of epilepsy. Unfortunately, a darker side of these medications soon emerged. Many people used barbiturates as a convenient method to commit suicide and barbiturate addicts are now commonplace. When detoxifying from these substances, the body may experience symptoms tragically similar to alcohol withdrawal, including agitation and *delirium tremens*.

Barbiturates quickly changed the pace of life within mental hospitals. Reducing the activity of the brain, these depressants turned the raving mad into the placid eccentrics rendered so well in *One Flew Over the Cuckoo's Nest*. The modern conception of the mental hospital as a place where people are drugged and zombified continues to raise controversy. The heavy drugging of mentally unstable people is far from ideal. As unhappy a situation as this is, the alternative— patients whose overactive brains have inflicted upon them a hellish existence—is far inferior.

Like alcohol, barbiturates work by affecting GABA neurotransmission. Barbiturates possess receptor sites alongside GABA receptors. When barbiturates interact with these specialized receptors, they enhance GABA's effects. This leads to an overall depression of nervous system activity. In moderate levels, this depression makes a perfect antidote to too much anxiety. In higher levels, barbiturates go beyond the modulation of GABA alone and can easily impose a lethal depression of neural activity, stopping vital processes, like breathing.

Though some barbiturates are still in use and highly successful in their ability to lessen anxiety or assist with sleep, the liabilities of these drugs have made physicians increasingly wary. When they possess good alternatives, doctors usually avoid prescribing barbiturates.

## Benzodiazepines

The benzodiazepines, including the famous diazepam (Valium), debuted in the early 1960s. Chlordiazepoxide (Librium) was the first of these successful depressants. These two are still popular throughout the world. Though they can be abused, physicians generally believe benzodiazepines to be less troublesome than barbiturates.

The name of the drugs, benzodiazepines, refers to the type of molecular structure all these medications share in common. It is due to this particular structure that benzodiazepines function as depressants. Many variations of benzodiazepine molecules have been attempted. Currently, over thirty-five medications of this type are available for prescription.

Benzodiazepines are enormously popular medications. In 1996, eight of the 200 most commonly prescribed drugs were benzodiazepines. Throughout much of the 1970s diazepam (Valium), called 'Mother's Little Helper' because of its common abuse by housewives, was the top-selling medication.[7] Currently, triazolam (Halcion) and zolpidem (Ambien) are the most popular hypnotics, helping millions of insomniacs to finally sleep. Flunitrazepam (Rohypnol), known as the 'date-rape drug,' is a sedative nearly ten times stronger than diazepam (Valium).[8] The combination of Rohypnol and alcohol, if it does not kill, will often lead to an extreme state of nervous system depression. The individual, if she doesn't pass out cold, will be in a trance-like state with hazy memory function. The frightening abuse of Rohypnol led to the banning of this benzodiazepine in the U.S.

Like alcohol, the anxiety-reducing effects of benzodiazepines can help to 'take the edge off.' In contrast to alcohol, these drugs can be more easily measured and are generally easier to control. Addiction, however, is a real possibility.

## Addiction

Addiction to drugs, of any type, often relies on the basic characteristics of drug metabolism in the body. Addiction works in two major ways—through psychological dependence and physical dependence. How quickly a drug affects the brain (called the 'rush' by addicts) determines its strength of psychological addiction. Crack cocaine, heroin, and nicotine enter the bloodstream and influence the brain quite rapidly. These substances all exhibit high rates of psychological addiction.

Quick onset benzodiazepines also tend to be more abused than the slower acting drugs of this class. Diazepam (Valium) possesses this trait of quick onset and likewise tends to be the most commonly abused benzodiazepine. Chlordiazepoxide (Librium) takes a while to achieve its depressant effects and tends to be less addictive in this way.

In contrast to the psychological addiction caused by fast onset drugs, physical dependence tends to occur when a drug rapidly exits the body. A drug's half-life, or the time it takes for half of the substance to be filtered out from the bloodstream, is a useful means to measure the drug's duration in the body. When a psychoactive drug has a short half-life and leaves the body quickly, it often produces withdrawal symptoms. A chemical with a long half-life that lingers in the body and gradually loses its influence evinces far fewer withdrawal symptoms and less overall physical dependence. Exploiting this pattern, addiction experts routinely put an individual detoxifying from alcohol or another substance on a slow-acting, slow-exiting benzodiazepine. The depressant action of the benzodiazepine lessens the withdrawal symptoms caused by the addict's drug of choice. The medications keep the nervous system at a low level of arousal/anxiety. Further, the benzodiazepine's slow-acting, slow-exit properties prevent addiction. The use of these drugs makes detoxification much easier to accomplish now than in past times.

One might wonder, given the patterns of addiction in fast-onset, fast-exiting drugs, why such substances would ever be used at all. Many of the most popular benzodiazepines, like Valium, are quick onset drugs. Though the drawback of quick-onset drugs includes its possibility to cause addiction, such quick onset is also one of its most useful properties. If a panic attack is triggered—causing extreme terror, sweating, and racing of the heart—one doesn't want to wait around for a medication to work. Similarly, if one can't sleep, a drug that slowly enters the bloodstream will not suffice. The insomniac wants a quick acting medication. Furthermore, the insomniac doesn't want to spend the entire next morning in a state of grogginess because the benzodiazepine slowly leaves her system. It's much nicer waking up refreshed because the drug has fully departed. As long as we have the conflicting desires to possess quick acting medications and to avoid the possibility of addiction, we will have to weigh the costs and benefits of such drugs.

### How Do Benzopdiazepines Work?

Benzodiazepines achieve their effects through GABA enhancement.[9] The benzodiazepines seem to act more selectively on certain receptors and areas than barbiturates. This selectivity generally makes them safer to use than the barbiturates. Benzodiazepine receptor sites exist somewhere within the GABA receptor complex. Benzodiazepines make GABA much stronger; its naturally inhibitory effects are amplified. Because of their common influence on the GABA system, benzodiazepines, barbiturates, and alcohol all facilitate each other. A person who tends to become dependent on any one of these (like alcohol) might also succumb to dependence on a barbiturate or benzodiazepine.

Benzodiazepines are particularly dangerous when mixed with alcohol. It is difficult to overdose on a benzodiazepine alone. Combined with alcohol, though, benzodiazepines often produce lethal levels of depressant action.

## Stimulants

Just as people often want to reduce the difficulties of life, benumbing themselves with various depressants, other times they want an intensification of the moment. Thrill-seeking, gambling, and dramatizing are but a few of the methods that help some feel truly alive. Stimulants are the chemical method to achieve this exaltation. By speeding up many aspects of the mind and body, stimulants exert a deep change in our underlying mood and experience.

The discovery of any new stimulant quickly becomes exploited. Less than a century passed from the time cocaine was pronounced by the finest minds as a cure-all until it became despised as a devil of addiction and a destroyer of society. The really powerful stimulants, like cocaine and methamphetamine, nearly always lead to individual and social disaster but not all stimulants are so sinister. The less powerful ones, like caffeine, help to fuel the tremendous energy and mental acuity that drives our modern accomplishments. Caffeination and the industrial revolution, for instance, go hand in hand.

# *Caffeine*

Caffeine is the most popular stimulant in the world. Roughly 240 million pounds of it are consumed each year.[10] Caffeine is a xanthine molecule, a common class of molecule found in plants and animals. Three xanthines which humans savor come from the coffee plant (caffeine), the tea plant (theophylline), and the cacao plant (theobromine)—from which we make chocolate. Caffeine, theophylline, and theobromine all stimulate the central nervous system to various degrees. One might wonder why such commonly enjoyed plants have these stimulating substances. Flowering throughout the year, these tropical plants would get eaten to extinction if they didn't have any natural defenses. They use their unique stimulants as insect repellants. The caffeine buzz humans so enjoy is not so appreciated by the fly or beetle. What keeps us coming back time and again to harvest these plants keeps bugs at arm's (or stem's) length.

## *The History of Coffee*

The most popular caffeine source is coffee, a venerable plant that now grows throughout the world and provides employment to millions in the poorer countries. As Mark Pendergrast notes in his book *Uncommon Grounds*: "...coffee is the second most valuable exported legal commodity on Earth (after oil), providing the largest jolt of the world's most widely taken psychoactive drug."[11] Over 13 billion pounds of coffee are produced yearly. Brazil dominates this production, representing nearly 25% of the market followed by Colombia with about 11% of world production. America drinks loads of coffee, averaging over 10 pounds of beans per person per year. While this seems excessive, individuals in the Scandinavian countries consume almost three times that amount![12]

According to a popular legend, coffee was discovered in Ethiopia by a goatherd named Kaldi. On an afternoon foray, the herdsman noticed his animals wildly frolicking, stamping, and dancing. Mystified by this energy burst, Kaldi found them nipping off the green leaves and red berries of an unknown plant. He worried that they might be poisoned but after venting all their energy, the animals returned to a relatively calm state. The next day the goats streamlined it to the same tree and began chomping the berries once again. Kaldi decided the stuff was worth a try so he chewed some of the leaves himself and danced with his goats the rest of the afternoon. Word quickly spread about the stimulating herb and the Ethiopians spent the next few centuries perfecting the art of coffee preparation.

Ethiopia, which lies along the northeast coast of Africa, rests uneasily close to the Muslim world. Christians before Islam was even developed, the Ethiopians have remained steadfast in their traditions and faith despite the great power of their Muslim neighbors. They traded with their neighbors and even had a brief moment of strength during which they ruled Yemen. During their suzerainty of Yemen, they may have leaked their secret to the Muslims. The Arabs quickly fell in love with the Ethiopians' stimulating, non-alcoholic beverage.

The Muslims named this drink *qahwa*, the Arabic word for wine. Coffee, café, and caffeine are but a few of the English derivatives of this Arabic noun. By the tenth century, coffee was noted in Muslim medical texts. For the next few centuries, coffee gradually spread throughout the vast Muslim world and became an essential trade item.

The concept of the café came about in the fifteenth century. These hotbeds of activity served important social purposes but also had the reputation of being immoral saloons. The more reverent Muslim rulers felt threatened both by this potential immorality and the political activity that naturally results whenever people congregate in numbers. Many leaders tried to eradicate this coffee-fueled danger in the sixteenth century when the Islamic cafes had reached their acme of influence. Though they were successful in prohibiting alcohol for centuries, the Muslims could not get rid of coffee. Caffeine addicts continued in secret until coffee-loving rulers, who could not demand so much of their sometimes-loyal subjects, lifted the prohibition.

Coffee became the jealously guarded treasure of its Islamic cultivators. The riches possible in the coffee trade kept its growers extremely protective of their plants. Nevertheless, interlopers managed to break the coffee monopoly. Dutch traders smuggled out a shrub and transplanted it in Holland. From this stolen plant the Dutch began an enormous business growing coffee in Java, Sumatra, and throughout the Dutch East Indies.

Coffee had percolated into Southern Europe in the early seventeenth century but once the Dutch took over production, coffee emerged as a Pan-European drink. Its medicinal uses took hold but, as occurs with any powerful pharmaceutical, non-medicinal exploitation quickly followed. Like the Arabs before them, Europeans featured coffee as a social drink and following suit started cafes throughout the Christian world.

## Teatime

> Tea, though ridiculed by those who are naturally coarse in their nervous sensibilities … will always be the favourite beverage of the intellectual.
> —Thomas de Quincey,
> *Confessions of an English Opium-Eater* (1821)[13]

Vying with the Dutch to provide exotic East Indian goods to Europe, the English tried to supplant coffee drinking with tea drinking. Though at first they took delight in coffee, the English feared that this increasingly popular drink might threaten their India-based tea trade. As a response, the tea barons made their product plentiful and cheap.

Though not as strong as coffee, the tea plant actually possesses more caffeine by weight than the coffee plant. Much less tea plant is used to produce the drink than coffee used to produce its liquor. The caffeine content of a cup of tea is only about half of that present in a cup of coffee. Although tea possesses the strong stimulant theophylline in addition to caffeine, it possesses this substance only in small quantities.

The most interesting legend about tea's origin tells the story of Bodhidharma—the Indian monk who brought Buddhism into China about fifteen hundred years ago.[14] According to the legend, Bodhidharma became so frustrated by his tendency to fall asleep while meditating that he finally tore off his eyelids. The many renditions of Bodhidharma in Asian art feature a wide-eyed, half-mad monk. From his discarded eyelids blossomed the tea plant whose stimulating leaves have helped meditating monks stay awake forever since. It is no small thing that the Buddha is literally "the Awakened One."

Much of the stuff called tea today is not tea at all but various herbal infusions (e.g. peppermint, ginseng, chamomile). Tea, originally pronounced "tay" by the English, comes from a specific type of plant common to India and China. Many types of tea can be prepared from this one plant. The top leaf of a tea plant is harvested as the premier tea, flowering orange pekoe; the second highest leaf is called simply orange pekoe, and the third just plain-old pekoe. Once plucked from the tree these leaves are rolled and left to dry and darken through the process of oxidation. The quickly dried green leaves form the basis for the beloved Japanese green tea. More slowly dried and slightly darkened leaves are selected as Oolong tea and the fully oxidized leaves enjoyed by the English as traditional black tea.[15]

## The American Caffeine Craze

> ...the average American's simplest and commonest form of breakfast consists of coffee and beefsteak...
> —Mark Twain, *A Tramp Abroad* (1880)[16]

As British subjects, colonial Americans drank plenty of tea and some coffee as well. The Americans were not wedded to any particular drink until they were forced to take sides. The English Stamp Act of 1765, meant to increase tax revenue by the taxation of various colonial imports, caused outrage in New England. The American outcry forced the English to rescind many of the import taxes. The English decided to persist in taxing tea, though, to illustrate their right to lord it over the colonies. The Boston Tea Party of 1773, perhaps the final break between England and America, caused tea to become the very symbol of British authority. Coffee became the American beverage of choice forever after.

Americans are among the most thoroughgoing coffee consumers, drinking about 25 gallons per year on average. In addition to this, the average American downs 50 gallons of soft drinks and over seven gallons of tea.[17] Overall, the caffeine intake in this country boggles the mind.

## How Does Caffeine Work?

Like GABA, the neurotransmitter adenosine serves to inhibit activity in the nervous system and generally slows things down. Mimicking the adenosine molecule, caffeine fits into some of its receptor sites. By blocking these receptors from their intended adenosine 'keys,' caffeine prevents adenosine's effects. In this sense, caffeine stimulates the nervous system not by 'doing' something but by blocking what normally would occur.[18] The English tradition of teatime in the mid-afternoon overrides the natural siesta for which the Spanish have such a strong preference.

In addition to its effects on adenosine, caffeine raises heart rate, blood pressure, and respiration by stimulating the release of epinephrine. Most people drink coffee for precisely this effect. In large doses, though, caffeine mimics a stress-response which is not generally good for the body.

Being so important to human culture, caffeine has attracted a great deal of research. Older caffeine studies warned about health hazards ranging from cancer to birth defects. Most current research holds moderate caffeine use to be harmless, if not somewhat beneficial for those without serious health problems.[19] It is known to be a powerful diuretic and laxative. By increasing the amount of fatty acids in the blood, caffeine seems to help physical endurance. The Olympic committee takes this effect seriously enough to ban high levels of caffeine in athletic competition. Caffeine generally causes tension in skeletal muscle and relaxation in smooth muscle, which is why it serves as a laxative. It may also lead to pronounced verbosity in some users.

While many studies show caffeine to be harmless, the regular usage of large doses of caffeine can be no more healthy for an individual than the regular experience of stress. Over time the stress response significantly wears down important processes of healing in the body. It's best to enjoy caffeine in moderation.

There has been concern that the high intake of caffeine (greater than 300 mg/day) during pregnancy lowers the birth weight of the child.[20] Another study warns that heavy caffeine use during pregnancy increases the risk of sudden infant death syndrome.[21] Pregnant women would be best advised to avoid all psychoactive drugs, including caffeine.

## *Nicotine*

Approximately one billion people use nicotine, the world's most lethal drug, on a regular basis. The number of nicotine-containing cigarettes smoked every year reach into the trillions, numbers impossible to really imagine. More premature deaths can be attributed to nicotine than to all other drugs combined. The health and productivity damages related to smoking are too vast to calculate. Researchers consider nicotine dependence to be as troubling and persistent as alcohol, cocaine, and even heroin addiction.[22] In spite of nicotine's known health dangers and the many social programs designed to forestall its popularity, almost thirty percent of adult Americans use it regularly.[23] Nicotine is obtained predominately through the consumption of tobacco products (cigarettes, cigars, and chew).

Like cocaine, nicotine—in the form of tobacco—is a 'New World' substance, one that had been unknown by Europe or Asia until Columbus's voyage in 1492. Wilbert notes that when Columbus landed in San Salvador he, "...had been offered tobacco by the Indians, puzzling what to do with the shriveled leaves and wondering why such withered matter should be considered an appropriate gift for such a momentous occasion."[24]

In contrast to the neophyte Europeans, the Native Americans had been using tobacco for 8000 years or more. Tobacco took on a profane character in European culture, being used by one and all for its pleasurable effects. In South America, it had always been reserved for the sacred elite and their healing traditions. Tobacco was one of the many substances shamans used to hasten alternate states of consciousness. The shamans would take the tobacco in quick, high doses and enter a dangerous borderline between life and death (nicotine being a potent poison) for the purposes of healing others. Exhibiting the symptoms of acute nicotine intoxication, tobacco shamans assume the stealthy ways of the sacred jaguar and assimilate the diseases of the sick.[25]

A short time after the explorers introduced tobacco smoking to Europe, it became widely practiced; first for medicinal purposes and then for recreational consumption. In early times smoking was referred to as 'tobacco drinking.'

Envious of the wealth tobacco generated for the Spaniards who colonized the New World, the English prompted their own tobacco growing settlements in the seventeenth century. Jamestown, Virginia was among the successes of these British experiments. The early development of the United States centers around tobacco production and its attendant wealth.

Though we think of smoking as the main use for tobacco, in the eighteenth and nineteenth centuries most people consumed it in the form of snuff or chew. Napoleon, for instance, consumed somewhere around seven pounds of snuff per month.[26] Until the 1930s, a communal snuff box remained in the Senate for lawmakers' use, though the habit had been out of fashion for decades.

By and large, nineteenth century Americans were chewers. The majority of tobacco in those days was processed into chewing tobacco. Gallons of tobacco and spit collected in public spitoons, available everywhere. This trend in tobacco consuming behavior didn't change much until 1900. In that year, Americans purchased about 7 pounds of tobacco per person. 4 pounds of this was chewing tobacco, 1.6 pipe tobacco, and a third of a pound was in the form of snuff. Only about a pound of tobacco (per person) in 1900 was used for cigarette smoking.[27]

Cigarettes transformed a nation of chewers into a nation of smokers in the early part of the twentieth century. One of the important steps in the transition to cigarettes was an invention the industrialist James Duke (of Duke University fame) first put to use. In 1883, his cigarette-rolling machine cranked out 200 cigarettes per minute. While that seems impressive, Duke's machine pales in comparison to modern ones that roll 3600 cigarettes in a minute! This innovation in the industry caused a drop in the price of cigarettes which, until then, had to be hand-rolled. The little devils were now both cheap and plentiful.

Besides its highly addictive nature and the noxious excess of its fumes, tobacco has almost always enjoyed status as a socially acceptable drug, at least for men; women smokers only became common halfway through the twentieth century. Most cultures have sanctioned smoking for much longer than they have condemned it. Before the

1970s, it seemed that anyone of class smoked which means, of course, that everyone followed suit. The percentage of smokers peaked in the mid-1960s at 41% of the U.S. population.[28]

## Tobacco and Health

In the United States, nearly half a million people die every year from tobacco-related causes. In their survey of tobacco's health implications, Shopland and Burns credit smoking with 35% of all cancer deaths, 22% of deaths from coronary heart disease, and 15% of the strokes people suffer. About nine of the ten people that die from lung cancer are (were) smokers.[29] Thankfully, smoking has become much less popular during the last few decades. Also, there is a great deal of hope for smokers who quit. The risk of premature death goes down by half in former smokers who abstain for more than five years. Those who have given up smoking for 15 years have premature death profiles on par with the average non-smoker.[30]

A long-term deprivation of oxygen is one of the most insidious biological effects of nicotine. This occurs along two routes. First, as nicotine causes a constriction of the capillaries, the fine blood vessels, large portions of tissue are slowly suffocated. The effects of this are often visible in chronic smokers whose skin seems particularly aged and pallid because of poor circulation. Second, nicotine binds to oxygen-carrying blood cells preventing their delivery of oxygen. Overall, smokers have about ten percent less oxygen in their systems than non-smokers.

The health and productivity costs of smoking affect every living person. The former U.S. Surgeon General, C. Everett Koop characterized smoking as: "…the chief, single, avoidable cause of death in our society and the most important public health issue of our time."[31] Every year, the health costs related to smoking continue to rise. Hanson and Venturelli nicely sum up the costs of smoking in the United States:

> In 1993, smoking-attributable costs for medical care reached $50 billion. Each of the approximately 24 billion packages of cigarettes sold in 1993 amounted to $2.06 spent on medical care attributable to smoking. Of this $2.06, approximately $.89 was paid through public sources. Thus, it costs the American taxpayer $.89 for medical care expenses for each pack of cigarettes smoked by oth-

ers, regardless of whether he or she smokes![32]

In spite of its risks, people continue to smoke for two major reasons. The first reason is straightforward—nicotine is pleasurable. Paradoxically, nicotine provides the smoker both relaxation and a favorable stimulation. Few drugs possess such a contradictory character. Alcohol, the other common relaxing agent, calms at the expense of mental clarity. The smoker enjoys the dual-pleasures of nicotine because it can both relax and make one more mentally efficient.[33] This allows smoking to be enjoyed at times when alcohol could not, like during work or while driving. The second reason people smoke is because they become addicted to nicotine. Nicotine is among the most addictive drugs available of any type, legal or illicit.

### How Does Nicotine Work?

Nicotine's potent ability to addict follows from its rapid absorption in the body. When smoked, droplets of nicotine-laden tar and vapors deposit themselves in the delicate tissue of the lungs. From the lungs, nicotine enters the bloodstream in mere seconds.[34] The rapidity of absorption is closely tied with a substance's ability to create psychological dependence. Smoking allows a very quick, very controllable high—convenient for active people.

Nicotine levels also diminish rather quickly. The half-life of nicotine is only around two hours. As we discussed earlier, the rate at which a drug leaves one's system generally relates to its ability to produce physical dependence. Nicotine's strong physical dependence makes withdrawal from it an unpleasant, agitating experience.

The effects of nicotine largely result from its stimulation of acetylcholine receptors. Acetylcholine, one of the most common neurotransmitters, is widely distributed throughout the nervous system. It is the main neurotransmitter at neuromuscular junctions, those places where the nervous system connects to and controls the skeletal muscles.[35]

By mimicking the acetylcholine neurotransmitter, nicotine binds to its receptors, stimulating them, and then rests there, preventing acetylcholine from binding to its receptors. Translated into sensations: smoking first stimulates and then relaxes.

In addition to altering acetylcholine, nicotine affects levels of many other neurotransmitters. Nicotine's ability to stimulate the release of the neurotransmitter dopamine in certain brain areas may lead to its feelings of reward and its ability to addict.[36]

Nicotine also causes the release of various stress chemicals including epinephrine and norepinephrine. Controlled levels of these chemicals create a feeling of alertness and mental acuity. Chronically raised levels of stress chemicals lead to a number of pernicious health deficits.[37]

Unfortunately, nicotine's potency at these sites can also be quite toxic. In surprisingly small doses, nicotine is a life-taking poison. It forms the chemical basis for a number of successful insecticides.

## Cocaine

> Sherlock Holmes took his bottle from the corner of the mantelpiece, and his hypodermic syringe from its neat morocco case. With his long, white nervous fingers, he adjusted the delicate needle and rolled back his left shirtcuff. For some little time his eyes rested thoughtfully upon the sinewy forearm and wrist, all dotted and scarred with innumerable puncture-marks. Finally, he thrust the sharp point home, pressed down the tiny piston, and sank back into the velvet-lined armchair with a long sigh of satisfaction...
> —Arthur Conan Doyle, *The Sign of the Four*[38]

Cocaine is a stimulant, providing loads of energy, and a euphoriant that produces a sensation of pleasure. Sherlock Holmes evidently appreciated the latter effect more than the former. Cocaine has been appreciated as an important cultural staple by the peoples of South America for five thousand years.[39] Despite this beneficial influence, the last century of cocaine abuse has permanently maligned the substance. What happened in recent history to transform this once respectable stimulant into one of the most dangerous illegal drugs?

### From Coca Leaves to Coca-Cola

The coca plant, native to the western part of South America, helped to shape the pre-Columbian cultures. As Sigmund Freud notes in *On Coca*: "Legend held that Manco Capac, the divine son of the Sun, had descended in primeval times from the cliffs of Lake Titicaca, bringing...them the coca leaf, this divine plant which satiates the hungry, strengthens the weak, and causes them to forget their misfortune."[40]

By chewing the coca leaves, the Incas were able to sustain a vast empire spread over difficult terrain. The coca plant enabled the sturdy Incans to hike mountainous routes from city to city and effectively administrate a sprawling empire. The footpaths these people blazed still crisscross the Andean Mountains as an intricate web. Freud cites a report of one South American's coca-sustained endurance:

> The man in question carried out laborious excavation work for five days and nights, without sleeping more than two hours each night, and consumed nothing but coca. After the work was completed he accompanied Tschudi on a two-day ride, running alongside his mule. He gave every assurance that he would gladly perform the same work again, without eating, if he were given enough coca. The man was sixty-two years old and had never been ill.[41]

For the pre-Columbian peoples cocaine never became a serious source of trouble because in the leaf form they took it—absorbing small amounts over a period of time through their mouth lining—cocaine did not produce the quick rushes that lead to addiction.

Though the Spanish colonials understood the power of the coca plant and used it to increase the productivity of their Indian slaves, it did not achieve any popularity in European culture until organic chemistry began to flourish in the middle of the nineteenth century. When cocaine was isolated from the coca plant in 1855 scientists quickly recognized the potency of the stimulant. Soon after, Carl Koller, a colleague of Sigmund Freud's, discovered the remarkable ability of cocaine to produce local anesthesia.[42] The procaine (Novocain™) dentists make such wide use of is closely related to the cocaine molecule.

One of the earliest investigators, turned advocate, of cocaine was the young Viennese doctor, Sigmund Freud. Freud, a desperately high achiever, suffered from periodic depressions. A less ambitious man might have overlooked these episodes and accepted such changes in mood and energy as natural cycles. But Freud preferred to be active all the time and detested the slack in mood and energy that his depressions brought with them. He soon found that cocaine obliterated such moments and kept him in top form all the time. As he wrote to his betrothed, Martha Bernays, at the time:

> Woe to you my princess when I come. I will kiss you quite red and feed you till you are plump. And if you are forward, you shall see who is the stronger, a gentle little girl who doesn't eat enough or a big wild man with cocaine in his body.[43]

Freud became so excited by the effects of cocaine that he sought to popularize the substance to a larger audience in a "song of praise."[44] He began distributing the drug to his closest friends and family without reservation. As Freud's biographer, Ernest Jones, quips: "…looked at from the vantage point of our present knowledge, he was rapidly becoming a public menace."[45]

One of his earliest writings did not address the unconscious, the Oedipal complex, or psychoanalysis; Freud's first major paper, *On Coca*, appeared in 1884 and makes him a founding father of psychopharmacology.[46] Here he maps out the future of cocaine usage:

> The main use of coca will undoubtedly remain that which the Indians have made of it for centuries: it is of value in all cases where the primary aim is to increase the physical capacity of the body for a given short period of time and to hold strength in reserve to meet further demands—especially when outward circumstances exclude the possibility of obtaining the rest and nourishment normally necessary for great exertion. Such situations arise in wartime, on journeys, during mountain climbing and other expeditions… its widespread utilization is hindered at present only by its high cost.[47]

As history has proven, these hopeful predictions did not yield good fruits. Before long, Freud came to understand cocaine's potential for abuse. One of his closest friends, Ernst von Fleischl-Marxow, in treating a chronic pain had become addicted to morphine, the common drug of abuse at that time. Freud believed cocaine would free Fleischl from his morphine addiction. Freud's genius proved correct—Fleischl gave up morphine, only now he had become a hopeless cocaine addict. Fleischl's addiction reached the summit of cocaine psychosis, a horrid insanity caused by large doses of the drug. By his own hand, Freud came to see the disastrous effects of cocaine addiction on someone very dear to him.[48]

Cocaine, in various extracts and tinctures, had reached a wide audience and attracted a good following by the turn of the twentieth century. In a short amount of time, though, the harmful effects of pure cocaine—including addiction, depression, and psychosis—forced the once-duped medical community to turn on this wonder drug.

In 1886, before the medical community had consolidated its opinions, an enterprising pharmacist and former Confederate Lieutenant came up with a fountain drink to lift peoples' spirits and energy levels. By combining a number of ingredients (whose exact formula is still a closely guarded secret), including coca leaf extract and kola nut extract, John Pemberton created Coca-Cola. Even in its original preparation Coca-Cola did not contain very much cocaine but the turn of public sentiment against cocaine forced the Coca-Cola company to completely remove this devilish little ingredient in 1903. Extracts of the cocaine-free coca leaf remain part of the secret flavoring to this day.[49]

In recent times, cocaine has lost any claim to innocence. Everyone seems to recognize this substance for the destruction it wields rather than the pleasure it brings. The trafficking of cocaine by enormously powerful drug rings is responsible for an abyss of suffering and depravity. To get an idea just how much cocaine is trafficked consider that, in 1998, the U.S. Drug Enforcement Agency seized 264,000 pounds of the drug.[50] This amount is but a tiny fraction of the cocaine that actually made it to the United States in that year. The abuse of cocaine in various forms, including 'crack' cocaine, continues to steal opportunity and hope from countless junkies.

## *Amphetamine*

Like so many of the drugs whose history we have surveyed, amphetamine began as a medically sanctioned drug. Its early uses as an asthmatic aid and a hunger suppressant wooed many doctors in its favor. Later, especially once amphetamine made the change into methamphetamine, the devastating repercussions of this drug turned public sentiment against it.

Thrill seekers are quite familiar with the 'adrenaline rush' experienced when the body registers risk. As an important hormone, epinephrine (a.k.a. adrenaline) regulates many processes in the body. The adrenal gland secretes epinephrine when an individual feels stress or senses danger. The 'fight or flight' syndrome—ushered in by a sudden rise in heartbeat, respiration, and nervous energy—is a consequence of its release. The intense state of mind and body produced by epinephrine flooding mobilizes the energy and attention of an animal so that it can effectively escape danger.

Before the 1920s, epinephrine was one of the few effective treatments for asthma. Epinephrine had to be administered either through inhalation or by injection into the blood; it does not readily enter one's system through digestion. In an effort to find an asthmatic drug that could be taken as a pill, the pharmacologist K.K. Chen began looking into a traditional Chinese treatment for the breathing disorder. Herbalists had long appreciated the herb, *ma huang* (*Ephedra vulgaris*), for its ability to increase energy and open breathing passages. Chen and colleagues isolated the active ingredient of *ma huang* and named it ephedrine. Its quick action opened the airways and allowed free breathing. Unfortunately, supplies of *ma huang* were limited and the drug became costly.[51] In 1927, chemist Gordon Alles synthesized a molecule that possessed many of the properties of ephedrine; he named it amphetamine, later to be marketed as Benzedrine.[52]

Doctors began prescribing amphetamine for asthmatics. One noted side effect was a decrease in appetite. Soon after this discovery doctors prescribed amphetamine as a dietary aid as well. By the late 1930s college students were routinely using the over the counter medication to perform cram study sessions.[53]

Since the benefits of amphetamine included bursts of energy and an ability to override hunger and fatigue, the drug found widespread usage in wartime just a few years later. Since the isolation of cocaine in the nineteenth century, the idea of utilizing stimulants to increase military prowess had come into practice.[54] In World War II, the German, Japanese, and British militaries provided amphetamine to their soldiers. The American military experimented with amphetamine but could not decide on its safety. As a result, American GIs got the drug from their British cohorts.

The Japanese usage of amphetamine was particularly acute. Not only did the military exploit the substance, civilians were encouraged to use it as an aid to increase efficiency in their wartime productions. After the war, there was such a stockpile of amphetamine that it was sold cheaply. Methamphetamine, a more potent type of stimulant, became especially popular with the Japanese. A wake of drug abuse and addiction followed in Japan after the depressing cataclysm of Hiroshima and Nagasaki.[55]

In America, amphetamine abuse did not reach worrisome levels until the 1960s and 1970s. Eventually, once the use of 'speed' (another name for amphetamine) had gotten out of hand the FDA put limits on the amount of amphetamine that pharmaceutical companies could manufacture. The drug trade in amphetamine became increasingly expensive and the ingredients of speed dubious. The speed problem went away for a while.

One of the unforeseen results of limited amphetamine availability was the illegal manufacture of speed-like substances. Hack chemists used a few cheap ingredients and came up with 'crank,' another name for methamphetamine. Methamphetamine had already been invented by the medical establishment but was in limited use for emergency situations, its existence was not widely known. Once backyard laboratories began producing crank, the public got a taste for it.

Methamphetamine is one of the most troublesome contemporary drugs. Its quick onset and inducement of euphoria make it one of the most addictive drugs available. Because it can be produced by relatively unsophisticated chemists from very cheap ingredients, the supply of it is great. One of methamphetamine's more worrisome aspects is its ability to cause psychosis and paranoia. In combination with a burst of energy, these states of mind lead to uncommon violence.

### How Do Cocaine and Amphetamine Work?

The effects of these drugs occur because of their influence on dopamine and norepinephrine. Amphetamine creates a sense of pleasure and energy primarily by increasing the release dopamine and, to a lesser extent, norepinephrine. Additionally, amphetamine prevents the reuptake of these neurotransmitters.[56] The net result is much higher levels of both chemicals. Cocaine functions by blocking the reuptake of dopamine. Because of this blockade, levels of dopamine rise in the synapses of the limbic system.[57]

Dopamine, a common neurotransmitter, is involved with the way we register pleasure and helps to balance our state of mind. When dopamine levels are unusually high, as is the case both in schizophrenia and in chronic abusers of these two drugs, a state of psychosis ensues. In fact, the worst drug-induced psychoses occur because of stimulants. A heavy abuser of cocaine or methamphetamine may experience the delusions characteristic of paranoid schizophrenia. As far as the brain is concerned, there is no significant difference between the dopamine levels of a schizophrenic and those of a stimulant junkie.

# Opiates

The opiates—raw opium, morphine, codeine, heroin, and other similar substances—are prized for their ability to lull difficulties away, like an untroubled sleep. As a class, they are sometimes called narcotics (from Greek *narkoun*, "to benumb").[58] The effects produced by opiates include analgesia (prevention of pain), pleasant repose, and deep euphoria. Opium has the ability to abolish the cares and sorrows of the world—a nice chemical alternative for sensitive types. Unfortunately, the serenity opium provides is a temporary and misleading one. When the reality of the world comes in again, at the end of the narcotic dream, it seems more tempestuous than ever before. Sadly, opiate addicts get lured into a terrible cycle whose calms are interspersed in a larger pattern of storms.

## Opium

All natural opiate derivatives come from a single source, the poppy plant (*Papaver somniferum*). People have long appreciated the milky white sap of the poppy for its miraculous abilities to annul pain and induce pleasure. We call this sap opium. Originally grown in the Middle East, the famed abilities of the poppy plant caused its cultivation to spread far and wide. Most opium now comes from Asia.

Like our most popular drugs, this one has been with us since society began. Six thousand-year-old cuneiform tablets from ancient Sumeria speak of opium's pleasures.[59] In the *Odyssey* (c. 800 B.C.E.), Homer recounts, with his characteristic taste for maulings and gore, an episode in which Helen uses an unnamed opiate:

> ...now it entered into Helen's mind to drop into the wine that they were drinking an anodyne, mild magic of forgetfulness. Whoever drank this mixture in the wine bowl would be incapable of tears that day—though he should lose mother and father both, or see, with his own eyes, a son or brother mauled by weapons of bronze at his own gate. The opiate of Zeus's daughter bore this canny power. It had been supplied her by Polydamna... in Egypt...[60]

There is little doubt that this Egyptian-born herb is opium. Coming from this civilized and ancient culture, opium's usage probably stretches far back into Egyptian history as well.

Galen (c. 129-200 C.E.), the most famous physician of ancient Rome, and his Muslim counterpart, Avicenna (980-1037 C.E.), recommended opium for many health conditions.[61] Its reliability in producing apparent changes in mind and body made opium, in its various preparations, one of the leading pharmaceuticals before the twentieth century.

The Islamic culture utilized opium extensively, as it was a plant native to the Middle East. Through their active trading, it is likely that opium was introduced to the Chinese by Muslims. By the year 1000 C.E., opium had been noted in Chinese medical writings. The smoking of opium, which allowed a more rapid delivery and absorption than oral ingestion, became quite a public nuisance in eighteenth century China. The Chinese government outlawed it in 1729. The law of supply and demand took effect and the British began supplying India-grown opium to the Chinese at a huge profit. They used these profits to buy tea and other Chinese goods.

Since opium was one of the few things the Chinese desired from the British, and given its high profit, the British focused more and more on this narcotic sap. Officials of the Chinese Empire did not appreciate the subversion of their laws. In 1839, things came to a head and two successive Opium Wars between China and England followed. With their superior navy, the British eventually won both conflicts. The Treaty of Nanking provided the British with a base for their trading activities, the island of Hong Kong. The British-Chinese opium trade did not fully cease until the beginning of the twentieth century.

The United States was relatively free from opiates until the 1850s. The construction of the American transcontinental railroad necessitated a huge supply of cheap laborers. The Irish and Chinese filled this void. The influx of Chinese on the West Coast brought with them the pleasures of opium smoking. Opium dens were set up throughout the boomtowns of the Old West to meet the demand of Chinese laborers, but cowboys and outlaws alike took to the habit. Though enjoyed by the few, the serenity of the opium dens couldn't properly compete with the raucous fervor of the saloons.[62]

## Morphine

In the early nineteenth century, as the science of chemistry was being refined, chemists began searching for the active component in opium. Friedrich Sertürner succeeded and named his discovery morphine after *Morpheus*, the Roman god of dreams. Morphine composes about ten percent of raw opium. By weight, then, morphine is about ten times as strong as opium. Doctors were duly impressed with morphine's analgesic properties. To this day, it is the most potent painkiller available.

Opium had already been used in patent medicines for much of the nineteenth century. After its refinement, the 'miracle cures' sold by unscrupulous mountebanks contained large amounts of morphine. These medicines were sold as much for recreational use as for physical ailments. At a time when the progress of medicine had only just begun, the availability of morphine containing 'snake oils' provided one of the few sure solutions to treat chronic pains.

With the invention of the hypodermic syringe in 1853, society possessed the ultimate drug and means of delivery for intractable pain.[63] The timing could not have been more favorable; America's bloodiest conflict, the Civil War, erupted soon thereafter.

During the Civil War morphine achieved wide usage and also led to this country's first real problem with addiction. After the war, addiction to morphine was so prevalent among veterans that it was known simply as "the soldier's disease." Scientists, so recently wooed by this effective drug, now sobered to its dangerous potential. Hoping they could produce a morphine-like analgesic free of its addictive properties, chemists began to tinker with the morphine molecule.

## Heroin

By cobbling two acetyl groups onto the morphine molecule chemists created a more powerful opium derivative called diacetylmorphine. This apparently minor change allowed the morphine to readily cross the blood-brain barrier. In 1898, Bayer Laboratories were the first to market diacetylmorphine, calling it Heroin. Heroin and aspirin were Bayer's first great successes.

Once inside the brain morphine and heroin are identical; heroin merely allows more of the molecule to enter the central nervous system. When they discovered heroin, scientists thought they had found the perfect, non-addicting analgesic. These researchers were far too optimistic—like Dr. Frankenstein before them, instead of 'improving' on nature they had fashioned a monster.

Somewhere around a million heroin abusers live in the United States alone. Heroin addiction enjoys status as the most serious drug problem ever known. Rightly so, for this is a powerfully addictive, natural substance further engineered to possess an addictive capacity artificial and unknown in the realm of nature. The abuser will bypass any amount of hunger or fear to secure the next 'fix.' With brave resolve, addicts of alcohol and even the surpassingly addictive nicotine can overcome their abuse. In contrast, heroin transforms even the strongest willed into cringing slaves who achieve their liberation only with superhuman courage and tremendous support. Without these singular efforts, the heroin addict is freed only by death.

Odysseus's encounter with the Sirens seems the exact metaphor for heroin's dual nature:

> ...crying beauty to bewitch men coasting by;
> woe to the innocent who hears that sound!
> He will not see his lady nor his children

in joy, crowding about him, home from sea;
the Sirens will sing his mind away
on their sweet meadow lolling. There are bones
of dead men rotting in a pile beside them
and flayed skins shrivel around the spot.[64]

The potency of the drug and its attunement to brain metabolism leads to a rare fate: the commingling of the highest pleasure and the most certain doom. To wean the addict from this enchantress is a near impossible task; like the sirens, the tantalizing song of this substance cannot be heard without the gravest danger.

The heroin on the streets today is far purer than in times past. While it is good that modern heroin contains less impurities and other ingredients, it is tragically more addictive than older supplies. The use of injectable heroin has many other dangers besides addiction alone. The spread of AIDS and hepatitis is widespread among this needle-sharing population. Moderns often forget that any breach of the body's largest, most protective organ—the skin—carries serious risk. Poor syringe technique commonly leads to the injection of bacteria, fungi, and other disease-causing organisms directly into the blood. Additionally, damage to the tissue at the injection site can lead to vein collapse. These complications are just the more colorful ones—malnutrition and constipation are chronic for heroin addicts as well.

## How Do Opiates Work?

I was necessarily ignorant of the whole art and mystery of opium-taking... But I took it:—and in an hour, oh! Heavens! What a revulsion! What an upheaving, from its lowest depths, of the inner spirit! What an apocalypse of the world within me! That my pains had vanished, was now a trifle in my eyes:— this negative effect was swallowed up in the immensity of those positive effects which had opened before me—in the abyss of divine enjoyment thus suddenly revealed. Here was a panacea... for all human woes: here was the secret of happiness, about which philosophers had disputed for so many ages, at once discovered: happiness might now be bought for a penny, and carried in the waistcoat pocket: portable ecstasies might be

corked up in a pint bottle: and peace of mind could be sent
down in gallons by the mail coach.
—Thomas de Quincey,
*Confessions of an English Opium Eater* (1821)[65]

In the last few decades, neurobiologists have uncovered many
of the mechanisms behind pleasure. Alcohol, nicotine, cocaine,
amphetamine, and opiates cause pleasure by exciting the brain's
'reward system.'[66] The opiates do this with more efficiency than any
other drug.

What is the reward system? It is the primary way that we feel
pleasure of any type. Everything that gives us satisfaction—a good
meal, a funny joke, sex—all somehow influence this one underlying
system. Because of this, a heroin addict can forego food, pride, and
any other gratification because he chemically induces a sensation
just as fulfilling as any of these things.

As we saw in the discussion of cocaine and amphetamine, raising the level of the neurotransmitter dopamine appears essential to
the sense of pleasure.

One of the major sources of dopamine in the brain, the ventral
tegmental area (VTA), projects two tracts of dopamine-carrying cells
throughout the limbic system and the frontal cortex of the brain.
These two tracts are called the mesolimbic and mesocortical pathways. Researchers have learned that electrical stimulation of the ventral tegmental area, the source of these two pathways, creates an
intensely rewarding sensation. Electrical stimulation releases
dopamine into the mesolimbic and mesocortical projections. By one
means or another, the ability of drugs to increase the level of
dopamine flowing in these pathways creates pleasure and controls
motivation.[67]

To use the terminology MacLean set forth in his 'triune model'
of the human brain, these pathways interlink the limbic system, the
seat of appetites and emotions common to all mammals, and the
neocortex, wherein lie the uniquely human mental attributes.
Somewhere between the ventral tegmental area and its farthest nodes
lies quintessential humanity. Through these same tiny stretches of
matter Mother Theresa found motivation to help the poor of Calcutta
and become the very ideal of the saint while Thomas de Quincey

discovered, "...the secret of happiness, about which philosophers had disputed for so many ages..." Of course, the dopamine projections that suffuse the limbic system and the frontal cortex are not the only structures that link these two zones but in creating the reward system they produce the biological substrate for pleasure. Without pleasure, without the normal functioning of these brain mechanisms, one can experience neither happiness nor motivation.

Before the route of the reward system was well understood, scientists made use of a good inference to discover a new class of chemicals in the brain. While the actions of opiates were still a mystery, researchers asked the overarching question behind their pleasure-inducing ability: "Why, in God's name, do we possess morphine receptors in our brains?" It seemed the height of strangeness that animals received so much reward by ingesting the syrup of an obscure Middle Eastern plant. This question led scientists to infer the presence of endogenous ("produced-within") opiates in the brain. In other words, there is a natural opiate-like mechanism for gratification; it is only a chance occurrence that derivatives of the poppy plant mimic the brain's own pleasure-creating molecules.

In 1973, Solomon Snyder, Candace Pert, and colleagues furthered this idea by discovering the first receptor sites for opiate molecules, thus assuring the presence of these drugs in the brain.[68] By stimulating these receptors, the consumed opiates trick the body into a feeling of pleasure and a state of analgesia. In general, opiates raise dopamine levels and stimulate the brain's endogenous pleasure chemicals.[69] These two actions are deeply interconnected but not entirely understood.

In 1975, Scottish researchers isolated the first natural opiates produced within the brain and named them enkephalins. This name did not take as well as 'endorphins' (from a contraction of endogenous and morphine). The presence of natural opiates lie behind our pleasures, through the stimulation of the reward system, and help in analgesia—the tolerance of pain. Many people have received injury during states of crisis that they did not register until the crisis passed. Endorphins provide us this ability to override pain when we must continue to act. Sadly, medical researchers are still in the dark about the exquisite details of this system, so millions with chronic pain continue to suffer.

The final source of indulgence for opiate abusers comes not from the pharmacological properties of the drugs themselves but from the pleasures produced by association, from the ceremony of administering these substances. The ritual of preparing the morphine or heroin for injection—tying the arm with a tourniquet, examining the dappled flesh for a healthy vein, and finally plunging the syringe like a harpoon into one's body—produces an engrossing bliss. As grisly as it all sounds, these steps become so closely allied with the opiate rush that, by association, they are conditioned to delight.[70] The conditioned responses we associate with our sources of gratification, those subtle and particular cues we register as part and parcel of our joy, identify us with Pavlov's dogs who learned to salivate upon hearing the chiming of a bell.

## *In Search of Pleasure*

Is pleasure simply the brute feeling of something nice: sugar on the tongue? Does the dopamine-driven reward system explain— *or explain away*—our feelings of delight? If pleasure were so simple a thing as this, in other words, were human beings simply reactive animals blind to the nuances of mind, then the zenith of the culinary arts would have been reached with the refinement of sucrose, table sugar. In fact, as we well know, pleasure exceeds our description of it—be that description chemical or poetic. In defining the sense of pleasure, the biologist, in whose world the discussion of receptors and pathways seems a caricature of humanity, should heed cues from philosophy and psychology. Here we must pause for a moment to juxtapose the neurobiology of reward with the philosophy of pleasure in an effort to understand the truth behind pleasure and the good life.

The good life cannot be separated from pleasure. Pleasure is inherent to any form of happiness. But, if happiness is to be defined as the attainment of pleasure then why should we not deem opiates a social mainstay rather than an illicit narcotic? We must recognize the chronic abuse of the opiates not simply as the foibles of those with inconstant character but as testaments to a way of life deeply appreciated by many who have sampled it. Aldous Huxley hit upon this question and explored a possible future for human society in his novel *Brave New World*. In that world, a rational society had organized itself around a blissful drug—soma. For all that future society's enlightenment, there existed a noteworthy lack of depth. A life of simple pleasures creates a simple mind.

The experience of pleasure imparted by opiates bypasses the 'person' altogether. The pleasures of the good life must be integrative, binding together disparate qualities and energies of the person so that the pleasure attained thereby enhances one's psychic unity, enlarging and making more sophisticated the sense of self. In contrast, unrefined pleasures—like the opiates—disintegrate the person. The individual simply need not be present; none of the personal traits, thoughts, or characteristics are necessary for the drug-induced experience of pleasure. One might immediately proffer sex to be the same but, in fact, anyone of sensitive constitution knows that the abilities of a lover can be great or minimal, depending on their creativity and sensitivity. Why should this be so if the height of the act is always the same physiological mechanism? Pleasures, in short, are mediated by the sum total of the person's constitution.

The finest modern study of pleasure and its mysteries has been undertaken by Mihaly Czikszentmihalyi who redefined the word *flow*. Flow is an experience (especially common to mountain climbers, chess wizards, and Zen masters alike) that harnesses all of a person's unique abilities and concentration. To some extent, everyone knows what flow is for the peak moments of one's life are almost always such experiences. Flow is a complete identification with a challenging and invigorating process that concentrates the person's skills and engenders rapt attention. Activities that impart the experience of flow must be challenging, but not too challenging—lest they inspire frustration rather than mastery. The happy person always has a hobby or set of activities that are rich sources of these optimal experiences.

Flow harmonizes a person's consciousness and brings it to a higher order. As Czikszentmihalyi writes:

> The optimal state of inner experience is one in which there is *order in consciousness*. This happens when psychic energy—or attention—is invested in realistic goals, and when skills match the opportunities for action. The pursuit of a goal brings order in awareness because a person must concentrate attention on the task at hand and momentarily forget everything else. These periods of strug-

gling to overcome challenges are what people find to be the most enjoyable times of their lives.[71]

The difference then between a true pleasure and a raw one is that a true pleasure enhances the person's psychological integration while a raw pleasure bypasses the personality stimulating the reward system directly. Even with this qualification, though, the raw pleasure is not 'bad' or 'wrong.' Of itself, no pleasure carries any moral or destructive tenor. The raw pleasures do tend to have consequences which make them far less preferable than states of flow. One commonly sees the raw pleasures light the fuse of self-destruction and psychological disintegration by creating addiction and dissociation.

The notion that pleasures can be broken down into a range of types reaches back to that land of ideas—ancient Greece. The Greek philosopher Epicurus distinguished between unstable pleasures and stable ones. Because of their short duration and dependence on others, drugs, sex, and the like would fall under Epicurus's distinction of unstable pleasures. Epicurus recommended an extremely simple way of life that involved the integration of stable pleasures. Using more modern terms, he taught a life of nearly constant flow—being totally invested in one's activities, thoughts, and work. Czikszentmihalyi proffers the same sort of life and sees a solution to the psychological unhappiness of our time through the expansion of the principles of flow into the recreations and duties of everyday life.

A further source of the refinement of pleasure is in their delay. Kierkegaard, an expert on the subtleties of rumination, exhibits this understanding of pleasure in *Either/Or* where he wrote: "Most men rush after pleasure so fast that they rush right past it."[72] In Kierkegaard's same age—that juncture between the Classical period, with its tendency to elaborate upon a theme and draw things out into the most sophisticated realms, and the self-indulgent Romantic period, with its insistence on the raw and the passionate—Jane Austen lighted upon such distinctions about pleasure. In *Emma*, Austen attests to the growing division between those who cultivate their appreciation of pleasure, admiring and expanding its subtleties, and the brutes who came to define pleasure in the lowest common vernacular when she writes: "One half of the world cannot understand the pleasures of the other."[73]

The poetics of desire always highlights upon themes of waiting and longing as much as finding and having. How many young children have waited by their mailboxes for agonizing weeks until some mail-order doodad finally arrived? My comic books days provided many such trials. The period of waiting for the gizmo always generates far more pleasure than the thing itself once it finally arrives and loses its luster. By delaying gratification, the human mind encompasses the source of pleasure—surveying its possibilities, imagining its fine distinctions—and generally teases itself to the heights of agony and ecstasy. Of all creatures, only humans can so postpone an object of desire, meditating upon it as a mantra, sometimes for many years. Surely, the Tantric Buddhists had this finer, higher pleasure in mind when they developed their elaborate sexual practices using them as methods to access the divine.

The delay of gratification evokes such a higher pleasure because it helps to create, exercise, and define the self. At the consummation of pleasure, the self ceases to be—only pleasure exists. At this stage, one might equally be a genius, a fool, or a mouse—all feel the same fulfillment. Before this, though, as one searches, imagines, and longs for pleasure, the distinctive traits and sensations of the individual are flushed. Somewhere between the individual and her pleasure, on the unique pathway of desire, lies true happiness. For happiness to be met, one's objects of desire must be challenging and complex enough to require the total unfolding of one's abilities and efforts without creating a despair born from impossibility. It is here that the savant finds meaning and enjoys happiness for he is tautly stretched between the individual and collective life. For this refined type of human being the desired object—be it truth, love, or heroin—is utterly superfluous. Pleasure is the journey, not the destination.

# Hallucinogens/Entheogens

If the doors of perception were cleansed, everything would
appear to man as it is, infinite.
  —William Blake, *The Marriage of Heaven and Hell*[74]

Most of us have the good fortune to possess a few sacred rec-
ollections— memories of some passing moments upon a mountain,
in a forest, or fishing from a giant lake. Whatever the particular character of our memory, these times loom large in consciousness for in
these brief pauses we felt God. Or so we thought. The experience,
stripped of theology or doctrine, is ineffable—we know merely that
colors shone in unearthly hues and that the vivid contrast around,
above, and beneath took on a razor sharp sheen. Most important of
all is the feeling—that exceptionally rare sensation—that we are not
separated from our surroundings, not caught up in our typical turmoil, but simply immersed into the cosmos at large. Then we wish
well to all that is. At last, we feel—*we know*—we are at home. These
intriguing moments are not so different from those induced by the
hallucinogens.

## Set and Setting

In speaking of these drugs, an important concession must be
made; they are neither faultlessly mystical nor predictably madden-
ing. Hallucinogens do very different things for different people. This
demands explanation. If we're dealing with chemicals here—which
we are—then shouldn't they be rather predictable? In some ways yes;
in others, no. For instance, aspirin does pretty much the same thing
most of the time to most of the people who take it. After all, the pre-
dictability of many drugs is why they're useful at all. If they were
unpredictable they wouldn't be therapeutically safe.

  The truth is that even our most tried and true drugs are not
entirely predictable. Because of an individual's unique biochemistry
at the time they use a drug, the drug may work 'normally' or it may
produce any number of adverse reactions. All too often, people suffering side effects are treated by their doctors off-handedly, for the doctor, just like the patient, expects the drug to be reliably safe. When a

drug is not predictable, for doctor and patient alike, some disbelief arises; the logic runs: "a drug is good, if something bad occurs, it can't be the drug." So, even with many of our common pharmaceuticals side effects and unexpected results occur some percentage of the time.

The hallucinogens, by affecting brain chemistry, are even more prone to unpredictability than other pharmaceuticals and psychotropics. The chemistry of the brain changes more often and in more intricate ways than any other organ of the body. We recognize this, among other ways, by changes in consciousness. At times we're in deep sleep, at other times aroused, sad, anxious, or angry. Within a single day we may experience dozens of chemical 'shifts' in our brain causing various changes in mood and the perception of events around us.

How do these changes occur? To simplify the matter, we are dealing with two variables: set and setting. Dr. Andrew Weil sums it up concisely: "Set is a person's expectations of what a drug will do to him, considered in the context of his whole personality. Setting is the environment, both physical and social, in which a drug is taken."[75] The brain's chemistry is more intricately linked to the environment than most other organs. The purpose of the nervous system is to monitor and react to the environment. By constantly monitoring and reacting to the environment, the nervous system attempts to keep the organism alive. The speed with which a person will tug his hand away from a hot surface reflects the dazzling electro-chemistry at work in the human animal. The downside of this adaptation is a certain amount of instability. At times, we definitely 'lose control.' Some environmental factor—a rude remark, a driving offense, a child's tantrum—sets us off and we react in spite of our best intentions and values. We also know that some people are more prone to lose control than others. This would be considered their 'set.' They are generally anxious, angry, unpredictable people. Others we know to be 'rock solid;' these people are rather predictable and seem quite 'stable.' The 'setting' would be the event and its context. Road rage is a good example. Usually no single driving offense sets a person off. The combination of frustrating traffic, hunger, and the incident together may turn even the meek into the ferocious—such is the setting.

Hallucinogens cause different reactions in people because of one's set and setting. A mildly psychotic person amid a crowd of imposing strangers in a foreign country who already has many anxieties about drugs should not use a hallucinogen, bad results are sure to follow. On the other hand, a stable person, who does not easily succumb to anxiety, surrounded by trusted friends camping in a beautiful mountain area (but not too far from a hospital) might comfortably use a hallucinogen for purposes of "mind expansion." If such a person respects the power and has an intimation of the effects of hallucinogens, the experience will likely be an adventurous one.

## Accessing the Divine Within

The term—hallucinogen—has stuck but most experts in the field think it an unfortunate misnomer. Only a few of these substances, in high quantities, cause visual or auditory hallucinations. In their common dosages, hallucinogens cause vivid imagery when the eyes are closed but scarcely import images into normal vision. Drugs of other classes have about the same probability of creating eye-open hallucinations. An addict coming off of depressants may experience hallucinations and high dosages of stimulants are likely to evoke nightmarish visuals.

What is a hallucination anyway? Its very definition suggests mistaken perception—but are religious experiences mistakes of consciousness? Would one be so bold to claim this in the case of Moses or Muhammad? Some critics continue to argue that the hallucinogens cause absurd mistakes in perception but many more hold these substances to be among the most sacred tools humans possess—keys for accessing the divine.

Some researchers prefer the term *entheogen* ("generating the divine within") when discussing many of the substances outlined below. This august sounding phrase entitles these drugs a bit more respect than they have previously received. Why accord these drugs such respect? As we'll discuss, the history of many of these substances is not one of abuse and recreation, as we have seen in our own recent times. The history of entheogens finds them as essential sacraments in a variety of ancient religious traditions. In discussing these substances, we are handling artifacts akin to crucifixes and idols—though far more powerful in the experience they typically impart. To decry these items as illicit, mind-bending drugs is to mistake their cultural importance and impose a modern stereotype upon ancient practices. Furthermore, the near universality of entheogen usage suggests something remarkable about man's essential nature. In his book, *The Natural Mind*, Dr. Weil likens man's pursuit of these substances to a basic instinct: "...the desire to alter consciousness periodically is an innate, normal drive analogous to hunger or the sexual drive."[76]

Entheogens definitely affect perception. In general, the alterations in perception lead to a striking intensification of stimuli: colors are brighter, sounds more distinct and more subtly experienced, smell and taste heightened, and touch sensitized to the finest textures. Sometimes, again in a higher range of dosage, an effect called synesthesia occurs. Synesthesia is the jumbling of perception: visual things may be heard, musical things seen, and all of them 'felt.' In short, the entheogens amplify the senses—both the senses that stream through one's eyes and ears and the perception of self, emotion, and mood.

In higher dosages, while experiencing 'true' hallucinations or synesthesia, the effects of these substances can be unsettling. They take the individual so far out of the normal routine of mental activity that the person may 'freak out.' While in this bizarre state, the person may feel she is permanently deranged or insane. A state of intense anxiety follows, the increase in heartbeat or sweating may feel a thousand times more intense, like nothing the person has ever experienced. The person on a bad trip thinks he will die or go insane. In sum, though these drugs are part of the typical array of recreational substances, they should not be recklessly exploited.

While the escapism provided by depressants or stimulants alters one's typical mental activity, the entheogens create another identity altogether. In some cultures, extended psychoactive 'trips' formed part of the initiation from childhood to adulthood. The prolonged break from 'normal' reality to an alternate one marked the juncture to adulthood and helped revamp one's identity to take on new roles.

The entheogen-induced state of derangement is not for the fainthearted. These substances shake one's core assumptions about the world. The psychic disintegration, which only in the very rarest cases lasts beyond the normal course of the drug's action in the body, may shatter the icon of that most holy of holies—the stable sense of self—and leave an uncertain relativity in its place. This is reflected in the 1960s maxim that after an LSD experience the initiated is never the same again. The entheogenic experience is one only to be attempted by the most mature, grounded, and knowledgeable few—those already awake to life's more disturbing truths. These drugs lead to mental states neither common nor easy to integrate—these drugs create a mystical experience.

## Materia Mystica

Some may scoff: how can drugs create a truly mystical experience? In his study, *Cleansing the Doors of Perception: The Religious Significance of Entheogenic Plants and Chemicals*, Huston Smith voices a similar wonder and disbelief in recollecting his own drug-induced religious experience: "How could what felt like an epochal change in my life have been crowded into a few hours and occasioned by a chemical?"[77] Religious leaders in ancient times voiced no such protest. The animistic worldview held that all animals, plants, and objects possessed a 'spirituality.' With this framework in place, the effects of a psychoactive plant would be recognized as an assimilation of its spiritual power. In this understanding, nothing 'material' was affecting any other material thing (i.e. chemicals affecting the brain). In the animist's world, the spirit of the plant moved man's own spirit. We moderns have so much trouble accepting psychoactive plants as conveying 'spiritual' experiences because we know, for a fact, that such plants work because of the peculiar chemicals they possess. We can even replicate these specific chemicals in a laboratory and be done with the plant altogether.

Albert Hofmann, for instance, accomplished this in 1938 when he synthesized LSD-25 from a type of molecule present in the ergot fungus. Hofmann later studied some of the traditional 'medicine' plants of the great Central American cultures. As he describes: "When we analyzed them we arrived at an unexpected result: these ancient drugs that we are apt to call magical and the Indians consider divine, contained as their psychoactive principles some of our already familiar ergot alkaloids."[78]

We know something the ancients didn't—we know that the

plant does not possess a spirit, the plant possesses a psychoactive chemical or a mixture of such chemicals. Our trouble is not with the plant as an arbiter of mystical experience, our real trouble is in admitting that a mystical experience is a chemical one, a fact we can no longer reasonably deny. As Smith notes:

> When the…philosophical authority on mysticism, W.T. Stace, was asked whether the drug experience is similar to the mystical experience, he answered, 'It's not a matter of its being similar to mystical experience; it is mystical experience.'[79]

According to those who know both mysticism and entheogenic drugs, the distinction between them is a forced one, an overlaid prejudice. The raw data of the experience is truly mystical.

One researcher, Walter Pahnke, attributes our disbelief in these agents as promoters of mystical experience to the Protestant ethic that anything 'good' must be thoroughly paid for by an exertion of effort and labor. Decidedly, the ingestion of a few capsules does not qualify as real effort. But, Pahnke insists, even within the Protestant heritage (and the Christian one more generally), these agents can be considered particular gifts of grace:

> "Gratuitous grace" is an appropriate theological term, because the psychedelic (literally 'mind manifesting') mystical experience can lead to a profound sense of inspiration, reverential awe, and humility, perhaps partially as a result of the realization that the experience is a gift and not particularly earned or deserved.[80]

How do we reconcile the bad reputation of psychedelic 'drugs' with the sanctity of the mystical experience they can produce? The prejudice against them is a cultural one—one more case example of the false stereotype. In *Hallucinogens and Culture*, Furst describes varying cultural perceptions of the entheogens:

> It is clearly society, not chemistry, that is the variable, since the same or chemically similar drugs can function so differently in different cultural situations, or be venerated over centuries as sacred, benign, and culturally integrative in some contexts but regarded in others as inherently so evil and dangerous that their very possession constitutes a serious crime.[81]

There is good reason for viewing entheogens as true threats to human culture for they upset many of our most important beliefs. Furthermore, they disrupt the theology that has hardened into a cultural concrete and provides the foundation upon which so many social institutions rest. To break up this concrete, many fear, would be to tear apart all of society's best adaptations. But alas, the psychedelic sixties came and went and though the tremors rattled social patterns, society remains surprisingly sturdy.

The states of mind created by our chemical brains, while truly religious experiences that gain us alternate perceptions of our world, do not occur because some immaterial being, a god, has conveyed them to our immaterial souls. Mystical experiences occur because our brains metabolize entheogenic chemicals, chemicals either taken into the body or produced within the brain itself. The perceived threat of entheogenic plants is real but it is not from a fear that the substances will turn one into a junkie (use of hallucinogens have rarely, if ever, given rise to dependency). The fear of entheogenic substances is the fear of truth—the truth of materialism, the truth that the human being, for all her miraculous abilities, perceptions, and insights remains wholly dependent on and derivative of the body's material basis. With this truth comes the concomitant fear that all matter passes away and that time dissolves both muscle and mind. Hallucinogens are dangerous indeed! At once they release man from his day-to-day, hum-drum world and render the reality of ecstasy; at the same time they confirm his worst fears—the very paradox of meaning and mortality.

Whether the mystic achieves his states of ecstasy through ascetic vigils, fasting, meditation, or by ingesting psychoactive substances—the identical experience occurs. Whether we subsequently label this experience as sacred or profane is merely a social and psychological prejudice, a further flight from the inevitable truth that we are physical beings affected, in our most intimate and religious moments, by physical causes.

The setting—the environment—yields our cherished moments as much as any other factor. If God truly exists, he certainly is predictable in the times and places he chooses to send his Holy Spirit to illuminate mortal minds. After all, what mystic would talk of God without his cave, mountaintop, or tranquilizing sunset?[82] What mystic has no method?

If entheogenic chemicals produce mystical experiences then why do some users have such frightening experiences and others such life-affirming ones? Bad trips are merely the experience of too much too soon. The eminent mythologist, Joseph Campbell, expresses this point well:

> I have attended a number of psychological conferences dealing with this whole problem of the difference between the mystical experience and the psychological crack-up. The difference is that the one who cracks up is drowning in the water in which the mystic swims.[83]

The drug, in contrast to meditation or some other, more subtle influence, literally 'throws' one into a mystical experience. Furthermore, the chaos and tone of that experience is generally dose-dependent, a greater dose induces a more powerful experience. There is no turning back once the drug courses through the bloodstream. In contrast, when meditating or fasting one can always open one's eyes, turn on the television, or get something to eat. One cannot so easily retreat from a drug-dependent trip. For good or ill, one must remain on this flight until it comes to a complete stop.

The mystic, if anything, is prepared for the experience he will find and if it still turns out to be frightening then it can always be attributed to a demonic being. The psychologically adept shaman calls upon benevolent spirits to counteract the frightening ones; thus placating the turbulence, the shaman gains confidence and relaxes—the solution to bad trips ancient or modern.

While the recreational abuse of entheogens is unfortunate, these substances still have their place in our own time. Psychologically, man is little different now than he has always been—after all we've been using the same model of brain for at least 100,000 years. Man always and everywhere lusts for the creative exploration of his nervous system. Whether this tendency is culturally or biologically programmed, humans thrive when they live within a framework where such explorations are guided and supervised by knowing elders (e.g. Classical Greece's Eleusinian Mysteries). If a framework for these experiences is not available then we will continue to witness each lost generation passing its illicit activities and irrational prejudices to the following one—always searching, and abusing, but never finding.

## Shamanism and Ecstasy Revisited

The entheogenic drugs form a backdrop for many ancient religions. Some theorists think these drugs and the experiences they induce responsible for religion itself. As Harner notes in his anthology, *Hallucinogens and Shamanism*:

> There can be little doubt that the use of the more powerful hallucinogens tends to strongly reinforce a belief in the reality of the supernatural world and in the existence of a disembodied soul or souls. An intriguing possibility is that hallucinogenic experiences may have also played a role in the innovation of such beliefs.[84]

As discussed in the first section, shamanism cannot be divorced from the state of ecstasy. Through this state and the attendant beliefs associated with it, some of our first ideas about a detachable, disembodied soul emerged. The state of mind created by the entheogenic drugs is a state of ecstasy, a radical alteration of consciousness. It is a mind-shattering, soul-rattling adventure that seems to tear one from his normally corporeal existence and allows insights into a separate reality. These experiences and the stories told about them may have led to the complex mythologies behind many ancient religions with their subsequent focus on the soul.

One of the characteristic features of shamanism is the shamanic flight—the ability to take off from their bodies on a 'trip' to explore transcendent realities. In *The Long Trip: A Prehistory of Psychedelia*, Devereux discusses shamanic flight:

> There are numerous ways in which travel in the spirit realm was envisaged. …we have seen repeatedly…that spirit flight is the pre-eminent form. It is the one most emphasized throughout shamanism worldwide: the allusions to flight, particularly through the medium of bird imagery, can be found in rock art, geoglyphs, in effigy mounds, on a shaman's robes, in ceremonial dancing and costume, in ritual paraphernalia, in shamanic gestural symbolism (such as the flapping of the armsatop ritual poles), and in the legends concerning shamans…[85]

Why such a recurrence of this flight motif? The uncanny effect of many entheogens in creating a sensation of bodily detachment, what in neurological terms would be called a derangement of proprioception (the body's perception of balance and tactile sensation), likely reinforced, if it did not originate, the shamanic flight. Drugs that influence proprioception can produce everything from a bizarre 'headiness' or 'weightlessness' to a virtual sensation of flight.

A peculiar cultural repetition of drug-induced flight occurred in the Middle Ages when witches on their 'flying broomsticks' made such a frightening appearance. Perhaps not far removed from pre-historic European shamanism (who can deny the shamanic abilities of Merlin, King Arthur's magician?), Medieval Wicca utilized psychoactive plants in their religious practices.

The herbs featured in this pagan tradition included deadly night-shade (*Atropa belladonna*), henbane (*Hyoscyamus*), mandrake (*Mandragora*), and thorn apple (*Datura*). In addition to being powerful hallucinogens, these plants are known to be quite toxic. Wicca's successful usage of this assortment implied a sophisticated knowledge of plants reminiscent of shamanism.[86]

Twentieth century scholars, recreating some of the Medieval witches' 'flying ointments' note the very kind of psychological sensations of flight recounted in the Medieval chronicles. Schenk experimented with henbane and reported the following experience:

> My teeth were clenched, and a dizzy rage took possession of me. I know that I trembled with horror; but I also know that I was permeated by a peculiar sense of well-being connected with the crazy sensation that my feet were growing lighter, expanding and breaking loose from my body. (This sensation of gradual body dissolution is typical of henbane poisoning.) Each part of my body seemed to be going off on its own. My head was growing independently larger, and I was seized with the fear that I was falling apart. At the same time I experienced an intoxicating sensation of flying.
>
> The frightening certainty that my end was near through the dissolution of my body was counterbalanced by animal joy in flight. I soared where my hallucinations—the clouds, the lowering sky, herds of beasts, falling leaves which were quite unlike any ordinary leaves, billowing streamers of steam and rivers of molten metal—were swirling along.[87]

The uncanny resemblance of this twentieth century scholar's account to both Medieval witches' tales and to the mythology of shamanism suggests a chemical lineage departing from the same ancestry—psychoactive plants.

Along with our culture in general, the character of our religious thinking has changed dramatically over time. Recent, institutionalized religions obtain their theologies from authority, an authority based almost entirely on scripture and its interpretation. Ancient religion, based in a totally illiterate culture, relied upon the authority of direct experience. Harner touches upon this: "We of a literate civilization may get both our religion and our religious proofs from books; persons in non-literate societies often rely upon direct confrontation with the supernatural for evidence of religious reality."[88] As arbiters of 'supernatural evidence' entheogens were perhaps as important in their time as Bibles and sacred writings in our own.

## *Soma and the Origins of Hinduism*

The history of the search for Soma is, properly the history of Vedic studies in general, as the Soma sacrifice was the focal point of the Vedic religion. Indeed, if one accepts the point of view that the whole of Indian mystical practice from the Upanisads through the more mechanical methods of yoga is merely an attempt to recapture the vision granted by the Soma plant, then the nature of that vision—and of the plant—underlies the whole of Indian religion, and everything of a mystical nature within that religion is pertinent to the identity of the plant.

—Wendy Doniger,
*Soma: The Divine Mushroom of Immortality*[89]

As a worldwide movement, religion seems to have transformed from its experiential and bardic roots to its legalistic, canonical character approximately 3000 years ago. Hinduism typifies this transition from shamanism, and its basis in the experience of ecstasy, to written religion. The most ancient texts of Hinduism are called the Vedas—they are the written histories of the ancient *rishis* (seers). These texts are among the only universals in an otherwise broad tradition of religious thought and practice. The Rig Veda sings the praises of the, since lost, drug/god called *Soma*. The *rishis* who first recited these hymns experienced their religion through *Soma* but later devotees codified the songs into the first sacred writings of India.

The Vedas were sung for countless generations in the mother Indo-European tongue. The *rishis* accompanied the Indo-European tribes that thundered into India approximately 3500 years ago. In their conquest they brought the shamanic religion of ancient Europe but the creativity and diversity of the Indian peoples forged a manifold religion called Hinduism.

The mystery of *Soma* is its disappearance. How could a plant, revered as a god itself, have disappeared from the sacred traditions of the Hindus? Certainly, a psychotropic plant that could provide visions as powerful as those recorded in the Vedas would not have been set-aside. Why then did it disappear altogether thousands of years ago?

R. Gordon Wasson has identified the *Soma* of the ancient Vedas with the fly-agaric mushroom (*Amanita muscaria*), a colorful mushroom that appears time and again in fairy tales and their illustrations. It is this powerfully psychoactive mushroom he believes to have inspired the *rishis'* divine visions.

The psychoactive effects of this mushroom have long been known. *Amanita muscaria* was the favored mushroom of Siberian shamans from time immemorial. The first witnesses to meet these people noted the Siberians' appreciation of the mushrooms. They also chronicled an even more eccentric behavior. Because the cold climate often precludes the growth of *Amanita muscaria*, they would become scarce and extremely valuable during the winter. The poorer of the Siberians would hungrily await outside the wealthier ones' tents after a mushroom session had begun. When the mushroom-eaters came out to urinate, their attendants would catch their steaming piss in a bowl and lap it down! Because the psychoactive chemicals (muscimole and ibotenic acid) leave the body but partially metabolized, one could achieve a powerful a state of intoxication from the chemical-laden urine.[90]

Until the Russians brought them alcohol, the Siberians relied almost exclusively on the fly-agaric mushroom to access alternate states of consciousness. Curiously, they may have learned about the mushroom's power by observing the behavior of their beloved reindeer. The reindeer possess a preternatural lust for the colorful fungi and delightedly munch them down and become inebriated.

The *Amanita muscaria* mushroom, like all mushrooms, is difficult to cultivate. To pre-moderns the appearance and disappearance of mushrooms seemed part of nature's rhythmic mysteries. They might predictably arise from the ground during a certain season but nothing could sway them to man's control. Seedless, they long retained vestiges of the supernatural. This mushroom, in contrast to many others, possessed another fickleness; its underground fungal structure only grew in the soil around pine, fir, and especially birch trees. Without these trees, and numerous other environmental constraints, the fly-agaric would not fruit. While the ancestral homelands of the Indo-Europeans featured the precise ecology for fly-agaric growth, many of the regions they annexed did not. In particular, this mushroom cannot grow in the lowlands of India. This likely explains the disappearance of *Soma* from ancient Hinduism.

The Rig Veda mentions a number of details about *Soma*. *Soma* is always associated with the mountains and comes from those areas. It is no mean coincidence that the coniferous trees whose soil *Amanita* requires are among the only plant life that flourish at high altitudes.

The branches, roots, flowers, or leaves of *Soma* are nowhere mentioned in the Rig Veda. Surely, the praise of a divine plant would note some part of its botany. In fact, the only plant-like appendage noted are *Soma*'s fleshy stalks. Other than its cap, the mushroom's stalk (called a stipe) is it's most noticeable feature.

*Soma's* color is mentioned repeatedly in the Veda. It varies from fiery red to a tawny yellow. Wasson's extraction of juice from the fly-agaric mushroom fits just these spectrums depending on the age and particular type of fly-agaric.

One passage in the Rig Veda says of *Soma*: "Like a serpent he creeps out of his old skin."[91] Few metaphors so exactly capture the transition from fungal puffball, just breaking the surface of the soil, into sprouting mushroom, whose cap breaks free and perches over its "single-footed" stipe (another of the Rig Veda's tropes). One of the most intriguing references to *Soma* is the following: "Acting in concert, those charged with the Office, richly gifted, do full honor to Soma. The swollen men piss the flowing Soma."[92] This surely refers to the knowledge that the urine of those who ate fly-agaric remains psychoactively potent.

The identification of *Soma* with the *Amanita muscaria* mushroom solves an age-old mystery and provides more evidence regarding the ecstatic origins of our most sacred traditions.

## The Mysteries of Eleusis

The ancient testimony about Eleusis is unanimous and unambiguous. Eleusis was the supreme experience in an initiate's life. It was both physical and mystical: trembling, vertigo, cold sweat, and then a sight that made all previous seeing seem like blindness, a sense of awe and wonder at a brilliance that caused a profound silence since what had just been seen and felt could never be communicated: words are unequal to the task. Those symptoms are unmistakably the experience induced by an hallucinogen.

—Wasson, Hofmann, Ruck, *The Road to Eleusis*[93]

In ancient Greece, religions were concealed behind and within other religions. Secret 'mystery schools' flourished all over Attica and tales of Dionysis and Orpheus were murmured about in the marketplace. About these occult rituals we have mere fragments left—tantalizing accounts that inspire awe and reverence.

The most influential of the Greek mysteries were those performed at Eleusis, just 20 kilometers from Athens. So well kept were the mysteries of Eleusis that many classicists consider it the most enigmatic problem left to us by the Greeks. And yet, for all that, the mysteries affected so many well-known Greeks and Romans, for so long a period (some 2000 years), that the pieces and clues they left us add up to a rendition of the mysteries that is vaguely complete—like a painting by a pointillist. The picture seen is a psychedelic one for at the heart of the mysteries lies the consumption of an entheogenic beverage.

The mythological backdrop of the mystery is unrevealing. It concerns the goddess Demeter, an ancient mother goddess credited with the bestowal of grain and agriculture upon mankind, and her daughter, the goddess Persephone. Persephone had been spirited away by Hades, god of the underworld, to become his Queen. In consequence, Demeter wailed as she searched about for her stolen daughter. She left her important duties behind. The Earth became arid and would no longer support man. Zeus stepped in and Hades conceded to release Persephone though by cleverness he caused it so that Persephone resided with her mother for part of the year and with him, in the Underworld, for the other part. This myth explained the rhythms of nature, the cycles of growth and harvest, life and death.

The rituals performed in the mysteries revolved around these mythological themes but were not limited to them. Indeed, the recounting of a myth hardly explains the affect the mysteries had on its initiates. Of the mysteries, Cicero wrote: "...we have learned from them the beginnings of life, and have gained the power not only to live happily, but also to die with a better hope."[94] And just as Plato had the most significant things to say about the soul, so does he reveal the most about the mysteries:

> Beauty it was ours to see in all its brightness in those days when, amidst that happy company, we beheld with our eyes that blessed vision, ourselves in the train of Zeus, others following some other god; then were we all initiated into that mystery which is rightly accounted blessed beyond all others; whole and unblemished were we that did celebrate it, untouched by the evils that awaited us in days to come; whole and unblemished likewise, free from all alloy, steadfast and blissful were the spectacles on which we gazed in the moment of final revelation; pure was the light that shone around us, and pure were we, without taint of that prison house which now we are encompassed withal, and call a body, fast bound therein as an oyster in its shell.[95]

The mysteries alleviated the fear of death. But what possible experience could accomplish such a feat? The rituals conveyed, ultimately, an alternate state of consciousness. This state of consciousness and its subsequent vision convinced the devotees that the normal mode of life was not the only one. Perhaps, the initiates might conclude, the teases of Orpheus are true! According to the traditions at Eleusis, if one understood the process of dying he could fare better than the uninitiated. This concept is similar to that purveyed in the *Egyptian Book of the Dead* (*Book of Going Forth by Day*) and the *Tibetan Book of the Dead*.

Plutarch relates the process of dying to a mystery initiation.[96] Of death, he writes:

...the soul suffers an experience similar to those who celebrate great initiations...Wanderings astray in the beginning, tiresome walkings in circles, some frightening paths in darkness that lead nowhere; then immediately before the end all the terrible things, panic and shivering and sweat, and amazement. And then some wonderful light comes to meet you, pure regions and meadows are there to greet you, with sounds and dances stolen, sacred words and holy views; and there the initiate, perfect by now, set free and loose from all bondage, walks about, crowned with a wreath, celebrating the festival together with the other sacred and pure people, and he looks down on the uninitiated, unpurified crowd in this world in mud and fog beneath his feet.

Numenius felt that Plutarch had betrayed the secret of Eleusis in writing this. But what did he reveal? The mystery was nothing less than a beatific vision, a mystical apprehension of the divine order of things. As Burkert notes: "In religious terms, mysteries provide an immediate encounter with the divine."[97] And that logician of logicians, Aristotle, speaking out of character: "... is said to have used the pointed antithesis that at the final stage of mysteries there should be no more 'learning' but 'experiencing', and a change in the state of mind."[98]

The startling thing about the Eleusis experience was its regular occurrence. Year after year people came to be inspired. Year after year they were. This is no 'appearance of the virgin' or other singular mystical experience. Eleusis could be counted on, the experience was expected. Whether the initiate be young or old, philosopher or servant, he would invariably leave the place shaken to his core.

No mere theatrics could have been behind the vision. Greeks, the Athenians in particular, virtually invented dramatic performance and were thoroughly versed in the power of the theater. The mystery was not another play. What could have convinced the best and brightest that something truly divine had transpired? The answer is quite clear—entheogenic drugs.

For some days before initiation, a fast was required. In fact, entrance to the *Telesterion*, the great hall where the mysteries occurred, was only granted after one recited: "...I have fasted, I have drunk the *kykeon*."[99] But it is the latter part of this 'access code' that truly reveals the secrets of the mysteries—the *kykeon*. The *kykeon* was a special beverage prepared just before entrance to the *Telesterion*. It consisted of water, barley, and mint. To chemists and non-chemists alike this seems odd; none of these are hallucinogens. It is the opinion of Wasson, Hofmann, and Ruck that there was 'something in the water.' This something came from a fungus that might grow on barley. It is none other than the ergot fungus, the same from which Hofmann derived LSD-25 in 1938. The water-soluble ergot alkaloids created the state of mind that sanctified the mysteries.

An important clue lies in the fact that the *kykeon* was a measured volume of drink. One could not get in after a mere sip: "…a definite dose had to be taken. The dose in that case would have been the exact quantity contained in the small pots carried in the hands of the men in the procession."[100]

That the *kykeon* actually possessed entheogenic properties seems beyond doubt. In the words of one initiate: "I came out of the mystery hall feeling like a stranger to myself."[101] The *kykeon* delivered a state of ecstasy to the initiates.

While the *kykeon* provides the key to the mysteries, the intricate rituals should not be overlooked. Those who orchestrated the mysteries were masters of set and setting and could amplify the entheogenic effect of the *kykeon* to its maximum. The techniques behind the Eleusis experience were guarded for dozens of generations by just two families. A member of the Eumolpidai played the role of high priest while two of the Kerykes fulfilled roles as torchbearer and herald of the ceremonies. These families provided the magic brew and enacted the sacred rituals that convinced all who came that something supernatural had occurred. Proclus, born shortly after the mysteries were condemned, learned some 'family secrets' from the daughter of the last high priest:

> They cause sympathy of the souls with the ritual in a way that is unintelligible to us, and divine, so that some of the initiates are stricken with panic, being filled with divine awe; others assimilate themselves to the holy symbols, leave their own identity, become at home with the gods, and experience divine possession.[102]

Burkert describes the actual rites as: "…patterned by antithesis, moving between the extremes of terror and happiness, darkness and light."[103] This, indeed, sounds like maximum effect: one was made terribly anxious and frightened before experiencing the vision. The release and joy of the actual experience then appeared all the more 'saving;' it transformed the bad trip into the good. In juxtaposition, deliverance was complete. The fear of death had been replaced with ecstatic consciousness and hope for the hereafter.

Wasson describes the nature of the experience, at least as he came to understand it after sampling an entheogenic mushroom for the first time:

> As your body lies there…your soul is free, loses all sense of time, alert as it never was before, living an eternity in a night, seeing infinity in a grain of sand. What you have seen and heard is cut as with a burin in your memory, never to be effaced. At last you know what the ineffable is, and what ecstasy means. Ecstasy! The mind harks back to the origin of that word. For the Greeks *ekstasis* meant the flight of the soul from the body. I am certain that this word came into being to describe the effect of the Mystery of Eleusis.[104]

When Christian authorities, empowered by Alaric, King of the Goths, finally put an end to the mysteries some worried that the world would fall apart. As Kerényi notes:

> They [the mysteries] were thought to 'hold the entire human race together,' not only because people continued, no doubt, to come from every corner of the Earth to be initiated…but also because the Mysteries touched on something that was common to all men. They were connected not only with Athenian and Greek existence but with human existence in general.[105]

With the mysteries of Eleusis lost, Western man lost his last shamanically supervised mystical experience. In the nearly two thousand years since Christian monks put an end to the ancient experience, a few mystics have appeared here and there within the church, sometimes embraced, sometimes burned, but no proper supervision, nay, even encouragement, has been given for experience of the sacred *mysterium tremendum*. Did the world fall apart in the meantime?

The writing of the Vedas and the great mysteries of Eleusis share an entheogenic heritage, a heritage that comes from a form of ancient shamanism. These two sacred traditions confirmed for their devotees a separation of soul and body, a divorce of the natural and the supernatural. But for all their supernatural testimony, these drugs are most certainly chemicals and work along definite neurological pathways. While their psychoactive properties gave rise to some of the mystical experiences that set the foundation for spiritualist dogma, our current knowledge of the entheogens literally 'undoes' the animistic matrix they once affirmed. The irony of the situation suggests a cosmic joke of the very worst type.

The entheogenic substances, like all the better sources of wisdom in life, create an ultimately paradoxical effect. At once they teach about the most ethereal and unearthly parts of human existence while also confirming our physical basis and its short duration.

## *Marijuana*

Like a tourist in the Four Corners area of the American Southwest, marijuana possesses the uncommon ability to set foot in many different places at once—the differing categories of the hallucinogens/entheogens, the opiates, and the depressants. At various doses, its properties qualitatively alter the user's consciousness. Of these properties, marijuana's ability to produce euphoria keeps people coming back to it time and again. Around the world people have been doing so for thousands of years.

The actual plant probably came from the Russian steppes near Eastern Europe, the homeland of the Indo-European culture. It still grows wild in these areas today. All the Indo-European-based languages possess a term for marijuana (cannabis/hemp) testifying to the deep influence of this plant.[106] The wanderlust of the Indo-Europeans spread their culture, including marijuana use and cultivation, across the mid-latitudes all the way to Asia and particularly throughout the Indian subcontinent.

Since ancient times the plant has been valued for its physical and psychoactive properties. The use of hemp fibers to weave cloth and to make rope remain vitally important even in our time. The high tensile strength of the plant's fibers has made it an ideal rope constituent for millennia.

Besides its utilitarian uses, the plant was surely appreciated by the ancients for its psychoactivity. Archeological evidence suggests marijuana usage in ancient Europe, at least before the Bronze Age. Its medicinal usage in China stretches beyond recorded history but was first chronicled in a pharmacopoeia of the emperor Shen Nung in 2737 B.C.E.[107] Herodotus, the wandering Greek historian of the fifth century B.C.E. relates cannabis usage by the Scythians, a northern tribe that bordered ancient Greece:

> They have hemp growing in their country, very like flax, save that the hemp is by much the thicker and taller... The Scythians then take the seed of this hemp and...they throw it on the red-hot stones; and, being so thrown, it smoulders and sends forth so much steam that no Greek vapour-bath could surpass it. The Scythians howl in their joy at the vapour-bath.[108]

The religious uses of marijuana occur mainly in India. Different preparations of the plant include the weakest, *bhang*, the more potent *ganja*, and the hashish-like *charas*. A marijuana drink made from *bhang* has long been prized and some children's candies even include a bit of the substance. Marijuana is a staple of the wandering holy men, the *sannyasi*, who mimic the god Shiva, another of the plant's devotees.[109]

Traditionally, marijuana smoking flourished in the Middle East, though it continues to suffer periodic persecution there. Because of Islam's prohibition of alcohol, smoking various substances emerged as its primary alternatives.

In 12th century Persia, followers of Hashishin ibn-al Sabbah, the so-called *hashishin*, became a feared militant sect of Islamic mysticism. The two words, hashish and assassin, derive from this notorious group. They targeted various opponents and Christian Crusaders for summary execution. Cannabis was part of the reward for their services. As preparation during their commando training, the novice *hashishin* were given marijuana as a "foretaste of Paradise" so that they might not fear danger and death.[110]

There is some evidence that European usage began, in small scale, during the Crusades.[111] More commonly, it is thought that the reintroduction of marijuana to European culture resulted from Napoleon's massive Egyptian campaign. Napoleon's advancement of Enlightenment principles included the importation of teams of scholars to study and journal the flora and fauna of Egypt as he attempted (but failed) to subdue the country. Whether from these scientific observations or from the French soldiers' importation of the likable substance, European doctors began experimenting with marijuana soon thereafter. Of course, as the pattern appears again and again, this medical usage quickly spread to less academic quarters.

The Romantic intellectuals of the nineteenth century, in pursuit of eccentric novelties and rare sources of pleasure, pounced upon marijuana once it came to their attention. Baudelaire, Delacroix, Gautier, Dumas, and Hugo were all members of the *Club de Hachichins*, a group of Parisian writers and thinkers who experimented with numerous drugs. Baudelaire, with poetic style, describes the various stages and effects of marijuana inebriation:

> …people completely unsuited for word-play will improvise an endless string of puns and wholly improbable idea relationships fit to outdo the ablest masters of this preposterous craft. But after a few minutes, the relation between ideas becomes so vague, and the thread of your thoughts grows so tenuous, that only your cohorts…can understand you.

> …your senses become extraordinarily keen and acute. Your sight is infinite. Your ear can discern the slightest perceptible sound, even through the shrillest of noises.

> Now the hallucinations begin… The strangest ambiguities, the most inexplicable transpositions of ideas take place. In sounds there is color; in colors there is a music… You are sitting and smoking; you believe that you are sitting in your pipe, and that your pipe is smoking you; you are exhaling yourself in bluish clouds. You feel just fine in this position, and only one thing gives you worry or concern: how will you ever be able to get out of your pipe?

> This fantasy goes on for an eternity. A lucid interval, and a great expenditure of effort, permit you to look at the clock. The eternity turns out to have been only a minute.

> The third phase…is something beyond description…it is complete happiness. There is nothing whirling and tumultuous about it. It is a calm and placid beatitude. Every philosophical problem is resolved. Every difficult question that presents a point of contention for theologians, and brings despair to thoughtful men, becomes clear and transparent. Every contradiction is reconciled. Man has surpassed the gods.[112]

The U.S. experience with marijuana began quite early. The American Colonies did an enormous amount of hemp farming. The bustling naval activity of the Colonial period made rope and sail-cloth (also woven from hemp) an essential trade commodity. Washington and Jefferson both attempted hemp farming but ceased their operations due to the labor-intensive nature of the crop.[113] No Americans of that era, though, seem to have discovered hemp's psychoactive features.

The exploration of marijuana as a 'drug' in the United States did not occur until the twentieth century. Marijuana, or reefer, smoking spread throughout African-American populations originally from foreign influences in and around the port of New Orleans around the 1920s.[114] Its association with the burgeoning music called jazz provided it a quick medium to spread from South to North and East to West. Since it was largely a black drug in these days, early legislation against it expressed the typical fears and prejudices of the time. The 'reefer madness' campaigns of the 1940s and 1950s held that its use led to degenerate and violent acts, an unlikely interpretation given marijuana's blissful, tranquilizing effects. By the 1950s jazz had deeply shaped the Beatnik subculture. They extolled the novel drug. From the beatniks, marijuana spread into a largely white population and set the stage for the hippie-overrun 1960s. Used both by Vietnam protesters and GIs alike, marijuana use peaked in the late 1960s and early 1970s and spread throughout all sectors of society.

Today, marijuana use is commonplace and quasi-tolerated both in the United States and abroad. In 1997, almost 50% of those between the ages of 26 and 34 claimed prior usage of marijuana.[115] The drug's popularity has created an insoluble problem for law enforcement agencies. Among the greatest concerns of such agencies is that marijuana leads to experimentation with other drugs. After all, once an individual has broken both the social stigma and federal laws concerning drug regulation and found a source to provide at least one type of drug, the barriers to further experimentation are less imposing; as such, marijuana is termed a 'Gateway Drug.'

Besides its history in popular culture, marijuana possesses a long history as a therapeutic medicine. The role of cannabis in numerous medical traditions (including Hindu Ayurveda) stretches far back in time. Even today, marijuana-derived substances possess medical import in the most advanced therapies of Western medicine. Because of marijuana's ability to reduce eye pressure, it has been used as a glaucoma drug. Marijuana's ability to calm both nausea and anxiety elect it an important role in cancer treatment. These characteristics along with its analgesic properties make it an ideal adjunct to chemotherapy.[116]

Despite its historical and medicinal importance, marijuana is considered a social scourge by those who oppose it. In the United States alone almost two million pounds of marijuana are confiscated by federal authorities every year (at an enormous cost of life and money) in an effort to check its widespread usage.[117] This represents but a fraction of the marijuana consumed each year. One might logically infer a substance's danger by the zeal with which authorities seek to control it. On this measurement alone, one would conclude marijuana to be a lethal drug. The most recent research does not support this fear.[118] Marijuana, while not without its risks and dangers (especially to lung tissue, when smoked), poses less inherent risk than many other substances that suffer no such restriction. Marijuana exhibits relatively low potential for dependence; some data suggests it to be about half as addictive as alcohol.[119]

### Plant and Preparation

The marijuana plant was classified by the taxonomist Linnaeus in the eighteenth century. He labeled it *cannabis sativa*. Since Linnaeus, controversy has arisen about the number of species in existence. Some believe that three distinct species of cannabis exist: *sativa, indica,* and *ruderalis*.[120] Others feel that the latter two 'species' are actually just different breeds of the *cannabis sativa* plant.[121] The *cannabis indica* plant is squatter than the towering *sativa*; this feature has made it preferable for illegal production with its typical space constraints.

In the late 1960s, the famed botanist Richard Evans Schultes used to spring to his students' aid when they were arrested for marijuana usage. Since the early laws were quite specific in naming the species of plant, Schultes would claim his students' usage was limited to one of the other species. The law caught on to Schultes's tactics and eventually broadened its terms.

A number of common preparations exist for cannabis. The psychoactive constituents course throughout the plant, so all of its parts may be ingested for the desired effect. Since the active ingredients of marijuana are especially concentrated in its flowering tops, these are the more prized parts of the plant. The most potent method of delivery is smoking (free-basing) the dried plant though some prefer the longer lasting and less intense oral consumption of the plant (as is more traditional in India). Hash or hashish, the distilled oils and resins of marijuana, are more potent and easier to smuggle than the unprocessed plant. Hash oil, a more concentrated form yet, can be inconspicuously consumed or smoked on other media (e.g. tobacco cigarettes). In these higher potencies, marijuana is increasingly likely to induce hallucinogenic experiences.

## How Does Marijuana Work?

The marijuana plant contains a number of unique substances. These chemicals are called cannabinoids. Pharmacologically, the most active cannabinoid is THC (*delta*-9-tetrahydrocannabinol).[122] In addition to this, a number of other cannabinoids (such as cannabidiol) likely potentiate THC's metabolism or otherwise possess their own psychoactive properties.[123] The manner of marijuana delivery may modify these chemicals to make them more potent.

Once in the body, the cannabinoids are fat-soluble and, like general anesthetics, penetrate many types of tissues and generally affect the permeability of cell membranes. The cannabinoids easily pass through the blood-brain barrier. Understanding the precise mechanism of such highly soluble substances is tricky because they cause a variety of metabolic changes.

Recent work has demonstrated the presence of at least two cannabinoid receptors in the human body. Through these sites the drug exerts its effect. The main cannabinoid receptor, the CB1 receptor, is the only known cannabinoid receptor in the central nervous system. These sites are "extraordinarily abundant in the brain" in the words of one researcher.[124] Such abundance suggests their importance in the regulation of many neural processes. The other cannabinoid receptor, CB2, well represented in cells of the immune system, is poorly understood at this time. As a class, cannabinoid receptors show up in many different species, including invertebrates:

> The evolutionary history of vertebrates and invertebrates diverged more than 500 million years ago, so cannabinoid receptors appear to have been conserved throughout evolution at least this long. This suggests that they serve an important and basic function in animal physiology. In general, cannabinoid receptor molecules are similar among different species. Thus, cannabinoid receptors likely fill many similar functions in a broad range of animals, including humans.[125]

When dealing with the receptors of psychoactive plants the question always emerges: why are there plant-chemical receptors in the human nervous system? Again, in most cases, endogenous brain chemicals of a similar type exist already. The resemblance of plant chemicals to these brain-generated substances is mere coincidence.

At least one marijuana-like neurotransmitter has been discovered. This substance, labeled anandamide (from Sanskrit *ananda*—bliss), produces quasi-marijuana effects in laboratory animals. Anandamide is produced within the human brain and binds to the cannabinoid receptors in many separate regions of the brain.[126] Anandamide concentrations run high in the nucleus accumbens, part of the dopaminergic 'reward pathway.' The reward system pleasurably reinforces important animal behaviors like feeding and sex. The arousal of a superhuman appetite when using marijuana probably relates to the similarity of the cannabinoids to natural reward chemicals.[127]

The cannabinoids are generally inhibitory neurotransmitters and their selective binding preference in areas of movement and memory help to explain the difficulties many users have with those two functions when under the influence.[128] The cannabinoids' augmentation of dopamine release (especially in the mesolimbic tracts) indicates their ability to induce euphoria. However, the fact that they accomplish this dopamine release in a different manner than other drugs of abuse may explain marijuana's tendency to be less addictive.[129]

### The Social Dilemma of Marijuana

More than any other restricted drug, marijuana incites social commentary. A number of proponents argue for its legalization. The extensive usage of marijuana by all types of people makes its prohibition more questionable than other restricted drugs. Indeed, some researchers have likened the current state of irrational prohibition, chemical loyalty oaths (mandatory drug testing), and the generally anathema status of marijuana to a form of "psychopharmacological McCarthyism."[130]

Whatever potentially harmful effects marijuana begets, few of its users cry foul about it. Far more people, for instance, claim a sense of psychological and physical bondage from the use of alcohol and nicotine, both sanctioned drugs. Whatever deficits chronic marijuana abuse may engender they are arguably far less destructive than those seen as a result of long-term alcohol or nicotine usage. In light of these reasons, the severe prosecution of marijuana users and suppliers appears excessive.

As a "Gateway Drug," it is argued that marijuana use leads to experimentation with other, more destructive types of controlled substances. On sheer logical grounds, this alone is not a legitimate argument; it is a judgment of guilt by association. For instance, one could note a much higher correlation between gun procurement and crimes of violence yet this has not caused a federal crackdown on firearms. There is nothing inherent to marijuana, nothing that clings to it as a causal agent, that leads to further drug experimentation. Alcohol, nicotine, and coffee are as psychoactive as marijuana, in differing fashions, and yet they are not considered to be Gateway Drugs. The chemical induction of alternate states of consciousness by any of these substances does not necessitate further experimentation—again no causative link exists between these agents and subsequent drug experimentation. The anthropologist Weston LaBarre, with his typically ironical criticism, answers this confusion of social policy: "Despite its much-proved danger, we accept alcohol blandly, but rabidly reject marihuana for its as yet unproved dire danger, since unknown euphoriants must surely be more dangerous than known ones."[131]

The correlation between marijuana use and subsequent drug experimentation is more likely a result of crossing the social and psychological barriers concerning the use of an illegal drug. Were such a drug sanctioned, the loss of stigma would make marijuana users less susceptible to further law-breaking behavior. Another possible reason that marijuana serves as a Gateway Drug relates to its vendors. By associating with drug dealers whose very business it is to encourage further experimentation, the novice marijuana user exposes herself to the dangers of this subculture and its generally criminal influences. Were marijuana only a fraction as accessible as alcohol or nicotine and sold by regulated and supervised distributors, the association with drug-dealing and the drug subculture would stifle experimentation with the more dangerous substances.

In the end, though, all such arguments are too refined. The larger political question towers in the foreground: in a conservative political structure that professes the relative freedom of the individual over mind and body (one and the same) how can a drug that is widely used and viewed both by lay people and scientists alike to be a predominantly benign substance be prohibited outright without the contravention of democratic principles? If such a model of government will progress towards its ideal then the power of unfounded prejudice must be finally discarded and replaced with well-reasoned and objective legislation. Were we truly free we might finally choose our poisons.

## LSD

The sacrament of the sixties, the bane of urban lore, LSD is one of the world's most potent psychoactive substances. In ridiculously small doses, like 50 millionths of a gram, LSD can send its user on a hallucinogenic trip that lasts 8-12 hours or more.

Without LSD one can hardly imagine how the last few decades of the twentieth century would have been different—no Timothy Leary, no Lucy in the Sky with Diamonds, no Woodstock. If there was a flame in the 1960s then LSD was its spark. Despite being the youngest of the drugs mentioned here, LSD possesses a fluorescent history with larger than life characters and mind-boggling plots. The LSD experience shaped music, unchained its users from the weight of social taboos, and set creativity loose making this time of freedom and free love the most extraordinary tumult in Western society since the days of the French and American revolutions. If its enemies were more insidious (consumption-culture, environmental decay, and communism-phobia), these revolutionaries' implements of war were more subtle (mind-altering drugs, the methods of civil disobedience pioneered by Gandhi and King, and rock music).

## History

LSD, whose full name is lysergic acid diethylamide (in German, *Lyserg-säure-di*äthylamid), was born in 1938 in a Sandoz pharmaceutical lab in Basle, Switzerland. Its father, Albert Hofmann, had been systematically studying the chemistry of the ergot fungus for some time.[132]

For centuries, lore about ergot had bestowed upon it properties favorable in childbearing. It was also the responsible agent in St. Anthony's Fire, a periodic plague during the Middle Ages that inflicted gangrene and madness on those who consumed ergot-infected grains. By synthesizing ergot's therapeutic agents, Sandoz hoped to avoid its less favorable qualities. Hofmann satisfied them and derived some medicines from variations on the basic nucleus of an ergot alkaloid, lysergic acid. From these variations, Sandoz patented and produced pharmaceuticals that aided childbirth (reducing contraction time) and assisted in senility and headache.

When Hofmann first synthesized his 25th variation of lysergic acid in 1938, he had expected to produce a circulatory and respiratory stimulant. The chemical structure of LSD-25 resembled a well-known agent of that type. The Sandoz pharmacology department noted LSD-25 to be about 70% as effective as another ergot substance for the induction of contractions. They also observed a certain restlessness in their research animals—but who's to judge when or why an animal is grumpy? Any other hoped for benefits were not found. They decided to shelf LSD-25 as a redundancy at best.

For the next five years, Hofmann conducted fruitful research with the ergot alkaloids but a lingering presentiment about the twenty-fifth variation of LSD kept nagging at him. In 1943, he decided to produce a fresh batch for further testing just to see if they had overlooked anything back in 1938. On Friday April 16, 1943, while a massive war raged all over Europe and the South Pacific (North Africa had only just been won by the Allies), Dr. Hofmann, in neutral Switzerland, underwent a bizarre experience. He sent the following report to his superior:

...I was forced to interrupt my work in the laboratory in the middle of the afternoon and proceed home, being affected by a remarkable restlessness, combined with a slight dizziness. At home I lay down and sank into a not unpleasant intoxicated-like condition, characterized by an extremely stimulated imagination. In a dream-like state, with eyes closed (I found the daylight to be unpleasantly glaring), I perceived an uninterrupted stream of fantastic pictures, extraordinary shapes with intense, kaleidoscopic play of colors. After some two hours this condition faded away.[133]

In its effects, this toxic exposure was thoroughly eccentric; even more unusual, though, was its mechanism. Aware of ergot's toxicity, Dr. Hofmann always employed meticulous methods when handling it. He could, at most, have been exposed to only a tiny amount of the LSD-25 he had produced and then only on the skin of his fingertips!

Deciding to get to the bottom of this bizarre experience, Hofmann, on April 19, ingested a touch of LSD-25, just 250 micrograms (millionths of a gram). By later standards, this is approximately 5 'hits' of LSD! He quickly realized that it was indeed this substance that had been responsible for his previous experience. After asking an assistant to accompany him on a psychedelic bicycle ride back home (automobiles were restricted during the war), Dr. Hofmann went through hours more of a nightmarish experience. As he wrote:

Even worse than these demonic transformations of the outer world, were the alterations that I perceived in myself, in my inner being. Every exertion of my will, every attempt to put an end to the disintegration of the outer world and the dissolution of my ego, seemed to be wasted effort. A demon had invaded me, had taken possession of my body, mind, and soul. I jumped up and screamed, trying to free myself from him, but then sank down again and lay helpless on the sofa. The substance, with which I had wanted to experiment, had vanquished me. It was the demon that scornfully triumphed over my will. I was seized by the dreadful fear of going insane. I was taken to another world, another place, another time. My body seemed to be without sensation, lifeless, strange. Was I dying? Was this the transition? At times I believed myself to be outside my body, and then perceived clearly, as an outside observer, the complete tragedy of my situation.[134]

A doctor visited Hofmann during this state and noted all his vital signs to be perfectly normal. As time progressed, the worst part of this intense trip gave way to more playful alterations in perception and finally, a welcomed rest. After he awoke the next morning, his vision possessed unusual clarity and he felt profoundly grateful to be back in the world of the living, and the sane. This was, in effect, the first acid trip in history.

Sandoz faced a difficult situation: what to do with this unusual substance? They decided to provide it to interested researchers. They hoped that the world of psychology might find a use for this highly potent, synthetic hallucinogen.

One of LSD's best researchers, Dr. Stanislov Grof, experienced his first LSD trip in 1956. Of the experience, Grof wrote:

> ... [it] radically changed both my personal and professional life. I experienced an extraordinary encounter with my unconscious, and this experience instantly overshadowed all my previous interest in Freudian psychoanalysis. I was treated to a fantastic display of colorful visions, some abstract and geometrical, others filled with symbolic meaning. I felt an array of emotions of an intensity I had never dreamed possible...I emerged from this experience moved to the core.[135]

To gauge just how powerful this substance is, keep in mind that these are not the words of a youthful 'hippie' but the seasoned impressions of an intellectual, a doctor, and a man who had studied, and undergone, psychoanalysis for many years.

Such an effect was rather common. Even among the cool scientists who first researched LSD, an unnatural enthusiasm followed. The rigorous methods of science were often sacrificed to the intuition that the scientists had stumbled upon something new under the sun. Soon the research supplies of LSD began to show up among groups of intellectuals and others far outside the realm of scientific research.

## MKUltra

About the same time that Dr. Hofmann discovered LSD, the Nazis were experimenting with drugs like mescaline in an attempt to find effective mind control agents. Using prisoners in their concentration camps as unwitting subjects (not a very pleasant set and setting), the S.S. would spike their beverages to note different reactions. While one would expect such things of the Nazis, one might not expect them of the U.S. government. At roughly the same time, though, members of the proto-C.I.A. group called the Office of Strategic Services (O.S.S.), were themselves searching for a 'truth serum' for use in interrogation.

The early history of the C.I.A. is peppered with the search for effective mind control agents. The importance of separating truth from lie became a driving force in spy technique. An abundance of double-agents and adepts at disinformation had to be sifted from genuine intelligence gatherers. The C.I.A. settled on a powerful form of marijuana as their best truth serum, for a while.[136]

In 1953, the head of the C.I.A., Allen Dulles, approved the MKULTRA program. This program aimed, "...to investigate whether and how it was possible to modify an individual's behavior by covert means," in the words of the project's chief chemist, Sid Gottlieb.[137] LSD was among the project's top concerns. They were especially impressed by its potency. Only an infinitesimal amount was necessary to produce a major 'trip.' As Marks notes in his book *The Search for the "Manchurian Candidate"*: "A two-suiter suitcase could hold enough LSD to turn on every man, woman, and child in the United States."[138] The C.I.A. imagined tainting a city's water supply to diminish the opponents' ability to defend themselves in time of war. Before the C.I.A. could really proceed in their use of LSD they had to know more about it. Using the Josiah Macy, Jr. Foundation and the Geschickter Fund for Medical Research as go-betweens, the C.I.A. funded dozens of LSD research projects at hospitals and universities across the country. U.S. citizens (and a few Canadians) would teach the C.I.A. all about LSD's capabilities.

One of the most insidious set of experiments was performed in Lexington, Kentucky at the Federal Addiction Research Center. The 'volunteers,' who were addict inmates at the Lexington facility, were promised use of their preferred drug (heroin, morphine) for participation in the LSD experiments. In one study, seven men were kept on LSD for 77 days. Because of LSD's ability to produce tolerance, these subjects were routinely taking triple and quadruple doses by the end of the period.[139]

Sandoz was the only company that produced LSD through the early 1950s. Based in neutral Switzerland, the U.S. expected no loyalty from the pharmaceutical company. Fearing they might sell large amounts of LSD to the Soviets, the C.I.A. sent two agents and $240,000 to purchase all of the firm's LSD stock. The President of Sandoz informed the agents that since LSD's discovery the firm had produced a total of just 40 grams. He made a deal to supply the C.I.A. with 100 grams weekly and to keep them informed of all LSD orders. Nevertheless, the C.I.A. was much assured when an American firm, Eli Lilly & Company, discovered a process to produce LSD without the ergot fungus. The C.I.A. now had all the substance they could want and the loyalty of an American firm behind it.[140]

As the C.I.A. progressed in their control of the LSD supply and their potential control of the mind, they began to step-up their experiments. Imagining how the drug would be used in practice—by slipping it into an unsuspecting agent's food or drink—they began to test the notion on themselves. For a while, C.I.A. staff 'in the know' never drank anything they didn't personally control. One agent brought his own bottle of wine to all office parties to avoid any surprises. Nevertheless, some would have to succumb and succumb they did. An agent who drank some spiked coffee left the office in a flight of terror only to be chased halfway around Washington, D.C. by his cohorts. The inner circle of these experiments proved themselves by their inability to be swayed by LSD. Slipped a dose, the head chemist, or Helms (the project director), or any of the top 'operators,' could still play the spy game—showing how totally in control of themselves they were. At least they would not fumble if the enemy blasted them with truth serum.

Taking the experiments to their final extreme, the C.I.A. began drugging people outside of the agency, people who had no knowledge of LSD or what it did. When they did this to Dr. Frank Olson, a Chemical Warfare scientist for the Army, tragedy ensued. Gottlieb dosed a bottle of Cointreau with LSD during a meeting with members of the Army's Special Operations Division. Olson took poorly to the LSD and after suffering through some days of paranoia, guilt, and worry—committed suicide. The C.I.A. coverup was immediate. Twenty-two years passed before the Olson family understood the cause of their husband and father's suicide.[141]

Despite the tragedy and negligence of the Olson case, the C.I.A. considered its LSD experimentation too vital to shelf. The MKUL-TRA program continued unabated. The C.I.A. had to reassess their modus operandi. They needed to find experimental subjects they could monitor but ones who could not be traced back to the agency. The Army's Frank Olson was too close for comfort. They had to remove themselves even farther from their test subjects. By targeting questionable types--like prostitutes and drug addicts--the C.I.A. felt a safe distance from any credible accusation. In one set up, the C.I.A. operated a small brothel in San Francisco where unsuspecting clients would be guinea pigs for LSD and assorted psychotropics. Since people in such compromised positions are not likely to go on record about a night of psychosis in a whorehouse, the C.I.A. possessed a truly covert laboratory for human behavior. Many a lecher was chastened by the experience.

MKULTRA's search for chemical means to control behavior continued in one form or another until the early 1970s. When Richard Nixon expunged Helms from the C.I.A., Sidney Gottlieb also retired. With these two out of the picture, the C.I.A.'s nefarious research into mind control ended—hopefully.

## Enter the High Priest

Whether in the hands of the C.I.A. or research academics, LSD went unnoticed by the public. It could be spoken about in circles of intelligentsia but, by and large, the majority of people remained ignorant of this drug. A handful of psychotherapists began using it in therapy, to help unlock the mysteries of the subconscious.

The first celebrity to go on record was none other than Cary Grant. All told, Grant experienced more than seventy acid trips. Shortly after his first experience Grant gave a candid interview:

> I have been born again. I have been through a psychiatric experience which has completely changed me. I was horrendous. I had to face things about myself which I never admitted, which I didn't know were there. Now I know that I hurt every woman I ever loved. I was an utter fake, a self-opinionated bore, a know-all who knew very little. I found I was hiding behind all kinds of defenses, hypocrisies and vanities. I had to get rid of them layer by layer. The moment your conscious meets your subconscious is a hell of a wrench. With me there came a day when I saw the light.[142]

Given this was the 1950s, no one really knew what he was talking about. But this was all about to change.

In 1960 a middle-aged psychologist, just riding the wave of some successful research, consumed a handful of foul-smelling mushrooms while summering in Cuernavaca, Mexico.[143] The psychologist's name was Timothy Leary and he was about to take his first psychedelic trip on psilocybin mushrooms in the tradition of the Aztecs who had celebrated religious practices in Cuernavaca half a millenium before. Leary's mushroom experience impressed him so much that he devoted the rest of his life to the entheogens and became the flashpoint for the psychedelic inferno of the 1960s.

Leary's most pressing question in personality psychology involved therapeutic change. How does one turn a hopeless neurotic into a robust, integrated personality? Like Cary Grant before him, Leary came to see his own personality structure with ruthless clarity after the psychedelic experience. This enlightenment was accomplished in mere hours, compared to the years of psychoanalytic work. Psilocybin, the primary agent in the Mexican mushrooms, disclosed one's 'hang-ups' as effectively as a highly-trained therapist and with chemical simplicity. Leary's mushroom experience in Cuernavaca changed him forever. He spent the next few months talking to everyone who'd listen and experimenting with massive doses of pure psilocybin, chemically synthesized from the mushrooms and free of their noxious taste.

The most brilliant figure in a crowd of luminaries, the charismatic Leary eventually founded a religion, was arrested by a federal judge who called him, "The most dangerous man in the world", and claimed personal responsibility for ten million peoples' 'acid trips.' His battle cry to 'tune in, turn on, and drop out' provided a countercultural ethos for dissatisfied American youth and a marching beat to oppose the Vietnam War. Leary and his cohorts hoped that widespread experimentation with LSD would wrestle people free from the social constraints and lifeless expectations of those times. They were right. The mixture of war protest, psychedelic drugs, and skepticism about traditional ways of life forged a cultural revolution that, if ill-organized, still managed to change American society in a radical way.

Leary and his fellow Harvard professor, Richard Alpert, led project after project to mine the psychedelic realms. During this time, the group switched their chemicals too. First using psilocybin, they settled on the more intense LSD as their psychotropic of choice. Though they began with healthy scientific curiosity, these projects ended in absurd attempts at psychedelic Utopias. Many other LSD researchers began to dismiss Leary. They were fearful that his democratic ways, his desire to turn on everyone to the psychedelics, would bring ruin to the field. They were right. While Leary should not bear sole responsibility for the government's eventual crack down on the hallucinogens, he surely deserves a large part of the blame.

Leary's basic theory about the hallucinogens, cribbed from Aldous Huxley, sees them as opening up the reducing valve of consciousness. The mind must select primary tasks for attention since we can only be aware of so much at any one time. If, for instance, one is battling on a war front, it is not a good use of processing capacity to consider the particular hue of the sky, the scent in the air, or some intriguing lines by Blake. To perform well, you must be focused on the things most likely to harm you. According to Leary, the hallucinogens expand the mind (psychedlic) to allow the numberless influences of the moment equal say. Leary thought character structure and personality to be 'encrustations;' the built-up residue of too much consciousness restriction, mere lime-deposits within the valve. Using these drugs, he hoped to dissolve the residue of 'hang-ups.' This accomplished, one could hope to live a more enlightened existence. Leary's aims were social and religious as much as they were therapeutic. His research into a class of potentially therapeutic drugs led him to believe that everyone was in need of therapy. The normally adjusted, 'sane' modern was, in fact, a mad collection of personality hang-ups and behavior residues. This breached the category of psychology research and turned into social and religious revolution. Despite taking place in the early sixties, this idea came to express the tenor of that whole decade.

Leary's excitement soon leapt past even a quasi-scientific framework and embraced every Eastern conception of the 'Other World,' the spiritual realm of pure consciousness. Leary, Alpert, and Ralph Metzner put out a psychedelic guidebook based on the *Tibetan Book of the Dead*. No scientist would take him seriously any longer, most even thought him dangerous. But Leary's lack of restraint and unchecked creativity made him a champion of the hippies. His method, or lack of them, also promised ruin for any real growth. Almost everyone ended up disillusioned, sure they had stumbled upon something momentous but uncertain how to integrate it into their lives.

Leary's first quasi-religious organization, The International Federation for Internal Freedom (IFIF), attempted to set up base in Zihuatanejo, Mexico. The lush tropical surroundings along an unblemished stretch of Pacific served as the perfect venue for their psychedelic forays. After a few months, though, the Mexican government, tired of their antics and wary of the drug use, deported the lot of them. From there, the crumbling organization, inspired by the visionary Utopia Aldous Huxley set out in his novel *Island*, tried to lodge in first one, then another, Caribbean outpost. Government after colonial government chased them away, worried that they were attempting to assist locals in revolution which, at times, they were.

Broke and homeless, the fledgling group benefited from Leary's socialite standing. A friend of Leary's, a wealthy New York heiress, provided shelter for the psychonauts at one of her family's estates. IFIF settled on a five square mile estate, mansion and all, 90 miles north of New York city. These luxurious surroundings were home to some of the group's more decadent experiments. Trouble kept brewing and after just a few months of community living, Leary disbanded IFIF. The group was finally arrested and expunged from the house by authorities, led by assistant district attorney G. Gordon Liddy.[144]

Leary couldn't ignore his calling. He thought it his destiny to spread the knowledge and usage of Hofmann's otherworldly molecule. He touted LSD as the ultimate aphrodisiac and Playboy chased him down for an interview. The statement was far from true but Leary considered any means justified so long as it served his end of popularizing LSD.

Unfortunately, LSD did not live up to Leary's promise of enlightenment. If traditional conceptions of enlightenment always convey some attenuation of ego then Leary's hundreds of trips weren't working. For all his good intentions, Leary, both in his call to destiny and the indulgences he took along that path, exhibiting a thoroughly inflated sense of self-importance.

Along with him, thousands of other hippies and LSD enthusiasts seemed to be losing their way. Taking the baton from a bedraggled Leary, others, like Ken Kesey and the Merry Pranksters, continued to sway the masses to use LSD. They organized massive "Acid Tests" (see Tom Wolfe's classic novel *The Electric Kool-Aid Acid Test*) in which crowds could sample LSD while listening to the psychedelic music of the Grateful Dead. But even when millions had been 'turned on' the vision of the clear light always hid behind the next bend, the next dose, or the next drug. As Stevens sums up in his chronicle *Storming Heaven: LSD and the American Dream*: "Instead of creating a taste for enlightenment, LSD was promoting a love of sensation, the more intense the better..."[145] These groups began experimenting with every kind of drug in search of illumination, bliss, or just a new kick.

Among the maelstrom of hippies and hippie leaders, some spoke with more seasoned wisdom. For instance, Richard Alpert, who had been one of Leary's co-conspirators in the massive popularization of LSD eventually came to see drugs as a stumbling block. While exploring India in search of real enlightenment he came across a traditional guru and began following the rigorous methods of meditation. His spiritual record, *Be Here Now*, became a key text for the seekers of his generation. Another student of the Eastern traditions, Alan Watts, gave perhaps the final word on drugs and enlightenment: "My retrospective attitude to LSD is that when one has received the message, one hangs up the phone. ...my feeling about psychedelic chemicals, as about most other drugs, is that they should serve as medicine rather than diet."[146]

## All Good Things...

The time of consciousness expansion was quickly contracting as the sixties came to a close. In 1968, LBJ, in his State of the Union address, made the eradication of the psychedelics a national priority: "These powders and pills threaten our nation's health, vitality, and self-respect." The criminalization of the psychedelics had begun even before this, however. In California, the fault line of psychoactivity, possession of LSD became a crime on October 6, 1966. Though illegal, California would experience its 'Summer of Love' in 1967 with LSD still gushing through the hippie subculture.

# Psilocybin Mushrooms

> There is a world beyond ours, a world that is far away, nearby, and invisible. And there is where God lives, where the dead live, the spirits and the saints, a world where everything has already happened and everything is known. That world talks. It has a language of its own. I report what it says. The sacred mushroom takes me by the hand and brings me to the world where everything is known. It is they, the sacred mushrooms, that speak in a way I can understand. I ask them and they answer me. When I return from the trip that I have taken with them, I tell what they have told me and what they have shown me.
> —Maria Sabina (a Mazatec Shaman),
> *Plants of the Gods*[147]

The European rediscovery of psychoactive mushrooms occurred rather late in this century. For thousands of years occult traditions in forgotten parts of the world persisted in their ceremonial use of these mushrooms. Largely due to the devotion of one amateur mycologist (student of mushrooms), these fungi returned into the bank of common knowledge.

In contrast to cannabis, which can be cultivated easily, or the peyote cactus, which grows prolifically in certain parts of Mexico, psilocybin mushrooms have only recently swayed to human cultivation. Mushrooms yield to cultivation only with the most fastidious, scientifically-controlled methods. In the wild, these mushrooms grow during very humid times of year, sprouting where they may, seemingly overnight. Their appearance, then, seems a miraculous occurrence to prescientific peoples.

Psilocybin mushrooms (of which there are numerous species) appear as the last stage of fungal reproduction. Mushrooms, of any type, stretch skyward as the fruiting bodies of fungi in order to disseminate spores, their units of reproduction. Because these spores are microscopic, the reproduction process of fungi has only recently been understood with specialized scientific tools. In traditional cultures the growth of mushrooms could only vaguely be predicted; their mysterious appearance defied the most advanced knowledge of plants. Combined with their powerful psychoactive traits, psilocybin mushrooms truly fit the profile of a divine substance.

The sixteenth century Spanish missionaries, whose charge it was to convert vast sections of Mesoamerican peoples to Catholicism, found the natives' knowledge of plants to be quite sophisticated. The explorers and missionaries possessed no basis of comparison, the lush botanical wealth of these regions had no such European analogue. In chronicling what they perceived to be a diabolical Aztec religion (which did, in fact, practice terrifying amounts of human sacrifice), the more meticulous missionaries took note of the role of sacred plants in this tradition. One Dominican friar, Diego Durán, recorded the following:

> The sacrifice finished and the steps of the temple and patio bathed in human blood, they all went to eat raw mushrooms; on which food they all went out of their minds, worse than if they had drunk much wine; so drunk and senseless were they that many killed themselves by their own hand, and, with the force of those mushrooms, they would see visions and have revelations of the future, the Devil speaking to them in that drunken state.[148]

Seeing in the mushroom rituals a Satanic perversion of the Catholic Communion, the priests sought to stamp out this tradition. Along with the vast writings of the Aztec and Maya, these plants were banished by the Church. While the Aztec writing system and most of its literature was summarily destroyed, the usage of mushrooms continued in small pockets of Aztec-descended culture. Preserved by the *curanderos* and *sabios* (healers and sages), a few of these plants, like the psilocybin mushrooms, have come to be rediscovered by ethnobotanists (those who study the cultural significance of plants).

In 1936, an anthropologist named Blas Pablo Reko, began consulting the Nahua-speaking (a language derived from Aztec) mountain peoples of Oaxaca, Mexico about their sacred plants. Joined by the godfather of ethnobotany, Richard Evans Schultes, Reko obtained samples of the mushrooms from a village of Mazatec. In 1939, Schultes published a paper identifying the legendary Aztec *teonanácatl* (Flesh of the Gods) as this mushroom, and subsequently classified them *Psilocybe mexicana*.[149]

Despite this identification, little research followed until the fifties. An unlikely researcher, R. Gordon Wasson, participated in a secret mushroom *velada* (night vigil) with the Mazatec *sabia* María

Sabina, herself an heiress of the primordial shaman heritage. The American enthnobotanist R. Gordon Wasson was no academic, however. At the time, in fact, he was a Vice-President of J.P. Morgan—a Wall Street banker! He later coined a term for his own field, ethnomycology—the cultural influence of mushrooms.

He and his wife, a Russian-born physician, had long kindled a fascination for mushrooms. During their honeymoon in the Catskills, Wasson, of English heritage, reviled his young Russian wife's delight in the discovery and culinary preparation of wild mushrooms. He was quite sure she would poison herself eating these dirty 'toadstools.' The two intellectuals observed their noteworthy attitudes on this point and nursed their fascination over many years. They eventually concluded that some cultures (largely Western European) had been taught to shun mushrooms and fear them as universally poisonous. These cultures they labeled 'mycophobic.' Other cultures, like the Slavic Russians, adored mushrooms and commonly distinguished dozens of them. These cultures they called 'mycophilic.' They eventually concluded this divergence of feelings to have arisen from ancient religious taboos. The strange husband-wife hobby vaulted them to the forefront of a niche field. In the 1950s, the Wassons devoted increasingly more of their time to their studies and, following Schultes's trail, were among the first non-Aztec to ever experience the psychoactive influence of these sacred mushrooms.

In 1957, a couple years after the experience, Wasson published an article in *Life Magazine* about the mushroom *velada*—the ceremonial mushroom vigil that intertwines rich Catholic motifs with native Aztec traditions. Some think this article the spore of the psychedelic sixties. Wasson's poetic descriptions of his mushroom experience reveal a great deal about their role in shamanic traditions. The language of Wasson's accounts leaves no doubt that the mushroom and other entheogens helped early man to discover the soul or, at the very least, confirm its existence as an entity separate from the body:

> Here as in the first night the visions seemed freighted with significance. They seemed the very archetypes of beautiful form and color. We felt ourselves in the presence of the Ideas that Plato had talked about. In saying this let not the reader think that we are indulging in rhetoric, straining to command his attention by an extravagant figure of speech. For the world our visions were and

must remain 'hallucinations'. But for us at that moment they were not false or shadowy suggestions of real things, figments of an unhinged imagination. What we were seeing was, we knew, the only reality, of which the counterparts of every day are mere imperfect adumbrations.[150]

To the discontent of both R. Gordon Wasson and María Sabina, the local *sabia* who led the *velada*, many in search of psychoactive novelties began disturbing the Mazatec in search of their secret, and sacred, traditions. Timothy Leary, whose story has already been related, was among the first of these hack anthropologists.

The mushroom *veladas* exhibit the bizarre mixture of Native and European traditions that mark so much of Latin American culture. And yet, behind these façades, deeper still, one sees the shamanic influence, the millennial-old traditions, that emerged in the oldest matrix of Euro-Asian culture and lie as essential traits in the religious worldviews of people all over the globe.

### Mushrooms and Mysticism—The Good Friday Experiment

With psilocybin in pill form, thanks to Hofmann, researchers commenced an intriguing set of experiments in the early 1960s. Later prohibition of the entire class of hallucinogens by the DEA virtually ended research into these substances.

The most famous experiment was performed by a medical doctor in pursuit of a Ph.D. in the study of religion, Walter Pahnke. His interest in mysticism led him to research the entheogens. He decided to base his dissertation on an experiment he designed to test the entheogens' ability to evoke mystical experiences. Entitled the Good Friday Experiment, this relatively simple idea gained enormous press.

Using a set of nine criteria to distinguish a mystical experience (unity, transcendence of time and space, deeply felt positive mood, sense of sacredness, objectivity and reality, paradoxicality, alleged ineffability, transiency, and persisting positive changes in mood and behavior[151]) Pahnke distributed (in a double-blind procedure) either psilocybin or a niacin placebo to twenty volunteer subjects, mostly students from the Andover Newton Theological Seminary.

The setting of the experiment attempted to promote the religious connotations of these drugs. Pahnke received permission from the Dean of Marsh Chapel at Boston University to conduct the experiment as part of the Good Friday services. He received use of a closed off basement where the two and a half hour service could be conveyed via loudspeakers.

Of the ten subjects who actually ingested psilocybin, all experienced mystical experiences along the lines of the criteria mentioned above. One, unfortunately, went a bit mad and escaped the building, only to be chased down by supervisors of the experiment. By the next day, this subject was back to normal but never considered his experience very pleasant.[152]

One of the 'guides' in this experiment (who also received psilocybin), the same Huston Smith mentioned earlier, reports a particular highlight he had that day. Smith experienced the acme of his mystical experience after listening to what he objectively considered a "trite" hymn but, "...the gestalt transformed a routine musical progression into the most powerful cosmic homecoming I have ever experienced."[153]

In general, the experiences of the subjects who received psilocybin that day in 1962, were profound and cherished over a lifetime. A retrospective study in 1990 found all the active subjects truly thankful for that day twenty eight years earlier.[154]

Pahnke offered some cogent conclusions about the experiment. For one, the use of psilocybin to engender authentic mystical experience allows it to be reproduced—a *sine qua non* for scientific research. But, as Pahnke is quick to report, psilocybin does not guarantee a mystical experience. The recurrent theme of set and setting in relation to the entheogens is at least as important in furthering the experience than is the chemical alone:

> Positive mystical experience with psychedelic drugs is by no means automatic. It would seem that the "drug effect" is a delicate combination of psychological set and setting in which the drug itself is the trigger or facilitating agent—i.e., in which the drug is a necessary but not sufficient condition.[155]

In the end, mysticism—the origin of religion—may be its final step as well. Huxley aptly entitled it the "perennial philosophy." But mysticism needs more study and more exploration. Its psychology and possible dangers must be better understood. In short, mysticism needs science.

Just as animism integrated early cultures with their environment, teaching people to believe that all things are spiritual, subject and object alike, now science accomplishes the same thing—teaching us that the material world creates our inner world as well, subject and object revisited. Unfortunately, we lay between these two worlds—animism and science—desperately holding on to one that we know to be false (but want to be true), and another we know to be true but is, as yet, new and frightening. Until we recognize the congruency of our highest aspirations with nature, we will remain distorted and confused—hunter-gatherers living in the age of the atom bomb and supermarket.

### How Do LSD and Psilocybin Mushrooms Work?

With some eagerness the famed Swiss pharmacologist Albert Hofmann obtained samples of *Psilocybe mexicana* from Wasson via Roger Heim, a French mycologist.[156] Hofmann was able to isolate and then synthesize the primary entheogenic chemical he entitled psilocybin. The various species of mushrooms in the *Psilocybe* (Greek for "bald head") genus contain other active chemicals, but most experts agree that psilocybin is the primary agent of the experience. Wasson and Sabina, after experience with synthetic psilocybin, found no difference from the natural mushroom experience.[157]

Both LSD and psilocybin possess a molecular structure called an indole ring. These molecules closely resemble the neurotransmitter serotonin and can fit into a certain serotonin receptor, called the 5-HT2 receptor. Current researchers hold this to be the primary site of action for the hallucinogenic effects of these substances.[158] How or why binding to the 5-HT2 receptors creates the entheogenic experience remains unknown.

## Peyote

The peyote cactus (*Lophophora williamsii*) has been used as a sacred plant in the Americas for at least 7000 years.[159] Shaped like a bulging carrot, most of the cactus stretches beneath the soil. Only the crown of the plant, like the top of a carrot, remains above ground. A few wooly patches grow on this button and occasionally a dainty flower blooms from it. Those who make use of the plant cut off this top section. A new button grows back from the subterranean portion. Peyote buttons can be dried and kept for a very long time without losing any psychoactive properties.

Numerous indigenous tribes of Mexico, including the Aztec, revered peyote until the arrival of Spanish missionaries in the 16th century. Christianity's condemnation of sacred plants largely supplanted peyote usage. Only a few of the more remote tribes continued to use the cactus for healing purposes.

The Huichol, residents of Western Mexico, remain steadfast in their native traditions and have used peyote for centuries. Each October, a group of Huichol make an arduous 200 mile journey to a locale where peyote grows wild. Actually, the journey is not quite so arduous as it once was. In the old days, it was a 200 mile epic infused with magic and ceremony. Now it is a road trip along the major highways. Modernization has crept into this cultural niche as well. The Huichol still undergo some special preparations and abstain from sex, food, and sleep during the journey. Upon seeing the first cactus, the Huichol shaman shoots it with an arrow, for in their mythology they associate peyote with the deer and enact a sacred hunt. The pilgrims then proceed to harvest countless buttons, for each adult Huichol will consume between 6-12 of the buttons during the peyote ceremony in January. Outside of this ceremony, the plant is rarely consumed.

A people who still rely on hunting for a good portion of their food, the Huichol represent, in LaBarre's words: "...almost the ideal type of the mesolithic shamanic myth."[160] By this he refers to his larger theory that the shamanism of mesolithic hunting peoples crossed over with them from Eurasia into the New World tens of thousands of years ago. The stability of these cultural traits, as portrayed in numerous tribes and in evidence from French caves, to Siberian folkways, to Huichol peyotism, reflect an enormously ancient and influential complex of religious themes among pre-modern peoples the world over.

The art and clothing of the Huichol reflect peyote's influence on their culture. Few of the world's art forms reflect such a mastery of bright color, obviously the workings of the intense visual acuity peyote provides. Their careful beadwork generally focuses around religious and symbolic themes, commonly depicting the holy trinity of these people—deer, corn, and peyote. The yarn paintings they specialize in can convince the aesthete that he himself is seeing a psychedelic vision—the colors and pronounced play of geometry and form blast the eyes with a visionary maze.

Towards the end of the 19th century the use of peyote among Native Americans enjoyed a widespread revival. As the resident tribes of Texas and the Southwest were increasingly marginalized and forced from their lands, many of them, like the Apache, sought refuge in Mexico. It is from these and other forays that the use of peyote diffused from Mexican Native American populations to U.S. tribes. By 1870, peyote had definitely gained a foothold among some tribes of the American Southwest. From the Apache peyote use spread to the Kiowa, the Comanche, and the Caddo. By the turn of the twentieth century the congregation of numerous tribes on reservations rapidly diffused the peyote religion. Oklahoma became the epicenter of this influence and numerous Plains tribes took to peyote as a unifying religion that transcended their normal tribal divisions. Such unity was more necessary than ever given the tremendous changes wrought in Native American culture by the invasion of Europeans.

Peyote has been an integral part of certain Native American tribal customs for centuries. More recently, the use of peyote has achieved a galvanizing effect, bringing together members of disparate tribes into a single church. Peyote enjoys a rare status in American culture for it alone of the classic entheogens possesses a marginal tolerance by federal authorities. After years of judicial proceedings that alternately sanctioned and prohibited the use of peyote by members of the Native American Church (roughly 200,000 strong), the church finally won its 1993 case before the Supreme Court.

Forte relates a telling anecdote that imparts the Native American view concerning this substance: "Once, when a journalist casually referred to peyote as a drug, a Huichol Indian shaman replied, 'Aspirin is a drug, peyote is sacred.'"[161]

### How Does Peyote Work?

Just as LSD and psilocybin resemble the neurotransmitter serotonin, mescaline, the psychoactive compound of peyote, resembles the neurotransmitter norepinephrine. Though the states of consciousness between LSD and peyote are not identical, their overwhelming similarity leaves us to question why two different neurotransmitter systems can produce such similar effects.

## MDMA/Ecstasy

For all its novelty, MDMA, or Ecstasy, is not truly new; the compound was synthesized by Merck Laboratories in 1914.[162] In the late 1960s people had begun experimenting with many obscure hallucinogens besides the 'majors.' Among these lesser known substances was MDA, an amphetamine derivative. When the DEA cracked down on the hallucinogens they numbered MDA among those to be scheduled. Underground chemists found MDMA to be quite similar, molecularly, to MDA. Citing this similarity, people cautiously began using it. To their delight, it provided a unique psychological experience.

Ecstasy does not resemble other hallucinogens/entheogens. When using it people don't experience the unusual alterations in perception that LSD or psilocybin provide. The most striking property of Ecstasy is the feeling of empathy it arouses. It promotes trust and kindles concern for others. Some have entitled MDMA the 'love drug.'

Despite it's lurid label, Ecstasy is not an aphrodisiac. In fact, during the better portion of the four hour trip the 'mechanics' of sexual performance are hindered, especially in men. Rather than an erotic arousal, Ecstasy heightens non-sexual feelings of unity and commonality. Again, we must be struck by the ability of a drug to produce sentiments so traditionally 'spiritual.' The spirit of loving community that the early Christians deemed holy—*agape* and *koinonia*—are here rendered in chemical form. The kind-hearted atmosphere of an Ecstasy rave is probably not different in kind from a Baptist prayer meeting.

The earliest camp to realize these special properties and use them for therapeutic purposes was a network of psychologists. One of the great difficulties in psychotherapy is generating enough trust for an honest rapport between patient and therapist. For wounded people, there may be so many layers of defenses against a trusting relationship that useful therapy becomes almost impossible.

In the 1970s a chemist, impressed with Ecstasy's empathogenic (empathy-producing) properties, discussed them with a friend of his, an elder psychotherapist on the verge of retirement.[163] The psychotherapist had occasionally used hallucinogens in therapy sessions. Intrigued, he decided to give this still-legal drug a try. He was so impressed with the breakthroughs he achieved with some 'stuck' patients that he became Ecstasy's chief proponent. He spread the word of his good results and a number of psychotherapists began using Ecstasy in their practices.

Two camps quickly emerged in Ecstasy's history—the elitists and the popularists. The elitists held that Ecstasy should remain a relative secret, used by therapists and those psychological explorers who had already logged many hours in the reaches of psychedelic space. The elitists wanted to investigate its uses fully. Newcomers, they feared, might abuse the drug, using it without regard to appropriate set and setting. More than this, though, they feared that the popularization of Ecstasy would bring it to the attention of government authorities and lead to its regulation. Though legal, production occurred on a rather small scale catering to the needs of psychotherapists and cognoscenti. This group, based in Boston, did everything to stave off publicity and prevent government intervention. One Dallas-based Ecstasy user felt that he had stumbled onto a gold mine. He sought investors and began large-scale production of the substance in 1983. The Texas group advertised the drug at bars and nightclubs and distributed it at these locales. Instead of a beer, one could easily purchase a tablet of Ecstasy from any Dallas bartender for about $20. These entrepreneurs were right, they were mining the mother lode and turning some major profits. Ecstasy was made a Schedule I drug by the DEA just two years later.[164] To be placed in this category, a drug must meet the following criteria: a high potential for abuse, no currently accepted medical use, and a lack of safety for use even under medical supervision.

## How Does Ecstasy Work?

The mechanism of ecstasy is uncertain. It may work by fostering a massive release of serotonin. Some research suggests MDMA to be neurotoxic. In particular, it is thought to selectively damage serotonin neurons.[165] The long-term consequences of such injury could be disastrous but at this time few of its users seem to be complaining. Like most drugs, when MDMA is irresponsibly abused—taken too often or taken in large doses—damage to one's body is almost certain. Furthermore, when taken at raves, during which people may dance all night, MDMA may be particularly dangerous. Its tendency to alter heat regulation can cause a great deal of bodily harm, including rapid electrolyte imbalance. When these imbalances progress, the brain may swell.

*Chapter 16*

# THE BROKEN BRAIN

Some of the strongest, and certainly the most unsettling, evidence for the thesis of materialism comes from studying the broken brain. Whether chemically imbalanced or physically injured the broken brain puts before us a powerful testament concerning the human mind. All of the latest findings, especially those gained from the highly refined imaging technologies, locate the various mental illnesses in quite specific places in the brain. Furthermore, the success of medications in treating everything from obsessive-compulsive disorder to schizophrenia illustrates these faults to be brain based. In studying just a few of these intriguing details, we'll come to see that even the subtlest properties of the spirit arise from matter alone.

## *Depression*

In his "memoir of madness," *Darkness Visible*, the popular writer William Styron records some of his own reflections as he inches through depression:

> One bright day on a walk through the woods with my dog I heard a flock of Canada geese honking high above trees ablaze with foliage; ordinarily a sight and sound that would have exhilarated me, the flight of birds caused me to stop, riveted with fear, and I stood stranded there, helpless, shivering, aware for the first time that I had been stricken by no mere pangs of withdrawal [from alcohol] but by a serious illness whose name and actuality I was able to finally acknowledge. Going home, I couldn't rid my mind of the line of Baudelaire's, dredged up from the distant past, that for several days had been skittering around at the edge of my consciousness: 'I have felt the wind of the wing of madness.'[1]

Styron reveals anxiety as one of the key symptoms of depression. Typically thought of as an accentuated experience of the 'blues,' depression is, more often, a roller coaster ride between anxiety, despair, and dizzying fear. One worries that he will never escape from this cavernous space of meaninglessness. The depressive feels she doesn't 'deserve' to escape from this bondage and notes myriad faults of character and failures of kindness that have landed her in these chains of torment.

As a mental 'disease,' depression rests uneasily between our interpretations of the individual as a physical or spiritual being. With thousands of years of spiritual interpretation, a cure for depression has not come forth. Religion can uplift the 'spirit;' providing philosophic comfort, communal support, and a glimmer of hope for people in desperate circumstances. As far as truly curing despair, though, religion rarely saves a soul. The experience of melancholia, as clinical depression was once known, can be cured neither by prayer nor penance.

Physicians of all times and places have sought a means to help those suffering this most common mental disease, one that will strike 1 out of every 5 people (in its deep, clinical sense) during their lives.[2] Each year, more than 30,000 in the United States die from suicide.[3] Other than in ancient Japan, where samurai committed *seppuku* (ritual disembowelment) to retain a trace of honor after being shamed, suicide usually follows upon the heels of depression. And since the samurai culture is not especially flourishing in this country, we must attribute these yearly deaths to the various faces of depression. The root cause of countless addictions and fatal 'accidents' lies in this condition as well. It is, in short, an epidemic; the black plague of our times.

The subtlety of this disease has always posed great difficulties. Is it really a medical condition? Many continue to argue that it is not. They proclaim depression to be a weakness of character, a pessimistic take on the world by those not tough enough to make it through life's challenges. For all its insensitivity, this perspective is a logical one for a person who conceives of human beings as spirits. To a dualist, the alteration of chemicals in the brain cannot be why one person feels joy and another despair. In fact, such a take on the human condition is blasphemous to a person of this persuasion. The relative joy, despair, and comfort we feel results from our relationship to God, our state of faith, and the intercession of grace. If the dualist is not so religious as all this, he still thinks in terms akin to these—character, after all, cannot be part of one's physiology but must come from that mental stuff outside of the body. The depressive, through faults of her own, lacks the will power and perseverance to weather the storms. In short, a depressive is pusillanimous—weak-spirited.

Most contemporary physicians, even religious ones, feel less and less comfortable with such 'common sense' interpretations of depression. The advent of successful antidepressant medication confirms brain chemistry to be the mediator of this dreadful mindset. The modification of brain chemistry by medication, if it does not provide an outright cure to depression, can greatly alleviate its worst symptoms and open a window for therapeutic change. Psychotherapies can then more successfully address the sources of anguish and stress that contribute to the person's mood disorder.

Depression humiliates the traditional conception of man as a spiritual being. This disorder has taught us important lessons about our physical underpinnings. In just the last few decades science has provided us with medications capable of revitalizing the spirit and renewing hope for depressives. With the ingestion of mere chemicals, a personality change ensues. Depression, once treatable only by time, can now be readily 'managed' with the available drugs. By using an antidepressant, a once solitary, somber, and pessimistic person transforms into a pleasantly social, optimistic person. The spirit of man, the subtlest parts of his character and motivations, can undergo a conversion experience 'inspired' by drugs alone.

## Hippocrates's Humors

The turn towards a biochemical explanation of depression is not new. Hippocrates (c. 400 B.C.E.) provided the first biological theory of mood long ago. The Hippocratic influence runs deep in our medical traditions. At the inception of one's medical career, a doctor still recites the Hippocratic oath that weds him to the sanctity of the trade. Hippocrates's theory of humors, a physical explanation for moods and character types, lasted for over two thousand years alongside the spiritual interpretation of man. Hippocrates describes the idea in summary:

The body of man has in itself blood, phlegm, yellow bile and black bile; these make up the nature of his body, and through these he feels pain or enjoys health. Now he enjoys the most perfect health when these elements are duly proportioned to one another in respect compounding, power, and bulk, and when they are perfectly mingled.[4]

The four humors—blood, black bile, yellow bile, and phlegm—each cause a distinct effect on character. The four basic characters then are sanguine, melancholic, choleric, and phlegmatic. The sanguine person, whose excess is blood, lives with passion and fortitude, blood being the most fundamental and energetic fluid. An excess of yellow bile, or choler, caused a person's character to be angry and ill tempered. The phlegmatic person, with too much phlegm, exhibited sluggish, apathetic traits. And too much black bile led to melancholia—the depressive type. This theory describes the person's most basic attitude about himself and the world as a function of his bodily fluids.[5] Of course, this theory is no longer in currency but its division of people into character types still provides us with some useful adjectives.

The theory of humors attributed to Hippocrates derives some of its originality from Hippocrates's philosophical predecessor, Empedocles. Empedocles held that all of nature came from four components: earth, wind, fire, and water. In *Greek Rational Medicine*, Longrigg, describes this influence:

> ...his [Hippocrates] own hypothesis is the counterpart of Empedocles' theory in that he not only limits the basic constituents of the body to four, but also, like that philosopher, attempts to explain man as a product of his environment, conforming to the same laws operating within the cosmos at large.[6]

These first Western philosophers, known as the pre-Socratics, commenced a revolution in describing the nature and cause of the world as one of matter and its interaction. To them, the world did not originate in a supernatural substance but from the interaction of a few basic elements in nature. This background remains at the heart of our contemporary theories of nature and causality.

Hippocrates, with his ultra-modern instinct for science, quipped that all things have causes. With this insistence comes the scientific pursuit of causes, the search for the natural basis behind the mysteries of the world and the human condition. Without this first principle science and medicine are condemned to the mythological sphere. The task of medicine, in contrast to previous traditions of purifications, prayers, and entreaties to the gods, became a thoroughgoing study of the natural world. The original state of man, according to the humoral theory, is one of balance and health. Only when the humors become unbalanced do problems arise. The physician's trade rested in his ability to use diet, exercise, herbs, and an insight into environmental influences to right the balance of the humors. All in all, the underlying philosophy of this system is remarkably advanced.

The humoral theory's enduring influence is an enigma. How could a wholly physical explanation of man's moods remain popular when it blatantly contradicted Church teaching about the soul? Should a person in Medieval times become melancholic, who treats her—the priest for her sins or the barber (bloodletting doctor) for her humoral imbalance?

Galen (c. 129-200 C.E.), the most famous Roman physician, was the critical link between Hippocrates's medical views and the Medieval world. Galen's invigoration of the Hippocratic ideas sustained the humoral theory for the remainder of Christian history. Unfortunately, Galen also popularized bloodletting as a means to balance the four humors. Untold lives were lost as a result of this dangerous practice. In his work, *Revels in Madness*, Alan Thiher addresses the Church's acceptance of Galen's materialist ideas:

> Galen's legacy to Western culture…was the doctrine that the body…is the main cause of madness. This may not seem consonant with a theology that viewed the anima [soul] as a part of the divine spirit; but, since Galen could be construed as showing a belief in a monotheistic God, Christian thinkers worked with enthusiasm to fit Galen's thought in the Christian worldview.[7]

As a telling relic, the theory of humors provides us one more piece of evidence that man has never wholly accepted the spiritual interpretation of life. On some level, the recognition of his sheer materiality never escapes him. Too many of the influences around us—the seasons, our diet, medications—alter our deepest sense of self, our soul's consciousness. The act of denial, that all-too-common revolt against knowledge, always registers on some level of consciousness and allows us to mix, in practice, what cannot be mixed in theory—body and soul.

# The Chemistry of Despair

The neurochemistry of depression hinges on two prevalent neurotransmitters, serotonin and norepinephrine.[8] Hormonal susceptibilities to depression remain a part of most theories as well. While we don't understand the fine details of depression, we know that low levels of serotonin and norepinephrine correlate to the depressive experience. The most successful antidepressant agents alter the function of one or both of these neurotransmitters and their receptors.

The selective serotonin reuptake inhibitors (SSRIs, such as Prozac) are quite specific in that they target the serotonin pathways of the brain. Most of the brain's serotonin originates in the raphe nuclei, a small patch of neurons in the brain stem. Neuronal axons stretch from this structure all throughout the brain. These axons interlace many structures in the limbic system, the brain structures thought to be most involved with emotional processing. Unusual levels of serotonin, by affecting these limbic structures, modify one's moods.

If underactive, certain parts of the brain lead to depression. As the theory goes, these regions simply do not have enough serotonin. Deficient serotonin production could be to blame and, consequently, a change in receptor systems. Alternately, the problem may lie in the efficiency of the 'reuptake system.' Rather than constantly producing new neurotransmitters, the brain does a fabulous job of recycling. Through the process of reuptake the neurotransmitters that have not bound to the dendrite receptors reabsorb into the axon for future use. In depressives, this reuptake may occur too quickly. Rather than lingering in the synapse to fully activate the adjacent dendrites, these neurotransmitters get vacuumed back from whence they came. The recycling program has gotten too zealous leaving the original purpose of the chemicals unfulfilled. It's as if you were halfway through with your soft drink when a conservationist snatches it from you and recycles it! Similarly, the brain regions responsible for depression, due to this eager reuptake process, don't get properly activated—thus they don't function correctly. As a result, one experiences the complex of disturbing symptoms so well known to depressives: lack of energy, lack of pleasure, sense of futility, cognitive deficits, and the like.

If the problem is more basic and there's simply not enough sero-tonin produced for the job at hand, then the antidepressant's abil-ity to block reuptake virtually normalizes serotonin levels. The net amount of serotonin has not increased but the net effect of serotonin has increased because it is allowed to linger in the synaptic cleft for a more avid stimulation of serotonin receptors. As mentioned above, the balance between serotonin levels and receptor number and sen-sitivity cannot be overlooked. It is not simply levels of the chemi-cals that matter but some see-saw adjustment of the neurotransmitter's receptors.

## *Seasons of Discontent*

As old as humanity, depression has long plagued us. Sometimes adaptive, depression can slow us down when we might otherwise be too active. Some theorists have correlated a type of depression called Seasonal Affective Disorder to the cycles of hibernation in other mammals.[9] In this theory, it is thought that our bodies, through the intervention of mood, slow down into a depressive state to conserve energy. At these times of years we tend to oversleep and wallow in fatigue; physical rest being forced upon us at the cost of our mental well-being.

How does the body sense the seasons in this seasonally linked disease? Patterns of weather were no less predictable in prehistory than today, so the body settled on the ingenious solution of deter-mining seasonal changes by using light levels. The mechanism of winter is not some willy-nilly temperature drop but the tilting away of the Earth from the sun. This leads to a cooling of certain sections of the globe (and a warming of others) as we progress on our 365 day revolution around the sun. Sensing the diminution of light, the brain alters its hormonal (especially the sleep-wake hormone, melatonin) levels which, in turn, affect neurotransmitter levels. Why do all this? Why change the happy homeostasis that is our mood?

For most of our evolution the harshness of winter meant a reduction in food sources, especially during ice ages. If, during these times, ancient man frolicked with the gaiety of summertime, he'd quickly fall short of calories and risk starvation. After all, the nuts and berries of summertime had dropped to the ground, leaving nothing but skeletal bushes behind. The few animals that survive through winter generally hole up and venture out but briefly. Hibernating, they conserve their calories. All the food supplies of spring and summer are pitifully low. But while animals experience this as just a slowing-down of activity, we have the additional mental aspects with which to contend. Animals are more purely behavioral beings whereas humans are mental/behavioral in our nature. Much of our behavior proceeds from our mentality—our thoughts, memories, and influences. If we're huddled in the cave, discussing the dismal plays of Sartre, we're burning a lot less calories than if we're out chasing our lovers through the forest. Our mentality becomes dark—why do anything? Our body forces a mentality upon us to—paradoxically—control the body.

A fine explanation, this theory provides only a partial solution to the vast range of depressions and their diverse causes. Depression, for all its woes, may have found such a place in our species because in some instances it proved highly adaptive. In times of danger and scarcity, the best strategy to survive may have been avoidance and rest. In our twenty-first century world, such prehistorical adaptations may have lost their value. Many doctors now swear by light therapy, encouraging SAD sufferers to purchase full spectrum lights and expose themselves to it during the dark mornings of winter. But, alas, there's always Prozac.

## *Alzheimer's Disease*

The most common type of dementia, Alzheimer's disease (AD) gradually, and hideously, deteriorates one's mental faculties. In my own family, I've seen two people dwindle away into fragments of their former selves. It is likely that I carry some of the genes for this disease and thus have a predisposition for it. If I live a long life, I may have to face this fearsome enemy.

Beginning in the hippocampus, the way station for the formation of memories, the disease generally spreads throughout the brain, devastating the cerebral cortex in particular. The overall number of Alzheimer's cases in the U.S. amounts to some 4 million people. The chance of getting AD doubles every five years between the ages of 65 and 95, from approximately .3% at age 65 to 10% at age 92.[10] In spite of this prevalence, AD is not a normal part of aging and not to be confused with the 'senior moments' everyone experiences as the years stack up. Alzheimer's is truly a disease process; the victim must have a genetic predisposition for it.

Alzheimer's Disease reduces the amount of brain tissue through a malignant progression of web-like tangles and plaques. These growths strangle the nerve cells and interfere with cellular communication. Eventually the disease lowers levels of key neurotransmitters. The intersection of these problems transforms the theoretically simple disease process into a syndrome—a combination of symptoms arising from a number of different causes. Study of the syndrome requires a careful disentanglement of one symptom, and its neural basis, from another.

During early phases, the redundancy of one's mental functions makes the disease seem rather minor; mainly the patient suffers difficulties with recent memories and concentration. As AD progresses and more and more tissue dies, the mental deficits become staggering. A very dangerous symptom, many AD sufferers wander off when not carefully monitored. Some tragic cases have resulted from this tendency. The person in the late stages of AD has lost all ability to remember, has difficulty controlling bodily functions, and cannot reason abstractly. One account of an Alzheimer's victim (Mr. E) records the following:

> A year and a half after Mr. E's initial visit to the geriatric center...Mrs. E first began discussing long-term placement for Mr. E with the treatment team. By this time, the dementia was severe: Mr. E paced most of the night, experienced frequent crying spells, and has become physically threatening to his wife. On one occasion, Mrs. E had gotten up during the night to find that her husband had turned up the thermostat to the maximum temperature, turned on all the burners of the stove, and turned the oven on at 500 degrees.[11]

The human tragedy of AD cannot fail to frighten: before family and friends, one's personality undergoes a progression of changes until it disappears altogether.

Because age is the most important risk factor, our society faces a health epidemic like never before. Once the baby boomers live into their seventh and eighth decades we will encounter Alzheimer's all around us. According to predictions, by 2050 the number of AD sufferers will equal the number of cancer patients.[12]

## Brain Damage

Brain trauma occurs all around us. Knowingly or not, we encounter brain damaged people almost everyday. Besides the more identifiable types, there are always the stroke victims, the slowly-sinking Alzheimer's cases, and those who are unwittingly growing tumors in their heads. Additionally, head injuries are a rampant health problem. In the United States alone, more than 2 million head injuries occur each year.[13]

Surrounded by brain injury as we are, most of us remain blind to it. We may get aggravated with a homeless person or a young troublemaker never perceiving the fact that they suffer from a true biological disorder. The offensive behavior of some noteworthy boxers is almost certainly the result of persistent blows to the head. When confronted by these strange people, we mutter something about them 'having a screw loose' but see their actions as proof of bad character rather than the result of a physical impairment. If a person in a wheelchair comes our way, we're eager to clear a passage or hold open a door; we feel their incapacity to be a blameless one. When disabilities are less visible, hidden away in the wiring of the brain, we tend to show little sympathy or patience. Our dualistic heritage still convinces us that all things mental are securely lodged in the realm of spirit. Bad behavior can only be caused by poor choices and sinister character, an exercise of will.

A callousness born from ignorance is excusable; brain damage, after all, is difficult to diagnose even with careful medical training. Depending on where the brain receives injury, a mental or behavioral deficit may be strikingly apparent or comparatively subtle. Damage to the vital structures in the hindbrain usually lead to death or send one into a deep coma, sometimes never to awake. Damage to the occipital lobes at the back of the brain may render one blind or partially blind—unable to perceive color or depth, for instance. Or, in rarer instances, as Dr. Oliver Sacks relates, a person can become "blind to blindness" altogether:

...in one patient under my care, a sudden thrombosis in the posterior circulation of the brain caused the immediate death of the visual parts of the brain. Forthwith this patient became completely blind—but did not know it. He looked blind—but he made no complaints. Questioning and testing showed, beyond doubt, that not only was he centrally or 'cortically' blind, but he had lost all visual images and memories, lost them totally—yet had no sense of any loss. Indeed, he had lost the very idea of seeing—and was not only unable to describe anything visually, but bewildered when I used words such as 'seeing' and 'light.' He had become, in essence, a non-visual being. His entire lifetime of seeing, of 'visuality,' had, in effect, been stolen.[14]

Such bizarre cases force us to reevaluate traditional concepts of the self. The notion of a stable, unitary, 'invulnerable' self makes little headway in explaining the brain damaged.

Reading a book by Oliver Sacks or Antonio Damasio provides a wealth of such strange cases. The annals of neuropsychology are full of people whose brain injuries correspond with dramatic losses in mental function. Many of these case histories lead to major philosophical questions. As you read about an Alzheimer's patient whose personality changes and whose 'spiritual essence' dissipates to leave a foreigner behind, you cannot avoid the identification of the mind with the brain. If this is the case, though, why wasn't the conclusion reached earlier? Why have philosophers and prophets so clung to the concept of a soul when brain injury so clearly defies this concept? The basic thesis of this book is that our inherent fear of mortality and the historical momentum of the idea of the soul has, until now, kept us believing the unbelievable. Nevertheless, one still wonders how the great thinkers throughout history missed all the evidence of the mind's utter dependence on the brain. Why didn't Plato see that head injuries changed peoples' souls?

Looking back on history with the divine vision afforded by a university library misinforms us. Bathed as we are in information—televisions, newspapers, books-a-plenty, and the internet—we forget how scarce information was to most people throughout history. For Socrates and Plato, for Augustine, even for Descartes, books were especially rare things. Until 1492, the year that the printing press was invented, books were reproduced completely by hand. Imagine what luck it took to come across a good volume, and how expensive it must have been!

We know in our own times how information can be altered along the path from the incident to our ears. Imagine then what life was like before the printed word when literally everything you heard about came through countless, error-prone people who were just passing along stories.

Surely, the wars in ancient times produced a bevy of head injuries. Men returned with wounds in their bodies and minds. But even with a surplus of cases such men disappeared in a thousand directions back to their local villages and farms. They were not all laying about the local VA hospital ready for study. In sum, the radically different nature of communications now compared to most of history prevented the reasonable construction of theories about the mind. The case examples that seem so telling to us were few and far between until recently.

In this section, we'll briefly survey a few of the more interesting type of brain injuries, especially those resulting from damage to the frontal lobes. Such damage can be quite common, for these structures—evolutionarily the youngest—are also the most vulnerable. Brain injury to the frontal lobes occasions profound alterations in personality. Healthy and effective in almost every other way—able to memorize facts, perform arithmetic, retain their IQ score—a person with frontal lobe damage can lose something as central as 'self.' Some evanescent part of the person may be forever lost, though in all other ways he remains the same. A great many of us are so insensitive and have been so misinformed by the mind/body distinction that we assume that any conscious person is a whole person, an 'ensouled' person. Frontal damage teaches us that while everything else may be working, the person has basically 'checked out.' How shall traditional, soul-based theology treat such people? Has the essential identity of the person flown skyward, leaving his body, all his memories, some complement of emotions, and his perceptions behind? Is such a person responsible for his actions after head trauma in the same way as he was before? When we talk to our brain-damaged friend are we interacting with a soulless automaton? The clumsy philosophy of yesteryear cannot plausibly account for brain damaged people.

## The Strange Case of Mr. Gage

The most famous case of frontal lobe damage occurred in 1848 to a young man named Phineas Gage.[15] We forget, in our young era of antibiotics and intensive care units, how rare it was to survive such head trauma back in the day. His story is one of the oldest and best documented cases of severe injury to this part of the brain.

At age 25, Gage had become a foreman for the Rutland & Burlington railroad. His job consisted in overseeing a construction group that was fast laying tracks across Vermont. While performing a routine duty, tapping a gunpowder charge into rock, Gage carelessly began tapping the charge down before sand had been heaped upon it for insulation. Setting off this makeshift gun, the tapping bar—a three and a half feet long iron shaft—exploded upwards piercing a large, clean hole through the right frontal lobe. Phineas Gage had effectively lobotomized himself.

Gage's young and robust nature helped him survive this physical trauma. Though he lived another 13 years, the man never truly recovered. His personality underwent a profound alteration. Using Freudian terminology, Gage had lost superego, ego, and was left only with id. His hearty appetites went unrestricted, he became lazy, irresponsible, impulsive, and was unable to hold down a job for any length of time, even the menial ones he usually took, and he suffered from abulia—a loss of goal-oriented behavior. Besides these alterations, though, he was otherwise the same man! But what does such a statement mean? He had his same body, could speak, act, react, remember things, seek pleasure, avoid pain, but his previous 'soul' had been literally blown out of his head. In the words of his friends: "Gage was no longer Gage."

## Lobotomy

In *One Flew Over the Cuckoo's Nest*, Ken Kesey exposed the worst sin of 20th century neurology—the prefrontal lobotomy. A practically random mutilation of the frontal lobes, the procedure was used on no less than 40,000 people—in the United States alone.[16] In Kesey's novel, R.P. McMurphy, an excessively free spirit, was reduced to a dribbling infant after one of these operations. As horrid as the lobotomy could be, turning neurotics into zombies, this psychosurgery (literally, "soul surgery") began as a medical procedure with all the best intentions.

Doctors have always used whatever means available to curb the diseased tendencies of disturbed minds. Through history we've seen trephination (not all that different from lobotomy), tinctures of lead and arsenic, insulin-shock, malaria therapy, and electroshock (which, somewhat updated, is still practiced) come and go as methods to exorcise (also still in use) the demons of insanity. So long as the delicate mechanisms of the brain fail to reveal their intricate secrets, our best procedures will be lumbering, blunt ones at best.

If the unstable mind can be compared to a symphony whose individual sections and instruments fail to harmonize, then medication therapies can be equated to knocking out the discordant percussionists or the string section. Even with our most refined knowledge about brain chemistry, medication treatments remain quite crude. But the lobotomy took the award for desperate cures, attacking mental illness with a knife. 'Fixing' psychological disorders with lobotomy is like trying to harmonize a symphony by driving a semi-truck across the stage.

A Portuguese neurologist named Egas Moniz developed the lobotomy in 1935. In 1949, he won the Nobel Prize for his work. Though he had long considered neurosurgery for the treatment of psychological disorders, Moniz had been freshly inspired to consider this approach upon hearing about a recent experiment in which two chimpanzees had had their frontal lobes removed. After the removal, the chimps no longer retained the ability to get anxious or frustrated. Moniz considered that a disruption of frontal lobe function may essentially separate the emotional and intellectual parts of the brain, thus serving to quiet a troubled mind.[17]

Drawing from a mental hospital, Moniz obtained its worst case patients, of all persuasions, as experimental subjects. His early procedure was to inject pure alcohol into those areas of white matter that connected the frontal lobes to the rest of the brain. Targeting these areas, he hoped, would prevent some of the large-scale damage (and surgical risks) that would occur if he attempted something akin to complete frontal lobe removal, as had been forced upon the chimps. The operation never took on much more refinement, its sole aim to destroy massive amounts of the white matter beneath the frontal cortex. Basing his 1936 book, *Experimental Surgery in the Treatment of Certain Psychoses*, on just 20 subjects, Moniz proclaimed the procedure a fundamental success—an innovative treatment for severe psychiatric disorders.[18]

His earliest convert, and a man who single-handedly performed thousands of the operations, was the American neurologist Walter Freeman. Freeman thought the technique too promising to be limited to the worst cases alone so he began prescribing it for even the slightest neuroses. His first operation was performed on a housewife from whom he had gained consent. Hardly a severe case, the patient was, in Freeman's words: "...a typically insecure, rigid, emotional, claustrophrenic individual," and a "past master at bitching..."[19] Shortly before the operation, the woman had nearly rejected her consent when she learned that her hair would have to be shaved. In Freeman's chilling words: "We got around her objection by promising to spare the curls if we could. Of course it was impossible, but after the operation she never mentioned the lost curls."[20]

Freeman understood the lobotomy's 'success' as a reduction of the sense of self. He wrote: "Since too intense preoccupation with the self seemed to be the sine qua non of emotional disorders, it followed that cutting down on this would enable the patient to focus his attention on the more constructive aspects of his life among his fellows."[21] In comparing surgical lobotomy to psychoanalysis, Freeman notes: "I have written of the Gordian knot that Alexander cut when he did not have the patience to unravel it, and suggested that psychiatrists might at times resort to the knife rather than attempt in their own compulsive fashion to try to unravel it."[22] The lobotomy had trespassed into the very sanctum of the self, reaching in and ripping out the offensive personality.

In performing surgery on the soul, Freeman's intentions were therapeutic but he seems to have possessed a peculiar insensitivity to all things fine. This insensitivity may explain his failure to perceive the more hideous shades of the operation. When discussing the wild sexual drive that is often aroused after this surgery, one of the traits of the so-called "lobotomy personality," Freeman gives the following advice to the wives of lobotomized men: "Physical self-defense is probably the best tactic for the woman. Her husband may have regressed to the cave-man level, and she owes it to him to be responsive at the cave-woman level. It may not be agreeable at first, but she will soon find it exhilarating if unconventional."[23] Rarely has "self-defense" been used so euphemistically. Another passage serves to illustrate his bluntness to subtlety. In discussing the lobotomy personality, with its noted destruction of the intellectual functions, he writes: "Society can accommodate itself to the must humble laborer, but justifiably distrusts the thinker...Lobotomized patients make rather good citizens."[24] To Freeman, then, the sacrifice of the higher intellect seemed a meager loss.

In 1946, Freeman crowned his surgical technique by developing the transorbital lobotomy. This method circumvented the more laborious and risky task of breaching the thick-boned parts of the skull by entering the cranium through a corner of the eye socket. Using a hammer, and in the earlier trials an ice pick from his own kitchen, Freeman would perforate the wafery bone behind the eyeball and then wrangle the pick around to sever neural connections. While infection was still a concern, the transorbital lobotomy saved a great deal of time. Freeman would often proceed in assembly line fashion, lobotomizing patients in under ten minutes. With this innovation, the numbers of lobotomies soared and a less skilled group of surgeons could perform them in mental hospitals, prison wards, and even medical offices. The previously depressed, anxious, or eccentric patients would return to their lives pleasantly quiet, exhibiting nothing more than a black eye from their brain surgery. A part of themselves had been forever knocked-out. Freeman hoped doctors would come to see the transorbital lobotomy as little different than a tonsillectomy.

In the 1950s psychiatry was revolutionized by the successful new generation of psychotropics, including Thorazine. These drugs could stabilize and sometimes truly 'cure' psychotic illnesses. Now, the crude technique of lobotomization appeared all the more extreme. The procedure gradually faded, criticism increased, and the tumult of the 1960s, with its hyperawareness of civil rights, helped to end most forms of psychosurgery. The dark ages of psychiatry had come to a close.

## *Anosognosia*

Anosognosia is the most insidious type of brain damage but also the most interesting. It indicates a lack of awareness of weakness or disability—a delusion about one's capacities. No matter how severe the behavioral or personal alteration, *the person doesn't know what she's lost!* Anosognosia resembles a mental blindspot—though an injury's effect can be noticed, measured, and recorded by others, the person herself perceives no change in self-concept. This disorder remains something of a mystery though it almost always occurs when there is damage to the right hemisphere of the cortex. When damage has occurred here, especially to the right frontal lobe, a massive amount of denial ensues.[25]

In *Phantoms in the Brain*, V.S. Ramachandran, the preeminent researcher of anosognosia, relates a number of the oddities that arise when questioning people who suffer from this disorder. In considering exactly 'how far a patient will go' in some delusion or another, he recounts a woman who'd recently suffered a massive stroke and had lost command of the left side of her body:

'Mrs. Dodds, can you touch my nose with your right hand?'
She did so with no trouble.
'Can you touch my nose with your left hand?'
Her hand lay paralyzed in front of her.
'Mrs. Dodds, are you touching my nose?'
'Yes, of course I'm touching your nose.'
'Can you actually see yourself touching my nose?'
'Yes, I can see it. It's less than an inch from your face.'[26]

Here, the exasperated Mrs. Dodds put up with as much of Dr. Ramachandran's nonsensical directions as she could tolerate. And, in the end, *she saw what she wanted to see.*

In many cases of right frontal lobe damage, the patient will proclaim to their doctors that a strange person is sharing their bed. Unable to recognize the paralyzed part of their body, the unresponsive arm or leg, they lose all awareness that such parts ever belonged to them—a condition called asomatognosia (lack of awareness of body parts). A common response is, "Doctor, someone is laying on top of me." Frequently, patients will snatch the unresponsive limb, using their right arm to grasp their left, they will attempt to fling it out of bed—only to find themselves tumbling out of bed with it! They have so lost the sense of their bodies that their perception of self convinces them that one part belongs to another person altogether. The perception of self—be that capacity a mental one or a physical one—depends totally on brain structures.

## ADHD

The traits of frontal lobe dysfunction exert themselves along a continuum. For all the severe cases of frontal lobe dysfunction, a great many more subtle ones prevail. People with Attention Deficit Hyperactivity Disorder (ADHD) have relatively little activity in this brain region compared to the rest of the population. Formerly called "minimal brain dysfunction," ADHD occurs in 3-4% of the population.[27] In the United States, that equals some 8 to 11 million people. By stimulating the prefrontal cortex, especially its dopaminergic pathways, stimulants—such as Ritalin—actually calm the hyperactive person and increase his ability to concentrate. Since the stimulant arouses frontal lobe brain tissue, the person can finally enlist this region to augment his concentration. Unfortunately, while Ritalin and other treatments may improve some aspects of ADHD functioning it comes at the cost of impairing other functions. Like most psychotropic treatments, therapy with Ritalin is a rather simplistic approach to treat a complicated disorder.

ADHD originates in the frontal lobes. These individuals, then, may test (if you can keep them still long enough) all across the charts, the same as 'normal' people. The capacities they possess outside of the frontal lobes are usually unaffected. Within the set of these people are great mathematicians, linguists, and scientists, at least insofar as innate ability goes. When it comes to the mass of information you must actually master to excel in any discipline, these people quickly fall behind because they lack the ability to concentrate. In some cases, the ADHD sufferer cannot stick to any plans or work towards goals (abulia). Distractibility is the overarching trait of this brain disorder. Along with distractibility may be a chronic hyperactivity and emotional impulsivity. Since the child isn't born with fully developed frontal lobes, a good deal of this behavior may be on the way to resolving itself as he matures. Only in the hopelessly distractible adolescent can you be sure that something truly 'dysfunctional' in the brain's development has occurred.

The psychologist sees the same type of distractibility in those who have suffered frontal injury. But the ADHD case, in contrast to a true injury case, possesses the ability to relieve his condition. The injury case, his brain tissue destroyed, cannot so easily regain the functions of the frontal lobes. If severe, the person may be wholly unable to concentrate; as spontaneous as a dog in a park. He may be unable to hold down a job for long. When his inability to stick to a routine doesn't fail him, his emotional outburst might just do him in. Such were the symptoms that Phineas Gage could never overcome after his terrible accident. The less aggrieved person, with just a bit of excited distractibility, may be the life of the party and comedian *par excellence*. As we learned in the section on alcohol, the depression of the frontal lobes accentuates the sense of spontaneity by freeing up one's inhibitions. Depending on the context, this kind of behavior is anything but dysfunctional; in many situations it is quite superior. At a party or in a ribald conversation such ability serves the person well. The 'dysfunction,' then, lies not in the behavior itself but in the person's incapacity to *ever* alter it. To study, to read, to perform experiments, to contemplate—all require a measure of indistractibility. Like Socrates poised in some inner landscape, deep thought depends on a temporary isolation from the distractions of one's environment. The serious-minded concentration that lies behind all the mental innovations of our species requires some amount of steady-gazed concentration. Without the frontal lobes performing optimally, such a gift is kept from the person.

# PART III

# GIVING UP THE GHOST

...every living thing comes from the dead.
—Plato, *Phaedo*

# The Beautiful Lie

Tell the beautiful lie.

Tell the children whose doting parents just died in a robbery or on a racing freeway that they are not really gone but in a joyous place of light, just a silent plane away, still watching over the family and working in their favor; always witnessing their kids' athletic victories with pride; always sharing their defeats with sympathy and concern; present always at their marriages with love abounding—father misty with tears, mother rendered mute by joy—father walking his daughter down the aisle in invisible glory. Tell the sweet children, tell the children always; the children still insensate to the leaves' browning, the leaves falling, and the termite-ridden husk of the tree robbed of its sap; still ignorant of the squirrels' winter starvation within— unknowing of the runt's short, cruel fate at the paws of his siblings and parent—they too soon to starve, the mama squirrel already shaking from eating too little and suckling too much; always tell the children, tell them that someday not too far off the great reunion awaits at the mighty oak table with places for all and boundless cornucopias and music and laughter and long-missed embraces...and always.

Assure the loving husband that his cancer-stalked and cancer-reaped wife longs for him until his own timely death when they shall again be brought together in a more lasting bliss free from disease and pain and worry and doctors. No more blood cells to be counted, no more injected morphine to dull the pain and the spirit, no more loss of hair and fading of life, no more closed eyes and still, shriveled hands daintily crossed in a pristine gesture of peace.

Promise the father who has lost his precious daughter that at the end of days they will hold each other and never again be wrenched apart by the cruelty of a blind mortal fate, or a blind drunk driver. Again shall they walk in green meadows, hand-in-hand, and chat about the flowers and the bees and the rippling brook full of fish. Again she shall ride upon his shoulders and see the world from the towering height of her papa's frame, the grand scope of his vision way up there. Again and again moreover.

Tragedy begone! Happiness, light, and life forever!

Each of us has told this beautiful lie to a mourner or to ourselves, mourning. It has saved many of us and kept us going in the face of mind-arresting tragedy. The happy illusion has deposited hope in bankrupt hearts and brought a long-missed dawn of happiness to what seemed an endless night of despair.

Is it cruel or insane to tell the truth? Can we possibly admit that there is no more—save memory—once the gate of death has crashed down upon a once vibrant life? Should we not preserve our beautiful—our truly necessary—illusion with every scrap of effort and with all our powers of faith? Shall we not happily condemn the man who would question our dear doctrine? And if even the quietest voice, if some little part of us hidden away in the farthest corner of our soul, should whisper a despairing tone shall we not strike him down? We shall—we must—do all these things lest we awaken to the all-pervading sadness of our all-too-real tragedies, to the tragedy at the heart of the world, to the tragic sense of life itself.

Is it monstrously cruel to tell this truth? Is it insane to admit the destiny of one and all? To admit that the unconscious leaf, the barely-conscious squirrel, and the supremely conscious human being share equal destinies? To judge from the world's great religions, and their billions, this truth should be denied. The majority of humans who have lived on this planet have long counted upon these faith systems and the ultimate hope they all place out on the farthest reach of the limb—that succulent fruit—the hope of a better life without end. But in reaching for that mythical fruit will we not finally fall and take the limb crashing down with us?

Before we make an honest decision, before we choose truth or illusion, we must carefully weigh, as best as we're able, what is gained and what lost. And if it's illusion you choose, fear not, for all these thoughts will recede like so much sand at the edge of shore. For one thing nature has provided us is a preternatural ability to deceive, and thus to defend, ourselves.

## Chapter 17

# CONTINGENCY: THE STING OF DEATH

> Our language and our culture are as much a contingency, as much a result of thousands of small mutations finding niches (and millions of others finding no niches), as are the orchids and the anthropoids.
> —Richard Rorty, *Contingency, Irony, & Solidarity*[1]

Death is sometimes acceptable in the very aged as it finally switches off a dimming lamp. It is more difficult when it swoops down upon a life bright with energy, in the midst of its projects, to snuff out its fire. In these losses, death reveals to us the central horror of life—contingency.

The conclusion of all postmodern thought, contingency teaches that nothing is 'supposed' to be. A marked tendency of thinking, well-represented in ancient philosophy, is the notion that everything aims towards an end. This notion goes by the name of teleology. If you think teleologically then you assume that nature strives for completion and the supremely meaningful integration of all things. One has only to read the Catholic priest, Teilhard de Chardin, to recognize the intensity with which even the scientifically literate may grasp for the lost hope of teleology. Contingency opposes this humanizing doctrine and remains the most challenging philosophic issue in our time and in times to come. No grand plan works itself out in the cosmos, neither human nor human-like intentions pull strings behind the veil of our ignorance.

Contingency means 'purposeless' or 'random;' it contrasts with 'by design' or 'Providence.' Whether a particular species of owl dies out, whether a supernova flashes, or whether democracy becomes the standard government of all peoples—no 'greater power' and no 'higher authority' *intends* anything of the sort. The things to which we attach our sacred meanings have no necessity. The real pang of this philosophy comes from this: no matter who you are—be you rich or poor, green-eyed or brown-eyed, famous or unknown—no matter the individual merits of your character, you may die today, you may die in the very next moment. Nothing precludes your imminent death. Considering this, one may conclude that all human effort and all culture emerged as methods of contingency avoidance, of "terror management."[2] The science of medicine, for instance, consistently expands its boundaries to wrest more and more control from disease and disintegration. As medicine improves, the sheer 'luck' (another synonym for contingency) of one's genetics and the random threats from one's environment become less and less controlling over life. So also do governments and police forces attempt to wrap people together and provide them a meaningful structure of protection and opportunity. Criminals are chained, wars avoided, and overall civic safety improved. Governments protect people from contingencies in other ways as well. In a more ruthless time, depending on the luck of your birth, you might enter the world absolutely destitute with no chance of opportunity. Alternately, you might be born into tremendous power and for no good reason lord it over thousands of lives. Democracy and socialistic economics try to minimize the inconsistencies of birth so that justice and equality become more universal. Nature, however, uses no such logic. One person is born strong and intelligent, another weak and mentally disabled; one into a family of cuddling and laughter, another into a family of abuse and neglect. As humans extend our knowledge and power, we desperately wash over the most blatant of these contingencies. But no matter how ingenious our methods or expansive our knowledge, we will always—at the end of days—pass into oblivion.

Contingency has been most aggressively tackled by religion. Using an imaginative framework, religious doctrines take the contingent and wholly deny it, claiming everything inhuman to be part of God's mystery. Religion is the sanctification of teleology, the assertion that all things exist by Providence. And against that champion of contingency, death? For the religious, death is no end, but a transition; justice not blind, but karmically harmonized over the eons (beyond the sight of our mortal eyes, that is). Much as religions have worked to annul the rights of contingency, they have, at last, failed. Nothing could prevent us from maturing, even if slowly. And all know from the experience of adolescence that maturation often comes in spurts, and painful ones at that.

Like a powerful medicine, contingency goes down bitterly. People find this concept so difficult because all of our thinking is founded on its opposite: we live through principles of meaningful order, reason-driven changes, and carefully planned, fully 'mapped-out' sets of actions. Of course, all such organization refers to human-directed activities—the manner in which we communicate to one another, structure our social groups, and comprehend our natural environment. When we look into a mindless puddle of contingent facts—like a pile of spaghetti strands that have landed atop one another—we instinctively begin to draw the strands apart in an attempt to discover their underlying pattern (provided we're not driven by the more pressing instinct of hunger at the moment). Why did they fall just so? What does it mean? In like fashion, priests and oracles have utilized the guts of animals, the leaves of plants, and the pattern of fallen sticks to foresee the future. Using such tricks the inherent destiny of life could be prematurely glimpsed. The idea of an uncertain future, one that pays no mind to particular individuals or nations, has never been an acceptable philosophy.

Before all mysteries large and small we experience the peculiarly human rapture of wonder. The more terrible the vastness, the more aroused our organizing intellect becomes. Our brain, like other erogenous parts of our body, engorges itself with blood before a naked mystery. We sense an impossible puzzle but still the whisper teases: "seek and ye shall find." The same teasing whisper drives all the great endeavors of humanity—the ceaseless quest for knowledge, the breakneck pursuit of meaning in love and relationships, and the expression of bittersweet finitude in art. Humans live, eat, and breathe meaning. The notion of 'meaninglessness' cannot be fathomed except as some shadowy opposition to our core sense of meaning. We vaguely begin to understand contingency when we create a vacuum by avoiding meaningful things and activities; this unnatural state is a difficult one to keep up, though, so strong is our organizing instinct, so ubiquitous our shared webs of meaning.

Human thought strives for pattern. Even when we perceive patternless phenomena—a patch of clouds in the sky or the noise of static on the radio—we begin to tease out images, seeing faces in the clouds, and we structure the randomness, hearing whispered sentences in the radio static. Contingency, then, defines a totally foreign, 'inhuman' concept. A random or meaningless act proceeds without 'mind.' Given that we experience everything through mind, even the passions of the so-called 'heart,' the idea of something being meaningless opposes our every intuition. Our brain-mediated organs of perception, far from recording the environment with objective fidelity, only perceive those things for which the brain is primed and 'accepts.' Thus does physiology give birth to the divide in our mentality that we label the conscious and the unconscious. In contrast to the meaning-constrained methods that we employ, the methods of nature proceed heartlessly from the grinding probabilities of random variation. In proposing evolution as the mechanism by which all things creaturely and substantial have come into being, Darwin deified the random.

Many claim that the sense of contingency has grown, and continues to grow, as mythology recedes and objective, scientific thought fastens itself upon our perceptions of the world. Something about the scientific worldview amplifies the perception of contingency. Perhaps, in attributing to cold processes what had previously been explained in terms of a human-like God, we see our natural surroundings with more clarity—in all their inhuman glory.

One of the first individuals of the modern era to recognize contingency was the philosopher Blaise Pascal (1623-1662). A child prodigy, Pascal attracted fame for his mathematical and scientific insight. Among other things, he discovered and explained the principles of the vacuum. For much of his short life he struggled to reconcile the sheer logic of math with the Christian religion. When he was 32, Pascal underwent a mystical experience that forever settled this debate for him. He fell back onto his traditional religious upbringing with abandon. But his precocious brain continued to entertain dark thoughts. The contemplation of what seemed to him a godless, inhuman universe made him cringe. The clash between the all-meaningful religious construct and the essentially meaningless scientific one aided him in discovering the vacuum of meaning, contingency:

"Why is my knowledge limited? Why my stature? Why my life to one hundred years rather than to a thousand? What reason has nature had for giving me such, and for choosing this number rather than another..."[3] Pascal had stumbled onto a horrifying series of insights that taught him that all the little accidents of life, those to which we generally attribute no significance, also lie at the heart of personal existence. An orderless series of accidents confirms us in one body, and one identity, rather than another. Just as Pascal was born preternaturally intelligent, he might as easily have been born with Down's Syndrome or deaf—and for no particular *reason*. Of course, any such alteration, originating in the tiniest accident as his chromosomes tumbled into place in the womb of his mother, would forever have changed the nature and type of life he led and we'd have no reason to discuss his life and thoughts. So does science threaten our comfort, our 'at-homeness' in the universe, teaching that even as we perceive a lack of meaning in nature, so would nature overlook our own significance. We are, in a most horrifying insight, utterly replaceable—our individual existences as ephemeral and unnecessary as a flea's. In a darker moment, Pascal—otherwise a very religious man—wrote: "...at the end a little earth is thrown upon our head, and that is the end forever."[4]

With Pascal began modernity's biting awareness of contingency. But the felt reality of contingency was not Pascal's doing. Contingency is a vacuum that exists around all things human when a notion of God, or divine order, gets expunged.

The consummate philosopher of contingency, who would redefine man within this vacuum of meaning, is Friedrich Nietzsche. In describing the 'death of God' in *The Gay Science*, Nietzsche makes an allegory out of the ascendancy of science:

> The madman jumped into their midst and pierced them with his eyes. "Whither is God?" he cried; "I will tell you. We have killed him—you and I. All of us are his murderers. But how did we do this? How could we drink up the sea? Who gave us the sponge to wipe away the entire horizon? What were we doing when we unchained this Earth from its sun? Whither is it moving now? Whither are we moving? Away from all suns? Are we not plunging continually? Backward, sideward, forward, in all directions? Is there still any up or down? Are we not straying as through an infinite nothing? Do we not feel night continually closing in on us?

Do we not need to light lanterns in the morning? Do we hear nothing as yet of the noise of the gravediggers who are burying God. Do we smell nothing as yet of the divine decomposition? Gods, too, decompose. God is dead. God remains dead. And we have killed him.[5]

As Nietzsche poetically describes, 'after God' one feels disoriented. When the traditional constructs of meaning dissolve, one loses all bearings: "Backward, sideward, forward, in all directions?" Contingency, the lack of felt necessity, of rule, of order, is the true sting of death. Just as the contingency of the world creates horror in the face of death, so is death the archangel of contingency. Death, the scraping dread of life's certain end, does more than anything to show us that the grand vision and patterns of life are fleeting and inessential.

In his autobiography, *Speak Memory*, the twentieth century writer Vladimir Nabokov reflects the spirit of the time and perceives contingency all about him. He begins: "The cradle rocks above an abyss, and common sense tells us that our existence is but a brief crack of light between two eternities of darkness."[6] For Nabokov, as for every feeling person, contingency insults the meaningful:

> I rebel against this state of affairs. I feel the urge to take my rebellion outside and picket nature. Over and over again my mind has made colossal efforts to distinguish the faintest of personal glimmers in the impersonal darkness on both sides of my life.[7]

Here Nabokov identifies birth to be as much of an assault on meaning as death. Birth—the miraculous act of appearing out of nothing and growing into self-consciousness—makes as strong an argument for life's contingency as annihilation. How can a soul honestly believe that he is born on some summer day, August 21, at some particular location, Tulsa, Oklahoma, at a precise time, 4:43pm, but will *never* die? If, as the immortality ideologies assure us, the individual soul exists as the very essence of God and shall, upon death, proceed to some higher plane wherein it shall live forever, then a birthday is a magnificent thing indeed! Every birthday, in this context, is *the* birthday—the birth of an immortal being, the one and only birth of an undying spirit who shall outlive every star and eclipse the mortal universe. In this context, all the accidents of personality and character—the lagging self-esteem from the club foot, the bitter resentment of poverty and neglect—become deified. As the essence of the personality these idiosyncrasies shall never die. We must be careful to note, as absurd a doctrine as this appears, *so does the real one*, the mortal human round. Again, Nabokov expresses as much with poignancy:

> Whenever I start thinking of my love for a person, I am in the habit of immediately drawing radii from my love—from my heart, from the tender nucleus of a personal matter—to monstrously remote points of the universe. Something impels me to measure the consciousness of my love against such unimaginable and incalculable things as the behavior of nebulae (whose very remoteness seems a form of insanity), the dreadful pitfalls of eternity, the unknowledgeable beyond the unknown, the helplessness, the cold, the sickening involutions and interpenetrations of space and time. ... When that slow-motion, silent explosion of love takes place in me, unfolding its melting fringes and overwhelming me with the sense of something much vaster, much more enduring and powerful than the accumulation of matter or energy in any imaginable cosmos, then my mind cannot but pinch itself to see if it is really awake. ... I have to have all space and all time participate in my emotion, in my mortal love, so that the edge of its mortality is taken off, thus helping me to fight the utter degradation, ridicule, and horror of having developed an infinity of sensation and thought within a finite existence.[8]

Developing "an infinity of sensation and thought within a finite existence," the sentient human cannot fail to perceive the strangeness of his position. In appreciating all things sophisticated and subtle, man mocks the accidents of his foundation. By conceiving something as lofty as human love and compassion, mankind seems an island amid a sea without edge. In respect to this, the existential philosophers discussed the absurdity of human existence. However, by pointing out its absurdity, these thinkers, like Jean-Paul Sartre, sound ever more absurd: "Every existing thing is born without reason, prolongs itself out of weakness and dies by chance."[9]

Why absurd? Existentialism's preoccupation with absurdity—the modern gloom that rises like bruises after a bout with contingency—simply mismeasures the human condition. Just as one wouldn't, as Descartes illustrated, try to measure the substance of mind (read brain properties) using rulers or scales, so one shouldn't perceive the meaning of a human life against a background of cosmic immensity. Unfortunately, we have made such poor measuring practices a habit, thanks to our acceptance of immortality ideologies. Were the octopus to consider his world using the framework of an opossum's life, it would seem absurd. Were a pygmy to judge his culture using a Swede's perspective, it would seem absurd. And if a mortal human animal imagines his life against that of an immortal sky god, then it naturally seems absurd and meaningless. The modern perception of contingency and its dismal reflection on meaninglessness are just the growing pains a child experiences as he develops into his adult frame and leaves the comforts of the crib.

## Chapter 18

# PROLONGED IMMATURITY

> If I wished to express the basic principle of my ideas in a some-
> what strongly worded sentence, I would say that man, in his
> bodily development, is a primate fetus that has become sexu-
> ally mature.
> —Louis Bolk, *Das Problem der Menschwerdung*[1]

One of biology's most significant discoveries reveals a pattern
of prolonged immaturity—called neoteny—among a number of animal species, including our own. Some creatures, it seems, retain distinctly juvenile traits well into adulthood. The most careful studies
of the neoteny phenomenon appear in *Ontogeny and Phylogeny* by
Stephen Jay Gould and *Growing Young* by Ashley Montagu. That a
pattern of prolonged immaturity should become favorable in the
natural world, in any species, boggles the mind. Every beast knows
that predators favor the sick, the elderly, and the *young*—all three
present an easier won meal to the skilled hunter than the well-func-
tioning adult of a species who will fight and flail to its mortal end.
To prolong immaturity is equivalent to prolonging sickness and disease. Besides the more obvious vulnerabilities to death, one cannot
reproduce in these states and reproducing, after all, is the *summum
bonum* of evolution. The state of immaturity features many weaknesses that the forces of destruction are hasty to exploit. If nature
selects for a condition of prolonged immaturity, there must be many
good and powerful reasons for it.

The case of man presents the strongest argument for the use-
fulness of prolonged immaturity. Foremost, this contingency endowed
us with a revisionary intelligence—a mind that can constantly adapt
to new conditions. Some theorists consider neoteny the most impor-

tant biological feature of our evolution. Neoteny may explain how the appearance and traits of man, despite coming from a genome that is ninety-nine percent similar to the chimpanzee's, can so differ from his cousin ape.[2] In essence, these thinkers argue that *Homo sapiens'* retarded growth takes credit for the tremendous variation between man and ape. The expression of our genes is timed differently than other primates (heterochrony). Like steel, which is more than 97% iron—with just a sprinkling of carbon—a range of surprisingly different properties unfold from the tempering process—its time in the fire.

Neoteny results in an excessively long, indeed, an endless state of physical immaturity. Compared to most apes, the human is quite weak, poorly insulated, possesses none of the robust chewing capacity nor the useful fangs, has a truly poor sense of smell, etc. One has only to inspect an adult gorilla up close (but not too close!) to understand how the fully-grown human is but a lanky prepubescent in comparison. The retardation of his physical development makes man structurally inferior to the apes. Such, it seems, was the exorbitant price of life-long learning capacity.

We have overcome the timeless obstacle—namely, that you can't teach old dogs new tricks—by never growing old. Biology favors childhood as the optimum time for learning in animals. Animals continue to learn throughout their life span but the most complete and efficient learning occurs during youth. In the experiment of man, nature seems to have selected a virtually endless childhood. Thus did we retain the youthful ability to learn and re-learn all our lives. The boon of this mental flexibility comes at the high cost of a juvenilization of the body for the entire life cycle.

In the last section, we discussed the importance of the cerebral cortex for our mental capabilities. Without the properties of this final sheet of cerebral neurons, we'd never know the pleasures of science, literature, or religion. One of the lingering questions from that discussion relates to maximization: why, if these cells are so especially useful, do we not keep evolving more and more of them? As we touched upon previously, for all its utility, the head isn't the sole factor in the success of our species. Mobility and balance are two important checks upon the development of the human head. The brain is, after all, just one of many organs that must work within the body's delicate equilibrium. Already, the brain's bill runs high—it commandeers some twenty percent of the body's oxygen and glucose.

Neoteny allows us the largest brains possible while keeping the size of a woman's hips tolerably wide and the shape of her pelvis reasonably efficient. As a smaller newborn, the maximally spherical head of the human neonate can barely fit through the mother's hips. Compared to other mammals, human birth seems egregiously difficult and dangerous.

The hallmark feature of the human infant is its massive head and proportionally tiny body. It takes many years for the human baby to grow into a body and mind that allow it a share of self-reliance. Noting this human specialty, Krogman writes: "Man has absolutely the most protracted period of infancy, childhood and juvenility of all forms of life, i.e., he is a neotenous or long-growing animal. Nearly thirty percent of his entire life-span is devoted to growing."[3] This eccentricity has its reasons, most importantly that a prolonged infancy gives us the ability to grow a bigger brain. Neoteny dangerously balances the advantage of growing a large brain with the cost of total dependency during a child's long maturation. Even our closest relative, the chimpanzee, has finished about forty-one percent of its brain growth by birth. By comparison, a newborn's brain possesses only twenty-three percent of its final mass.[4] The human brain does not finish growing until age 20! As Gould puts it, we are essentially an "extrauterine embryo," still growing and developing outside of the womb at staggering rates.[5]

Neoteny necessitated many careful adaptations in our kind. Most importantly, the danger posed to such a terribly undeveloped infant required new strategies of care and protection. No other animal so needs the protection and goodwill of its kind than the human baby. For the first few years of life, the infant wholly depends on its parents and elders to meet its every need. When these many needs are distilled, we may say that the infant more generally requires love—the warmth and assurance of security and help. Love, the mysterious glue that binds human male to female and ties them both to their progeny, stands as the highest biological necessity of this triad. The family is humanity's consummate end—in it we find our most essential meaning and joy.

The adult human, with all her splendid abilities, could not develop without thorough care during youth. Additionally, the adult could not raise her offspring to a mature age without the tight-binding affections that exist between she and her child. What we have long considered the most supernatural and spiritual properties of man—her proclivities to love, care, and sacrifice—prove themselves to be absolute necessities in our natural context. Without these curiously sophisticated affections, the human experiment would have been a singular failure eons ago.

The relatively immature bodies of human adults necessitated a much more social form of hunting and security. Strength in numbers provided the juvenilized apes a share of the protection that the truly adult males (e.g. the silverback gorilla) furnished in their own communities. The father, mother, child triad could simply not provide enough protection in whatever ecology they chose to inhabit. Fortunately, social interdependence proved a highly effective manner of strength. Bound together, the individual families provided each other the amount of protection, vigilance, and care necessary for the breeding of their vulnerable young.

Without the total care and intervention of our parents and community, no human being could make it past the first few years of life. compare this to a sea-turtle, for instance. At birth, the sea turtle is likewise helpless: birds hungrily await the hatching of these green morsels and swoop down upon them during the race from the womb of the beach to the protection of sea. For all this vulnerability, though, they're surprisingly robust little mavericks: if a hatchling can make it past the first few seconds of life, the rest is a cakewalk. No reliance on parents, no education, no social development—the sea-turtle is living a life of gritty independence from the age of 5 minutes old. Neoteny can only work where a strange animal exists—an animal both smart enough and willing to provide food and protection for its infants for many years. We are, by nature, long-term investors. An adult sea-turtle invests a few calories in reproduction, the human adult commits years of total devotion to his children. An animal as weaponless as the human could not perform this feat of parenting alone. Very social and mutually supportive beings were necessary to make prolonged immaturity work for our species. This biological reality necessitated the triad nature of the family—with its specialized hunting father, nurturing mother, and flailing child.

A grand feedback loop, our intelligence led to strong social support and survival success. This led to our ability to nurse vulnerable infants for prolonged periods which created bigger brains and intelligence which led to more advanced social forms and survival success and so on. After many precarious epochs, we've reached our current state of massive brains, endless childhood, and superbly complex social structures. All these many elements had to march 'lockstep' through the generations to evolve our present state of complexity.

## Absolute Dependence

The great Protestant theologian, Friedrich Schleiermacher, thought religion's most essential characteristic the sense of absolute dependence: "...to feel oneself absolutely dependent and to be conscious of being in relation with God are one and the same thing..."[6] To grasp the significance of this principle, one must ask, "What am I control of?" Whether pauper or billionaire, neurotic or swashbuckler, the answer always returns: relatively little. Freedom is checked by dependence and liberation rendered meaningless without the more common sense of involvement and commitment. Whereas everyone recognizes in themselves an alternation between freedom and dependence, the truly religious (in Schleiermacher's words, the "pious") experience a consciousness of absolute dependence. The keenest sense of self, the truest and most intense experience whatsoever, emerges in this felt dependence. The individual self, one may suppose, flashes most brightly just as it recedes into the whole from which it emerged.

Few theologians possessed such fine insight into the human condition but none so missed the point of his insight—that the feeling of absolute dependence is a projection, onto God, of man's early experience.

Another great nineteenth century thinker, Ludwig Feuerbach, backed up Schleiermacher's teaching. In *Lectures on the Essence of Religion*, he argued against Schleiermacher's critics and wrote: "When we consider the religion of so-called savages...and of the civilized peoples as well, when we look into our own inner life...we find no other appropriate and all-embracing psychological explanation of religion than the feeling or consciousness of dependency."[7]

Feuerbach agreed with Schleiermacher on the primacy of this religious sentiment, but rejected it as a theistic dogma and uncovered in it the existential condition of man: "...the *first* definition of 'god,' derived from *practice*, from *life*, is simply that a god is what man requires for his physical existence, which is the foundation of his spiritual existence...in subjective terms: man's first god is need, and specifically physical need..."[8]

While Feuerbach plumbed the significance of this dependency, it was Freud who localized it to the formative period of youth. Beyond the particular models Freud formulated (the Oedipal complex, phallic envy and the like)—dogmas which have generally fallen from favor in contemporary psychology—Freud's ideas remain the crux of modern psychology. Neoteny strongly supports the psychoanalytic notion that much of one's current turmoil can be traced to poorly resolved crises of childhood. In *The Future of an Illusion*, Freud wrote: "The defense against childish helplessness is what lends its characteristic features to the adult's reaction to the helplessness which *he* has to acknowledge—a reaction which is precisely the formation of religion."[9] Like a Rorschach test onto which the person projects his concerns, one's religion accurately conveys the unconscious shape of the self as it was formed in childhood. Piety, in the end, is the human experience of one's dependent origination from culture and family. Freud's colleague, Ernest Jones, phrases this idea more succinctly: "Religious life represents a dramatization on the cosmic plane of the emotions, fears, and longings which arose in the child's relation to his parents."[10]

As the brain forges all its essential connections, as its neurons go through myelination and pruning, the human infant is bathed in the sense of dependency, the anxiety of need, and the uncertainty of safety. That early, bewildering world, a period that William James characterized as a "blooming, buzzing confusion,"[11] gave rise to a foundational level of wonder in the human psyche. Just as a substratum of our mind wallows in a pool of anxiety (and which must be filtered through various of Freud's "defense mechanisms"), so the more pleasant side of this preverbal world emerges in the sense of wonder. To this sense we owe the awe we feel when atop a mountain, overlooking an ocean, or listening to Handel. To this sense we owe religion, poetry, philosophy, and science. These influences and anxieties coalesce into the very life-blood of religion. The feeling of dependency and wonder pierces the heart of religious thinking and holds it up to inspection. Because of their preverbal, preconceptual origins, religious notions will never be dismissed solely by rational argumentation. Just as no argument, no matter how ingenious, could repudiate the human experience of love, so no sophistry will diminish religious longing, only the eradication of neotony and childhood could accomplish such a horror. Perhaps, though, in understanding the psychology of religion, one will be less apt to fall under the sway of those dubious prophets that arise in each generation. The rational individual can be skeptical about the particular contents of a religious doctrine but still heed the more universal sentiments he feels in the perception of the *mysterium tremendum*—the sense of the holy. Such a person can be human, but genuinely cosmopolitan.

With some precision, we can detail the physical manifestations of human neoteny—the flat, child-like face, the reduction of body hair, the shape of the ear, the high relative brain weight, the delicate skull bones, small teeth, etc.[12] We know, also, that the importance of this physical retardation lies in the enlargement and sophistication of the human brain. What, though, are the psychological ramifications of this process? The overarching principle in neoteny is the retention of juvenile traits. If extrapolated to the psychological sphere we could suppose that the early patterns of psychological thinking become an underlying fixture of the adult psyche.

The youthful mindset possesses an extraordinary sense of wonder; indeed, we often discuss the 'magic of childhood.' All remember the bright-eyed interest that every crawling, flying, blooming, and creeping organism aroused in us. A wheel can be the source of endless amusement and a summer day in the woods holds far more discoveries for the youth than a linear accelerator does for his adult counterpart. The child possesses an inordinate degree of playfulness, interest, imagination, and amusement. We note these same qualities in those we call 'ingenious,' the brilliant poets and thinkers who present a new take on the world. These rare few retain the child's virginal sensitivity to all phenomena. The genius, like the child, approaches every problem—no matter how sacred or hackneyed—

as a fascinating new toy to be obsessed over. The freshness and suppleness of the childhood mind remains the heart of invention and creativity, the trademark of human genius and adaptation.

We might say that the 'method' and character of childhood thinking surpasses the adult's. Montagu refers to the adult mindset—with its apathy, authoritarianism, and sheer dullness—as "psychosclerotic."[13] Just as old arteries harden and lose their youthful flexibility, so does the mind harden into a state of boorish complacency. The adult mindset, despite these dangers, far exceeds the youthful mindset on other fronts. Most importantly, the contents of the adult's mind—its wealth of experiences (both its own and others')—give the adult a far grander scope of the world and a more subtle appreciation for its rich patterns. In sum, the adult mind possesses wisdom that the child's mind does not. If the adult, in good stead, retains the vigorous flexibility of a young mind and combines with it the achieved wisdom of a life then a sage is made to brighten the world.

The mind of the child must stretch and strain to make sense of the bewildering environment. Childhood is a vital time of adaptation to the dangers of environment. As the psyche first breaks hold from its primitive sense of physiological irritation (feed me, pet me, warm me) and becomes self-aware, in exact proportion to its cerebral growth, so too must it resolve the many character-forming confrontations with strife. Like a ship at sea, the youth must bash against the rocks until he learns how to safely navigate around them. In this confrontation, as the person first meets freedom, danger, and death—all steeped in the murky waters of anxiety—and defining himself against them, he becomes his own person. While we would prefer it otherwise, the wisdom of growth teaches Dostoevsky's truth, namely: "Suffering…is the sole source of consciousness."[14] This long and difficult process, though it will span a lifetime, intones its resounding note in the first few years of life.

The person learns how to react and resolve difficulties primarily through the observation of others around her—mainly, those towering, omnipotent figures called parents. But while the child can model its elders' behaviors, it cannot get inside their heads and model the nuances of their thought. Because of this, even when the child appears to resolve crises, a profoundly inadequate set of interpretations may persist unchanged. For all its verve, erroneous thinking marks the childish mentality. This immature content will change only when the individual works through these beliefs and interpretations. Until the contents of the child's mind take on the complexity of adulthood, no ingenuity of method will save it. Difficult analysis and questioning must follow—such, indeed, is the quintessential nature of adolescence. Anything that makes revision of these contents harder (i.e. dogma, authority, fear) robs the person of the necessary suppleness for wisdom and—like fatty foods to the heart—accelerates psychosclerosis.

The person's behavior is built upon the early patterns and training of its family and peers. Should these people sensitively minister to the infant's needs, and more subtly, *how* they minister to them, forever determines the person's basic feelings about life. If he's neglected or excessively punished, he may perceive reality as dark and dangerous. If raised in a caring and warm environment the individual will think of the world as a place worth knowing. The scope of the individual's life projects—whether she'll be outwardly directed, inwardly directed, happy, or constantly in despair—shape themselves according to the needs, wants, and general *tone* of its infantile environment.

The question then arises: if all is set down in childhood, then what's the point? Is adulthood merely a lifelong reaction to the web of neuroses spun in the first few years? Some might answer yes but this opinion, upon scrutiny, seems unjustified. The human brain possesses the ability to re-learn even its most basic lessons over and over again. This is neoteny's most precious gift. The re-learning of one's behaviors, especially one's most ancient, fossilized habits, imposes a wall of difficulties, not the least of which is that the better part of these habits are unconscious! That such change is possible, though, cannot be doubted. Though difficult to win, the victory of mental agility—psychological health and happiness—is the easy, and truly good, life. This goal requires an unflinching analysis, an analysis ultimately of one's religious life. Therein, clinging to the roots in the soil of childhood, lie one's underlying ideas about the world and the poorly resolved crises of a blundering youth. Bringing a lifetime of experience, bringing the wisdom of thousands of years to bear upon these hastily met challenges of infancy promises each person a new religion and interpretation of the world.

Traditional religious doctrines, born from the juvenile mindset of a pre-intellectual youth, relate to the world through the skewed perceptions of this phase. The vulnerable infant's appropriate reaction to danger involves crying and screaming in repetition, like a mantra. Incapable of self-protection, the infant learns to call upon greater powers when threatened. To the child's delight, mama and papa come rushing in to fight his foes. Praying closely resembles this strategy. The qualities that had once adhered to a real figure, the caregiver, now exist in ghostly abstraction as a personal god, or perhaps, in the guise of an intelligent, caring universe imbued with karma. Whereas praying is the analogue of this infantile reaction for religious people, non-religious people simply cry and scream. When the adult still does not receive care and ministration he proceeds to the next line of infantile defense—flight. Totally vulnerable and lacking real power, the infant can only try to run or hide from her crisis. Either a total stillness (depression) or a frantic turning and crawling away (anxiety) from the threat remains the best response. As an adult, of course, we know that these are not very good strategies to meet a threat. Where a threat is overwhelming, the adult must band together with his peers; he must form a social network to address the menace. This, in psychological terms, would involve discussing one's fears and difficulties with friends and counselors. Where at all possible, of course, the threat should be confronted face on—either alone or with a group. The success of support groups—like Alcoholics Anonymous—attests to the more adaptive responses of the adult mentality. That many of these groups utilize vague beliefs in deities and rely upon prayers or mantras shows that the adult always keeps something of his childish dependency close to heart.

For the normal infant, the methods of averting danger and obtaining safety remain undeveloped until later ages when mental skills can be called into play. Safety, after all, is something of a given. The good parent does such a thorough job of keeping the infant from harm that it's own methods get little exercise. For the majority of people, then, life appears relatively safe. A smaller group of people, to the sadness of us all, did not receive the necessary protection from safety and harm as children. Behind every sociopath and psychopath lies at least one very poor parent. This dangerous minority constantly alternates between fear and anger. In various forms they are thieves, sadists, and religious zealots—always breaking the normal rules of life in an attempt to get back what they missed at the beginning. We all suffer for the failure of their parents. We cannot, as a society, undo the errors of these parents. The best method here, as in all health, remains education and prevention.

The lion's share of the infant's time involves the acquisition of food and care. Here the infant is completely dependent on her parents and community. To receive their goodwill the infant may exercise an adaptation of constant need—the infant may constantly cry, scream, and the like to receive the necessary attention. Or the infant may ingratiate itself to its beneficent parents, lavishly smiling and practicing the most adored gestures and sounds to arouse the delight of its elders. For so many infants then, the message forever becomes ingrained: you are rewarded for your performance, the more dramatic and complete, the better. With this comes the essentially ethical nature of so many religions: the notion that God (who by definition needs nothing!) values us according to the intensity of our performance, just as our parents did. For the majority, then, religious life is a vigilant performance of action and effort. Since the impersonal universe rarely addresses us with the affection and care that our parents did in youth, the performance becomes progressively intense until either a delusional state is reached, despair becomes ever-present, or mature reflection breaks through and calls an end to the absurd game. What is mature reflection? It is the learned awareness that the waddling comfort of infancy is a stage, not a perennial right, of life. LaBarre formulates the paramount task of maturity: "A child has to learn that the dead universe, whether physical or 'spiritual,' is bent neither on attacking nor on cherishing him or her."[15]

*Chapter 19*

# Narcissism and the Reality Principle

The human situation resembles a massive Rube Goldberg device: one of those elaborate, gimmicky illustrations that shows how a match, chicken, bowling ball, hammer, and a goodly length of string can be organized into a 'work-saving' invention and, perhaps, turn on a lamp. Similarly, life—which should be simple—brims over with ridiculous complexity. During the passage from birth to death the person invents himself, usually with far more ingenuity than required.

Man's symbolic self is as eminently real as any piece of his flesh. The symbolic self, with its thousand blazing fictions, lived before the man, temporarily filled his brain, and survives long after him. Like the air we breathe—which has passed through the lungs of Cleopatra, Jesus, and Shakespeare—when we die we exhale, just as we did all through life, the air that is shared among all before and all to come. The modern sense of 'individuality' is misleading; in truth, each of us is a living history. Without your particular family and culture, without your particular language and nation, you would not be you. Would you believe in the god that you do, would you believe in the nation that you do, if you were not born here, to these people, at this time? The self receives its world from its culture, family, language, and shared systems of meaning. In what individual, in what body, emerged the virtues of honor or love? Like Plato's magical Ideas, these truths are a fluid, transcendental currency that manage somehow to stay alive through successive generations and achieve immortality through a lineage of mortal lives. From a river of symbols, we each fill the pitchers of our identities and, broken upon death, release them downstream to fill newly fired vessels.

Because symbols can be stored outside of the human brain, in song or writing, they survive the contingent death of every individual. The symbolic self lives and breathes a series of such abstractions, the nature of which truly define the individual. On the other hand, this very same person will certainly die. She knows that the cycles of menstruation that exist within and through her—and create fertility—reflect the cycle of each human life. From the ovum, a person takes root, swells with flesh and vitality, and then, after a day or a century, withers and drops away. Each body will weaken, its miraculous properties of mind and memory wane, and leave a corpse dead to ideas and sentiments. While every individual should perceive her place in a family, community, and nation as truly irreplaceable, on another level—the grander scope of nature with its cosmically reducing vision—one perceives her stomach fluttering insignificance, a terrifying smallness before all things large.

The individual who has met Freud's reality principle is a series of contradictions that make sense only as levels upon levels of congruent roles. The symbolic and physical realms are irreconcilable, one cannot truly reduce one to the other. And yet, at some point these two planes meet—they agree and correspond—and sound a harmony. In contemplating, in accepting, the reality of one's physical existence and its necessary demise, a bell of meaning rings and thus we realize that there are no separate realms, no separate mind and body. A crucial truth unites all conscious things for they all share a reality within definite bounds. Like a piercing line of existential truths, reality runs through all the planes of our being. Should we not integrate such existential truths, the planes of our being will stubbornly oppose each other. The body's physical desires will never accept the discipline the mind will place over them and a sturdy neurosis will result. Similarly, the symbolic mind will deny the reality of the body altogether, holding it to be a temporary and insignificant container of the infinitely more valuable mental contents. In short, we will remain an embarrassingly incomplete being at war with itself.

The true human being, the healthy person, is a champion of tension and hard-headed courage. Nietzsche reflects: "Man is a rope, tied between beast and overman—a rope over an abyss. A dangerous across, a dangerous on-the-way, a dangerous looking-back, a dangerous shuddering and stopping."[1] Using similar insights, the Stoics, Epicureans, and hosts of wisdom schools declared that the good life is the one that lives according to nature, living according to what we would term the reality principle. Becker captures this admirably:

> The Greeks knew the fictional nature of human meanings and saw the only dignified way out for man: it was up to man to take responsibility for the accidents of his life even though he was innocent of them; it was up to him to make his life a duty, a contract with fate and the gods, an offering to them. Only in this way could he take command of it, rise above it, and attain his proper nobility in the animal kingdom: he becomes the animal who knows and who knowingly gives the gift of his life. He resolves the paradox of his existence by seeing and accepting the truth of it.[2]

Why do the Greeks appear over and over in discussions of contingency and meaning? Greek philosophy and culture possessed a much richer and fuller perception of contingency than our own. Anyone who knows the epic and tragic literature of these people understands how acutely they understood the uncompromising laws of necessity. They possessed a fully developed and sophisticated culture before the emergence of Christianity and are thus the finest 'Other' against whom we can understand our own uniqueness. The unlikely confluence of Greek and Christian sentiments mixed to create our heritage.

Our Christian metaphysics has consciously denied contingency and painted a façade over reality for centuries. The most eager of these attempts involved the absolute denial of death. The omnipotent God made everything for a specific reason with man at the center of his vision. Once the Earth rested at the central point of a small universe, the human soul existed on a separate plane from the natural world, and anything contrary to this perspective was the essence of evil, the work of the devil. St. Ignatius of Loyola, reflecting the truth of his 16th century world, could unashamedly write: "All other things on Earth, then, have been created because of man himself, in order to help him reach the end of his creation."[3] But, to our undoing, science provided insights into a natural order that reduced man's importance, changed the possible nature of God, and made contingency ubiquitous. To understand the modern condition, the Greeks provide a more fitting parallel than anyone else in human history. It is to the Greeks, of course, that we owe the legend of Narcissus.

A beautiful wildflower, myths about the narcissus seem always to be entwined with death.[4] Little wonder, for in valuing the self above all else, the narcissist loses touch with reality and dies to the world.

According to one myth, the narcissus owes its origin to Zeus himself. The king of the gods created the majestic flower to help his brother, the god of death Hades, attract the beautiful Persephone, daughter of Demeter. Unfortunately, the ruse worked: as the maiden traipsed across the fields to retrieve the blossom, the ground opened underneath her and the dark Hades carried her down to his abode.

A second myth, far richer in mythological themes, describes a supremely attractive young man named Narcissus. His good looks had all the nymphs chasing after him but Narcissus had no room for love in his heart and spurned them each and all. The loveliest of the nymphs, Echo, tirelessly persisted after Narcissus but he would not have her. When she offered herself to him he declared, "I will die before I give you power over me." The nymph echoed, "I give you power over me," but Narcissus left her heartbroken.

At last, the gods turned against the love-spurning Narcissus. The goddess of righteous anger, Nemesis, cursed: "May he who loves not others love himself." Soon after, Narcissus caught a glimpse of his image in a pond and became heartbroken like the rest, beholding a beauty he could not grasp. Entranced by his shimmering reflection, his face merged with the water and the youth drowned. A narcissus flower bloomed from the marshy soil where he died.

The themes of the myths, like the terrible motifs in the psychology of the narcissist, address a turning away from love and the loss of a self addicted to its reflections. The narcissist retreats from love because he fears losing control; he will not relinquish the illusion of independence. Love transcends the self; its primordial forces surpass self-restraint. Temporary insanity, that curious legal plea, is almost totally limited to 'crimes of passion.' Even the blind scales of justice take the overwhelming forces of the heart into account. Any who experience love sense its awesome powers and its ability to render a person vulnerable. The narcissist fights any such loss of control and desperately attempts to subtract all contingency from the equation of his life. As the beautiful youth told his admirer Echo—as a nymph the very representative of nature—"I will not give you power over me." And, with the genius that only mythmakers seemed to possess, in repudiating any effects of contingency—any loss of control—the narcissist ironically loses all control. In small quantities, contingency inoculates while an outright avoidance of it leaves one vulnerable to a catastrophic infection. As Echo reflected back to Narcissus, "I give you power over me." The anti-narcissist, who would have accepted Echo's call, has power over nature, power over contingency. In contrast, he who declares, "I will not..." to nature most certainly will before much time passes. In turning against nature and the binding principles of love, the narcissist loses control over the self. In failing to discover himself through others, the narcissist never discovers the real self. Now the simulacrum of self—harsh independence—squeezes out every other facet of self. The vital insides die leaving only an attractive husk to serve as the self. But the healthy self is *interde-*pendent. As Montagu notes, the individual is a myth, the only people that really exist are interdependent, vital parts of a community: "In the concept of the individual we have created separateness where separateness does not exist, where, in reality, the genuine condition is relatedness."[5] When, staring at his own image, Narcissus drowns the identical theme repeats itself: rather than acknowledging the interpenetrating forces of life—the water—the narcissist perceives only his own reflection.

As an ideal, the human being accepts, deeply and religiously, as much of the outside world as he possibly can. And to balance, the person projects his essence, stamping as much of his personality onto his surroundings as possible. Such an individual is truly alive and authentically religious. Always projecting the self but never internalizing the outside world, the narcissist languishes upon an extreme of this polarity. The narcissist has denied nature, rejected the reality principle, and seen only a projection of his lovely image; his finest face forward. The very waters that should provide him life end up swallowing him whole.

## Stages Along Life's Way

In common terms, narcissism can be thought of as a love of self that surpasses all decency and good sense. While most people are slight narcissists, and can laugh at their pretensions when they come to light, the true narcissist seems a living joke. Her ruthless self-concern and vanity is grossly apparent to everyone but herself.

Narcissism emerges either as an error or a defense. The happy fiction of self-importance that parents and well-wishers weave around us as children occasionally outlasts its proper stage and extends into adulthood. Such examples of narcissism are merely mistakes; what should have naturally sloughed off as so much larval cocoon clings tightly around the still gestating adult, arrested in its development.

Freud considered primary narcissism a normal stage of development for the young child. The child, in fact, must go through this stage for a durable ego to develop. In degrees the fledgling ego of the human animal must be tersely initiated—through the trauma of birth—gradually inflated throughout the first years of life and then slowly molded, like cooling glass, according to the realistic constraints of the adult world. Should things go wrong somewhere along this sequence, and they almost always do, then the glass of the ego will remain scarred and fractured (to which we owe the multiplicity of character types) or even shatter into cutting shards (to which we owe the insane).

Like a plant, the prenatal child possesses every want so that a central figure of self has no proper role. The distance, as it were, between desire and satisfaction is zero. As Buddhism infers, the painful wants and desires that bring suffering into life come from the strongly individuated ego. When there are no wants, neither is there suffering nor, to a large degree, a self. Bathed in a pool of life and contemplating Nirvana, the unborn child possesses warmth and food, protection and blissful rest. Neither anxiety nor ambition are to be found; no trace of fear furrows the brow nor does one cringe before the tyrannies of responsibility and authority. The organic state of the child growing in the womb must be as near to unconscious bliss as the human organism ever gets. A far cry from what we'd define as a human being, this state is, at once, the perfected human condition and the unrealized self. Something of everyone's dreams point in the direction of this bliss. But the vital person cannot rest still in contentment, a whole other set of desires spur us on to field a volley of obstacles in the violent game of life. Freud called the womb 'oceanic' and thought most mystical states a regression to this blissful unity of child and mother, sprout and soil. The eminently religious sense of transcendence, that indissoluble bond between the mystic and his universe, appeared to Freud all too similar to the state of the child— warm and whole—in the womb. All good things come to an end, though, and the child must be born to face the world. Freud's creative student, Otto Rank, described the process of birth—the difficult wrenching of the once complete organism into the pain of breathing and the searing brightness of the outside world—as a key trauma in each person's life.[6]

While the infant is far removed from the fulfillment of the womb, he is granted a new gift, that of selfhood. Now, an ever-widening margin appears between thought and desire, desire and gratification. To he that can creatively and patiently postpone a gratification, we award the title—adult. The ego begins when one must tolerate the delay of gratification. With each cry, the baby potentiates a change in his world—the mother or father comes running to his aid. Though the world appears increasingly difficult to the young ego, as needs proliferate and comfort wanes, at least it seems—in the form of parents—ready and willing to minister to one's desires. The doting parents make the infant a minor deity. Freud writes:

> The child shall have a better time than his parents; he shall not be subject to the necessities which they have recognized as paramount in life. Illness, death, renunciation of enjoyment, restrictions on his own will, shall not touch him; the laws of nature and of society shall be abrogated in his favour; he shall once more really be the centre and core of creation—'His Majesty the Baby,' as we once fancied ourselves.[7]

The sensitive parents will meet the child's needs and quietly inflate the young ego to enormous proportions. This stage, Freud entitled 'primary narcissism.' The young speaker is often heard to accentuate *I*, *Me*, *My*, and *Mine* with bravado. The youngster, in these bounteous surroundings, develops a core feeling about the self, an unflagging sense of worth and value.

The magic state of childhood must go by the wayside to allow the individual a proper development of the ego. Outside of the home, in the neighborhood and in schooling situations, the youthful god recognizes that his divine rule does not extend so far. When the parents aren't about both his status and his wants must shrink. No longer is the narcissistic child the center of attention nor the champion of all good causes, he is just one among many struggling to do right—to 'fit in,' and struggling, perhaps, to regain some bit of his lost glory. The checks of reality and the chides of his fellows hopefully come in slow succession, allowing the youth a relatively painless reformation of self-worth and identity. As the youth ages, he learns to displace the robust feelings of primary narcissism into the realm of ideals, dreams, and fantasies. Freud notes:

> He is not willing to forgo the narcissistic perfection of his child-hood; and when, as he grows up, he is disturbed by the admonitions of others and by the awakening of his own critical judgment, so that he can no longer retain that perfection, he seeks to recover it in the new form of an ego ideal. What he projects before him as his ideal is the substitute for the lost narcissism of his childhood in which he was his own ideal.[8]

Another god has fallen earthward to become a man. Now the man lives towards a future, towards goals and efforts that might win admiration and love, if not a measure of importance. The ego ideal serves as a future hope of boundless admiration, unconditional love, and blissful fulfillment—the promissory note against his lost primary narcissism. The assumption of time, of progress towards an ideal in the future, suggests that the ego ideal perceives something of the reality principle. The contents of the ego ideal, in the healthy person, gradually conform to more and more reality as one voyages through life and achieves wisdom. While the youth may forthrightly declare his intention to become a successful doctor, millionaire, president, astronaut, and writer, the adolescent may settle just for the dream of being a successful writer, the adult wish nothing more than a happy family, the divorcee long for friendship, and the elder for quiet place to sit and watch the pigeons. Sadly, the achievement of wisdom and the appreciation of the moment—the essential truth of life—manifests only when one has few moments remaining. No matter our present life projects, always below lingers the glory of that lost kingdom. However difficult the crises of youth, the residue of primary narcissism provides a lasting sense of self-regard upon which any stable character must be constructed. In the end, if nothing else, we know that we deserve happiness.

While this kind of narcissism, primary narcissism, shows itself as a necessary and healthy stage of development, a darker form of narcissism may erupt as well. Subtle shadings of a secondary, or pathological, narcissism will appear according to the imperfections of parental technique, the superabundance of childhood needs, or any number of cancerous influences. Because of this, alas, we all live in some degree of *hamartia*—'missing the mark,' that is; tragically suffering from an original fall from the grace of wholeness. Besides this relatively normal state, though, a far more profound amount of narcissism may occur in a few lost souls. These few suffer a most unholy lot for they have inherited the sins of their fathers.

Pathological narcissism arises as a defense mechanism when the lack of a psychological cocoon during infancy allows too many assaults and traumas pelt the soft and fledgling ego. From an early age, the ego becomes the battleground of a many front war. Its opponents are the id (the instinctual needs and desires governed by the pleasure principle), reality (which necessarily opposes so many requests of id and ego), and the superego (the internalization of parental restriction and punishment). From this brutal process, scars and deformations of character come about. Like a broken oyster shell, the fleshy interior, if not altogether destroyed and rotten, will harden and deform to preserve itself. It may, through great effort, gloss itself with a pearlescent casing to hide its withered insides. Without fully developed defense mechanisms (denial, projection, repression, etc.), the childish ego creates an overtly narcissistic construct, regressing in a vain attempt at self-defense. The broken, fragmented self seeks desperately to assure its own integrity, even if only through a façade of self-importance. The persevering self-worth that the healthy ego retains from the primary narcissism nourished by giving parents is wholly absent in the sorry case of the pathological narcissist. Without the healthy ego's sense of esteem, the narcissist must not only work like everyone else for his 'daily bread'—the saving sustenance of admiration—but must labor endlessly in an attempt to replenish what has been empty since the beginning. Always paying interest, the narcissist can never acquire capital. The pathological narcissist spends a lifetime seeking inordinate amounts of praise and approval, both from self and others, to pay off the massive psychic debt that its dysfunctional parents incurred during the child's infancy. How many personal and historical tragedies can be traced to this single process?

Like most errors, pathological narcissism proceeds from a normal precursor: the love of self—one's natural 'centeredness.' Its basis lies beyond the family alone and finds a plentiful source in man's biology. Each creature must place its own needs and safety above others; such reads the law of necessity. With his ballooned brain, unfortunately, the human person possesses an ability to inflate this creaturely disposition into a perversion of the most unnatural kind. Alford, in his comprehensive *Narcissism*, makes the distinction between a regressive and progressive type of adaptation, slightly different from Freud's primary and pathological narcissism. Alford writes: "…narcissism is neither sick nor healthy. It is the human condition. What is sick or healthy, regressive or progressive, is how individuals come to terms with their narcissism, understood as a longing for perfection, wholeness, and control over self and world."[9] It is precisely this—how one comes to terms with her narcissism—that forever defines the person's real psychological health. And what is the catalyst and framework for the progressive type of narcissism? Freud would label it the reality principle.

The healthy self emerges only when the person has properly surveyed the environment and understood the realities of her situation. Having taken all things into account, the mature ego possesses something akin to wisdom, a knowledge of the structure of the whole, including an appraisal of one's own place in this whole. In *The Search for the Self*, the psychologist Heinz Kohut wrote, "Wisdom is achieved largely through man's ability to overcome his unmodified narcissism, and it rests on his acceptance of the limitations of his physical, intellectual, and emotional powers."[10] Like an accountant, the seasoned ego understands that nothing comes for free and that the costs of each desire must be carefully reckoned. The ego comprehends the world according to the reality principle. Fueled by the pleasure principle, the id may desire sex. Taking the baton, the ego, with its appreciation for reality, will make sure the desire is met within normal social constraints. The id would happily chase after its desire without any concern for law, consequence, or well-being. The id (literally 'it') might be considered the voice of the organism, scarcely a human one at all; it voices avarice and acquisition. The difficult and circuitous route by which the ego sates the id's demands gives rise to the complex structure of human character.

The unconscious id always strives after more and better life while the ego, speaking the language of reality, understands that the price of birth is death. Where the id feels little more than the present and would never admit its cessation in death, the ego must check its impulses and pay heed lest it prematurely drop the whole organism into death's grasp. The ego—the proper human self—lives in a pool of anxieties for it accounts the high costs and glaring dangers of the real world. Narcissism, somewhere above the primitive id but below the integrated ego, denies the reality principle and hopes to avoid the dangers and contingencies of life by imagining a transcendent self that flies over all things difficult and ugly.

## The End of Narcissism?

It is the search for total mastery and control, no matter what the scale, that marks an activity as narcissistic. What is needed, of course, is a balance, characterized not so much by a pulling back from the quest for mastery as by an appreciation that this quest must always tolerate vast amounts of contingency and imperfection: in one's self, in one's knowledge of the world, and in the world itself. In other words, this balance can be struck by continuing to pursue the whole, while recognizing that one can never know or possess it.

—C. Fred Alford, *Narcissism*[11]

Contingency creates narcissism by assaulting the juvenile ego but it can also be narcissism's worst enemy. By confronting too much contingency too soon, the undeveloped self quickly puts up a narcissistic defense. Like a taut balloon, the narcissist registers every little threat, every accident and mistake, and rears backwards. The narcissist recognizes, on some level, that the tiniest prick of contingency will burst its dangerously overinflated self. In contrast to a robust and elastic self, the narcissist's remains precariously thin and vulnerable. A misspoken word, the lack of an invitation or compliment—anything that deems the person average rather than exemplary—brings on a crisis. To the narcissist everything short of praise seems an attack. In contrast to the developed ego, that seeks criticism so that it can more carefully achieve the reality of its goals, the narcissist has ears only for the honey of praise.

The body, of course, is the ultimate insult to the narcissist. The all-too-common war on the body (anorexia, dieting, steroid abuse) is symptomatic of the far more virulent disease of narcissism. With its myriad imperfections, the body shames the narcissist. He would be a god among mortals free from all time and all imperfection. Few gods possess such vulnerability to sleight and injury (excepting Yahweh, of course). Tragically, narcissistic injury results in narcissistic rage. To the latter we owe the great majority of human evil throughout history.

The rabid intensity with which characters like Hitler and Stalin opposed all sources of disorder and humiliation (and what is humiliation except the recognition of the reality principle?) gave rise to humanity's worst mistakes. The post-World War I German nation suffered terrible assaults to its sense of self. The contingencies of poverty, political weakness, and world humiliation—like assaults to a shaky ego-structure—aroused intense narcissism that reacted to its past wounds with typical narcissistic rage. By attributing all contingencies to the Jews, Hitler provided a physical manifestation of Germany's psychological and historical contingencies. To all outside of the construct, the Nazi agenda against the Jews seemed the most ridiculous type of irrationality. As they faced a world armed against them, the Nazis still devoted vast sums of energies to the Jews' destruction. These efforts exhibited the very essence of magico-religious sacrifice. Within its psychological framework, the Nazi's projection of contingency upon the Jews offered absolution from their narcissistic injury. It was the Jews who were responsible for their World War I defeat. It was the Jews who kept the economy depressed. It was the Jews that kept their otherwise superior race from conquering the entire world in a single stroke. The Nazi's true fight was a psychological one—they wanted more than anything to make a deliberately ordered culture free of all contingencies; they were, in short, narcissistic to the worst degree. Because of this narcissism, Nazi Germany ultimately failed to appreciate the reality principle, readily took on far more enemies than they could possibly handle, and gave up the few advantages that came their way (what all-powerful, Providential force needs 'breadcrumbs'?). Hitler, in particular, exhibited all the simple-minded traits of the juvenile—all or nothing thinking, reliance on fantasy, fits of anger, etc.—with none of the child's mental flexibility.

Similarly, the Soviet Union under Stalin deified the clarity and workings of the contingency-free machine with their five-year plans. These megalomaniacal agendas required superhuman efforts. With their impossible dreams, they hoped to renovate all the loss and disorder of the early Soviet experiment. In opposing all contingency from its idealistic schema, the Politburo freely excised entire populations of its people and, like the Nazis, projected all its evils onto human targets. These 'traitors' could be sacrificed and expunged like a machine—exuding oil and consuming fuel—that magically transforms raw, messy material into a refined, human-stamped product. Failure could not be caused by the constraints of reality, but must be due to human sabotage. Stalin's paranoia illustrates the tremendous fear and need for security that imbues the infant's mindset.

While just these two examples show narcissism to be the cause of so much destruction in our own time, we can only imagine the scope of narcissistic rage throughout human history. What, in the end, is the cure of narcissistic insanity? There is none. One will always live within its horizons—we are self-concerned, after all. But this, as we early defined, is not ill. To seek progressive narcissism the "longing for perfection, wholeness, and control over self and world," remains appropriate and good. To strive after such goals with no appreciation of contingency, or a flat denial of it, gives rise to regressive narcissism whose realities on the personal level can achieve a level of rage and irrationality that Stalin and the Nazi programs wrought on a social level. Countless suicides proceed from this rage. The appreciation of death, the fact of reality that we most strongly deny, bursts the cancerous membrane of narcissism. To one and all, death drives home the reality principle as nothing else can. When confronting and accepting the reality principle Freud's agenda must remain foremost: *make the unconscious conscious.* Conscious of our worst fears, we cannot so easily project them onto the outside world. Thus does our inner world and our outer world begin to synchronize.

*Chapter 20*

# THE EPIC OF GILGAMESH

We've begun to explore death as a fear of contingency and as the worst challenge facing the poorly formed, narcissistic ego. Now we'll trace the universality of this fear and get to its underlying significance.

## *Looking at Medusa*

Mythology has long been the preferred method of encountering death. It still whispers subtle truths to us. Perseus, one of the mythic heroes of the ancient Greeks, achieved his fame by beheading the hideous, snake-haired Medusa. This heroic task posed such a great danger because a mere glance at Medusa reduced the seer to stone. The goddess of wisdom, Athena, aided Perseus in his challenge by lending him a mirrored shield. With this divine weapon, Perseus could behold Medusa in reflection and hack off her head. At the end of the myth, Athena placed Medusa's head on the divine shield, the shield of Zeus. Thus death became one of the masks of God.

Like Perseus, each of us is charged with the heroic task to find Medusa and behead her without facing her directly. If she finds us before we're ready, or have the proper weapons, we shall be turned to stone. Shellshock, the psychic death of warfare, attests to this horrible truth.

Like Medusa, death is so frightful that we spend our whole lives avoiding its dreaded visage. We shape our cultures and characters in the avoidance of death. Why? What lies behind this great fear? Death possesses Medusa's vision—the power to render us lifeless and incapable of action. It is Athena's gift, that of reason—the mirror of nature—that provides us the ability to gaze upon death with some amount of protection. Should we accomplish Perseus's task we will behead our foe before it beheads us. The heroic journey of confronting the fear of death and rendering it powerless over us confers upon us a new vision of life. Having beheaded it, we can make death our shield. Death defeated becomes the ultimate protection from life's many dangers.

## Gilgamesh

One of the most ancient writings available to us, a 5000 year old myth called *The Epic of Gilgamesh*, nicely elaborates the basic themes of mortality. Written in cuneiform, *Gilgamesh* achieved wide popularity in its time and showed up in multiple copies—variously Sumerian, Babylonian, Hittite, and Assyrian—over many centuries. Though couched in the bizarre mythic language appropriate to a time and place so distant and foreign from our own, the underlying themes and challenges of the story retain a humanity sympathetic even today.

The text begins with the wailing of a people; those under Gilgamesh ask their gods for help against his tyrannical rule. Gilgamesh, the paragon of masculine strength and power, "two-thirds god and one third man"[1] has broken the boundaries appropriate to a ruler—forsaking his duty to serve his people, he has enslaved those under him and taken liberties that no leader should. A potent narcissist, Gilgamesh fails to see the reality of interdependence. The gods hear his peoples' plea and answer it. Off in the wilderness, they create Enkidu, a wild man who could rival Gilgamesh in strength but who is innocent of civilization. In the wilderness, Enkidu "he who fed with gazelles on grass,"[2] lives with the animals and protects them from capture. Discovered by a hunter, news of Enkidu and his wiles travels to the city and Gilgamesh sends a temple prostitute to tame the wild man.

The prostitute seduced Enkidu, "She made him know, the man-as-he-was, what a woman is."[3] After spending many days and nights with the prostitute, Enkidu returned to his animals but they fled from him, afraid. Enkidu "...could not gallop as before. Yet he had knowledge, wider mind."4 The wild man no longer belonged to the wild and accompanied the prostitute back to Uruk, the city of Gilgamesh.

The people of Uruk recognize Enkidu as the equal of Gilgamesh and the two clash in a rousing brawl to prove supremacy. Their fight shakes the whole town but when they finally collapse together, they are fast friends. Shortly, they begin some great adventures. The two leave Uruk to fight beasts and to conquer. Together they slay the fierce monster Humbaba, protector of the great cedar forests. Then they face and conquer the mighty Bull of Heaven. Against lions they triumph. Each challenge faced together, they overcome. But their victories will be their undoing, for the gods decide that these two revelers are too powerful a team—one of them must die.

Paralysis comes upon Enkidu and he quickly loses his strength—death will claim him first. Now that he is dying, Enkidu curses the hunter and the prostitute who found him in the wild and brought him to the city. The high god, Shamash, chides him and shows him the many good things that came about since his arrival to the city: how he found deep friendship with Gilgamesh, was treated as high nobility and enjoyed all the fruits of civilization, and will be mourned by all of Uruk when he dies. Enkidu begins to appreciate these blessings and undoes his curses, now thankful that he has come to the city, even if he will die there. A short time later, he passes away.

From Enkidu's death derives the second and more poetic stage of the epic. Ignorant of death until he has lost his dear friend, Gilgamesh--"The one who saw the abyss..."5  -begins to mourn deeply. "For Enkidu, for my friend, I weep like a wailing woman, howling bitterly. He was the axe at my side, the bow at my arm, the dagger in my belt, the shield in front of me, my festive garment, my splendid attire... An evil has risen up and robbed me."6 Of our own death, most of us remain pleasantly benumbed, disbelieving the fact that we will actually pass away. The surging power within us will not admit its boundaries. To register death and to make it real, it takes the loss of someone dear, an equal. It is not the imagined prospect of one's own death that crushes but the real death of a loved one. This makes death a reality rather than an idea. From Enkidu's death, Gilgamesh understands the horrifying nature of mortality and begins his quest to escape death. Knowing Enkidu to be his equal, Gilgamesh understands that death is his own fate and is frightened: "Me! Will

I too not die like Enkidu? Sorrow has come into my belly. I fear death; I roam over the hills."[7]

Gilgamesh learns that only one person has escaped death—Utnapishtim. Utnapishtim resembles the biblical character Noah. He survived the Flood and for this the gods awarded him immortality. Gilgamesh sets off on a quest to find Utnapishtim. He crosses deserts and journeys for years until he has withered into a skeleton of the man he once was.

As he approaches a sea, Gilgamesh encounters a Barmaid who asks him why he appears so ragged. Gilgamesh tells her of his quest to overcome death:

> My friend whom I love dearly underwent with me all hardships. … The fate of mankind overtook him. Six days and seven nights I wept over him until a worm fell out of his nose. Then I was afraid. In fear of death I roam the wilderness. The case of my friend lies heavy in me. … On a long journey I wander the steppe. How can I keep still? How can I be silent? The friend I loved has turned to clay. Enkidu, the friend I love, has turned to clay. Me, shall I not lie down like him, never again to move?[8]

The Barmaid tells Gilgamesh that no one has ever made the journey that he wishes to undertake but she gives him directions nonetheless. Utnapishtim lies across the vast sea and further still. In one version of the story, she tells Gilgamesh to end his futile journey and to:

> …Let your belly be full, make merry day and night. Of each day make a feast of rejoicing, day and night dance and play! Let your garments be sparkling fresh, your head be washed; bathe in water. Pay heed to a little one that holds on to your hand. Let a spouse delight in your bosom…[9]

In short, the Barmaid tells Gilgamesh that death cannot be 'solved' and that life must be lived as pleasurably as possible, within its natural constraints. Gilgamesh cannot be persuaded, his heart is too overwhelmed with grief and tragedy to accept such solace.

Gilgamesh approaches the waters of death and there meets the boatman who aids him in the crossing. At long last, he arrives in the land of Utnapishtim—"at the source of all rivers"[10]—and finally encounters the immortal man. Strangely, Utnapishtim seems to revel in doing nothing, Gilgamesh mocks him with the words: "Your heart burns entirely for war-making, yet there you are, lying on your back."[11] With all time before him, Utnapishtim is blind to its value. Gilgamesh goes on to recount his woes to the immortal man: "I turned, wandering, over all the lands. I crossed uncrossable mountains. I traveled all the seas. No real sleep has calmed my face. I have worn myself out in sleeplessness; my flesh is filled with grief."[12] Utnapishtim shows no sympathy for Gilgamesh. He tells Gilgamesh how blessed he is compared to all other mortals, how his flesh is two-thirds divine, how his victories brought him fame. He goes on, in the traditional voice of wisdom, so similar in tone to *Ecclesiastes* and *Job*:

> Do we build a house forever? Do we seal a contract for all time? Do brothers divide shares forever? Does hostility last forever between enemies? Does the river forever rise higher, bringing on floods? ... From the beginning there is no permanence. The sleeping and the dead, how like brothers they are! Do they not both make a picture of death? The man-as-he-was-in-the-beginning and the hero: [are they not the same] when they arrive at their fate? ... As for death, its time is hidden. The time of life is shown plain.[13]

Gilgamesh is little consoled, for this wisdom offers no solution to the death he hopes to overcome.

Gilgamesh asks Utnapishtim how he obtained immortality. Utnapishtim, impressed by Gilgamesh's relentlessness, decides to tell him a "secret of the gods."[14] With great pomp, Utnapishtim unfolds, for the first time, the legend of the Flood, amazingly similar in detail to the one recorded in the Hebrew Bible. After he survived the Flood, saving his family and two of every animal in his ark, Utnapishtim gained the notice of the destroying god who had brought the Flood on: "Has life-breath escaped? No man was meant to live through the devastation!"[15] But the other gods show the destroying god that he had been hasty, that mankind must survive. The council of gods bless Utnapishtim. He and his wife were transported to the 'source of all rivers' and granted immortality.

Utnapishtim becomes impatient with Gilgamesh in his refusal to accept fate. Even after hearing the secret of the gods—the tale of the Flood—Gilgamesh doesn't understand. He still wants his own immortality. Utnapishtim has Gilgamesh test himself, he must keep awake for six days and seven nights to prove himself worthy.

Gilgamesh quickly fails and sleeps for many days. Awaking and being told how long he slept, Gilgamesh pleads once more to the immortal: "What can I do, Utnapishtim? Where can I go? A thief has stolen my flesh. Death lives in the house where my bed is, and wherever I set my feet, there Death is."[16] Utnapishtim will not respond to Gilgamesh. Annoyed with the difficult mortal, Utnapishtim prohibits the boatman from ever crossing over the waters of death again. Utnapishtim commands the boatman to bathe Gilgamesh and award him new clothes so that he may be on his way back home. Then he sends the two away.

Taking pity on Gilgamesh and his intent quest, Utnapishtim's wife asks her husband to send Gilgamesh away with some reward for his difficulties. Utnapishtim calls Gilgamesh back and tells him of a life-extending plant beneath the sea. Overjoyed, Gilgamesh dove down to collect the miracle herb. He started on the journey back to his city. On the way, a snake robbed him of the plant, quickly shed its old skin for a fresh new one, and slithered away. Gilgamesh returned to Uruk empty-handed. As he approaches his city, he suddenly marvels over its beauty and takes pride in its fine construction. The long journey has given him new eyes—a vision for the meaningful. At last, he can see that his existence, if short, has mattered.

What does one learn from this strange little tale, older than the sands? Above all, this ancient story shows how the themes of myth and literature rarely change. Gilgamesh recounts how humanity has always, and must always, discover itself in the struggle against death. No solution to the problem can be had, each individual—be he the toughest warrior, most powerful king, or least significant bum—will die. *Gilgamesh*, more than anything, is a poetic expression of journeying through the life-cycle. The many messages of the epic intertwine like living vines along the central axis of the struggle of life, of growing into proper maturity.

The great similarities between Gilgamesh and Enkidu are more than similarities, these two characters are really two phases of the same person. Both these men—one representing the earliest, primeval man, the other the spoiled fruit of civilization—show ignorance of social order. Like the Greek tragic heroes, *hubris*, excessive pride, will be their undoing. Both Gilgamesh and Enkidu fail to understand the proper place of the individual within nature and his own culture, the human habitat.

The virginal wild man, ignorant of death, civilization, and his own distinction from the animals, roams free over the hills. Enkidu is both the first man and a true threat to civilization. Living off grass and opposing the hunters, Enkidu represents the ignorant bliss of the egoless human beast. His humanity is as yet undeveloped; he lacks individuation: "He fed with the gazelles on grass; with the wild animals he drank at waterholes."[17] No matter how we may romanticize such a character, in truth, Enkidu is inhuman. In a word, his existence is 'inappropriate.' He poses a challenge to the social order and prevents the necessary, if sad, hunting of the beasts. Gilgamesh perceives this threat and sends the hunter off with a temple prostitute to civilize the wild man. Cultivated by the prostitute, the wild Enkidu becomes human, learns language, and achieves selfhood. No longer will the animals welcome him, he simply hasn't the ability to return to the state of innocence. Having woken up to his identity as a human being, he realizes he cannot return to his prior life among the beasts—that has been barred to him forevermore. Enkidu must go to the place of men, to the city. His growing ego delights in the thought of challenging the famous Gilgamesh and for the first time he feels pride: "I will cry out in Uruk: 'I, I alone, am powerful. I am the one who changes fates, who was born in the wild, might of strength belongs to me.'"[18]

If Enkidu was born excessively immature and representative of primary narcissism, the bounty of the infant, Gilgamesh is the secondary narcissist. In contrast to being egoless, Gilgamesh arrives with a precocious sense of ego and mastery: "Who like Gilgamesh can boast, 'I am the king!' From the day of his birth Gilgamesh was called by name."[19] Born "two-thirds divine, one third mortal," Gilgamesh possesses an abundance of the godlike sense of mastery, the overpowering human will. In sheer opposition to the herdlike mentality of the first men, Gilgamesh seeks to name everything his own. From this excess, Gilgamesh becomes tyrant over his people and disturbs the social order in just the opposite way that Enkidu does. If Enkidu's problem is an ignorance and rejection of the ways of civilization, Gilgamesh's is excessive knowledge ("of him who knew all, let me tell the whole story"[20])—excessive power—wielded over the group. When these two poles meet, a terrible clash occurs followed by a lasting and complete bond—the original narcissism meets its cultivated pair. They are two of the same, their few differences perfectly complement to create a whole. Together, they seek the high adventure of great heroes and the glorification of the self.

Naturally, when half of this whole dies, the other half feels the intense pang of death—the ultimate separation. Having lost primary narcissism, never again to be felt, the secondary narcissist feels the constant struggle of reality and the fight against death. Still weaning from a godlike sense of ego and power, Gilgamesh simply cannot accept death for it completely denies the omnipotence of the will and the insignificance of the person in the larger scheme. No matter how intense the desire, no matter how strong the body, each will pass away. The core of the story, then, is this falling away from the narcissistic self towards the seasoned and mature ego.

The difficult quest and ultimate failure of Gilgamesh had been the necessary grindstone against which his coarse ego needed smoothing. The mature wisdom of the Barmaid to cease his quest and live a life of pleasure and family, the hallmark wisdom of all mature philosophies, still fell upon unhearing ears. Utnapishtim, the elder with endless time and thus endless patience, quickly grew tired of this childish man who would not accept the way of things. Even the secret of the gods, the story of the Flood, failed to move the stubborn Gilgamesh. And why was this tale so pivotal, why such a sacred mystery? Why does the story of the Flood, more than any other part of this intriguing epic, survive and proliferate in nearly every ancient culture? Because the story of the Flood answers the question of human mortality.

The wholesale death of the Flood, intent upon the destruction of all humanity, always preserves one seedling—the Utnapishtim or Noah—who will gather samples of each creature and store them in the ark. While death destroys *nearly* everything, something yet remains. The immortal man, at the 'source of all rivers,' saves himself and the germ of all creatures. The gods will not destroy all mankind—just as the death of the individual is not total death—humanity must, and does, survive. Even when all remnants of the last generation seem washed clean from the face of the Earth, when all appears forgotten, the essential man—the humanity that can be recognized in a strange tale of ancient Sumeria—remains, far off, both away from and at the source of all—and each—human existence. His culture washed away, man begins again. In the germ an essence survives that transcends time and place and language. The great epics find their source in human physiology for it is man's existential struggles that always center him in humanity itself.

The myth of individuality makes us fear our death as *true* death, as if the plucking of a flower destroys every bloom. In fact, no matter how we distinguish and individuate ourselves, the reservoir of humanity exists as fully in one person as another; from a pauper the next king is born.

*Gilgamesh* also intertwines man's salvation with the other creatures, and vice versa. The story of the Flood is quite careful in reiterating this truth. Man does not survive alone—to survive each kind of creature must survive with him. Just as we share the same land, just as each animal is a necessity to every other, so must man protect and sustain the animals he depends on and the creatures that depend on him. The secret of the gods is that man, no matter how insignificant he may seem when he faces personal annihilation, endures in mankind. The individual survives in the society. The human experiment, despite the wicked heights it climbs, remains essential. Mankind is no mistake, our existence is justified in the pattern of the whole. Neither creatures nor gods survive without this paragon beast. But we cannot exist without the rest of our vertebrate kin. Just as every part only makes sense in the whole, so does the whole proceed from its many parts. With every lost ecosystem and endangered species, something essential in us dies and—as a thief in the night—when enough of these oversights come to pass, so will we.

What of the curious little tale of the snake who eats the final gift of Utnapishtim, the herb of youth? In a brilliant passage, the snake, after snatching the plant away, drops its old skin and slithers away rejuvenated. Similarly, to achieve youth, one must allow the old to die away—Gilgamesh's final lesson. It is time for him to give birth to the next generation—to the next Gilgamesh—by releasing his hold on life. The ultimate phallic symbol, the snake instucts us, by shedding his skin and being 'reborn,' that the difference between us and our progeny is quite small. Human life, for all its wondrous variation, is forever the same. The next generation, like the one before it, will be full of merchants and artists, comedians and liars, and a whole new set of mothers and fathers.

After losing all hope of achieving personal immortality, just when Gilgamesh should theoretically be most dejected and broken, he is, in fact, finally ready to enter his old city—to enter life—on its own terms. When he approaches Uruk, Gilgamesh recognizes, for the first time, the real beauty of its design: "Inspect the base, view the brickwork. Is not the very core made of oven-fired brick? Did not the seven sages lay down its foundation?"[21] Long ago, one of the few constructive tasks he accomplished as tyrant was the building of Uruk's walls. He acknowledges, then, that his greatest, most lasting fame will not come from his glorious battles or the beauty of his body, but from the practical and long-lasting city walls. Gilgamesh left the city an ignorant and arrogant child and returned a wise elder. He left deluded by independence and returned interdependent, taking pride in his accomplishments and respecting those of others (the seven sages). The pride that had so swelled the narcissistic self now rests on the more stable foundation of social order and accomplishment. In finishing his quest, in giving up the search for personal immortality, he finally recognizes that each person comes out of and dies into the immortal human endeavor. The great sufferings he bore finally taught him that while his own existence must pass, all was not in vain.

## Chapter 21

# THE CULT OF IMMORTALITY

...all religion has sprung historically from the cult of the dead,
that is to say from the cult of immortality.
—Miguel de Unamuno, *The Tragic Sense of Life*[1]

When Enkidu died, death became a reality for Gilgamesh. The
remainder of the epic conveys Gilgamesh's failure to escape this reality. Though he searched relentlessly for it, Gilgamesh could not win
immortality for himself. Gilgamesh's fear is universally human; since
his time, the great religions of the world have sprung up to relieve
man's fear of personal annihilation. With scarcely an exception, the
major belief systems promise immortality to their devotees. Death is
the cutting edge of the sword of contingency. Immortality doctrines
treat the festering, narcissistic wounds suffered in the duel with our
fiercest—and most practiced—opponent. By accepting an immortality ideology, the individual embraces the solution of regressive
narcissism, battling the complexities of adulthood using the simpler
defenses of youth.

Religious neurosis, by far the most popular means of dimin-
ishing the anxiety of contingency and death, has for long stretches of
history been relatively stable. The adaptation then, while neurotic, has
served a useful purpose by concealing life's more unpleasant truths.
As long as the child remains a child, Santa is a pleasant and amus-
ing fiction. If the Renaissance and Enlightenment, the rise of science
and ensuing cataclysms of the twentieth century indicate a burgeoning
adolescence—and the population explosion a tweaking of its hormonal urges—then the fictions of yesteryear must be revealed as
such. Wallowing in childish fantasies, the adolescent splits his real-

ity in two: awkwardly balancing the reality he held in youth with the increasingly complex one he must accept as an adult. Contemporary worldviews pose tremendous challenges to the neurotic mechanisms of religion. In consequence, the religious 'solution' loses more stability with each passing year. Fanaticism, evangelism, reaction, and orthodoxy regress in desperate moves, fitfully stretching skyward to obscure a sun grown too bright. An unholy endeavor, indeed; religious zealots around the world are trying to crawl back into the womb and, in consequence, are killing their mother cultures and anyone else who blocks the way. At this time of crisis, we must thoughtfully confront the singular question—how to adapt to the anxieties of contingency and death? We have the rare opportunity to analyze the historical precedents of our neuroses with an eye towards a better, more integrated state of psychological health that places a harsh honesty above flattering lies.

If one question looms above all philosophy and lodges itself in the mind of every child, adult, and elder, it is this: will I die? Though the answer seems fantastically simple, never has a living person answered this question simply. Entire lives burn themselves up obsessing over the question. Every time we hear of a miraculous or eerie experience our ears perk up—maybe, just maybe, there is something more. Whole peoples form themselves around and against the underlying question of life. Religion in every culture emerges from it. Until we understand death, we do not understand life. Without forming some notion about death, either accepting it or rejecting it, we fail to make a decision about life. For how, in the face of an ever-present annihilation, do we live? By virtue of an authentic approach to death do we win an authentic life? Hordes of prophets, saints, and philosophers can write us prescriptions against death but each of us must finally make peace with this most terminal of all diseases. In the end—indeed, throughout the entire journey of life—one is alone with this question and must answer it in utter solitude.

How many world religions—the ones able to count millions of adherents in their registers—believe in the annihilation of the individual person, the self, the soul? Buddhism, one answers, but that's only if one really probes Buddhism and the Buddha's teachings. For the commoners, though—for the masses with their shrines, relics, and burning incense—Buddhism speaks a different language. For these folk, the Buddha is just the local savior. Buddha is another name for the Lord; for Brahman; for the God of Abraham, Isaac, and Jacob; for the Father of Jesus who sacrificed his only son... to Himself; for the Great Spirit; for Allah to whom the Prophet submitted himself in a cave above Mecca. In all times and places the vast majority choose the truth of this living lie, one told by zealous messengers, rather than choose the inevitable truth which witnesses the death of each and every thing. To admit that life is fleeting and that the hard-won character of a human destiny, a destiny tempered in the hottest fires for many decades—a Gandhi—falls into the same pile of dust as the mindless, humming cicada... it is simply too much. The blind world that places the singing divinity of a human soul on the same level as that of a grubby insect and, in the end, consigns both to the same trash heap... Even our bountiful intellects and unfathomable hearts cannot forgive such an affront to the affections. Neither Plato nor Christ could accept this holocaust of souls. As the Apostle Paul wrote in a desperate tone: "If only for this life we have hope in Christ, we are to be pitied more than all men. ... If the dead are not raised, 'Let us eat and drink, for tomorrow we die.'"[2]

It seems nothing could outweigh the happiness and hope that our wonderful illusion about death provides us. For those who have suffered an acute loss nothing can take precedence over the solace of immortality. For the grandmother, who in the fullness of age must watch as leukemia steals the life of her grandchild; for the grandmother the truth cannot be accepted. The temporary insanity of a beautiful mirage is far preferable. If there is water yet, perhaps one can walk a little farther.

Deep grief itself is a psychosis—a shattering divorce from standard reality. Such grief may need the therapy of a healing psychosis. Fighting fire with fire, though always dangerous, may be the last hope to prevent an all-out inferno, a breaking of the vessels of selfhood. This therapy may preserve one's will to endure. For the time being, the heart must take precedence over the head. Just as no one but a smug miser would go around at Christmas and dispel the happy myth of Santa Claus, so neither should the atheist try to steal away the poultice of immortality from a neighbor in deep grief.

To the mourner, the idea of immortality serves as a much-needed blanket on a freezing night. Such a blanket, while unnecessary for much of the year and terribly uncomfortable in summer time, may be the difference between life and death during a hard winter. A time comes, though, when the child must find out that Santa is a happy fiction given as a gift to the innocent and inexperienced. A time comes when, as grief recedes and we begin to count ourselves among the living again, we must accept the reality of death. It will never be easy to do so but—naked in the cold—we find ourselves not dying from this trauma but getting stronger both in ourselves and for others. We can be stronger and tougher than we ever imagined ourselves capable. We also find ourselves comforting each other, huddling together to share warmth. And in the sacred communion that only the cold know we may find our burdens much lightened, if not transformed into something bearable and humanly beautiful.

## *After Life?*

Oh threats of Hell and Hopes of Paradise!
    One thing at least is certain—This Life flies;
One thing is certain and the rest is Lies;
The Flower that once has blown forever dies.[3]

I sent my Soul through the Invisible,
Some letter of that After-life to spell:
    And by and by my Soul return'd to me,
And answer'd "I myself am Heav'n and Hell."[4]

—Omar Khayyám, *Rubáiyát*

One of the primary tenets of any belief system holds that one should not ask too much. How often the curious child is first patiently rebuffed and then harshly reprimanded when he continues to query: "Will my dog be in heaven when I die?" An elder will tolerate only so much of this sort of thing before indicating the silliness of such questions. The common frustration, if not anger, exhibited by indoctrinators reveals the tenuous nature of their most precious beliefs. Sanctity lies in a total acceptance of mystery and ignorance, an item more pleasantly heralded as *faith*. Touted as an act of humility, the totalitarian insistence of faith reveals how ironically arrogant the stance is: to be absolutely unquestioning shows far more pretension than being genuinely curious. As Norman O. Brown concludes in

*Life Against Death:* "True humility... requires that we learn from Copernicus that the human world is not the purpose or the center of the universe; that we learn from Darwin that man is a member of the animal kingdom; and that we learn from Freud that the human ego is not even master in its own house."[5] Realistically, we cannot fault faith systems for their insistence on certainty—none of them could last very long were adherents permitted to freely examine a creed's intelligibility. The zaniest notions become the most sacred and least amenable to thoughtful discussion.

Few of all religious ideas show as little sensibility as the notion of an afterlife. While many people deposit great amounts of hope in this doctrine, anything beyond the briefest exploration reveals the bankruptcy of this concept. In truth, no reasonably thought out understanding of the afterlife makes any sense at all.

All the faiths of the West possess doctrines of immortality. Christianity and Islam uphold personal immortality as a pillar of faith. Judaism is less certain on this point. While Judaism does consider immortality, it is only in terms of a bodily resurrection at the end of time. A rare few seem to have bypassed the waiting period between death and the final resurrection: the prophets Elijah and Enoch both ascended to God in bodily form.[6] Written in the second century before the common era, The *Book of Daniel* exhibits strong support for the resurrection. Around the time of Jesus, the Pharisees believed in immortality while the Sadducees quizzed Jesus on the logic of the afterlife and opposed it as so much irrationality.[7] Maimonides later affirmed the doctrine, though segments of Judaism remain uncomfortable with the idea to this day.[8]

Eastern traditions pose a doctrine of immortality that hardly deserves the label since the aim of these traditions is precisely the dissolution of the ego-identity. Western ideas about immortality are quite discrete: one is born in this life with an individual soul and lives forever after death. Eastern ideas are far more continuous: one goes through hundreds, if not thousands, of incarnations before attaining the maturity to renounce one's personal existence. Since immortality without the person is not immortality at all, we will discuss only the Western versions of the afterlife.

Underlying all Western ideas about the afterlife lies an ambiguity about the body. Islam heartily embraces an immediate, post-death afterlife though almost always describes it in the language of the body. The doctrine necessarily precludes bodily existence, however. After death, the Muslim's body rots in the ground; only an immaterial self could survive. Christianity equivocates between the afterlife as ensuing immediately after death, in a spiritual realm, or at the end of the world on a post-Messianic Earth. Popular interpretations lean towards the afterlife commencing right after the death of the body. This interpretation assumes that the body serves only as a vehicle for the mentality of the person, her soul. Free of it, the soul flies up to empyrean realms. The doubtful evidence of 'near death experiences' necessitates this interpretation as well. The general popularity of the soul doctrine attests to the influence of Orphic and Platonic ideas above even scriptural support. Scripturally-based interpretations show predominant support for the doctrine of Resurrection. At the Last Judgment the dead will arise, in fresh bodies, to be sorted according to their desserts: eternal bliss for the blessed and everlasting torture and damnation for the wicked. In these more literal readings lies the assumption that the person and his body are inseparable.

The Resurrection, while more robust in scriptural support, possesses a host of rational flaws. Without the body we cannot even imagine a proper existence. But the body is as vestigial in heaven as our prehistoric appendix is now. Why retain a body—*forever*—that evolved for earthly use? In the afterlife, of what use are our tree-swinging arms? Why possess legs adapted to strolling across the savanna? Teeth for gnawing stalk and meat? Why possess such great lengths of intestine? Will one need an anus? A penis? Why have testicles or ovaries—or any of their related hormones—if reproduction will be banished from that everlasting life? What about family resemblance and the countless testaments of heredity? Will the African retain his dark skin for protection against the sun while Europeans keep their lighter skin for greater production of Vitamin D? Will Chinese Emperors play chess with Huck Finn? Will Ape-men hold conversations with Isaac Newton? If we retain our bodies then the contingencies of birth and culture become 'infinitized.' The supermodels will retain their striking beauty forever while the ugly will always remain at the periphery of the 'in-crowd,' just as they did in high school. Evangelists discount all such differences but in so doing they strip the individual of all personality. Robbed of these many and varied contingencies the person does not win afterlife, only some 'essentialized' part of the individual remains. What, after all, is the person without culture, body, language, personality, 'hang-ups,' et cetera? The perfect person is the inhuman person. If the perfect person wins immortality then no human being does. Doesn't the mere concept of this heaven—this place where all things human are silly and useless—insult human existence as we know it?

The afterlife painted by Islam is the most unashamed one, a veritable Paradise of sensuality. The pious can expect a life of ease and comfort somewhat akin to that lived in the present by Middle Eastern oil sheikhs and their hosts of children. Born and bred in the desert, Islam promises a lush garden—the consummate oasis—to its adherents.[9] Virginal maidens attend one's every need in this luxurious garden. The bountiful Allah gratifies those who held his stifling precepts while on Earth.

The afterlife of Christianity comes in many forms depending on the metaphors and sophistication of its believers. The theologically ignorant hope for sensual delights—a life of ease, immersion in one's favorite activities and hobbies (football games/NASCAR races...*ad infinitum*—Hosanna on the Highest). It doesn't take much imagination to reveal the limitations of such an afterlife. Too much of any good thing quickly taxes the senses and blunts one's affections—many an episode of the *Twilight Zone* has explored just such a theme to reveal how our intimations of heaven quickly turn into hell itself. The more refined hope for a life like this one, though free of its defects: a family without any losses, good food, love bountiful, meaningful activity, time with friends; in short, a thoroughly robust life without grief or contingency. Such a vision renders a wholesome message for it sanctifies the highest meanings and pleasures of this world. Most cannot easily imagine happiness outside of its earthly manifestations. The metaphysically-minded theologians and poets pose a much more radical transformation of life in the hereafter. One will sing hymns of praises to God—Christ at his right hand—and wile away the millennia beholding the bright majesty of the All Powerful, a bit like Christmas Caroling in a suntan booth forever and ever...amen. While few could glean delight from this activity beyond the first few thousand years, a rarer bunch can imagine no better way to spend their eternal existence.

No matter how vibrant the colors one uses to paint heaven, the Christian exhibits a startling vagueness about this blessed abode. To speak of heaven is merely to use superlatives devoid of real content. The existence one shall possess in heaven is infinite while existence on Earth a mere flash. This paltry existence is but a precursor to that far more real, infinitely more lasting existence. And while the finest lives on Earth integrate a good deal of suffering and difficulty, the heavenly life abounds in joy and peace wholly devoid of suffering. In spite of these ridiculously uneven slates—perfection versus tragedy—the vast majority of Christians cling to this mortal life and exploit every medical advantage. No matter how painful the cancer or devastating the dysfunction, numberless Christians prefer these states of misery to the unutterable bliss lying just on the other side of death. If the Christian possesses even a figment of the belief in heaven, this behavior appears insane. Why not engage in every thrill-seeking, danger-laden activity at hand? At some level of consciousness, the Christian doubts his immortality far more than he admits. Unconsciously, he testifies to a profound fear death and this fear is often proportional to the intensity of religious activity.

Besides the poverty of its imaginative contents, the concept of immortality possesses defects in its very structure. Any notion of self quickly turns into a meaningless one given an eternal framework. The heaven of sensual delights, though nice for a conference weekend, reduces the personality of the individual to its most basic level—here the id is supreme. A boorish gratification of one's every whim extracts all value from human existence and seems little different from a heroin junkie's existence on Earth. The slightly modified heaven of earthly delights—family, friends, and an indulgence in all the finer pleasures of relationships, without grief—makes little sense. Life without suffering is life without challenge. Without suffering, no compassion develops. The relationship without vicissitude fails to be a relationship of any profundity. The higher relationships are born from the mutual care aroused by suffering and the shared hope fostered in challenge. The 'beer buddy,' always there to enjoy a drink and a laugh, doesn't fulfill the heart's longings and never stands up to the friend of war who kept you going when you would quit, and die.

Personal existence, stretched out infinitely, breaks down into insanity itself. No matter how kindly the childhood home and mother's chicken dinner, after the millionth day, one will simply go mad. The human ego is not built for endless duration. The concerns and needs we address are necessarily dependent upon and framed within time. Outside of time, these needs and pleasures melt into nonsensical propositions. If the journey of life ceases to be a journey, then it ceases to be a life.

The theologians' heaven—singing, majesty, contemplation of God's beauty—implies a total transformation of personhood and its context. This existence ceases to be a personal one at all and may be considered an Eastern dissolution of self into the Godhead. Once everyone ceases to do personal things and engages in a standard universal, a fawning submission before ineffable beauty, one sacrifices one's personality. At such a stage friend and lover, brother and son, all disappear. Hunger and admiration, play and sex, all dissolve into the singular experience—*the singularly inhuman experience*—of God worship. Every depiction of an existence worth living for disappears with the personality. Such an impersonal existence could be immortal but the person would have ceased to exist at death as surely as if he were simply mortal.

Besides the issues of personal immortality, a notion of eternal life implies many other gross complications. One of the most absurd assumptions of immortality is that a mentality of time and place—a human existence that never lasts more than a few score years—decides, through pious action or dogged obedience, its eternal fate. To clarify the point, we'll consider the case of King Claudius in *Hamlet*.

A weak character, the second brother, who by chance was born into the ruling family of Denmark, and by chance born one son too late, spent a life in the shadow of his elder brother, King Hamlet. Claudius desired both his elder brother's kingdom and his delicious wife besides. Claudius secretly poisons his brother during a nap. All turns out amiably save for the return of King Hamlet's ghost. Angry at the injustice of having his position and wife stolen through treachery, he is perhaps even more fumed over the fact that he was dispatched to the netherworld without the last rites. His sins still upon his head, then, the elder Hamlet must pass through the cleansing fires of Purgatory before he can advance to Heaven. By virtue of his spiritual lingering, the elder Hamlet is able to relate his sad fate to his sole son, the young Hamlet. The rest of the plot conveys Hamlet's anguished decision to find the right circumstances, and the requisite will, to avenge his father's death by murdering his uncle.

Hamlet devises a method to reveal his uncle's guilt. After all, the ghost of his father may be a misleading demon a là Descartes. The younger Hamlet must be sure of his uncle's guilt before he can imagine going through with a murder. Shortly after confirming the truth of the ghost's words, Hamlet finds his uncle unattended, praying at an altar. Hamlet readies himself for the strike of revenge...

> Now might I do it pat, now he is praying;
> And now I'll do't. And so he goes to heaven,
> And so am I revenged. That would be scanned.
> A villain kills my father; and for that,
> I, his sole son, do this same villain send
> To heaven.
> Why, this is hire and salary, not revenge!
> ...
> No.
> Up, sword, and know thou a more horrid hent.
> When he is drunk asleep; or in his rage;
> Or in the incestuous pleasure of his bed;
> At gaming, swearing, or about some act
> That has no relish of salvation in't—
> Then trip him, that his heels may kick at heaven,
> And that his soul may be as damned and black
> As hell, whereto it goes.[10]

Hamlet reasons, all too well, that the vengeance he would have on his uncle is no vengeance at all. If he awaits some slightly different conditions then his Uncle, instead of going Heavenward, will spend his eternity in hellfire.

Hamlet's reasoning highlights the critical problem of any merit-based schema of afterlife (be that merit won by virtue of a belief in Christ, submission to Allah, or by virtue of one's deeds). The absurdity is that one mortal moment—the intricate conditions of a single moment in a human's life—can determine one's everlasting fate. The resounding clash of this illogic must be thoroughly considered. What kind of just God, what kind of humane metaphysical system, would entail that a single action or a single mortal life could ever justify one's eternal fate? Indeed, even the fire-breathing God of the Old Testament, Jehovah, told Abraham that he'd spare Sodom and Gomorrah's destruction if just ten righteous souls could be found there.[11] Using the criteria of this harsh God, one's eternal fate would avoid hellfire if just a few moments of goodness were discovered in one's life. Such is not the case, however, in traditional Christian theology. In common theology, the unbaptized baby—innocent of every sin except the Original Sin inherited through Adam's transgression (reminder: he picked some fruit he wasn't supposed to)—is barred entrance to Heaven. As Jesus said (at least in the Gospel of John), "Unless a man be born again of water and the Holy Spirit he cannot enter into the Kingdom of God."[12]

In the real world, a momentary lapse of judgment can alter one's entire existence. Sexual activity without protection can render one mortally infected or pregnant, either of which will radically change the direction of one's life. However, the notion that an exceptionally long human life of 120 years could or should determine an eternity bears no comparison whatsoever. A second can change the course of 120 years, but 120 years compared to eternity, because of the quantity of the denominator, implies a qualitative transformation. It is the difference of a drop of water in the sea, versus a drop of water in a billion seas, and even more! Compared to eternity, no mortal duration deserves mention. Yet in the theology of Western religions, the saints and prophets would have us believe that a short human life is quite capable of justifying its eternal merits. In truth, the time expanse of human existence, and the character born of such limitations, could never—*in a just system*—determine one's eternal fate.

In his introduction to *Immortality*, the philosopher Paul Edwards discusses the "Age Regression Problem".[13] This problem relates another irrationality fundamental to immortality doctrines. What age will one be forever? If a five year old dies does he remain five forever? Does the eighty year old man turn eighty one in heaven? Some philosophers argue that the person returns to the age of her peak, posited at 30 or 35 years of age. Does the undeveloped character of the five year old—free of the challenges of life—somehow transform into a mature 35 year old? If so, how will his mother recognize him when she dies? Will she meet the beloved five year old unchanged in her mind or the adult son whom she does not know? Shorn of his last fifty years, will the 80 year old return to some magic time at his physical and mental peak when he was, essentially, a completely different person with none of the wisdom that his decrepitude taught? The complications one can imagine because of this problem are too many to relate. Questions of age and identity emerge full-blown when placed in the context of the afterlife.

The person derives his peculiar character from meeting the challenges and conditions that a mortal life provides. One's personality does not arrive, full-blown, at any particular age nor is it innate. Appearance, gender, physical abilities/disabilities, mental and psychological predispositions, and the intersection of a million random occurrences all combine to forge an individual. Projected onto eternity, freed of one's mortal and personal limitations, the person disappears. Perfected, the individual gives way to the species—to the idealized capacities and characteristics of the human being. At such a point, the individual is gone and God emerges. At such a point, the person is truly dead.

## *Unamuno*

The heart and head clash thunderously when addressing human existence. While the head always questions, the heart answers with impassioned certainty. Most saints refuse the head and its conundrums and speak to the heart directly. The Buddha answered some debaters:

> If you are shot with an arrow and one comes to pull it out do you stop him and ask first, 'Who shot me thus?' Do you restrain his helping hand and query, 'Do you think the arrowhead fashioned from stone or metal?' While the life-blood drains from you do you stop the fellow come to your aid and ask him, 'Is this arrow bound with cat gut or deer hide?'

To the wounded, there seems no point in tarrying about. Whatever heals is right, be it truth or lie. The wounded heart draws healers in close; the head may never again be heard. Consider Nicholas II, the last Czar of Russia: he and his wife embraced the services of the dubious Rasputin because the 'Holy Man' could stanch their son's hemophilia. In the end, Rasputin's presence helped discredit the royal family. The need of this colorful healer wedged Nicholas farther apart from his people during the critical time when Lenin and his crew were gaining their trust. In accepting a cure without care, we may gain temporary advantage over some disease but may inadvertently infect ourselves with a more insidious one. Desperately saving one part from death, we may sacrifice the whole.

Even the brightest minds will finally bow under a heavy heart. Reason, after all, leaves one hungry; reason weans. Faith holds its believers tightly to breast. The 'sacrifice of the intellect' has long been a requirement in traditions of faith. In the seventeenth century, Pascal was preeminent among those who would choose illusion over reason. In nineteenth century Denmark that modern Hamlet, Søren Kierkegaard, finally professed "a leap of faith" as the best solution to human existence.[14] In his appropriately titled *Concluding Unscientific Postscript*, Kierkegaard taught that "truth is subjectivity."[15] For him, ultimately, truth could not be found in science or community, but in the singular relation of the individual to his God.

Even the secular twentieth century had its intellectual sacrifices. The Spanish philosopher, Miguel de Unamuno, modeling himself upon Cervante's immortal hero—Don Quixote de la Mancha—chose absurdity, chose personal immortality, and put all rationality aside. Every argument he considered and his own considerable intellect told him that life is passing, that human existence lives on in no other plane besides this one: "Everything passes! That is the refrain of all who have drunk, lips to the spout, at the fountain of life, of all who have savored the fruit of the Tree of the Knowledge of Good and Evil."[16] Unamuno knew the truth of death because he was a philosopher and an honest man. But he was also a whole man, in his terms, "a man of flesh and blood." As such, he claims, he *deserved* immortality. No argument could separate him from his stubborn desire to live forever. Unamuno highlights a living experience: the unending struggle between reason and hope. In his passionate work, *The Tragic Sense of Life*, Unamuno writes:

> ...ratiocinations do not move me, for they are reasons and no more than reasons, and one does not feed the heart with reasons. I do not want to die. No! I do not want to die, and I do not want

to want to die. I want to live always, forever and ever. And I want to live, this poor I which I am, the I which I feel myself to be here and now, and for that reason I am tormented by the problem of the duration of my soul, of my own soul.[17]

Unamuno howls for immortality. Like the immortal Quixote, Unamuno would deny the whole world before he'd alter his own. He lacks the ability to be a part of the whole and accept death; he wants to be the entirety itself, undying and infinite. A potent narcissism adheres to this doctrine. It requires the unembarrassed testimony of an Unamuno to see how real this narcissism still is:

The visible Universe, the one created by the instinct of self-preservation, strikes me as too narrow. It is like an over-small cage against whose bars my soul beats its wings. I need more air to breathe: more, more, always more! I want to be myself and, without ceasing to be myself, to be others as well, to encompass the totality of all things visible and invisible, to extend myself to the limitless in space and prolong myself to the endless in time. Not to be everything and not be it forever is the same as not being at all. At least let me be altogether myself and be so forever. And to be altogether myself is to be all others. All or nothing![18]

All or nothing thinking—the very hallmark of a childish mentality—underlies the cult of immortality. Mature reasoning accepts shades and lives with compromise; the immortality of contribution, of parenthood, of poetry means nothing to these types. Like the pre-diplomatic child, the narcissist demands that its desires be met in their entirety without concession.

Just as the Maya performed human sacrifices to keep the sun on its daily round, the cult of immortality daily sacrifices untold numbers of intellects—*human minds*—to sustain its beloved *mythos* for one more day. The heart, given precedence, will gladly sacrifice the intellect. In his quixotic gesture, in his unwillingness to become anything less than a whole man, Unamuno utters the truth that everyone intuits. He reveals the core problem that all face when deciding between reason and faith: the two are oppositional. Unamuno calls this frightful space—this holy land of war and conflict—the tragic sense of life. The tragedy of life, according to Unamuno, is that the foundation of humanity is built upon reason and passion and that these two musical chords can never sound a harmony. If you sound one, you silence the other, and vice versa. As such, to live with both, as a whole person must do, means to be in conflict with oneself and in despair. Every one of us who still questions lives in this tragic place.

Why tragic? Unamuno undoubtedly takes from Hegel here. Hegel defined the essence of tragedy as the conflict of two 'rights,' of two just causes.[19] When neither party in a conflict is wrong, when neither side is 'evil,' tragedy ensues:

> ...the tragic history of human thought is simply one of struggle between reason and life—reason bent on rationalizing life and forcing it to submit to the inevitable, to mortality; life bent on vitalizing reason and forcing it to serve as a support for its own vital desires. This is the history of philosophy, and it is inseparable from the history of religion.[20]

There is neither solution nor even happy medium in this conflict of two rights. To faithfully cater to the heart one must perform a terrible operation, hacking away their intellect in a gruesome act of self-vivisection. Like Abraham, the faithful will thrust a pointed blade into the heart of an innocent child if the tyrannical Lord so commands him.[21] On the other hand, to live in perfect rationality, to give up the desire for immortality and universal meaning, one crushes life's most intense desire—to avoid death outright.

Is Unamuno wrong? Has he oversimplified or altered the facts of the case? Hardly. But what are the agents of opposition here? The heart and head ultimately harmonize before the doctrine of *mortality*. Given the heart's compassion one cannot demand immortality for one knows that destruction is a real part of all things natural. If one were to except himself from this whole he would sacrifice his reason but he would also end up stamping out his compassion as well. Does an individual's beauty and uniqueness, deserving as it may be, deserve more than any other beauty? The flower shall not wilt nor the star dim in the mind of the immortalist. The heart cannot sate its burning desire with its own survival; finally, *everything* good and beautiful must persist into eternity. Unamuno addresses this: "That distant star shining up there in the night will one day be extinguished and turn to dust and cease shining and existing. And as with the one star, so it will be with the whole of the starry sky. Poor sky!"[22] If the law of death comes to all, why should man demand sole exception?

His heart knows that it too must pass. Justice demands as much.

*Chapter 22*

# THE MECHANICS OF
# BELIEF AND DISBELIEF

At the center of human psychology multiple forces work themselves out, battling often and achieving only an occasional peace. When coming up with models of the mind, all the great psychologists have perceived it to be a divided entity. Few psychologists have imagined the mind as a monolithic, unified thing. Plato used the metaphor of a chariot pulled by two horses. In writing his most substantial dialogue, the *Republic*, Plato used the city-state as an analogy for the mind with the idea that justice in the person and in the state are the same—a harmonious interchange of diverse roles and needs, a 'political' organization.[1] Similarly, Freud discussed the attempt of the conscious and the unconscious, the id, ego, and superego to keep some kind of balance among each other, cooperatively staving off anxiety. Freud's many ideas came from investigating the interaction of these various agencies of the mind.

Everyone's daily struggle resides in the vigilant effort to maintain, if not increase, self-esteem. To accomplish this is no easy task. The ego is besieged and always struggling against a world that pays no heed to its attempts to keep afloat. Indeed, the basic parameters of existence hold up an unsatisfying mirror to the person. In the context of 'the big picture' the ego appears infinitesimal and insignificant. From this, then, comes man's ceaseless vanity. As history and theology show time and again, man makes himself, his culture, and his planet the very center of the cosmic forces, the epicenter of the quake, the reason that all else exists. Man deceives himself.

The processes of belief lie at the core of psychological processes because they support the vital desire each person has to maintain self-esteem on the edge of an abyss. From this kernel of esteem, man derives his basic motivation. If given one unmovable point, Archimedes said he could use leverage to move the entire world. As both saints and tyrants have proved, from an unassailable diamond of esteem, the world can be shaped to one's very will—a carpenter can become God Himself and a racist thug can nearly conquer modern Europe.

## *Self-Deception*

Self-deception seems paradoxical. After all, one person can deceive another but how can he deceive himself? Doesn't the individual have knowledge of truth and lie and can't he easily see when he's being honest and when deceitful, at least to himself? The answer is a counterintuitive "no." The person, against what we've generally been led to believe, is not a perfectly unified entity. When we don't want to see, we are blind, when we don't want to doubt, we believe, and when we want bliss, we bathe ourselves in ignorance.

Self-deception occurs when a person possesses two conflicting beliefs: suppose one ardently believes in the immortality of the human soul but is then presented evidence to the contrary. The evidence is undesirable, it conflicts with an important set of beliefs. Rather than live in a state of anxiety because one's cherished beliefs are challenged, the crisis resolves itself by being 'overlooked.' One simply forgets the conflicting evidence or stores it away, unheeded, in a lesser visited region of the mind. In his book on the subject, Fingarette compares self-deception to sleep, a process that is partly willed and partly automatic.[2] A slight, nearly unconscious drive must exist to avoid a difficult truth and *voilà*, the difficulty disappears as if by magic. Fingarette describes: "...the self-deceiver is able to retain both beliefs inasmuch as, not noticing one of them, he does not compare the two and hence does not appreciate their incompatibility."[3] Like an illusionist, the mind possesses the uncanny ability to veil unwanted data by rendering it 'imperceptible.' Because of this common ability, a scientist can be a fundamentalist Christian and a Prozac-prescribing psychiatrist can believe the individual person to be an immaterial spirit.

In his ominous novel, *1984*, George Orwell discusses 'double-think,' a concept remarkably similar to self-deception: "Doublethink means the power of holding two contradictory beliefs in one's mind simultaneously, and accepting both of them."[4] The political elite of *1984* use doublethink as a technique to control the masses. By effectively boggling their minds, the masses—now inept at thinking clearly—can be more easily directed to whatever course the elite pleases. Orwell describes the process of doublethinking in more detail:

> To tell deliberate lies while genuinely believing in them, to forget any fact that has become inconvenient, and then, when it becomes necessary again, to draw it back from oblivion for just so long as it is needed, to deny the existence of objective reality and all the while to take account of the reality which one denies—all this is indispensably necessary.[5]

Like Plato before him, Orwell is using the analogy of the state as a vehicle to observe the processes of the mind on a larger scale. By magnifying the intricacies of personal psychology one can see the social ramifications of 'mental cheating.' From it come the injustices of the state and the evils of the world. He goes on to write: "It need hardly be said that the subtlest practitioners of doublethink are those who invented doublethink and know that it is a vast system of mental cheating. In our society, those who have the best knowledge of what is happening are also those who are furthest from seeing the world as it is."[6] In *1984*, the leaders of culture are those who confuse and cater to confusion. In short, their world is a horrific pyramid scheme where through excessive greed and lust for power, any amount of tyrannical and mind-bending lies will be tolerated—so does the Archimedean point, the esteem indulging lie, shift the entire world. The wide base of this pyramid, in contradiction to the truths of engineering, is supported by the illusions crafted at the summit. As history shows, the mass of people too clearly evade democracy in favor of dictatorship—allowing the few to rule the many—and choose to be fanatically religious rather than calmly humanistic, exchanging their individual consciences for the conscience of a prophet. In *What Is Enlightenment?*, Kant wrote:

> Enlightenment is man's emergence from his self-imposed imma-

turity. Immaturity is the inability to use one's understanding without guidance from another. This immaturity is self-imposed when its cause lies not in a lack of understanding, but in lack of resolve and courage to use it without guidance from another. Sapere Aude! 'Have courage to use your own understanding!'—that is the motto of enlightenment.[7]

Self-deception derives from mental laziness and moral weakness. It conveys a temporary quietude to its practitioners. As always, it is the desire for instant gratification that predicts this moral failure. The final cost of this mental cheating is high: for eventually the injustice on the large scale—the crime, exploitation, and inequality rampant in a deceitful state—exist in like measure on the smaller scale, as personal neurosis in all its terrible forms. As Becker defines it, neurosis is: "...the miscarriage of clumsy lies about reality."[8]

Once the mind becomes an unreliable witness and can no longer attest to reality except through the prejudices and pettiness of its own desires, the ability to see right from wrong and truth from lie erodes the foundation of character.

## *Cognitive Dissonance*

Self-deception is a general term for the mental inconsistencies that plague a poorly exercised mind. One of the better studied processes of belief is cognitive dissonance, a species of self-deception. First detailed by the psychologist Leon Festinger in 1957[9], cognitive dissonance led to a flurry of experiments that proved its universality across cultures. In their fascinating study of 'doomsday cults,' Festinger and his colleagues defined the process of dissonance:

> Dissonance produces discomfort and, correspondingly, there will arise pressures to reduce or eliminate the dissonance. Attempts to reduce dissonance represent the observable manifestations that dissonance exists. Such attempts may take any or all of three forms. The person may try to change one or more of the beliefs, opinions, or behaviors involved in the dissonance; to acquire new information or beliefs that will increase the existing consonance and thus cause the total dissonance to be reduced; or to forget or reduce the importance of those cognitions that are in a dissonant relationship.[10]

Though it sounds rather technical, dissonance is a thoroughly familiar concept to all of us, for we all engage in self-justification a great deal. Aronson clarifies an important assumption: "...dissonance theory does not rest upon the assumption that man is a *rational* animal; rather, it suggests that man is a rational*izing* animal—that he attempts to appear rational, both to others and to himself."[11] Countless studies and nearly all of psychology illustrate that the individual does a great deal of rationalizing to himself and others. One always wants to appear justified in his actions and beliefs.

To use the example at hand, consider the person who professes a long-cherished belief in the immortal soul. To this person, the body and its functions are an embarrassing bit of physiology. The person is, in fact, an immaterial spirit. Nevertheless, our immortalist is presented common information about the abilities of chemicals to transform his 'spirit.' The person, if he retains even a shred of objectivity, knows that these beliefs thoroughly conflict. On the one hand, the immortal spirit should not be affected by coffee and drugs—mere molecules. On the other hand, the immortalist knows this to be the case. Henceforth, in the person's mind, a state of anxiety arises. To reduce this uncomfortable state a few things may occur, perhaps in conjunction. First, the person will bolster his immortality belief by using whatever evidence seems to strengthen it, to make its beliefs more consonant. The quasi-data of 'near death experiences,' ghosts, precognition, telekinesis, psychic abilities—in short, the whole spectral world of parapsychology—will become received truth, a previously overlooked field of the highest importance. Though in less forlorn times, the immortalist may have eschewed this information as so much quackery and may even have renounced it as devilish witchcraft or the like, now—in a time of war—the one time foe is welcomed ally. It is no wonder that the age of science also ushered in the 'New Age.'

Additionally, the immortalist may engage in a new temperance. He that worships spirits and thinks of himself as one will denounce alcohol, coffee, drugs, and the like because they tell him that he is a physical being thoroughly affected by physical causes. By evading these chemical witnesses, the spirit seems ever more certain. To his children, chemicals and their ilk become the last taboo. Over the body, the immortalist must wield a tyrannical power. He will enlist one of two primary defense mechanisms against the body—either repressing it or engaging in a reaction formation. The repressive will punish the body and perceive natural functions to be sinful. Powerful ascetic practices are performed to 'strengthen' the spirit. With a reaction formation, the spiritualist overcomes the threat of the body by becoming obsessed with it. Like an anorexic, the immortalist discards the body by more intensely focusing on it. The yogi gains careful control over all sorts of physiological functions. He can stand on his head for hours or go without food for weeks, sustained by chi, prana, or some such metaphysical nourishment. Achieving totalitarian control over his physiological functions, the yogi is reassured that it is the spirit that is truly in charge, the body remains a paltry vehicle under the spirit's dominion. These hard won abilities of one part of the body to control other parts, or—in spiritualist terms, the subjection of 'matter' to 'mind'—make the ideas about the spirit more consonant. By buttressing his most cherished beliefs with evasion and control, the unwelcome data—drunkenness, hunger, sleepiness, and the like—are seemingly diminished and rendered less difficult. The state of psychic discomfort and the great threat, that one is mortally wrong, has now passed.

A still easier technique to reduce dissonance can be found in social support. However strong our individual beliefs, however loudly we proclaim them to ourselves, they sound more convincing coming from someone else's mouth. On a self-improvement binge, the person may repeat that he has a good memory, is attractive, or has high self-esteem 100 times a day in an effort to convince himself of the hoped for attribute. However, hearing one of these suggestions from an admired friend, parent, or teacher just once seems a thousand times more effective. I can't be crazy if the president proclaims my same strange beliefs. Sadly, the most interior portions of the mind are more carefully shaped by others than they are by oneself. When one's cherished beliefs become threatened the most powerful means of bolstering that belief—and reducing cognitive dissonance—comes from convincing others of its truth.

In their study of doomsday cults, *When Prophecy Fails*, Festinger, Riecken, and Schachter found that before the intended 'end of the world,' these groups tend to be rather elitist. They profess their beliefs to seekers but generally keep to themselves. Such rare truths are singled out for the narcissistic elect, not the hordes of unbelievers whom the gods, angels, UFOs, or the like have not contacted about the coming end. When the dates inevitably come and pass, the cults are faced with tremendously powerful evidence that their belief system is delusional. The less committed 'believers,' at this point, will usually steal away, renouncing that they ever had anything to do with the cultists. They may claim they were only into it because of a girl, or because the group had good parties, or that they did it on a lark. After a while, in convincing others, they may convince themselves; they never 'really' believed any of that stuff at all. The more committed members of these groups—who may have quit jobs, left families, sacrificed reputations, and generally made asses of themselves—are now faced with the horrifying truth that they are all but insane for having given up all that they did. In fact, as social psychology details, the great sacrifices they engaged in were themselves part of the process of belief. If one believes herself to be a prudent, rational person and, at the same time, gives away all her money and possessions because the end of the world is coming then two things occur in her unconscious: either she's not truly rational and prudent (unacceptable) or the belief really is true (acceptable). Choosing the latter, the person now 'has to believe.' The massive commitment increases one's certainty and bolsters the sense of privilege in being a member of the group. After the end of the world passes, and the sun rises again, the person must again face, at some level of consciousness, these same two propositions. Rather than admit a gross error and try to start anew—wise from the experience—the heavily committed people are the very ones who then go out and begin preaching the truth of their seemingly washed up belief system. To patch up their torn system, they may claim that the end of the world did occur—in the spiritual realm—or that the date was wrong but that the end was still coming, sometime in the future, or that the grace and faith of the small group 'saved' the entire world from the predicted cataclysm. With these spurious amendments, the tight-lipped believers now transform themselves into charismatic proselytizers spreading the good news to the world. If they are at all successful, and they often are, then the new mass of converts serves to convince the original group of its redemptive message. After all, how could so many people believe something that was patently wrong? In a short time, the silly belief spoken from a million sets of lips gains the air of authority and becomes 'commonsense.' Instead of seeing themselves as gullible and foolish they continue to indulge themselves in a sense of their special significance—they are messengers of the inspired message, prophets of a new order.

Cognitive dissonance is an uncomfortable state of mental conflict that can be relieved in a number of ways. The dissonant state can be improved by discounting the dissonant information, slightly altering the original belief, increasing the consonant evidence, or by increasing social support for the original belief. Using any, or all of these methods, a belief—no matter how spurious—can achieve invulnerability. At some point, whatever the contrary evidence, however much 'reality' comes into conflict with the stipulated belief, the doctrine remains sancrosanct. At this stage, in the realm of psychology, a person is pronounced delusional or perhaps psychotic—broken off from reality. In cultural spaces, such a person is touted as being faithful. What is madness to some, is grace to others.

# Chapter 23

# MOURNING ONE'S OWN DEATH

Mourning one's own death, one awakens to life. Just as one must properly mourn the death of a beloved, so one must carefully and thoroughly mourn his own demise. One does not resolve the grief of a lifelong partner with, *"c'est la vie."* A long and painful process of integration must take place that acknowledges the tragedy of loss but infuses it with meaning and hope towards the future. And yes, there is even hope in a life that ends in certain demise. One is then left with the only true hope available—hope for the present. But to harvest this hope, one must work very hard. The prospect of one's own death—in truth a far more devastating and bewildering loss than any other—cannot be met with Stoical phrases. Such acceptance is superficial at most. The reality of death must be coolly and carefully brought into and through consciousness over a period of time. One must become cognizant of death in moments both of joy and agony. Such integration makes of death a reality and takes one through a process of grieving that leaves the self more robust and integrated than ever before. An incomplete mourning, here as elsewhere, leaves one confused, in despair, and psychologically fragmented—the poor resolution to trauma. And death is definitely traumatic! In "Eros and the Trauma of Death," Harry Slochower writes: "The 'trauma of birth' occurs only once. The trauma of death is experienced over and over again in the course of a man's lifetime. The *knowledge* of death is the most continuous, most persistent and inevitable, perhaps the most fateful trauma for man."[1] Facing death, one experiences the deep grief of losing himself and his entire world. At one level of the psyche, the individual death is the death of the whole world. What a frightening prospect! It takes incredible fortitude and insight to make peace with this. Having done so, one truly deserves the title of human being because being human is living with truth.

We tremble at the realization that death may come at any time unannounced, not after a long life of fulfillment and contribution but in the most mundane and absurd moments when we are least prepared to face it and not half-finished with the projects of our lives. This feeling, this horrifying insight, was termed "dread" (*angst*) by Martin Heidegger, the existentialist philosopher; a more appropriate word could not be found. Dread—it implies a long suffering state imbued with the knowledge of a forthcoming fall, a massive tragedy both known and expected. Such is each life in the face of death. Even those who have not lost a child or suffered some such grief, even we blessed ones who manage to pass through life so little scarred, must finally face the terrible fate of an obscene annihilation. In the end, we are all equal in the tragedy of death and the grief of losing ourselves—that place of intersection for everything dear and sacred. In itself, what is death but the final cataclysm and source of all fears? By properly mourning one's own death the individual brings, from the future, death's gifts into the present.

What are death's gifts? Contemplating the reality of death dissolves pettiness, immortalizes the moment, and demolishes narcissism. Death provides us an eminently richer and more authentic experience of life. These gifts, though, are not given with a free hand. One must accept, as certain, the truth of death. One cannot equivocate on this most important of issues—speaking out of both sides of the mouth and 'doublethinking' depending on one's mood. To make one's mind whole and honest, death must be accepted as fact. Feuerbach summarizes the importance of this in *Thoughts on Death and Immortality*:

> Only when the human once again recognizes that there exists not merely an appearance of death, but an actual and real death, a death that completely terminates the life of the individual, only when he returns to the awareness of his finitude will he gain the courage to begin a new life and to experience the pressing need for making that which is absolutely true and substantial, that which is actually infinite, into the theme and content of his entire spiritual activity.[2]

It seems unusual that such a distinction between the appearance of death and the certainty of it should be necessary. The powerful, deceptive voice of the unconscious opposes the reality of death. The unconscious conceals truth from us. It turns us into actors in the drama of life. But playing a role, as a way of life, is time consuming, exhausting, and ultimately demeaning. One can have an earnest conversation with a fanatical believer—watching his eyes, body language, considering each word and reference—and yet the whole time be in a state of shock. How does this person take such fantasy seriously? Does he really believe in this science-fiction take on reality? Does he really believe that angels stop and start for him, that God pines over his heartaches; that all of this—the experience of life—is an AAT (angelic aptitude test)? How does he deny the entire world and the logic of reality?

In *Thoughts for the Times on War and Death*, Freud discusses the disbelief we encounter regarding death:

> Our own death is indeed unimaginable, and whenever we make the attempt to imagine it we can perceive that we really survive as spectators. Hence the psychoanalytic school could venture on the assertion that at bottom no one believes in his own death, or to put the same thing another way, in the unconscious every one of us is convinced of his own immortality.[3]

Here we have something of a mystery: if we do not really believe in our own death then why do we shudder before its prospect? In fact, this testifies to the numerous divisions, deceptions, and glaring inconsistencies that plague the self-deceiver.

It is quite surprising, when one thinks about it, that death seems so *unreal* to us. Certainly we practice the art of 'disappearing,' of dying-to-the-world, every night when we sleep. Suddenly we're here—living, thinking, feeling—and the next moment we're virtually dead for some eight hours. We wake up the next morning and all proceeds again on its daily cycle, 16 hours of life, eight hours of death, a 2:1 ratio of life to death in the 72 years we call living. In fact, a lifetime of 72 years only contains 48 years of life (if one is not an insomniac, that is). Perhaps the wake/sleep cycle makes us think that death (which after all appears enough like sleep that the Greeks imagined the god of death—Hades—and the god of sleep—Hypnos—to be brothers) is a temporary condition like sleep. Just as one wakes up from 'nothingness' each morning, so we imagine that we will wake up from that more lasting sleep of death. Indeed, the Jewish concept of resurrection uses all the language of sleep when discussing man's final 'awakening.'

Besides these seemingly natural reasons to doubt death's finality, we must respect the quantities of psychic energy devoted to death denial. The life-hungry organism generates untold quanta of denial to stave off the reality of annihilation. Though we see decay and death everywhere around us, everyday of our lives, the majority of people—throughout history—could yet believe themselves immortal! The more evidence we encounter to oppose our denial of death, the more steadfastly we must continue to deny such evidence. We invest so much energy in our various denials that we begin to think them the very pillars of our character. And, of course, they are. We have good reason to struggle and oppose contrary evidence, for challenges of this sort do evince a crisis. However, the crisis is, at last, a necessary and liberating one. With the destruction of denial, a profound sense of freedom ensues. W. Somerset Maugham nicely captures these epiphanies in his novel *Of Human Bondage*. In one passage, after the main character 'solves' the meaning of life and discovers the blessings of death, he notes:

> Life was insignificant and death without consequence. Phillip exulted, as he had exulted in his boyhood when the weight of a belief in God was lifted from his shoulders: it seemed to him that the last burden of responsibility was taken from him; and for the first time he was utterly free. His insignificance was turned to power, and he felt himself suddenly equal with the cruel fate which had seemed to persecute him; for, if life was meaningless, the world was robbed of its cruelty. What he did or left undone did not matter. Failure was unimportant and success amounted to nothing. He was the most inconsiderable creature in that swarming mass of mankind which for a brief space occupied the surface of the Earth; and he was almighty because he had wrenched from the chaos the secret of its nothingness. Thoughts came tumbling over one another in Philip's eager fancy, and he took long breaths of joyous satisfaction. He felt inclined to leap and sing. He had not been so happy for months. 'Oh life,' he cried with his heart, 'oh life, where is thy sting?'[4]

Like a long-clenched fist opened for the first time, the destruction of a denial leaves one more relaxed than ever before. When one surveys his character and begins to smash down all the supports of denial, projection, transference, etc. (Freud's 'defense mechanisms') a miraculous transformation occurs—one understands that all these seeming 'supports' were, in fact, so much illusion and clutter. True living requires no support. A good life does not need denial mechanisms to further its joy in itself. The sense of liberation that ensues after rejecting these rejections of the world comes from the freed up strain of releasing one's overwrought defenses. A diminishment of the superego follows as well.

Freud defined the superego as the inner tyrant, the internalizing authority of parents, school, church, and society telling you, upon threat of doom, what not to do: "Do what I say or else!" But what is the else? Authority doesn't emerge from nothing, the threat of authority issues from the fear of punishment. In the case of the internalized authority bound up in the superego, the implied threat comes from death. The superego implies: "Do what I say or I'll destroy you." Freud thought the real fear of authority was castration fear. Castration fear, though, is the fear of having life, and the ability to extend life through reproduction, taken away. In the end, the great fear of life is death. Cured of this fear, the superego still has a voice but an ever softening one. Without death to back up its threat, the superego can be listened to as so much guidance; guidance to be taken or discarded, but never feared. Maugham captures these sentiments in the passage above. The great moments of freedom the character Philip experiences result from the breakdown of the superego: "...oh life, where is thy sting?"

With the loss of the superego, without deterrence, do we turn into sadists and killers? Does the adjudication of conscience, without threat and punish, melt one's ethics into a puddle of nihilism? The great illusion of ethics is that we must be tricked into doing what is right. In other words, the authorities believe that doing what is right and good are not good in themselves. We must be beaten, threatened, and cajoled into living the good life. This is a medieval psychology. At the end of the day, doing good makes one feel good. Morality is not a divine dispensation, it is part of a natural human ecology. Acting with righteousness is adaptive. Were not values adaptive, morality would never exist. What of the immoral? Immoral actions and immoral people are caused by one thing: an inability to appreciate another person—improper socialization. The golden rule expresses a self-evident truth when one's mind is healthy.

Just before one walks into the dread desert of nihilism, the mirage collapses and the superabundance of life and meaning reveal themselves; it turns out that authentic freedom and true meaning are only to be had in the borderlands between society and individual, nihilism and morality, truth and illusion. Only as an outlaw does one discover the inherent laws of life. The character remains, the self feels more robust than ever, and the terrible tension held in these pillars of character—these mechanisms of denial—rot away into the worthless dust that they are. The world needs no Atlas to bear it upon broad shoulders. The fears and terrors that neurosis suckled whither away. Like so many ambassadors of the dark empire, the phobias and fears one lives with are representatives of the specter of death. With this fear alleviated, so too do these lesser demons skulk away. One is left in a state of liberation—the highest human achievement, freedom from the accidents of existence. The acceptance of an all-consuming death, more than any other felt idea, gives the thinker control over her own life.

## *Religion and Ethics*

One of the most common arguments in favor of religion, and a seemingly humane one, states that spiritual doctrines play an important role in the realm of ethics. However much religion may insult the intellect, it sobers the wrongdoer from the drunkenness of criminality. Voltaire, an otherwise scathing critic of religion, wrote: "…if God did not exist, we would have to invent him."[5] There has long been this fear that if men were free from the threat of hellfire, they'd go running about in the streets raping, stealing, and setting things ablaze. While the subject of religion and ethics deserves a whole separate volume, we'll touch on a few relevant points here.

'Religion' and 'ligament' derive from the same Latin source. Just as the ligaments (from Latin, *ligare*-"to connect and unify") provide the essential binding and strapping that give the body's pile of meat and intestines support, so our religious (re-*ligare*) conceptions help us to unify and bind peoples to their communities. Like the body, these formless collections suddenly take on an organized and robust structure when religion binds a society together.

Both these words possess a 'systems' orientation. They imply that various pieces can be harmonized into systems for mutual benefit. Like the cardiovascular or respiratory systems, many different organs come together to provide an overall function—the circulation of blood or the interchange of gases. The things that integrate disparate elements are, at once, both practical and transcendent. They transcend the more natural conclusion that different things cannot come together and sound harmony. Yet anyone knows that the greatest things: societies, bodies, even musical chords, result from the blending of differences.

There is an unstated theme in the etymology of 'religion.' To bind, one needs certain materials; in particular, ropes, straps, and the like. These, in fact, are the tropes used to connote religion's purpose in society. In our age, the poetic metaphor is nearly lost. Why would the Romans associate ropes and knots with religious belief? When one envisions the world of construction before the industrial revolution, all becomes clear. The simple tools that the ancients would class under *ligare*, were requirements for any construction. In an era before cranes, bulldozers, and electricity, people unified their forces with ropes. Suddenly, a thin piece of nothing—some twisted fiber—gains life with the setting on of human hands. The strength of one man joins another and so on, until, by human force alone, vast monuments were raised to the sky. The marvelous structures of the ancient world—the Parthenon of Athens, the Roman Coliseum, Stonehenge, Chartres, and the pyramids of Giza—were built by the combined strength of people, people pulling ropes. Religion unifies and amplifies the mental capabilities of these same crowds and supports whole societies. It is no wonder that the majority of these ancient wonders were built by the religious authorities. Even at the beginning, the poets understood that religion and construction were the same human acts expressed in two spheres.

Religion has changed, though. While it previously unified, it now divides. Despite the anthropologists' recommendation to accept every faith system with a blind equanimity, in truth, such a policy only goes to reinforce the worst kinds of mental dishonesty. The Bible-gesticulating Christian, in spite of his genteel interaction with his Jewish or Buddhist neighbors, believes, quite firmly, that they will spend their infinity in hellfire while he'll enjoy the orgiastic bliss of immortality in heaven. The public and the private realm here clash with a deafening boom. The individual faith system, especially in the context of a modern, cosmopolitan world, must go by the wayside lest we wallow in dishonesty and occasional bursts of violence. While faith systems once bound together, they now rend apart. In the modern world, just as in the ancient one, religion justifies robbery, murder, and injustice. The Muslim martyrs of 9/11 proved as much to the world. And the weekly, if not daily, acts of terrorism in Israel, by one side or the other, are justified in part by religion just as the creation of the Jewish state was justified by an ancestral claim based on the Bible.

In truth, we become more wholly religious by a confrontation with our most universal ties to each other and our shared world. While doctrines and dogmas often serve as a way to distinguish differences between people, brain structure remains the same across all boundaries of sovereignty, color, and language. A heavy blow to the head does the same thing to anyone anywhere. Furthermore, billionaire and bankrupt are alike brothers against the most fundamental mortal dilemmas. Nature has imposed a stricter equality upon her creatures than any revolutionaries ever could; for no matter how intelligent, how beautiful, or how wealthy, we shall all know the very same fate—poet and falling leaf. We are all consigned to equal destinies.

When life-eternal depends on God, men give themselves to those who tell them what God says, for in their heart of hearts they know that God does not speak to them. Others who have no taste for religion choose the path of achievement and the cult of the name. When one imagines that some achievement will assure their continual memory (as if a memory in another's mind could mean anything to the insensate dead) then his life is not his own but just a machine of accomplishment, in the same manner that the pyramids were 'immortality machines.' Achievement becomes the aim of all one's actions and everything living gets conned into the ultimate scam.

The acceptance of death obliterates all illusions and grants control. It bestows true freedom upon the person who will look it in the face. But this freedom, can anyone bear it? Will we not be burnt up and destroyed by the intensity of the fire? Yes, of course we will. We each know this and because of this we hold ourselves back. We restrict life and turn it down so that it is no more than a flicker, scarcely enough to warm the hands. Even this flicker can be too much, we give it away to someone else so that we only feel the faint warmth when we are with our lover or near the leader who will share our warmth with us. Once in a great while a person tears through the sky, a blazing meteor, and we look and marvel, but we also fear. When and where will he fall? The massive weight of such a life, when it crashes to the surface, rumbles and shakes all around. Maybe, we think, if we don't attract too much notice, if we just chug away and do our duty, death will forget us. Death notices the radiant ones. If, through the practice of a negative magic, we spend our lives in a death-like trance perhaps the reaper will pass us by, mistaking us for a fallen husk. It is always our fear of death that makes us fear life.

## Death and Time

Time eludes those who admit no boundaries and when time is elusive one squanders it. Time becomes real when one acknowledges its scarcity. This is done automatically when the individual contemplates death. The philosopher Herbert Fingarette writes:

> Even when unexpected and spontaneous, the apprehension of death transforms the moment, be it the sound of my wife in the kitchen, or sitting at work in my study, or turning to watch dawn arrive. This momentary apprehension of an eventual end to my life, insofar as it has any imaginable content, is in fact an appreciation, a clearer, brighter vision, of what is here and now.[6]

In the vicinity of annihilation, time coalesces into a palpable substance and the dream of the alchemists, gold from base metal, manifests in hand. Such is the true and only magic we may work. At the point of a black hole, just before total consumption into the horizon event, time stops. So does the living individual make an infinity out of the moment.

For the 'unachieved,' time is a mystery. When one hasn't much to do, time drags on and on but engaged in a project, one's time becomes scarce and, in its preciousness, is carefully milked. Any good life possesses a variation of two states, keeping engaged in life's projects but occasionally taking the vacation where time becomes a dilated experience of consciousness. The vacation, by its juxtaposition to the business of life, fosters the same appreciation of time that scarcity does. This is why vacations seem more 'real' than normal life. The inflation of time makes life more real. Routine, habit, and complacency rob time, hence life, of this reality. To those whose time is scarce—in work and play—no words shall instruct; these people already possess the treasure. For many others, though, for whom the moment is of no particular consequence—a chance to peruse a magazine or watch a sitcom—time must be revealed in all its scarcity. Death teaches time. Death teaches the moment.

The person who internalizes the finality of death achieves a revitalization of time. While a good life may be had in the relative appreciation of time, watching it shrink when busy and expand when at rest, the truly achieved life lets not a moment pass unnoticed. At a banquet, such a person does not let a grain of rice go to waste. Even in the most routine of necessities, the sole of the foot and the crown of the head are felt, the wind and its aromas inhaled, the beating of one's heart appreciated as primal music. Schleiermacher, the Protestant theologian, understood the real Christian doctrine of immortality: "To be one with the infinite in the midst of the finite and to be eternal in a moment, that is the immortality of religion."[7]

Knowing death to be a solid boundary, life becomes being-towards-death. This gives all of life context and amplifies the integrating forces of the self. A beginning and an end transform the waffling uncertainties of the present into a meaningful moment in the context of one's whole life. Without an appreciation for boundaries, the most important of which is certainly death, one lacks an appreciation of *value*. Basic economic theory understands value to be the result of scarcity. When the person doesn't perceive the ultimate scarcity of life itself, disaster results. Our cultural 'miseducation' blinds us to the value of everything that supports life. The progression towards environmental collapse exemplifies the failure to appreciate scarcity. The bad habits of death denial rob us of scarcity and value. If life is limitless, so must all of life's necessities be limitless. Death abolishes this blinding influence and makes time a real substance, the true currency of personal wealth.

Heidegger taught that one cannot 'transfer' or escape one's own death. Apprehending this, death becomes the most individualizing event of the person's life. Birth was 'given' by parents (how many of us were really present at birth?), childhood and the first yawns of selfhood were basically extensions of one's parents and their culture, but, having apprehended the reality of one's own death and then living towards it, the person becomes his own. If death is the cost of birth, then *you* purchased your life. While this is only so much rhetoric, the lived reality of owning your actions and plans in the face of death anneal the actions of life into a strong and cohesive unity—in short, death forges the self.

The acknowledgement of death imbues one's projects with a sense of urgency. The intensity of this urgency will not allow the moment to be sacrificed as a mere means to an end. Only a passing urgency makes one forgetful of the moment; true urgency—the kind revealed by a death sentence—makes of each moment a kingdom. She for whom death is a reality knows that each moment must be fully exploited. In doing so, perhaps we will be less likely to exploit nature and other people. Exploiting the only thing of real value, our personal capacities—to be manifested in the gold standard of time— we can achieve a wealth that makes all the sundry goods of the world seem shoddy and pale in comparison. But here as elsewhere, we have been misled and trained against the truth. Rather than harvest the moment, our role models plant and plant for some eternal harvest and neurotically starve among fields of plenty. Believing real life to be some future achievement, they lose the reality of the present. In *The Book*, Alan Watts addresses the irony of this: "...unless one is able to live fully in the present, the future is a hoax."[8] So many have been taken in by this hoax and lost all their fortunes as a result. The error of this method shines glaringly all around us. There are too many well-known examples to embarrass any single person.

First, the young, hypnotized into the reality of grades, awards, and promotions, learns that everything real exists in the future of the ego ideal; far off in time, the narcissistic horn-of-plenty calls us to a quest. For the questing pilgrim the treasure is always a world away. In such a youth, a kindling ambition grows by leaps into a blazing inferno from which the fires of hell take their inspiration, and next to which they seem a comforting stove. One must attend the right college, then win the right job and spouse. The kids are tortured until they conform to the same Satanic laws. And, after a lifetime of achievement, the heart—choking on the fat of life it hadn't time to chew or digest—sputters and fails. All the riches, the sonorous poetry of the moment, fell upon deaf ears. The moment would only be had when the bank account was just so large, the house just so decorated, the reputation just so deserved, the children just so successful... Another drop of fuel, a human being, has been burned up in the devil's combustion engine leaving nothing but pollution to poison the living.

The pragmatic laugh at this idolatry of the present. "Nothing will be done, no great achievement undertaken." Most great achievements are so much illusion anyway. But, after all, some things need to be done. Even in undertaking time consuming projects, the moment can be harvested. The wisdom of work has always been simple—do what you love; the string of well-lived, well-worked moments not only justify themselves in the completion of a careful project but in each moment along the way. In the same way that a weekend hike is not (or should not) be about getting to the peak, so any worthwhile project is not about the completion. The truly valuable projects justify themselves both in their means and their ends.

## The Good Life

The worst embalmer of life is not death but pettiness. In devotion to superficial attachments, desires, and concerns one attempts to forget life's more profound duties and challenges. Forgetfulness, otherwise known as repression, encourages us to squander our time and live a life without real meaning. How did we ever get so swindled? How does the cheap and shoddy convince us to part with the surpassing beauty and wealth that only the authentic life can offer— plastic for stone, polyester for silk? One can only imagine that the fear of reality with its cold boundaries and impersonal rules cajoles us into such meanness. Like the irony of the narcissist who kills himself in an attempt to extract more life—who becomes smaller in an attempt to become larger—the irony of pettiness teaches that in escaping from the inhuman we make of our inner and outer selves mere replicas and extract all the native humanity from life.

In the face of death one naturally dissolves pettiness and brings profundity to all aspects of life. Death elicits courage and with this surpassing human trait all the fearful and inhuman aspects of life become additional proofs of courageous humanity. Having the strength to invest life with hard work and to withstand immense suffering, all in the face of death, makes of man his own ideal. Developing the ability to withstand death's jeers and threats strengthens one's muscles for meaning. With these come an ability to integrate all the lesser accidents and contingencies of life into a meaningful whole. Such a person can infuse even the most accidental with a quintessentially human meaning.

Anxiety, sometimes touted as the predominant disease of our time, is fear's quiet hum. To the weak, everything seems fearful—the stranger, the government, deep relationships, driving. If not their sole source then at least looming behind all these stands the giant—death. Just as David defeated Goliath and became King, so in our own lives after conquering this giant all smaller fears will bow before us. In *The Power of Myth*, the modern sage Joseph Campbell, wrote:

> The conquest of the fear of death is the recovery of life's joy. One can experience an unconditional affirmation of life only when one has accepted death, not as contrary to life but as an aspect of life. Life in its becoming is always shedding death, and on the point of death. The conquest of fear yields the courage of life. That is the cardinal initiation of every heroic adventure—fearlessness and achievement.[9]

The martial arts ones practices when tangling with death do not disappear with the conquest of this fear. The skills one has developed leave a lasting calmness and confidence before anxiety's myriad sources.

So much of what truly deserves the adjective 'evil' comes from pathological, or regressive, narcissism. The inability to form meaningful relationships, the poverty of true affection and value, the minimization of everything outside of oneself—all these acids are excreted as narcissism's waste products. The beginning of almost every psychological disease cycle lies in narcissism or is supported by it. In our society these weaknesses are writ large (as Lasch nicely describes in *The Culture of Narcissism*). The sense of entitlement, the increasing tension between have and have-nots, and public pronouncements of spite and resentment all arise from the feeble thoughts of a poorly integrated self. Before all these hideous behaviors and perverted thoughts one can only feel an alternation of pity and anger. But neither of these emotions serve any good cause. Death and contingency give rise to the narcissistic defense. So must they undo it. Walking towards death with increasing recognition strengthens the self, baptizes one into reality, and brings strength of character where the weakness of defense mechanisms once depleted one's stores. The narcissist will not acknowledge weaknesses and vulnerabilities. If he can be initiated into the reality of death the narcissistic defenses will unravel and the arduous, *but honest*, development of character will commence, a bit late but never too late.

# Chapter 24

# PHILOSOPHIES OF REDEMPTION

The deep instinct for how one must live, in order to feel oneself 'in heaven,' to feel 'eternal,' while in all other behavior one decidedly does not feel oneself 'in heaven'—this alone is the psychological reality of 'redemption.' A new way of life, not a new faith.

—Friedrich Nietzsche, *The Antichrist*[1]

Few of the philosophies developed throughout human history actually attend to man's happiness as a serious consideration of thought. Like the greedy businessman who is sure that some day, after his fortune has climbed to a sufficient height, all will be well with his soul, so the greedy philosopher in searching everywhere for the truth—except in the here and now—searches in vain. Far too much philosophizing has been devoted to fantastical issues (how many angels can fit onto the head of a pin?) and metaphysical quandaries completely indifferent to man's fundamental condition. Sadly, even great thinkers seem to have the knack of passing over the difficult, existential conditions of life.

Thankfully, within this florid jungle of false opinions a few orchids have bloomed. These mature philosophies resuscitate the ideal of the good life. They are 'redemptive' philosophies precisely because they do not claim the need for Christian redemption. Here Nietzsche, as is his delight, plays with linguistic and historical subtleties. Certain religious traditions, Christianity foremost among them, claim that life needs redemption. The individual 'owns' his life when he submits to a code and when he accepts a faith. But it is faith—a preconceived set of ideas *against* the experience of life—that dirties one's experience; it is a filtration system that infects rather than purifies, an anti-filtration system, a method of pollution. Against pristine nature, against natural methods and experiences—*against life itself*—one has faith. It is a dirty trick that has worked too often in history: to deem something pure, one needs to declare that everything is polluted and in need of purification. But to redeem oneself *against* such redemption, to remove faith, one needs mature philosophy. Among these mature philosophies, those that in Nietzsche's words offer "A new way of life, not a new faith," Buddhism, Epicureanism, and Stoicism standout.

Why, now, is there such a need for these mature philosophies? If, as this book details, the soul is a fiction—a premature, wholly mythological way of thinking about the brain—then dozens of ancient religious traditions are undermined. Such is the dawning realization among so many of us. Without the soul and immortality—the pillars of faith for so many Western religions—then the weaker of such structures come crashing down. And whether most people think of themselves as religious or not, the fundamental ways that they frame their existence is adopted from the underlying religious tradition of their community. A characteristic feature of these traditions is the understanding of oneself as a character in a great drama. You—the soul within you, that is—are part of a great Orphic tradition, an angel fallen from above. In these philosophies you are not an individual, dying creature that comes and goes, a flutter of consciousness in the dark sea, but an everlasting, recycling character. You are playing hide-and-seek with God. Such an interpretation lends you a narrative self, a self wholly entrapped in a story. Yes, in these religious dramas there is a meaning to life. It is your task to seek this meaning out, discover it, and behold a revelation.

A side-effect of these religious interpretations is the enthronement of the narrative self, a thoughtless acceptance of oneself as actor. The less consciously religious—most of us, that is—fall into the habit of becoming someone else. Rather than settling into one's own skin, the mark of success is to become like a certain actor, politician, or other celebrity.

In *Agon*, Harold Bloom could imagine the whole of literary history—the genesis of all our novels, characters, and dramas—as an effort of each writer to usurp the place and influence of his chosen predecessor; his Oedipal precursor, lover of the Muse. Instead of writing out of one's genius, instead of conveying some unique take on the world, most writers try to sound like—*try to be*—someone else. Only the most rare can write and think with his own thoughts.

*Mimesis* (imitation) is the dominant tone in all Western culture. In a great perversion of Plato's philosophy, only the replica of something is real. The conclusion thus speaks: Do not be yourself, do not accept your own thoughts—*do not hear them*—you begin to exist when you resemble someone else. You *redeem* yourself when you live another's dream. Such is genuine reality. Most history then is the sad flight of people to be like Pericles, Caesar, Homer, Napoleon, Flaubert, or Michael Jordan. No one, it seems, wants to be himself or live his own life.

But a self born from a philosophy of redemption is another thing entirely. For such a self there is no narrative, no story or dramatic backdrop. You are not making your way from A to Z and you are not taking an angelic aptitude test. In your own redemption, in the act of living well, you can only become yourself. To be redeemed is to accept your own person completely without goal or expectation. You will not begin to live when you lord it over Iraq, win the Oscar, or meet Jesus. Yes, life is meaningless. But explore this statement, chew the concept well. People are so afraid of meaninglessness that they turn and run before having a good look. How often I have started in panic and strenuously paddled my sea kayak away from a fin in the water. Every single time a second look has revealed the fin to be a dolphin's. And, at least once so far, coming closer to this dolphin brought me an experience of surpassing beauty.

Meaninglessness is not monstrous upon inspection. The great sages did not live as actors, but realized their own presence in the moment. To live without such meaning simply means that you are not embedded in a story beyond that of the visible present. You are not a character or an actor. You are not a fallen angel with amnesia. You are just what you are. You were born, grow, and will die. For the sage, life is not about one Big Story but lots of little ones: the story of a friend, the story of a day, the story of a moment. Is there meaning to this? No, there is no greater meaning than the *experience* of it, the infinitely layered experience of life itself. The only meaning of life is action in the present. You will not find a hidden revelation in all this any more than a happy infant finds some great meaning in smiling and laughing. Or any more than the sun finds meaning in its fireball of fusion. Break free from the concept of a narrative, step out of the artificial story, and begin life searching for nothing more than awareness and experience. This is the beginning of a mature philosophy.

Some pertinent characteristics can be found in all mature philosophies. None duck the uglier facts of life; in them death meets a steady gaze. By acknowledging contingency, these philosophies need not strain and deceive to build up powerful illusions against life's realities. By integrating the very worst in life, they sanctify the entire venture. In the words of Epicurus: "Vain is the word of a philosopher which does not heal any suffering of man."[2] In Buddhism, Epicureanism, and Stoicism self-reliance, simplicity, alleviation of fear and pain, and an increase of pleasure (at least of a certain type) find the highest importance. Philosophies that do not at least contain some mixture of these elements deserve little consideration, except as intellectual puzzle-solving to pass an afternoon.

The importance of self-scrutiny is common to all these philosophies. In their own way, each of these schools held the individual's interpretation of life to be of the utmost importance. To live in a tempest of emotion, tossed and turned by every chance event, is to live in the heart of *Maya*—the Hindu word for illusion. As the Stoic philosopher Epictetus wrote:

> *Men are disturbed not by the things which happen, but by the opinions about the things.* ...It is the act of an ill-instructed man to blame others for his own bad condition; it is the act of one who has begun to be instructed, to lay the blame on himself; and of the one whose instruction is completed, neither to blame another, nor himself.[3]

That the majority of our suffering derives not from outside, but from inside—from our own interpretation of the events which beset us—marks the height of wisdom. Modern psychology has put these theories to the test. Albert Ellis and Aaron Beck developed techniques of cognitive psychotherapy that harnessed this insight of Epictetus. By teaching their patients to change their interpretations of events—their belief systems—they've shown startling success in the treatment of psychological turmoil. A number of careful studies attest to the clinical success of these therapies. Wisdom, ancient or modern, makes life better, *makes your life better*.

## Buddhism

The awareness of contingency traumatizes the pathological narcissist. But the agony of a mortal narcissistic injury can also be the birth pains of a healthy human being. The trademark of any mature philosophy is the acceptance of life's contingencies. Only by a forthright recognition of the dark and difficult truths can we hope for integration. The essential truth of the Buddha's teachings involves the recognition that life is full of suffering, which might in our terms be called contingency. The doctrine does not mean to impugn the world but to recognize life's impermanence and meaning's shiftiness. Through this recognition, the spell of narcissism is broken and a more authentic, socially-based existence proceeds. The pig-headed, narcissistic philosophies insist on things working out in our favor, meeting our dearest wishes. All pain is only apparent. In the end, after this life, we will be rewarded threefold—like the long-suffering Job. This kind of intense avoidance creates far more problems than facing up to life's troubles as an adult. The traditional story of the Buddha (Awakened One) develops along these very themes.

Born into royalty, Siddhartha Gautama (the Buddha) would know every pleasure life had to offer; his father considered his son's comfort a duty. Upon his heir's birth, the elder of the Sakyamuni clan asked the counsel of wisemen and astrologers, "What will my son be." The wisemen gave the king high hopes, Siddhartha Gautama would be a world ruler. A moment passed and they wavered... he could also be an enlightened one. Showing no tolerance for the riches of religion, the Buddha's father sought to make his son a world ruler. He reasoned that if the boy knew nothing of the world's ills then he would more easily become a conqueror and ruler; freed of life's contingencies he would find no need for religious comforts. The Buddha's father swaddled the child in every comfort and delicacy and the youth grew up strong and brilliant.

Suddhodana kept his son always within the confines of the palace but Siddhartha grew curious about the outside world. He enlisted his charioteer's aid in sneaking out from time to time when his father's watchful gaze grew lazy. In these forays, the Buddha came to witness the Four Sights.

On his first trip outside, Siddhartha saw an enfeebled old man. His father had so sheltered the youth that even the fatigue of age was unknown to him. The Buddha asked his driver, Channa, about the old one. Channa told him that such was the way of all men. If a person lived long enough his vitality drained away and weakness set in. On the next trip, the Buddha saw a person by the road thoroughly ill and in a pile of filth. He asked the driver and was told about the constant ills that plague mankind. On his third trip outside of the palace, the Buddha saw a corpse. This truly startled him. Channa informed him about death and how it eventually came to every man. Well into his twenties, the Buddha had lately been awakened to life's vicissitudes. He still had his palace, he still possessed a beautiful wife who had just given birth to his first son. The Buddha claimed inheritance to an entire kingdom in Northern India. In spite of all this, he was utterly broken. So long ignorant of life's essential laws, he could now think of nothing else. Sickness and death seemed to pervade all things and rob life of its meaning. He began to wonder about the point of human existence. Why live at all if it came to this? On his next outing, the Buddha saw a sage and confident old monk strolling along with a gleam in his eye. The monk seemed to have met all the challenges of the world and still retained an air of dignity. Siddhartha sensed that something deeper lay behind all the apparent horrors of life. Siddhartha Gautama—a husband, father, and prince—escaped the palace and began his quest for Enlightenment.

With fierce discipline, the Buddha followed the ascetic path and tried many forms of yoga to no avail. Deep down, he always felt a sense of misgiving along these paths. Going his own way, the Middle Path—neither ascetic nor indulgent—the Buddha achieved Enlightenment on his own terms. Thus he conveyed that peace can be found only in the personal journey, not by following the examples set by others. The Buddha came back to the world to teach a simple way of life, cognizant of the Four Noble Truths.

The doctrine of the Four Noble Truths assumes a sickness in the human condition. Like a traditional healer, the Buddha specifies the sickness, gives his prognosis, and offers medicine. The First Noble Truth, the sickness, is suffering. All life is suffering and almost every act to minimize suffering creates delusion and plants seeds of future suffering. The Second Noble Truth finds the source of suffering in desire. In fact, these two truths are woven together. Just as suffering gives rise to desire, so desire amplifies suffering. Because of a bad education, the idea that suffering can be ended in some further desire, some further yearning or grasping, only deepens one's troubles, like jerking about in quicksand. The Third Noble Truth holds that the only solution to desire is to end desire. But how does one end desire? In one form or another isn't everything desire? To clarify and resolve these many difficulties, the Buddha taught the Fourth Noble Truth. This, perhaps, is the Buddha's only lie; in fact, the Fourth Noble Truth holds within it eight more—the existential medicine.

The Eightfold Path of Buddhism finds the quenching of desire in (1)Right understanding, (2)Right purpose, (3)Right speech, (4)Right conduct, (5)Right Livelihood, (6)Right effort, (7)Right mind-fulness, and (8)Right meditation. Rather than an extended discussion on the subtleties and ramifications of these recommendations, we shall conclude that the Buddha teaches a method, not a belief. He encourages action, not faith. In this clarification lies the essential fact: philosophies of redemption aim towards integration and personal fulfillment. Buddhism points to a practical happiness instead of practical madness (flight from reality).

How do such simple truths really address life's difficulties? The Parable of the Mustard Seed nicely captures the spirit of these existential truths. A young woman named Kisa Gotami had lost everything. Her family and husband passed away, leaving her homeless and desolate. The only joy left her was an infant, which then died. In her utter grief she lost her mind and wondered aimlessly never letting go of her child's dead body. The villagers were helpless. No one could undo her tragedy and there was no Prozac in those days to salve wounded psyches. Finally, someone suggested that she go to the Buddha to be healed. In all times and places, Enlightened Ones are thought of as miracle workers capable of supernatural healing. When told about the Buddha, Kisa Gotami developed new hope. Perhaps this saint could revive her child. She went on a long trek to meet him. The Buddha perceived the depth of her loss, the eccentricity of her mind, and counseled her appropriately, "Yes, I can help you," he answered to her requests. "But first I'll need you to gather some mustard seed for me." With great joy Kisa Gotami went to collect the mustard seed, a common cooking ingredient in that region. As she parted from him, the Buddha added, "Oh, be sure to get it from a house who has suffered no loss of child, parent, servant, or the like." Kisa Gotami, still holding her slack infant, hurried off. She went from one house to the next and was pitied. When she asked for mustard seed, she was treated graciously while the women and men measured some out for her. But in checking whether they had lost anyone, each and every person she met had a long, sad story to tell. Kisa Gotami went from house to house, first hopeful then despondent— everyone, literally everyone, had suffered great loss. As she contemplated all the loss she had experienced, she mourned, then went to the forest's edge. She buried her infant, and cried once more. Afterwards, she returned to the Buddha. He gazed into her eyes compassionately. "Nothing lasts," he told her. He gave her the same look of dignity and hope that he had once seen on a wandering old monk. She started on the path to true healing.

In recognizing our tragedies to be universal we deflate the pain that we hold so close to our breast, as our own. Compassion, or suffering with others, ends up as one of the realizations and practices of any mature philosophy. Nothing can be undone, nothing ever is undone, yet people persevere for the simple reason that they have no other choice. The only freedom left anyone in the face of a personal tragedy is the manner in which they respond to it. Will we, like Kisa Gotami, imagine our fate worse than any other and inflate it like our own narcissistic egos? Madness and heartbreak are the sure result. The Buddha earned the title of an Awakened Teacher not by undoing things but by changing minds. That, in the end, is the only thing that makes or breaks us as human beings.

It is interesting to note the neotenous development of the Buddha's life. Just as it is biological neoteny that gives rise to the wondrous human brain, so the existential neoteny of the Buddha's youth seems to have allowed him an enlarged view of the human condition and its 'solution.' He was slow to recognize life's contingencies—slow to mature—but finally he matured beyond everyone else and taught the quintessential doctrines of a mature philosophy.

## The Wisdom of Epicurus

Just as the Buddha's philosophy originated in the tumult of a sensitive soul, so the great philosophies of ancient Greece developed from the cultural crisis of a brilliant people. The strength of Greek culture arose from the solidarity of the community. As the individual city-states began to collapse, their destruction hastened by such power mongers as Alexander the Great, the traditional sources of identity and value began to disintegrate. Plato encouraged a flight from this imperfect world to the perfection of the next, as we traced in Part I. For Plato, the proper aim of philosophy was preparation for death. Embracing and systematizing Orphism, he taught truth to be imperturbable because of its basis in the transcendent, away from the contingencies of history and society.

The philosophy of Epicurus came about, in large part, as a reaction to Platonism. Epicurus wanted life to be philosophy's subject and man's happiness a reality in this life and in this world. Epicurus found Plato's metaphysical tone forced, his notion of the immateriality of the soul absurd, and his distrust of the senses paranoid. As Greek as it was in some ways, Plato's exaltation of immateriality jarred the sensibilities of these people. Epicurus, though his philosophy opposed many traditional values, especially that of *agon*—the constant competitiveness that permeated the Greek psyche—in the end taught a more traditional philosophy than Plato.

To fight the transcendence of Platonic theory, Epicurus turned back to the Presocratics for support. In these enigmatic thinkers he found a thoroughgoing materialism. Taking Democritus's atomic theory to be a sufficient explanation of matter, Epicurus affirmed all things to be of one substance, including man and his soul. Epicurus thought all things resultant from chance, so he made no effort to reconcile the individual and the universe. European culture would not return to such a place for some 2000 years. The conclusion of materialism, as we've seen throughout the present work, is the certain death of the person. While Plato denied the reality of death, Epicurus faced it without flinching.

Epicurean philosophy, so little discussed in our time and misunderstood when mentioned, possessed a wide appeal during Greek and Roman history. Christianity, or Jewish Platonism, eventually suppressed this Greek philosophy. Bignone discusses the popularity of Epicureanism versus Platonism during the classical era:

> ...the Epicurean philosophy resisted the ruin of the ancient world, because more than any of the others it held firm two beliefs which in the ancient world were the profound reasons for life: a belief in reality and in a knowledge of it, as well as a belief in the achievement of happiness. When anxiety about the supernatural overcomes, and earthly reality seems to be full of illusion and error, and true knowledge no longer inquires through the way of experience, but through mystical and religious apocalyptics, when earthly existence itself is irredeemably condemned, and man aspires to nothing other than to leave it as soon as possible, only then will the philosophy of Epicurus vanish...[4]

With eloquence, Bignone describes the conditions for Epicureanism's demise, conditions which found fulfillment in the epoch-making philosophy of Jesus and Paul.

Epicureanism is a simple philosophy. It teaches the good life. For Epicureans, true happiness is to be found in the simple pleasures afforded to all. Mature philosophies see in great ambition—the quest for fame, wealth, or power—so much nonsense and confusion. As Epicurus wrote: "He who is not satisfied with little, is satisfied with nothing."[5] From bad education, confusion, and narcissism the heroic individual, like Tantalus, grasps for a world that recedes ever farther from him the more he reaches. So do the Stalins, at the greatest height of their power, feel nothing but paranoia and insecurity.

For Epicureans, life should not be a long and circuitous route to happiness but a meditation upon stable pleasures. No philosopher understood pleasure and its distinctions better than Epicurus. From birth, the human creature seeks what is pleasurable and avoids what is painful. If we do not account for these things, we cannot treat the human condition. Two thousand years of Christian prejudice would have us believe that hedonism smacks of immorality. Epicurus considered the life of pleasure to be the only source of ethical action:

> Prudence teaches us how impossible it is to live pleasantly without living wisely, virtuously, and justly, just as we cannot live wisely,

virtuously, and justly without living pleasantly. For the virtues arise naturally with the pleasant life; indeed, the pleasant life cannot be separated from them.[6]

Since Epicurus's time, a long, dark history of neurotic megalomaniacs attests to his wisdom by their reverse example. In truth, when has there ever been a good Christian ruler during European history? For all their stated Christianity, the rulers of the West, as a group, have been immoral if not cruel. It is only when rulers are closet humanists that good has been accomplished. The power-hungry scarcely understand pleasure, rarely live wisely, compromise their virtue along the path of ambition, and consider justice to be found in might alone.

For all his talk of pleasure, though, Epicurus's notions are anything but the unalloyed hedonism we typically associate with that word. He refined all the traditional ideas about hedonism. The greedy pleasures of the body, that in their indulgence seem only to rouse more lust, Epicurus called *kinetic* (moving) pleasures. These pleasures always come about as the result of some movement—chewing or screwing—and take on the character of movement, in that they rarely rest without getting stirred up again. Epicurus passed over the kinetic pleasures for the *catastematic* (stable) pleasures: peaceful contemplation, rest, and time with friends. Stable pleasures could be controlled by prudence and strengthened one's mental stability. Over these stable pleasures, one wields control. In the end, the *summum bonum* for Epicureans was not pleasure but lack of pain. The quintessence of Epicureanism can be captured in a single sentence: "Everything we do is for the sake of this, namely, to avoid pain and fear. Once this is achieved, all the soul's trouble is dispelled…"[7]

One might imagine a philosophy of hedonism to cultivate and refine pleasures. In fact, Epicurus thought we should simplify our pleasures. Rather than savoring the gourmet meal, and subsequently longing for another of like quality, Epicurus thought one should satisfy his hunger with the simplest, most nutritious food available. A full stomach admits no hunger whether full of rice or caviar. Eating seeks to liberate us from the bondage of hunger. It can accomplish this without expensive foods. Self-sufficiency and the need for very little make life's problems shrink until they can be solved with scarce effort. Having the ability to rid oneself of pain, no matter what one's condition in time and place, offered a sense of security far richer and more stable than any indulgence in fine pleasures.

Death appeared a simple problem in light of this understanding. Since death rendered one unconscious and therefore free from pain, nothing in it could inspire fear. *Ataraxy* (tranquility) became the height of human pleasure. The calm mind, undisturbed by any of the chance events that came its way, provided a constant source of gratification. Since the good life for Epicureans did not involve achievement, fame, wealth, knowledge, or any of the other typical goods, they could hope for nothing in an afterlife. For them, the properly organized mind found all it needed in the present. The one delight they indulged in, which would necessarily be discontinued at death, was friendship. But even the removal of this mattered little because no 'self' would remain to perceive this lack: "Death, therefore—the most dreadful of evils—is nothing to us, since while we exist, death is not present, and whenever death is present, we do not exist."[8] The Epicurean triumph in the present seems a strange and foreign concept to we who invest so much in the tomorrow. As Epicurus wrote: "He who has least need of tomorrow will most gladly greet tomorrow."[9] It is our constant desire to achieve in the tomorrow which makes of it a day for anxiety and exhaustion. At heart, Epicureanism appears to be a Greek version of Buddhism.

Given his doctrines, one might think Epicurus atheistic. While he was not an outright atheist, his understanding of human perfection gave him insight into the nature of the gods. First, the gods were not spiritual, but possessed more enduring bodies than man. The divinities he imagined had nothing to do with the needy or vengeful gods to whom the person could pray for support or forgiveness: "The blessed and immortal is itself free from trouble nor does it cause trouble for anyone else; therefore, it is not constrained either by anger or by favor. For such sentiments exist only in the weak."[10] Epicurus encouraged contemplation of the gods as ideals of tranquility; the rest of human religious practices should be scrapped as so much fear-inducing nonsense.

## *Stoicism*

Stoicism opposed Epicureanism. Upon a careful review, though, these schools came from the very same stock. They were cousins, if not brothers. In their opposition, they exhibited nothing more than sibling rivalry. The Stoic school began in the philosophy of Zeno of Citium. In contrast to Epicureanism—whose principles changed little after Epicurus—Stoicism underwent a great deal of growth over centuries. It reached its peak in the Roman world with Seneca and the Emperor Marcus Aurelius. Before Christianity, Stoicism was the true faith of the empire.

Like Epicureanism, Stoicism taught a philosophy of materialism that necessitated the individual's death. Seneca used the testimony of body language to strengthen the belief in the soul's materiality. He considered the blush of embarrassment and the grimace of anger and pain: "Do you think that such evident marks of the body are stamped upon us by anything else than body?"[11]

Besides their materialism, the Stoics retained a strong belief in divinity, although it was an impersonal one, a divine reason that existed within and organized all of nature. The Stoics were thorough Pantheists and did not seek help, understanding, or any other boon from their god—*logos* (Reason). As much as the Epicureans, the Stoics felt the good life to be man's ideal and his own responsibility.

Since they thought reason behind all things, the Stoics believed in the necessity of Fate. Nothing could be different as it is, nothing wished otherwise, since all expresses the perfection of divine order—Providence. With Darwinism as background, Stoicism would have to carefully question this belief in Providence. The notion of Providence fostered resignation in the Stoic. *Apatheia*, or the complete removal of emotion, suggested a higher ideal to them. Emotions were essentially the result of wishing things different and the Stoics would have nothing different than it is.

How could one live a life of freedom within such a conception? The only freedom accorded the Stoic was the choice to consent to Fate. If one is tied to a slowly-moving car, one can fight, but will end up being dragged. If one consents to the movement and walks in step with it, freedom from emotion is achieved and life becomes harmonious. The ascetic, in fighting the body's needs, always loses. But a Buddhist-like middle way consents to the body without becoming slave to it. In the end, a dignified gratefulness accords the Stoic more virtue than the mindless, and unhappy, rebel. The fundamental precept of all Stoics, no matter their slight differences, is to live according to Nature.

Romans usually laughed at the Epicurean ideal of pleasure. The hardy Romans were not willing to give up suffering. Difficulties made one tough and crafted one's character. As one matured into Stoicism, he resigned himself to the difficulties of the world and thus achieved an apathetic peace of mind. The military state would not tolerate the effete dignity of the hedonist, far better the resigned dignity of the Old Warrior who suffered much but emerged victorious. And, in contrast to Epicureanism's individualism, Stoicism bred strong, community-minded individuals. In *Letters from a Stoic*, Seneca wrote: "The first thing philosophy promises us is the feeling of fellowship, of belonging to mankind and being members of a community…"[12] Stoics were unwilling to retire from the world and appreciate the life of tranquility. They would bring their equanimity to the community and bear any responsibilities with a well-weathered disposition. In a way, Stoicism was just another way of bringing the *Pax Romana* to one's interior. The empire held together impossibly different nations through sheer discipline of will and a careful bureaucracy. So could the self be bound together with a rigorous imposition of will and courage. Fortitude, civic virtue, and simplicity would be the trademarks of the Stoic.

From mental toughness and courage, a tolerant ability to withstand death and contingency developed. Marcus Aurelius, the emperor of a world empire, could write even-handedly:

> Think continually how many doctors have died who often knit their brows over their dying patients, how many astrologers who had foretold the deaths of others as a matter of importance, how many philosophers who had discoursed at great length on death and immortality, how many heroic warriors who had killed many men, how many tyrants who had used their power over men's lives with terrible brutality, as if immortal themselves. How often have not whole cities died… Go over in your mind the dead whom you have known, one after another: one paid the last rites to a friend and was himself laid out for burial by a third, who also died; and all in a short time. Altogether, human affairs must be regarded as

ephemeral, and of little worth: yesterday sperm, tomorrow a mummy or ashes. Journey then through this moment of time in accord with nature, and graciously depart, as a ripened olive might fall, praising the Earth which produced it...[13]

Neither chance nor death could upset the Stoic, immune as he was to the fears of life that so many other philosophies cultivate. Fully aware and appreciative of death, mature philosophies never instruct a wanton liberation to 'get it while you can' but, in simplicity and resolve, extol a life of dignity and meaning.

## *The Sage*

Be like a rock against which the waves of the sea break unceasingly. It stands unmoved, and the feverish waters around it are stilled.
     —Marcus Aurelius, *Meditations*[14]

The ideal of the sage shows remarkable similarity in all cultures. Each tradition, in its own way, seems to breed these striking individuals. The ideal of the good life and its attained perfection in the model of the sage shone particularly bright within the philosophies of Epicureanism and Stoicism. These schools addressed physics, epistemology, and the other branches of philosophy but held ethics and the ideal of happiness foremost. And in Buddhism, one need hardly mention the ideal. Enlightenment, or finding one's Buddha-nature, conveys the ideal of becoming a sage and an embodiment of virtue.

What are the universal traits of the sage? Above all, he possesses a mental peace within that resonates outward. The sage is not a philosopher because he doesn't need words to speak. Wordlessly, the sage teaches a way of life; still, he commands with authority. The sage, in the concentration upon self and the attainment of tranquility, ultimately serves humanity better than any other philanthropist. The model of life the sage upholds brings hope and peace even to those who fall far short of such living. By teaching that happiness lies always within—even in the worst times and places—the sage utters the highest human truths. The sage exemplifies an even-keeled temperament while: "The mean soul is puffed up by successes, but brought down by adversity."[15]

Far from fighting death and contingency, the sage wholly accepts life's more dismal realities as parts of the whole, shadows within the light. By denying these evils an ability to disturb, the sage integrates them into a more encompassing notion of peace. In discussing the Epicurean and Stoic ideal, Giovanni Reale, writes:

> [The sage] ...is a man who is profoundly convinced that the true good and the true evil do not arise from things but only from the opinions which we have about things. Gods, other men, all things, and even destiny *can touch us only if and as far as our opinion about them makes this possible. The correct evaluation of things makes us invulnerable.*[16]

By internalizing all of the world (exactly opposite of the narcissist), the sage gains power over himself. Having accustomed himself to the whirling, unpredictable nature of things, the sage remains at peace in the center of the cyclone. Epicurus, himself the enlightened example of his own school, understood that peace could be achieved in reality, in spite of its troubles: "The man who has best settled the feeling of disquiet that comes from external circumstances is he who has made those things he can of the same kin as himself; and what he cannot, at least not alien."[17]

By creating peace in the present and knowing harmony in the world, the sage attains godlike status. In fact, the sage surpasses God because the human, in his limitations, in his mortality, in his relative powerlessness, shows a compassion that no god with power, immortality, and perfection could understand. Free from ambition, the sage touches the height of human power—the power to create happiness.

*Chapter 25*

# CONCLUSION

The more a man can take reality as truth, appearance as essence, the sounder, the better adjusted, the happier will he be.

—Otto Rank, *Truth and Reality*[1]

The human soul is a myth. It teaches wonderful truths: each of us is more than a body that persists for a few decades. Each of us is the act of love, the act of memory, the act of individuality, the act of enlightenment, the human being. We are each vital links in a chain of family and history. But like all the myths, the myth of the soul must yield to modernity. We are not ghosts. We will not live forever. We are noble, ingenious, but wholly mortal animals.

Perceiving the soul to be a misunderstanding, a hasty and premature attempt to explain brain processes, do we simply discard it as we did the theory of a flat Earth? Or must we pause and consider the fact that this error has been in place for thousands of years and has shaped our fundamental ideas about human nature and destiny? In fact, that time has come and gone. Man has known, at some level, the truth about the human soul,—and the certainty of individual mortality,—for a very long time. Those who stubbornly fight for the myth of the soul deceive themselves and mislead others.

Self-deception is ultimately not a problem of perception—the truth, in fact, is known—rather it is a problem of courage. So too does our acceptance of truth and our ability to apprehend the boundaries of our existence exist as an aspect of character, not as a dispute of knowledge. Truth is for the strong. The question then becomes, "Are we strong enough, are we honest enough, and are we creative enough to be true to ourselves and the world?" Optimists will answer the question yes, pessimists will overlook it altogether. In *Beyond Good and Evil*, Nietzsche wrote: "It is the profound, suspicious fear of an incurable pessimism that forces whole millennia to bury their teeth in and cling to a religious interpretation of existence..."[2] Honesty in living requires an acceptance of things too hostile, rude, or frightening to welcome. Nevertheless, contingency—the cold, pulsing heart of existence—must be integrated into one's perception of the world. Life itself demands that we become comfortable with the uncomfortable. For no matter how faultlessly we live or how gently we walk, we will always require violence in order to obtain us food, we will always emit stinks and noises as a process of digestion, we will always be vainly self-concerned, we will always objectify those who would be our mates—seeing them initially as means to pleasure—and we will always stand naked before the threat of doom, weaponless against the overpowering monster of death. Such is life, such must life be.

# ACKNOWLEDGEMENTS

This book took the better part of four years to write, so in recalling who I need to thank, I have to put forth a special effort of memory. I'm extremely thankful of the friends and family I have, as their support and good cheer gave me sustenance when the most unrewarding parts of this text were being fashioned. My doubts of ability or style were never confirmed as I always had a surplus of kind words from my friends.

I would like to thank Sean Smith Ph.D. of The Salk Institute for reviewing my sections on the neurosciences. His critique and feedback were quite valuable. Daniel Liechty, Ph.D., D.Min., a friend from the Ernest Becker Foundation, was helpful with his insights into Becker's work. Dan took the time to read my manuscript and offered some thoughtful suggestions. My former advisor in the Stanford Religious Studies Department, Professor Van Harvey, was kind enough to read the entire first section and suggested some important changes. This was a special honor for me since it was largely his classes that set me on the trail of these arguments and ideas. Any errors or misrepresentations in this book, despite the best efforts of these reviewers, is my fault alone.

Finally, I'd like to thank my employers, Chris MacPhail of Wired Markets and Beatrice Golomb, M.D., Ph.D. of the UCSD Statin Study. My employers' patience with my schedule, helpful comments, and appreciation for my outside activities allowed me to pursue a project that would otherwise be impossible to finish.

# NOTES

## Part I—A History of the Soul

### Chapter 1: Where We Are—The Cartesian Split

1 René Descartes, *Meditations on First Philosophy*, trans. Ronald Rubin (Claremont, CA: Areté Press, 1986), pp. 4-5. [Meditation I]
2 René Descartes, *Discourse on the Method*, part IV.
3 Descartes, *Meditations on First Philosophy*, p. 44.

### Chapter 2: The Prehistoric Beginnings of the Soul

1 Eliade, *A History of Religious Ideas*, Vol. 1, trans. Willard R. Trask (Chicago: The University of Chicago Press, 1978), p. 9.
2 Eliade, *A History of Religious Ideas*, Vol. 1, p. 10.
3 Jean Clottes and David Lewis-Williams, *The Shamans of Prehistory: Trance and Magic in the Painted Caves* (New York: Harry N. Abrams, 1998).
4 Donald Johanson, Lenora Johnson, and Blake Edgar, *Ancestors: In Search of Human Origins* (New York: Villard Books, 1994), p. 299.
5 Jean Clottes, "France's Magical Ice Age Art: Chauvet Cave," *National Geographic*, August 2001, Vol. 200, No. 2, pp. 104-121.
6 Weston LaBarre, "Anthropological Perspectives on Hallucination, Hallucinogens, and the Shamanic Origins of Religion," in *Culture in Context: Selected Writings of Weston LaBarre* (Durham, NC: Duke University Press, 1980), p. 83 and Weston LaBarre, *Shadow of Childhood: Neoteny and the Biology of Religion* (Norman, OK: The University of Oklahoma Press, 1991), p. 130.
7 Paul Radin, *The Trickster: A Study in American Indian Mythology* (New York: Schocken Books, 1972), p. 52.
8 Miguel de Unamuno, *The Tragic Sense of Life in Men and Nations*, trans. Anthony Kerrigan (Princeton, NJ: Princeton University Press, 1972), p. 173.
9 Xenophanes in Kathleen Freeman, *Ancilla to the Pre-socratic Philosophers* (Cambridge: Harvard University Press, 1948), p. 22.
10 Xenophanes in Kathleen Freeman, p. 22.

## Chapter 3: Shamanism

1   Mircea Eliade, *Shamanism: Archaic Techniques of Ecstasy*, trans. Willard R. Trask (Princeton, NJ: The Princeton University Press, 1964), p. 509.
2   Eliade, *Shamanism*, p. 509.
3   Eliade, *Shamanism*, pp. 480-481.
4   Eliade, *Shamanism*, p. 4.
5   Aldous Huxley, *The Perennial Philosophy*, (New York: HarperCollins, 1990).
6   Joseph Campbell, *The Masks of God: Primitive Mythology* (New York: The Viking Press, 1959), pp. 252-253.
7   Eliade, *Shamanism*, p. 27.
8   Eliade, *Shamanism*, p. 30.
9   Eliade, *Shamanism*, p. 84.
10  Epicurus, *The Essential Epicurus*, trans. Eugene O'Connor (Amherst, NY: Prometheus Books, 1993), p. 63.

## Chapter 4: The ancient Egyptians

1   *The Gospel of Matthew*. 2:13-15 (All biblical citations from NSRV).
2   *Exodus*. 12:40
3   Stephen Quirke, *Ancient Egyptian Religion* (New York: Dover Publications, 1992), p. 105.
4   Quirke, p. 67.
5   Guillemette Andreu, *Egypt in the Age of the Pyramids*, trans. David Lorton (Ithaca: Cornell University Press, 1997) p. 144.
6   Stephen Davies, "Soul: Ancient Near East Concepts," in *The Encyclopedia of Religion*, Vol. 13, ed. Mircea Eliade (New York: Macmillian Publishing Company, 1987), pp. 432-433.
7   Davies, p. 162.
8   Andreu, p. 149.
9   Andreu, p. 150.

## Chapter 5: Zoroastrianism

1   Mircea Eliade, *A History of Religious Ideas*, Vol. 2, trans. Willard R. Trask (Chicago: The University of Chicago Press, 1978), p. 310.
2   Richard Frye, *The Heritage of Persia* (Cleveland: The World Publishing Company, 1963), pp. 31-32.
3   Gherardo Gnoli, "Zoroastrianism," trans. Ughetta Fitzgerald Lubin, in *The Encyclopedia of Religion*, vol. 15, ed. Mircea Eliade (New York: Macmillian Publishing Company, 1987), pp. 585-586.
4   A.V.W. Jackson, "Zoroastrianism," in *The Jewish Encyclopedia*, Vol. 12 (KTAV Publishing House), p. 696.

# Chapter 6: The Soul of Plato

1 A.E. Taylor, *Socrates* (Garden City, NJ: Doubleday, 1953), p. 132.
2 Friedrich Nietzsche, *The Birth of Tragedy*, trans. Walter Kaufmann (New York: Vintage, 1967), p. 95.
3 Walter Burkert, *Greek Religion*, trans. John Raffan (Cambridge, MA: Harvard University Press, 1985), p. 322.
4 Tertullian, *De Carne Christi*, 5, *The Ante Nicene Fathers* (Grand Rapids, MI: William B. Eerdman's Publishing Co.).
5 Burkert, p. 321.
6 Xenophon, *Memorabilia* (The Loeb Classical Library), trans. E.C. Marchant, (Cambridge, MA: Harvard University Press, 1929).
7 Aristophanes, *Clouds* (The Loeb Classical Library), trans. Jeffrey Henderson, (Cambridge, MA: Harvard University Press, 1998).
8 American School of Classical Studies at Athens, *Socrates in the Agora* (Meriden, CT: Meriden Gravure Company, 1978).
9 W.K.C. Guthrie, *Orpheus and Greek Religion: A Study of the Orphic Movement* (London: Methuen & Co. Ltd., 1952), p. 242.
10 Guthrie, pp. 216-246.
11 Aristophanes' *The Clouds* and *The Birds* may be seen as an attack on Orphic ideas as much as an attack upon Socrates himself.
12 E.R. Dodds, *The Greeks and the Irrational* (Berkeley: University of California Press, 1951), p. 209.
13 Vittorio Macchioro, *From Orpheus to Paul* (New York: Henry Holt & Company, 1930), p. 46.
14 John Warden, *Orpheus: The Metamorphoses of a Myth* (Toronto: University of Toronto Press, 1982), p. viii.
15 Plato, *Republic*, trans. Paul Shorey, *Plato: The Collected Dialogues*, eds. Edith Hamilton & Huntington Cairns (Princeton: Princeton University Press, 1961), 2: 364 e.
16 F.M. Cornford, *From Religion to Philosophy* (Princeton, NJ: Princeton University Press, 1991), p. 197.
17 Erwin Rohde, *Psyche: The Cult of Souls and Immortality Among the Greeks* (New York: Harcourt, Brace, and Co., 1925), p. 544.
18 H.D.F. Kitto, *The Greeks* (London: Penguin Books, 1957), p. 174.
19 Macchioro, p. 130.
20 Jaeger, *Paideia*, Vol. 1, trans. Gilbert Highet (Oxford: Oxford University Press, 1967), pp. 168-169.
21 Plato, *Symposium*, trans. Michael Joyce, *Plato: The Collected Dialogues*, eds. Edith Hamilton & Huntington Cairns (Princeton: Princeton University Press, 1961), 220 c-d.
22 F.M. Cornford, *Principium Sapientiae: The Origins of Greek Philosophical Thought*, ed. W.K.C. Guthrie (New York: Harper & Row, 1965), pp. 86-87.
23 Plato, *Symposium*, 214 a.
24 Plato, *Symposium*, 220 a-b, 221a-b.
25 quoted in Mircea Eliade, *Shamanism: Archaic Techniques of Ecstasy*, p. 29.
26 quoted in Mircea Eliade, *Shamanism: Archaic Techniques of Ecstasy*, p.

29.
27 Plato, *Apology*, trans. Hugh Tredennick, *Plato: The Collected Dialogues,*
   eds. Edith Hamilton & Huntington Cairns (Princeton: Princeton
   University Press, 1961), 23b.
28 Plato, *Apology*, 33c.
29 Plato, *Apology*, 40b.
30 Plato, *Phaedrus*, trans. R. Hackforth, *Plato: The Collected Dialogues*, eds.
   Edith Hamilton & Huntington Cairns (Princeton: Princeton
   University Press, 1961), 249d.
31 Plato, *Apology*, 30e-31a.
32 Plato, *Apology*, 31a.
33 Plato, *Phaedo*, trans. Hugh Tredennick, *Plato: The Collected Dialogues,*
   eds. Edith Hamilton & Huntington Cairns (Princeton: Princeton
   University Press, 1961), 74e.
34 Plato, *Phaedo*, 67d.
35 Plato, *Phaedo*, 66b-e, 67a.
36 Mark Twain, *Autobiography*, ed. Charles Neider (New York: Harper,
   1959).

## Chapter 7: Judaism

1 Jane Smith, "Afterlife: An Overview," *The Encyclopedia of Religion*, Vol.
   1, ed. Mircea Eliade (New York: Macmillian Publishing Company,
   1987), p. 110.
2 Jack Bemporad, "Soul: Jewish Concept," *The Encyclopedia of Religion*,
   Vol. 13, ed. Mircea Eliade (New York: Macmillian Publishing
   Company, 1987), p. 450.
3 David Stern, "Afterlife: Jewish Concepts," in *The Encyclopedia of
   Religion*, vol. 1, ed. Mircea Eliade (New York: Macmillian Publishing
   Company, 1987), p. 120.
4 John Noss, *Man's Religions*, 6th Ed. (New York: Macmillan Publishing
   Company, 1980), p. 394.

## Chapter 8: The Body of Christ

1 Jeffrey Burton Russell, *A History of Heaven* (Princeton: Princeton
   University Press, 1997), p. 46.
2 One of the more complete discussions of 'soul' terminology is found
   in Rudolf Bultmann, *Theology of the New Testament*, vol. 1, trans.
   Kendrick Grobel (London: SCM Press Ltd., 1952), pp. 191-248.
3 *1 Corinthians 7:40*
4 see especially, Gerd Lüdemann, *Paul: The Founder of Christianity*
   (Amherst, NY: Prometheus Books, 2002).
5 Karl Barth, *The Resurrection of the Dead*, trans. H.J. Stenning (New
   York: Fleming H. Revell Company, 1933), p. 197.
6 John Hick, *Death and Eternal Life* (New York: Harper and Row
   Publishers, 1976), p. 194.
7 Elaine Pagels, *The Gnostic Gospels* (New York: Vintage Books, 1989) p.

xix.

8    *The Book of Thomas the Contender*, trans. John D. Turner, *The Nag
     Hammadi Library*, Revised Edition, ed. James M. Robinson (San
     Francisco: HarperCollins, 1990), 138.16-19, in NHL p. 201.
9    *The Gospel of Thomas*, trans. Thomas O. Lambdin, *The Nag Hammadi
     Library*, Revised Edition, General Ed. James M. Robinson (San
     Francisco: HarperCollins, 1990), 32.1, in NHL p. 126.
10   *The Gospel of Philip*, trans. Wesley W. Isenberg, *The Nag Hammadi
     Library*, Revised Edition, General Ed. James M. Robinson (San
     Francisco: HarperCollins, 1990), 36, in NHL p. 130.
11   *The Gospel of Philip*, 80.24-81.14, in NHL p. 157.
12   *The Gospel of Thomas*, 38.31-39.1, in NHL p. 130.
13   *The Gospel of Philip*, 56.21-26, in NHL p. 144.
14   *Corpus Hermeticum*, XV, 6, cited in Hans Jonas, *The Gnostic Religion*,
     Second Edition (Boston: Beacon Press, 1991), p. 282.
15   *The Book of Thomas the Contender*, 139.2-12, in NHL p. 202.
16   Hans Jonas, *The Gnostic Religion*, Second Edition (Boston: Beacon
     Press, 1991), p. 251.
17   *The Gospel of Thomas*, 39.25-26, in NHL p. 130.
18   *The Gospel of Thomas*, 41.28-30, in NHL p. 132.
19   Jonas, *The Gnostic Religion*, p. 254.
20   Hick, p. 196.

# Part II—The Soul Matter
## A Conflict of Soul

1    Pindar, *Pythian 8*.

## Chapter 10: The Basics

1    M. Crabbe, *From Soul to Self* (London: Routledge, 1999), p. 1.

## Chapter 11: Of Neurons and Neurotransmitters

1    H. Song, C.F. Stevens, and F.H. Gage, "Neural stem cells from adult
     hippocampus develop essential properties of functional CNS neu-
     rons," *Nature Neuroscience* 5(5) (2002): 438-445
2    James H. Schwartz, "Neurotransmitters," in *Principles of Neural
     Science*, 4th Ed., eds. E.R. Kandel, J.H. Schwartz, and T.M. Jessell
     (New York: McGraw-Hill, 2000), p. 281.
3    L. Traskman-Bendz et al, "Prediction of Suicidal Behavior from
     Biologic Tests," *Journal of Clinical Psychopharmacology* 12 (2 supp)
     (1992): 21s-26s.
4    Eric Kandel, "Disorders of thought and Volition: Schizophrenia," in
     *Principles of Neural Science*, 4th Ed., eds. E.R. Kandel, J.H. Schwartz,
     and T.M. Jessell (New York: McGraw-Hill, 2000), pp. 1201-1203.

5    D. Hoyer, et al, "International Union of Pharmacology classification of receptors for 5-hydroxytryptamine (serotonin). Pharmacology Reviews, 46, 158-203.

## Chapter 13: Anatomy of the Brain

1    Paul MacLean, *The Triune Brain in Evolution* (New York: Plenum, 1990).
2    Claude Ghez and W. Thomas Thach, "The Cerebellum," in *Principles of Neural Science*, 4th Ed., eds. E.R. Kandel, J.H. Schwartz, and T.M. Jessell (New York: McGraw-Hill, 2000), p. 832.
3    N.A. Akshoomoff and E. Courchesne, "A New Role for the Cerebellum in Cognitive Operations," *Behavioral Neuroscience* 106(5) (1992): 693-698.
4    S.M. Hansen-Grant et al, "Neuroendocrine and Immune System Pathology in Psychiatric Disease," in *Textbook of Psychopharmacology*, 2nd Ed., eds. A.F. Schatzberg and C.B. Nemeroff (Washington, D.C.: American Psychiatric Press, 1998), pp. 171-194.
5    Jerome Beck and Marsha Rosenbaum, *Pursuit of Ecstasy: The MDMA Experience* (Albany, NY: The State University of New York Press, 1994).
6    Robert Sapolsky, *Why Zebras Don't Get Ulcers* (New York: W.H. Freeman & Co., 1994), pp. 25-32.
7    Elkhonon Goldberg, *The Executive Brain* (Oxford: Oxford University Press, 2001), p. 2.
8    Goldberg, pp. 107-110.
9    Antonio Damasio, *Descartes' Error* (New York: G.P. Putnam's Sons 1994).

## Chapter 14: The Binding Problem...

1    Paul Theroux, *The Mosquito Coast*, (New York: Cape Cod Scriveners, 1982), pp. 365-366.
2    Petrarch, *Letter to Boccaccio*.

## Chapter 15: Psychoactivity

The following books were critical in the development of Chapter 15 (in order of their importance):

I)    Oakley Ray and Charles Ksir, *Drugs, Society, and Human Behavior*, 8th Ed. (New York: WCB/McGraw-Hill, 1999).
II)   Solomon Snyder, *Drugs and the Brain* (New York: Scientific American Books, 1986).
III)  Glen Hanson and Peter Venturelli, *Drugs and Society*, 6th Ed. (Boston,

MA: Jones and Bartlett Publishers, 2001).

For the major topics, I highly recommend these fascinating and accessible texts. For more specific interests, the individual notes that follow should be useful:

1 William Shakespeare, *Othello* (New York: Washington Square Press, 1957), Act 2, Sc. 3, Lines 294-296.
2 Samuel Butler, *The Notebooks of Samuel Butler*, ed. Henry Festing Jones (London: A.C. Fifield, 1951), p. 255.
3 H-y. Yi et al, *NIAAA Surveillance Report #49: Trends in Alcohol-Related Fatal Traffic Crashes—1975-1997* (Bethesda, MD: U.S. Public Health Service, 1999).
4 Ernest Hemingway, *Ernest Hemingway Selected Letters*, ed. Carlos Baker (New York: Charles Scribner's Sons, 1981), p. 420
5 J.C. Ballenger, "Benzodiazepines," in *Textbook of Psychopharmacology*, 2nd ed., eds. A.F. Schatzberg and C.B. Nemeroff (Washington, D.C.: American Psychiatric Press, 1998), p. 274.
6 Ray and Ksir, p. 167.
7 Hanson and Venturelli, p. 164.
8 Hanson and Venturelli, p. 174.
9 J.C. Ballenger, "Benzodiazepines," in *Textbook of Psychopharmacology*, 2nd ed., eds. A.F. Schatzberg and C.B. Nemeroff (Washington, D.C.: American Psychiatric Press, 1998), pp. 274-275.
10 R.M. Gilbert, "Caffeine Consumption," in *The Methylxanthine Beverages and Foods*, ed. G.A. Spiller (New York: Alan R. Liss, 1984), pp. 185-214.
11 Pendergrast, *Uncommon Grounds* (New York: Basic Books, 1999), p. 1.
12 Amleto D'Amicis and Rinantonio Viani, "The Consumption of Coffee," in *Caffeine, Coffee, and Health*, ed. Silvio Garattini (New York: Raven Press, 1993), pp. 1-16.
13 Thomas de Quincey, *Confessions of an English Opium Eater*, ed. Alethea Hayter (London: Penguin Books, 1986).
14 Nancy Wilson Ross, *Three Ways of Asian Wisdom* (New York: Simon and Schuster, 1966), p. 152.
15 Ray and Ksir, pp. 294-297.
16 Mark Twain, *A Tramp Abroad* (Oxford: Oxford University Press, 1996), p. 571.
17 United States Census Bureau, *Statistical Abstract of the United States: 1999*, 119th Ed. (Washington, DC: 1999), Table No. 252.
18 Jack James, *Caffeine and Health* (London: Academic Press Limited, 1991), pp. 24-26.
19 Silvio Garattini, ed., *Caffeine, Coffee, and Health* (New York: Raven Press, 1993).
20 I. Santos et al, "Caffeine Intake and Pregnancy Outcomes: A Meta-Analytic Review," *Cadernos de Saude Publica* 14 (1998): 523-530.
21 R. Ford et al, "Heavy Caffeine Intake in Pregnancy and Sudden Infant Death Syndrome," *Archives of Disease in Childhood* 78 (1998): 9-13.

22  Jack Henningfield, Caroline Cohen, and Wallace Pickworth, "Psychopharmacology of Nicotine," in *Nicotine Addiction*, eds. C.T. Orleans and John Slade (Oxford: Oxford University Press, 1993), pp. 24-45.

23  U.S. Census Bureau, Table No. 238.

24  J. Wilbert, "The Ethnopharmacology of Tobacco in Native South America," in *Effects of Nicotine on Biological Systems*, eds. Franz Adlkofer and Klaus Thurau (Basel, Switzerland: Birkhäuser Verlag, 1991), p. 7-8.

25  J. Wilbert, p. 14-16.

26  E.C. Corti, *A History of Smoking* (London: Harrap and Company, 1931).

27  Michael Fiore, Polly Newcomb, and Patrick McBride, "Natural History and Epidemiology of Tobacco Use and Addiction," in *Nicotine Addiction*, eds. C.T. Orleans and John Slade (Oxford: Oxford University Press, 1993), p. 89.

28  United States Department of Health and Human Services, *Smoking, Tobacco and Cancer Program 1985-1989 Status Report*, U.S.D.H.H.S, Public Health Service, National Institutes of Health, National Cancer Institute, National Institute of Health Publication No. 90-3107, 1990.

29  Donald Shopland and David Burns, *Medical and Public Health Implications of Tobacco Addiction*, in *Nicotine Addiction*, eds. C.T. Orleans and John Slade (Oxford: Oxford University Press, 1993), pp. 105-128.

30  Shopland and Burns, Appendix 6-B, p. 122.

31  United States Department of Health and Human Services, *The Health Consequences of Smoking: Cancer. A Report of the Surgeon General*, U.S.D.H.H.S, Public Health Service, Office on Smoking and Health. DHHS Publication No. (PHS) 82-50179, 1982.

32  Hanson and Venturelli, pp. 305-306.

33  David Warburton, "The Pleasures of Nicotine," in *Effects of Nicotine on Biological Systems*, eds. Franz Adlkofer and Klaus Thurau (Basel, Switzerland: Birkhäuser Verlag, 1991), p. 473-483.

34  Henningfield, Cohen, and Pickworth, p. 25.

35  Kjell Fuxe, Kurt Anderson, Anders Härfstrand, Peter Eneroth, Miguel Perez de la Mora, and Luigi Agnati, "Effects of Nicotine on Synaptic Transmission in the Brain," in *Nicotine Psychopharmacology*, eds. S. Wonnacott, M.A.H. Russell, and I.P. Stolerman (Oxford: Oxford University Press, 1990), pp. 194-225.

36  Fuxe et al., pp. 196-208.

37  Robert Sapolsky, *Why Zebras Don't Get Ulcers* (New York: W.H. Freeman & Co., 1994).

38  Arthur Conan Doyle, *The Sign of the Four* (London: John Murray, 1963), p. 1.

39  Richard Evans Schultes, "Coca and Other Psychoactive Plants: Magico-Religious Roles in Primitive Societies of the New World," in *Cocaine: Clinical and Biobehavioral Aspects*, eds. Seymour Fisher, Allen Rasin, E.H. Uhlenhuth (Oxford: Oxford University Press, 1987), p.

223.

40   Sigmund Freud, "On Coca," in *Cocaine Papers,* trans. Steven
     Edminster, ed. Robert Byck (New York: Meridian Books, 1975), p. 50.
41   Freud, *Cocaine Papers,* p. 51.
42   Hortense Koller-Becker, "Carl Koller and Cocaine," *The Psychoanalytic
     Quarterly* 32 (1963): 309-373.
43   Sigmund Freud, "Letter to Martha Bernays: June 2, 1884," in Ernest
     Jones, *The Life and Work of Sigmund Freud,* Vol. 1 (New York: Basic
     Books, 1953), p. 84.
44   Jones, p. 84.
45   Jones, p. 81.
46   Robert Byck, ed., *Cocaine Papers,* p. xx.
47   Freud, *Cocaine Papers,* pp. 63-64.
48   Jones, pp. 89-92.
49   Mark Pendergrast, *For God, Country, and Coca-Cola* (New York:
     Charles Scribner's Sons, 1993).
50   U.S. Census Bureau, Table No. 361.
51   Snyder, *Drugs and the Brain,* pp. 130-131.
52   B. Angrist and A. Sudilovsky, "Central Nervous System Stimulants," in
     *Handbook of Psychopharmacology,* Vol. 11, eds. L.L. Iversen, S.D. Iversen
     and S.H. Snyder (New York: Plenum, 1978), p. 111.
53   Angrist and Sudilosky, p. 114.
54   Freud, *Cocaine Papers,* p. 64.
55   T. Hemmi, "How We Handled the Problem of Drug Abuse in Japan,"
     in *Abuse of Central Stimulants,* eds. F. Sjoqvist and M. Tottie
     (Stockholm: Almqvist and Wiksell, 1969), pp. 147-153.
56   K.E. Moore, "Amphetamines: biochemical and behavioral actions in
     animals" in *Handbook of Psychopharmacology,* Vol. 11, eds. L.L. Iversen,
     S.D. Iversen and S.H. Snyder (New York: Plenum, 1978), pp. 41-98.
57   W.L. Woolverton and K.M. Johnson, "Neurobiology of Cocaine
     Abuse," in *Trends in Pharmacological Sciences* 13 (1992): 193-200.
58   Oxford English Dictionary.
59   Hanson and Venturelli, p. 228.
60   Homer, *The Odyssey,* trans. Robert Fitzgerald (New York: Vintage
     Books, 1990), Book 4, Lines 235-246, pp. 53.
61   Ray and Ksir, p. 335-336.
62   Ray and Ksir, p. 335-341.
63   Snyder, *Drugs and the Brain,* pp. 32-33.
64   Homer, *The Odyssey,* trans. Robert Fitzgerald (New York: Vintage
     Books, 1990), Book 12, Lines 48-56, p. 210.
65   de Quincey, pp. 71-72.
66   George Koob, "Drugs of Abuse: Anatomy, Pharmacology and
     Function of Reward Pathways," in *Trends in Pharmacological Sciences*
     13 (1992): 177-184.
67   I. Kupfermann, E.R. Kandel, and S. Iversen, "Motivational and
     Addictive States," in *Principles of Neural Science,* 4th Ed., eds. E.R.
     Kandel, J.H. Schwartz, and T.M. Jessell (New York: McGraw-Hill,
     2000), pp. 1009-1012.

68  Snyder, *Drugs and the Brain*, pp. 38-59.
69  Gaetano DiChiara and R. Alan North, "Neurobiology of Opiate Abuse," in *Trends in Pharmacological Sciences* 13 (1992): 185-193.
70  Ray and Ksir, pp. 353-354.
71  Mihaly Czikszentmihalyi, *Flow: The Psychology of Optimal Experience* (New York: Harper & Row, 1990), p. 6.
72  Søren Kierkegaard, *Either/Or*, Part I, eds. and trans. Howard Hong and Edna Hong (Princeton, NJ: Princeton University Press, 1987), p.29.
73  Jane Austen, *Emma*, ed. James Kinsley (Oxford: Oxford University Press, 1995), p. 74.
74  William Blake, *Songs of Innocence*.
75  Andrew Weil, *The Natural Mind* (Boston, MA: Houghton Mifflin Company, 1972), p. 29.
76  Weil, p. 19.
77  Huston Smith, *Cleansing the Doors of Perception* (New York: Jeremy P. Tarcher/Putnam, 2000), p. 15.
78  Wasson, R. Gordon, Albert Hofmann, Carl A.P. Ruck, *The Road to Eleusis* (New York: Harcourt Brace Jovanovich, 1978), P. 29.
79  Huston Smith, p. 24.
80  Walter Pahnke, "Drugs and Mysticism," in *The International Journal of Parapsychology*, Vol. 8, No. 2 (1966): 295-313.
81  Peter T. Furst, *Hallucinogens and Culture* (San Francisco, CA: Chandler & Sharp, 1976), p. 17.
82  Cf. Walter Pahnke, pp. 295-313. [Perhaps there is more of a biochemical basis to such "natural" experiences than has been previously supposed. Certainly many ascetics who have had mystical experiences have engaged in such practices as breathing and postural exercises, sleep deprivation, fasting, flagellation with subsequent infection, sustained meditation, and sensory deprivation in caves or monastic cells. All these techniques have an effect on body chemistry. There is a definite interplay between physiological and psychological processes in the human being.]
83  Joseph Campbell with Bill Moyers, *The Power of Myth*, ed. Betty Sue Flowers (New York: Anchor Books, 1988), p. 16.
84  Michael Harner (ed.), *Hallucinogens and Shamanism* (New York: Oxford University Press, 1973), p. xiv.
85  Paul Devereux, *The Long Trip: A Prehistory of Psychedelia* (New York: Penguin Books, 1997), p. 220.
86  Michael Harner, "The Role of Hallucinogenic Plants in European Witchcraft," in *Hallucinogens and Shamanism* (New York: Oxford University Press, 1973), p. 128-129.
87  Gustav Schenk, *The Book of Poisons*, trans. Michael Bullock (New York: Rinehart, 1955), cited in Michael Harner, p. 139-140.
88  Michael Harner, p. xi.
89  Wendy Doniger O'Flaherty, "The Post-Vedic History of the Soma Plant," in R. Gordon Wasson, "*Soma: The Divine Mushroom of Immortality*," (New York: Harcourt Brace Jovanovich, 1968), p. 95.

90 Richard Schultes, Albert Hofmann, Christian Rätsch, *Plants of the Gods*, (Rochester, VT: Healing Arts Press, 2001), pp. 82-85.

91 R. Gordon Wasson, *Soma: The Divine Mushroom of Immortality*, pp. 41.

92 Wasson, *Soma*, pp. 29-31.

93 Wasson, R. Gordon, Albert Hofmann, Carl A.P. Ruck, *The Road to Eleusis* (New York: Harcourt Brace Jovanovich, 1978), p. 51.

94 Marcus Tullius Cicero, *Laws* (The Loeb Classical Library), trans. C.W. Keyes, (Cambridge, MA: Harvard University Press, 1928), Book II, 36, p. 415.

95 Plato, *Phaedrus*, trans. R. Hackforth, *Plato: The Collected Dialogues*, eds. Edith Hamilton & Huntington Cairns (Princeton: Princeton University Press, 1961), 250 b-c.

96 Walter Burkert, *Ancient Mystery Cults* (Cambridge, MA: Harvard University Press, 1987), pp. 91-92.

97 Burkert, p. 90.

98 Burkert, p. 89.

99 Carl Kerényi, *Eleusis: Archetypal Image of Mother and Daughter*, trans. Ralph Manheim, (New York: Pantheon Books, 1967), p. 177.

100 Kerényi, p. 178-179.

101 Sopatros, *Rhet. Gr.* VIII, 114f. in Walter Burkert, *Ancient Mystery Cults* (Cambridge, MA: Harvard University Press, 1987), p. 90.

102 Burkert, p. 113-114.

103 Burkert, p. 93.

104 Wasson, Hofmann, Ruck, p. 21.

105 Kerényi, p. 12.

106 Weston LaBarre, "History and Ethnography of Cannabis," in *Culture in Context: Selected Writings of Weston LaBarre* (Durham, NC: Duke University Press, 1980), p. 93.

107 William Emboden, "Ritual Use of Cannabis Sativa: A Historical-Ethnographic Survey," in Peter Furst (ed.), *Flesh of the Gods: The Ritual Use of Hallucinogens* (New York: Praeger Publishers, 1972), p. 217.

108 *Herodotus* (The Loeb Classical Library), Vol. 2, trans. A.D. Godley (Cambridge, MA: Harvard University Press, 1971), Book IV, 74-74, pp. 273-275.

109 Ernest Abel, *Marihuana: The First Twelve Thousand Years* (New York: Plenum Press, 1980), p. 17.

110 Emboden, pp. 220-222

111 LaBarre, "History and Ethnography of Cannabis," p. 99.

112 Charles Baudelaire, *Artificial Paradises: On Hashish and Wine as Means of Expanding Individuality*, Trans. Ellen Fox (New York: Herder & Herder, 1971), pp. 18-23.

113 Ernest Abel, *Marihuana: The First Twelve Thousand Years* (New York: Plenum Press, 1980), p. 80.

114 Abel, p. 214.

115 U.S. Census Bureau, Table No. 238.

116 For a thorough discussion of marijuana's medical properties see Institute of Medicine, *Marijuana and Medicine: Assessing the Science*

*Base*, Janet Joy, Stanley Watson, and John Benson (eds.) (Washington, DC: National Academy Press, 1999).

117   U.S. Census Bureau, Table No. 361.

118   Institute of Medicine, pp. 83-136.

119   J.C. Anthony, L.A. Warner, R.C. Kessler, "Comparative Epedemiology of Dependence on Tobacco, Alcohol, Controlled Substances, and Inhalants: Basic Findings form the national Comorbidity Survey," in *Experimental and Clinical Psychopharmacology* 2(1994) : 244-268.

120   Ray and Ksir, pp. 401-402.

121   Emboden, p. 214.

122   Institute of Medicine, p. 25.

123   Institute of Medicine, p. 36.

124   Institute of Medicine, p. 41.

125   Institute of Medicine, p. 42.

126   Institute of Medicine, pp. 43-47.

127   Eliot Gardiner, "Cannabinoid Interaction with Brain Reward Systems—the Neurobiological Basis of Cannabinoid Abuse," in *Marijuana/Cannabinoids: Neurobiology and Neurophysiology*, eds. Laura Murphy and Andrzej Bartke (Boca Raton, FL: CRC Press, 1992), p. 322.

128   Institute of Medicine, pp. 51-53.

129   Institute of Medicine, p. 58.

130   L. Grinspoon and J.B. Bakalar, Marijuana, The Forbidden Medicine (New Haven, CT: Yale University Press, 1993).

131   Weston LaBarre, "Anthropological Perspectives on Hallucination, Hallucinogens, and the Shamanic Origins of Religion," in *Culture in Context: Selected Writings of Weston LaBarre* (Durham, NC: Duke University Press, 1980), p. 65.

132   For a complete account, Albert Hofmann, *LSD: My Problem Child*, Trans. Jonathan Ott (Los Angeles, CA: Jeremy Tarcher, 1983), pp. 5-21.

133   Hofmann, *LSD: My Problem Child*, p. 15.

134   Hofmann, *LSD: My Problem Child*, pp. 17-18.

135   Stanislov Grof with Hal Bennett, *The Holotropic Mind* (San Francisco: HarperCollins, 1993), pp. 15-16.

136   John Marks, *The Search for the Manchurian Candidate*, (New York: New York Times Books, 1979), pp. 4-6.

137   Marks, p. 57.

138   Marks, p. 58.

139   Marks, p. 63.

140   Marks, pp. 65-67.

141   Marks, pp. 73-86.

142   Lee Guthrie, *The Life and Loves of Cary Grant* (New York: Drake Publishers, 1977), pp. 163-165.

143   Timothy Leary, *High Priest* (New York: The World Publishing Company, 1968), pp. 12-34.

144   Jay Stevens, *Storming Heaven: LSD and the American Dream* (New

York: Harper & Row, 1987), pp. 188-271.

145  Stevens, p. 342.

146  Alan Watts, *In My Own Way* (New York: Vintage, 1972), p. 402.

147  Richard Schultes, Albert Hofmann, Christian Rätsch, *Plants of the Gods* (Rochester, VT: Healing Arts Press, 2001), p. 156.

148  Diego Durán, *Historia de las Indias de Nueva España*, IICap LIV 24; quoted in R. Gordon Wasson, *The Wondrous Mushroom* (New York: McGraw-Hill, 1980), p. 202.

149  Richard Evans Schultes, "The Identification of Teonanacatl, a narcotic Basidiomycete of the Aztecs," in *Botanical Museum Leaflets* (Cambridge, MA: Harvard University, 1939), pp. 37-54.

150  Wasson, *The Wondrous Mushroom*, p. 16.

151  Walter Pahnke, pp. 295-313.

152  Smith, p. 101-104.

153  Smith, p. 101.

154  Rick Doblin, "Pahnke's 'Good Friday Experiment': A Long-Term Follow-Up and Methodological Critique," The Journal of Transpersonal Psychology 23, no. 1, (1991), 1-28.

155  Pahnke, pp. 295-313.

156  Robert Forte, "A Conversation with R. Gordon Wasson," in *Entheogens and the Future of Religion*, ed. Robert Forte (San Francisco: The Council on Spiritual Practices, 1997), pp. 72-73.

157  Hofmann, *LSD: My Problem Child*, pp. 141-142.

158  Richard Glennon, "Pharmacology of Hallucinogens," in *Handbook of Substance Abuse*, eds. Ralph Tarter, Robert Ammerman, Peggy Ott (New York: Plenum Press, 1998), pp. 222-223.

159  Richard Schultes, Albert Hofmann, Christian Rätsch, *Plants of the Gods*, (Rochester, VT: Healing Arts Press, 2001), p. 145.

160  Weston LaBarre, *The Peyote Cult*, 5th Ed., (Norman, OK: The University of Oklahoma Press, 1989), p. 257.

161  Robert Forte (ed.), *Entheogens and the Future of Religion* (San Francisco: The Council on Spiritual Practices, 1997), p. 1.

162  William McKim, *Drugs and Behavior*, 4th Ed., (Upper Saddle River, NJ: Prentice Hall, 2000), p. 331.

163  Alexander Shulgin, *Pikhal: A Chemical Love Story* (Berkeley, CA: Transform Press, 1991).

164  Jerome Beck and Marsha Rosenbaum, *Pursuit of Ecstasy: The MDMA Experience* (Albany, NY: The State University of New York Press, 1994), pp. 18-22.

165  Una McCann, Melissa Mertl, and George Ricaurte, "Ecstasy," in *Handbook of Substance Abuse*, eds. Ralph Tarter, Robert Ammerman, Peggy Ott (New York: Plenum Press, 1998), pp. 567-574.

## Chapter 16: The Broken Brain

1   William Styron, *Darkness Visible* (New York: Vintage, 1990), p. 46.

2   Blazer, D.G., Kessler, R.C., & McGonagle, K.A. (1994). The prevalence

and distribution of major depression in a national community sample: The National Comorbidity Survey. *American Journal of Psychiatry*, 151, 979-986.

3   U.S. Census Bureau, Table No. 149.

4   Hippocrates, "Nature of Man 4," in *Hippocrates* (The Loeb Classical Library), Vol. 4, trans. W.H.S. Jones, (Cambridge, MA: Harvard University Press, 1979), pp. 11-13.

5   J.F.A. McManus, *The Fundamental Ideas of Medicine* (Springfield, IL: Charles C. Thomas, 1963), p. 40.

6   John Longrigg, *Greek Rational Medicine* (London: Routledge, 1993), p. 91.

7   Allen Thiher, *Revels in Madness* (Ann Arbor: University of Michigan Press, 1999), p. 42.

8   K.I. Nathan, D.L. Musselman, A.F. Schatzberg, and C.B. Nemeroff, "Biology of Mood Disorders," in *Textbook of Psychopharmacology*, 2nd Ed., eds. A.F. Schatzberg and C.B. Nemeroff (Washington, D.C.: American Psychiatric Press, 1998).

9   Madden, P.A.F., Heath, A.C., Rosenthal, N.E., & Martin, N.G. (1996, January). Seasonal changes in mood and behavior. *Arch. Gen. Psychiat*, 553, 47-55.

10  C.H. Kawas and R. Katzman, "Epidemiology of Dementia and Alzheimer Disease," *Alzheimer Disease, 2nd Edition*, Eds. R.D. Terry, R. Katzman, K.L. Bick, and S.S. Sisodia (Philadelphia: Lippincott Williams & Wilkins, 1999), pp. 95-102.

11  Allen Frances and Ruth Ross, *DSM-IV Case Studies* (Washington, D.C.: American Psychiatric Press, 1996), p. 42.

12  C.H. Kawas and R. Katzman, "Epidemiology of Dementia and Alzheimer Disease," *Alzheimer Disease, 2nd Edition*, Eds. R.D. Terry, R. Katzman, K.L. Bick, and S.S. Sisodia (Philadelphia: Lippincott Williams & Wilkins, 1999), p. 96.

13  National Head Injury Foundation. (1993). *Fact Sheet and Pamphlet*. Washington, D.C.: Author.

14  Oliver Sacks, *The Man Who Mistook His Wife for a Hat* (New York: HarperCollins, 1990), pp. 40-41.

15  For a more complete retelling of this story, see Antonio Damasio, *Descartes' Error* (New York: G.P. Putnam's Sons 1994).

16  David Shutts, *Lobotomy: Resort to the Knife* (New York: Van Nostrand Reinhold Company, 1982), p. 250.

17  Shutts, pp. 30-48.

18  Shutts, pp. 47-56.

19  Walter Freeman quoted in David Shutts, *Lobotomy: Resort to the Knife* (New York: Van Nostrand Reinhold Company, 1982), p. 61.

20  Freeman quoted in Shutts, p. 62.

21  Freeman quoted in Shutts, p. 101.

22  Freeman quoted in Shutts, p. 101.

23  Freeman quoted in Shutts, p. 103.

24  Freeman quoted in Shutts, p. 134.

25  V.S. Ramachandran and Sandra Blakeslee, *Phantoms in the Brain* (New

York: William Morrow, 1998), p. 142.
26  Ramachandran and Blakeslee, p. 129.
27  American Psychiatric Association, *Diagnostic and Statistical Manual-IV* (Washington, DC: American Psychiatric Press, 2000).

# Part III—Giving Up the Ghost

## Chapter 17: Contingency: The Sting of Death

1  Richard Rorty, *Contingency, Irony, and Solidarity* (Cambridge: Cambridge University Press, 1989), p. 16.
2  Greenberg, J., Pyszczynski, T., & Solomon, S. (1986). The causes and consequeneces of a need for self-esteem: A terror management theory. In R.F. Baumeister (ed.), *Public self and private self* (pp. 189-212). New York: Springer-Verlag.
3  Blaise Pascal, *Pensées* (New York: E.P. Dutton & Co., 1958), p. 61. <208>
4  Pascal, p. 61. <210>
5  Friedrich Nietzsche, *The Gay Science*, trans. Walter Kaufmann (New York: Vintage, 1974), p. 181. <125>
6  Vladimir Nabokov, *Speak Memory* (New York: Vintage Books, 1989), p. 19.
7  Nabokov, p. 20.
8  Nabokov, p. 296-297.
9  Jean-Paul Sartre, *Nausea*, trans. Lloyd Alexander (New York: New Directions Publishing, 1964), p. 133.

## Chapter 18: Prolonged Immaturity

1  trans. Stephen Jay Gould, *Ontogeny and Phylogeny* (Cambridge, MA: Harvard University Press, 1977), p. 369.
2  Ashley Montagu, *Growing Young*, 2nd Edition (Granby, MA: Bergin & Garvey Publishers, 1989), p. 44.
3  W.M. Krogman, *Child Growth* (Ann Arbor, MI: University of Michigan Press, 1972), p. 2.
4  Gould, p. 372.
5  Gould, p. 361.
6  Friedrich Schleiermacher, *The Christian Faith*, Vol. 1, eds. & trans. H.R. Mackintosh and J.S. Stewart (New York: Harper & Row, 1963), p. 17.
7  Ludwig Feuerbach, *Lectures on the Essence of Religion*, trans. Ralph Mannheim (New York: Harper & Row, 1967), p. 25.
8  Feuerbach, *Lectures on the Essence of Religion*, p. 294.
9  Sigmund Freud, *The Future of an Illusion*, ed. & trans. James Strachey (New York: W.W. Norton & Co., 1961), p. 24.
10  Ernest Jones, "The Psychology of Religion," in *Psychoanalysis Today*, ed. Sandor Lorand, (New York: International Universities Press,

1944), p. 316.

11  William James, *The Principles of Psychology*, 2 vols. (New York: Dover, 1950).

12  Montagu, table 3, p. 255.

13  Montagu, p. 4.

14  Fyodor Dostoyevsky, *Notes from the Underground*, trans. Jessie Coulson (New York: Penguin, 1972), p. 41.

15  Weston LaBarre, *Shadow of Childhood* (Norman, OK: University of Oklahoma Press, 1991), p. 102.

## Chapter 19: Narcissism and the Reality Principle

1  Friedrich Nietzsche, *Thus Spoke Zarathustra*, in *The Portable Nietzsche*, ed. & trans. Walter Kaufmann (New York: Viking, 1982), Prologue, p.126.

2  Ernest Becker, *The Birth and Death of Meaning*, Second Edition (New York: Free Press, 1971), p. 197.

3  Saint Ignatius of Loyola, *The Spiritual Exercises of Saint Ignatius*, trans. Pierre Wolff (Ligouri, MO: Ligouri/Triump, 1997), p. 11.

4  Edith Hamilton, *Mythology* (New York: Penguin, 1969), pp. 86-88.

5  Montagu, p. 89.

6  Otto Rank, *The Trauma of Birth* (New York: R. Brunner, 1952).

7  Sigmund Freud, "On Narcissism: An Introduction," in *The Standard Edition of the Complete Psychological Works of Sigmund Freud*, ed. & trans. James Strachey (London: The Hogarth Press, 1957), vol. 14, p. 91.

8  Freud, "On Narcissism," p. 94.

9  C. Fred Alford, *Narcissism* (New Haven, CT: Yale University Press, 1988), p. 3.

10  "Forms and Transformations of Narcissism," in *The Search for the Self*, ed. Paul Ornstein (New York: International Universities Press, 1978), vol. 1, p. 458.

11  Alford, p. 192.

## Chapter 20: The Epic of Gilgamesh

1  *Gilgamesh*, trans. John Gardner and John Maier with the assistance of Richard Henshaw (New York: Vintage Books, 1984), Tablet 1, Column ii, line 1.

2  *Gilgamesh*, Tablet 1, Column iv, line 3.

3  *Gilgamesh*, Tablet 1, Column iv, line 19.

4  *Gilgamesh*, Tablet 1, Column iv, lines 28-29.

5  *Gilgamesh*, Tablet 1, Column i, line 1.

6  *Gilgamesh*, Tablet 8, Column ii, lines 2-7.

7  *Gilgamesh*, Tablet 9, Column i, lines 3-5.

8  *Gilgamesh*, Tablet 10, Column ii, lines 1-14.

9  Jeffrey Tigay, *The Evolution of the Gilgamesh Epic* (Philadelphia:

University of Pennsylvania Press, 1982), p. 168.

10 *Gilgamesh*, Tablet 11, Column iv, line 196.

11 *Gilgamesh*, Tablet 11, Column i, lines 5-6.

12 *Gilgamesh*, Tablet 10, Column v, lines 25-30.

13 *Gilgamesh*, Tablet 10, Column vi, lines 26-39.

14 *Gilgamesh*, Tablet 11, Column i, line 10.

15 *Gilgamesh*, Tablet 11, Column iii, line 173.

16 *Gilgamesh*, Tablet 11, Column vi, lines 230-233.

17 *Gilgamesh*, Tablet 1, Column ii, lines 39-40.

18 *Gilgamesh*, Tablet 1, Column v, lines 1-3.

19 *Gilgamesh*, Tablet 1, Column i, lines 44-45.

20 *Gilgamesh*, Tablet 1, Column i, line 2.

21 *Gilgamesh*, Tablet 11, Column vi, lines 305-307.

# Chapter 21: The Cult of Immortality

1 Miguel de Unamuno, *The Tragic Sense of Life in Men and Nations*, trans. Anthony Kerrigan (Princeton, NJ: Princeton University Press, 1972), p. 45.

2 *First Letter to the Corinthians*. 15:19-32

3 Omar Khayyám, *Rubáiyát: A Critical Edition*, ed. Christopher Drecker & trans. Edward FitzGerald, (Charlottesville, VA: University Press of Virginia, 1997), LXIII, p. 105.

4 Khayyám, LXVI, p. 105.

5 Norman O. Brown, *Life Against Death: The Psychoanalytic Meaning of History* (Middletown, CT: Wesleyan University Press, 1970), p. 16.

6 2 Kings 2:11-12. 2 Enoch 1:8-9.

7 *Gospel of Mark*. 12:19-27

8 Arthur A. Cohen, "Resurrection of the Dead," in *Contemporary Jewish Religious Thought*, eds. Arthur A. Cohen & Paul Mendes-Flohr (New York: Charles Scribner's Sons, 1987), pp. 807-813.

9 "al-Jannah," in Cyril Glassé, *The Concise Encyclopedia of Islam* (New York: Harper & Row, 1989), pp. 206-207.

10 *Hamlet*, Act III, scene 3, lines 76-98.

11 *Genesis* 18:22-32.

12 *Gospel of John* 3:5. See also T.M. De Ferrari, "Baptism," in *New Catholic Encyclopedia*, vol. 2 (Washington, D.C.: The Catholic University of America, 1967), pp. 62-68.

13 *Immortality*, ed. Paul Edwards (Amherst, NY: Prometheus Books, 1997), pp. 59-62.

14 See especially, Soren Kierkegaard, *Philosophical Fragments*, trans. Howard & Edna Hong (Princeton, NJ: Princeton University Press, 1985).

15 Soren Kierkegaard, *Concluding Unscientific Postscript*, trans. Howard & Edna Hong (Princeton, NJ: Princeton University Press, 1992).

16 Miguel de Unamuno, *The Tragic Sense of Life in Men and Nations*, trans. Anthony Kerrigan (Princeton, NJ: Princeton University Press, 1972), p. 45.

17  Unamuno, p. 51.
18  Unamuno, p. 43. [italics mine]
19  Cf. Kaufmann, Walter, *Tragedy and Philosophy*, (Princeton: Princeton University Press, 1968), pp. 200-212.
20  Unamuno, p. 127.
21  *Genesis* 22:1-10.
22  Unamuno, p. 152.

# Chapter 22: The Mechanics of Belief and Disbelief

1   Plato, *Republic*, trans. Paul Shorey, *Plato: The Collected Dialogues*, eds. Edith Hamilton & Huntington Cairns (Princeton: Princeton University Press, 1961), 368e-369c.
2   Herbert Fingarette, *Self-Deception* (Berkeley, CA: University of California Press, 2000), p. 98.
3   Fingarette, *Self-Deception*, p. 14.
4   George Orwell, *1984* (New York: Harcourt Brace Jovanovich, 1949), p. 176.
5   Orwell, p. 177.
6   Orwell, p. 177.
7   Immanuel Kant, *Perpetual Peace and Other Essays*, trans. Ted Humphrey (Indianapolis, IN: Hackett Publishing, 1983), p. 41.
8   Ernest Becker, *The Denial of Death* (New York: Free Press, 1974), p. 178.
9   Leon Festinger, *A Theory of Cognitive Dissonance* (Evanston, IL: Row, Peterson, 1957).
10  Leon Festinger, Henry Riecken and Stanley Schachter, *When Prophecy Fails* (New York: Harper & Row, 1964), p. 26.
11  Elliot Aronson, "Dissonance Theory: Progress and Problems," in *Theories of Cognitive Consistency: A Sourcebook*, eds. Robert P. Abelson, et al. (Chicago: Rand McNally & Company, 1968), p. 6.

# Chapter 23: Mourning One's Own Death

1   Harry Slochower "Eros and the Trauma of Death," in *The Interpretation of Death*, ed. Hendrik Ruitenbeek (New York: Jason Aronson Publishers, 1973), p. 193.
2   Ludwig Feuerbach, *Thoughts on Death and Immortality*, trans. James A. Massey (Berkeley, CA: University of California Press, 1980), p. 17.
3   Sigmund Freud, "Thoughts for the Times on War and Death," in *Collected Papers*, vol. 4, trans. Joan Riviere (New York: Basic Books, 1959), pp. 304-305.
4   W. Somerset Maugham, *Of Human Bondage* (New York: Penguin Books, 1992), p. 524.
5   Norman Torrey, "Voltaire," in *The Encyclopedia of Philosophy*, Vol. 8, ed. Paul Edwards (New York: MacMillian, 1967), p. 267.
6   Herbert Fingarette, *Death: Philosophical Soundings* (Chicago, IL: Open Court, 1996), p. 8.

7   Friedrich Schleiermacher, *On Religion*, trans. & ed. Richard Crouter (Cambridge: Cambridge University Press, 1996), p. 54.
8   Alan Watts, *The Book* (New York: Vintage Books, 1966), p. 80.
9   Joseph Campbell with Bill Moyers, *The Power of Myth*, ed. Betty Sue Flowers (New York: Anchor Books, 1988), p. 188.

## Chapter 24: Philosophies of Redemption

1   Friedrich Nietzsche, *The Antichrist*, in *The Portable Nietzsche*, ed. & trans. Walter Kaufmann (New York: Viking, 1982), p. 606. <33>
2   Epicurus, *The Essential Epicurus*, trans. Eugene O' Connor (Amherst, MA: Prometheus Books, 1993), p. 97.
3   Epictetus, *Enchiridion*, trans. George Long (Buffalo, NY: Prometheus Books, 1991), v, p. 14.
4   E. Bignone, *L'Aristotele perduto e la formazione filosofica di Epicuro*. 2 vols. (Firenze: La Nuova Italia, 1936), p. 1:111, quoted in Giovanni Reale, *The Systems of the Hellenistic Age*, ed. and trans. John Catan (Albany, NY: State University of New York Press, 1985).
5   Epicurus, p. 99.
6   Epicurus, p. 67.
7   Epicurus, p. 65.
8   Epicurus, p. 63.
9   Epicurus, p. 100.
10  Epicurus, p. 69.
11  Seneca, Epistle 106.2. frag. 84.29von Arnim
12  Seneca, *Letters from a Stoic*, trans. (Penguin Books, 1969), letter v
13  Marcus Aurelius, *The Meditations of Marcus Aurelius*, trans. G.M.A. Grube (New York: The Bobbs-Merrill Company, 1963), p. 35. [Book 4, 49]
14  Marcus Aurelius, pp. 55-56. [Book 6, 36]
15  Epicurus, p. 100.
16  Giovanni Reale, *A History of Ancient Philosophy, Vol. III: The Systems of the Hellenistic Age*, trans. John Catan (Albany, NY: SUNY Press, 1985), p. 375.
17  Epicurus, p. 75.

## Chapter 25: Conclusion

1   Otto Rank, *Truth and Reality*, trans. Jessie Taft (New York: W.W. Norton & Company, 1978), p. 42.
2   Friedrich Nietzsche, *Beyond Good and Evil*, p. 71, <59>

# INDEX